Children of La Frontera

Children of La Frontera:

Binational Efforts to Serve Mexican Migrant and Immigrant Students

Edited by
Judith LeBlanc Flores

Foreword by
Eugene E. Garcia

Clearinghouse on Rural Education and Small Schools
Charleston, West Virginia

Clearinghouse on Rural Education and Small Schools
Appalachia Educational Laboratory
PO Box 1348, Charleston, WV 25325

Second printing, July 1997

Cover illustration by John MacDonald, Williamstown, MA
Cover design by Richard Hendel, Chapel Hill, NC
"Recuerdos/Memories" by Gloria L. Velásquez is from
I Used to be a Superwoman,
published by Santa Monica College Press.
Reprinted with permission.

Library of Congress Cataloging-in-Publication Data

Children of la frontera : binational efforts to serve Mexican migrant and immigrant students / edited by Judith LeBlanc Flores ; with foreword by Eugene E. Garcia.

p. cm.
Includes bibliographical references
ISBN 1-880785-12-9 (pbk.)
1. Children of migrant laborers—Education—United States. 2. Children of immigrants—Education—United States. 3. Mexicans—Education—United States. 4. Mexican Americans—Education—United States. 5. Socially handicapped children—Education—Mexico.
I. Flores, Judith LeBlanc.
LC5151.C45 1996
371.96'75'0973—dc20 96-5323
CIP

This publication was prepared with funding from the U.S. Department of Education, Office of Educational Research and Improvement, under contract no. RR93002012. The opinions expressed herein do not necessarily reflect the positions or policies of the Appalachia Educational Laboratory, the Office of Educational Research and Improvement, or the Department of Education.

The ERIC Clearinghouse on Rural Education and Small Schools is operated by the Appalachia Educational Laboratory (AEL), Inc. AEL is an Affirmative Action/Equal Opportunity Employer.

Recuerdos

De Johnstown, Colorado
  el desahije, los patrones,
  leña partida, agua fría.

De Alamosa, Colorado
  pizca de papas, colchones de paja,
  velas, aceite, cortinas de lona.

De Denver City, Tejas
  sudor, construcción,
  barrio de morenos, niños amontonados.

De Loveland, Colorado
  colonia aislada, escuelas blancas,
  lonches fríos, ropa usada.

De Greeley, Colorado
  college degree, automatic dishwasher,
  air conditioning, iced tea.

Memories

In Johnstown, Colorado
  thinning sugarbeets, the patrones,
  chopped wood, ice-cold water.

In Alamosa, Colorado
  picking potatoes, straw mattresses,
  candles, oil lamps, canvas curtains.

In Denver City, Texas
  sweat, construction workers,
  brown barrios, hoards of children.

In Loveland, Colorado
  segregated neighborhoods, white schools,
  cold lunches, used clothing.

In Greeley, Colorado
  college degree, automatic dishwasher,
  air conditioning, iced tea.

— Gloria L. Velásquez
from *I Used to be a Superwoman*

Contents

Foreword—*Eugene E. Garcia* ix
Preface—*Judith LeBlanc Flores* xv
List of Contributors xvi

Part I. Background: Historic and Current Conditions for Mexican Migrant and Immigrant Education

1. Introduction 3
Judith LeBlanc Flores and *Patricia Cahape Hammer*

2. Migrant Farmworkers and Their Children: What Recent Labor Department Data Show 19
Philip L. Martin

3. Education in Mexico: Historical and Contemporary Educational Systems 25
Victoria Andrade de Herrera

4. The Newest "Outsiders": Educating Mexican Migrant and Immigrant Youth 61
Harriett Romo

5. Stories and Poems by Migrant Writers 93
Compiled by Silvia Kelly and Robert Lynch

Part II: Federal and State Programs

6. Mexico's Role in U.S. Education—A Well-Kept Secret 103
Robert Miller

7. Reauthorized Migrant Education Program: Old Themes and New 117
Al Wright

8. Migrant Education Binational Program 125
David P. Dolson and Gildardo Villaseñor

9. Genesis of the Migrant Binational Program 135
Arlene R. Dorn

10. Teachers for Mexican Migrant and Immigrant Students: Meeting an Urgent Need 153
Norma Varisco de García and Eugene E. Garcia

11. Exploring Binational Educational Issues: A Report from the Border Colloquy Project 165
Betty Mace-Matluck and Martha Boethel

12. Binational Health Care for Migrants: The Health Data Exchange Pilot Project and the Binational Health Data Transfer System ... 183
Héctor Eduardo Velasco Mondragón, Johnson Martin, and Henry Stevenson Perez

Part III: Working in Districts, Schools, and Classrooms

13. Bilingual, Bicultural, and Binational Cooperative Learning Communities for Students and Teachers 203
Margarita Calderón

14. Programming for Success Among Hispanic Migrant Students .. 229
Mary V. Montavon and Jeri Kinser

15. Latino Voices in Children's Literature: Instructional Approaches for Developing Cultural Understanding in the Classroom 239
John M. Kibler

16. Incorporating Mexican American History and Culture into the Social Studies Classroom 269
Kathy Escamilla

17. Teaching Mathematics for Understanding to Bilingual Students 285
Walter G. Secada and Yolanda De La Cruz

Part IV: Working with Families

18. Voices of Latina Migrant Mothers in Rural Pennsylvania 311
Stephanie L. Bressler

19. Involving Migrant Families in Their Children's Education: Challenges and Opportunities for Schools 325
Nancy Feyl Chavkin

20. Involving Hispanic Parents in Improving Educational Opportunities for Their Children 341
Alicia Salinas Sosa

Foreword

EUGENE E. GARCIA, PH.D.
UNIVERSITY OF CALIFORNIA, BERKELEY

As teachers look at the students in their classrooms today, they see a scenario much different from the classrooms of their own childhoods. Today 1 in 3 children nationwide is from an ethnic or racial minority group, 1 in 7 speaks a language other than English at home, and 1 in 15 was born outside the United States. The linguistic and cultural diversity of America's school population has increased dramatically during the past decade, and it's expected to increase even more in the future. While three quarters of Americans now claim European descent, by 2050 only half will. The concept of "minority" group will become obsolete as no group will form a majority.

Educating children from immigrant and ethnic minority group families is a major concern of school systems across the country. For many of these children, U.S. education is not a successful experience. While one tenth of non-Hispanic White students leave school without a diploma, one fourth of African Americans, one third of Hispanics, one half of Native Americans, and two thirds of immigrant students drop out of school.

Confronted with this dismal reality, administrators, teachers, parents, and policy makers urge each other to do something different—change teaching methods, adopt new curricula, allocate more funding. Such actions might be needed, but will be meaningless unless we begin to think differently about these students. In order to educate them, we must first educate ourselves about who they are and what they need in order to succeed. Thinking differently involves viewing these students in new ways that may contradict conventional notions, and coming to a new set of realizations.

This is particularly the case for educators and communities along "*la frontera*," an extensive geographical region bordering the United States and Mexico that is, intellectually and empirically, a significant social and economic zone quite distinct from either nation. This volume does much to explore this geographical, social, economic, and intellectual zone. My opening remarks to this significant volume will attempt to set a broader *context* for the *text* delivered in the contributions that follow.

These Are Not The Students We Expected To Be Teaching

In contrast to racial, ethnic, and linguistic diversity among students, the vast majority of teachers and administrators are Euro-American and speak English as their native and only language. Many are experiencing the daunting personal and professional challenge of adapting in adulthood to a degree of diversity that did not exist in their childhood. No place is the challenge greater than along *la frontera.*

The average teacher and administrator in his/her 30s or 40s grew up in the 1950s or 1960s. People who were raised in the postwar period, before desegregation, were likely to have attended schools with those of their own ethnic group. Not until young adulthood did they encounter the civil rights movement and other expressions of ethnic presence at the national level. Nor did they experience the swift increases in diversity that have occurred recently. They and their parents grew up expecting a much different world from what they now face.

The parents and teachers of today's teacher, now retired, grew up in the 1930s and the 1940s, after the period of massive immigration from Europe to the United States had ended. Today's retiree entered school at a time when the United States had a much larger proportion of foreign-born persons than today. But this diversity was perhaps not so evident because of segregated ethnic enclaves in housing and schooling and less widespread mass communications. And over the course of their lifetime, people now in their 70s experienced decreasing diversity. The melting pot ideology matched their own observations; the children of immigrants abandoned their native language and culture as they were urged to become 100 percent American. That just doesn't happen along *la frontera.*

But the 30-year period straddling the mid-century mark was an anomaly in our history. Until the 1930s, the story of the United States was a tale of immigration. The grandparents of today's teacher, who grew up in the early 1900s, and many of whom were immigrants themselves, experienced increasing ethnic and linguistic diversity during their formative years.

It Is Low, Not High, Levels of Immigration That Are Unusual

To many Americans, the immigration movement that brought our ancestors to this country is a closed chapter, part of our national past. But from the perspective of the entire spectrum of American history, immigration has been the norm rather than the exception. Two generations of adults have grown up in a very unusual low immigration period, an environment that has shaped our perceptions of our country. The new reality is that the America of 2000 will resemble the America of 1900 more than the America of 1950. Today's kindergartners will experience increasing diversity over their lifetime, as the generation of their great-grandparents did.

From 1900 to 1910, nearly 9 million immigrants entered the United States, increasing the total population by 10 percent. In the 1980s, about the same number of immigrants came to the United States, but they accounted for only a 4 percent increase in a now much larger U.S. population. In the early decades of the century, and back as far as 1850, as many as 1 in 7 persons in the United States were foreign born. The current rate of 1 in 13 is high only in comparison to the low immigration decades of the 1950s and 60s, when 1 in 20 Americans were foreign born. By 2020, when today's kindergartners are in the work force, the foreign-born population in the United States is again projected to reach 1 in 7 persons.

La Frontera Has Always Been Multicultural & Multilingual

Because the United States is so closely identified with the English language, many people assume that Anglo-Americans have always formed the majority group in U.S. society. But the 1990 Census reveals that only 13 percent of Americans claim English ancestry. They are outnumbered by the 15 percent whose families originated in Ireland, many of whom did not speak English as a native language. An additional 5 percent identify their ancestry as "Americans"; many of these are Scottish-Americans whose families have been in the United States for 9 or 10 generations. Thus, at most, about one third of Americans trace their ancestry to various cultures and languages of Great Britain.

German tops English as the heritage of the largest number of Americans; nearly one fourth claim German ancestry. The prominence of German immigrants a century ago is similar to that of Hispanics today; nearly 30 percent of foreign-born immigrants in 1900 came from Germanic-language countries, and the same percentage in 1980 came from Spanish-language countries.

Today, nearly 1 in 5 Americans live in households in which a language other than English is spoken. Along *la frontera,* it is 3 in 5. Three fourths of those households are Spanish-speaking.

Educating students from immigrant families may seem like an entirely new challenge, but it is not; such students have always been in American schools in large numbers. Throughout most of our history, 1 out of 4 or 5 White Americans grew up in immigrant families.

Although the United States has never been a monolingual, monocultural society, its people have been overwhelmingly of European origin. Until 1965, immigration laws favored Europeans, and immigrants spoke languages and brought cultures with which Americans, and U.S. school systems, had some familiarity. But today less than a quarter of immigrants come from Europe; most come from Latin America and Asia. In addition to large numbers of Spanish speakers, schools encounter students whose native language is Korean, Tagalog, Hindi, Farsi, Hmong, or Mandarin.

What Worked in the Past May Not Work Now

One mission of educators is to prepare young people for an occupational life. The economic environment in which today's students will seek employment has changed radically in the past few decades. Manufacturing jobs used to provide a good living for ethnic minority group members and for immigrants. Most jobs in the industrial sector did not require a high level of education or academic competence in English.

But those jobs have disappeared. The new economy will require workers who have more than basic skills; employees must be able to think critically and engage in group decision making, to communicate effectively orally and in writing, and to adapt to changing conditions by learning new skills. A larger proportion of jobs in the future will require the kind of educational preparation that has traditionally been provided to only the top students.

The American economy is now intertwined with the global marketplace; workers who can interact easily with people of different cultural and linguistic backgrounds will be prized. Even the domestic workplace that today's students will enter is changing, as employees and customers are becoming more diverse. Business leaders are well aware that most of their new employees will be minorities and women. Observers of American business trends comment that many companies have gone beyond debating whether they need to change; they are now actively managing diversity. If one of the purposes of education is to train young people for productive work lives, then schools will need to prepare all students for employment in a more ethnically, culturally, and linguistically diverse occupational environment than in the past. Along *la frontera*, NAFTA propels this understanding.

One Size Doesn't Fit All Students

Students from *la frontera* families are often defined by the characteristics they share—a lack of English fluency. But such a definition masks their diversity and underestimates the challenge facing schools. Schools serve students who are new immigrants, ignorant of American life beyond what they have seen in movies, as well as African Americans, Mexican Americans, Asian Americans, Native Americans, and European American students whose families have lived here for generations. Students representing dozens of native languages may attend a single school; in some school districts more than 125 languages are spoken by students. In many schools, a majority of the students come from immigrant or ethnic minority families. Some schools face a mobility problem; student turnover is high and the ethnic mix can shift radically from year to year.

Along with linguistic diversity comes diversity in culture, religion, and academic preparation. Some students visit their home country frequently, while others lack that opportunity. Some students have had excellent schooling in their home country before coming to the United States, others have had their schooling interrupted by war, and still others have never attended school. Some are illiterate in their own language, some have languages that were only oral until recently, and others come from cultures with long literary traditions.

Assimilation Doesn't Equal Success Along *La Frontera*

How can schools cope with the diversity presented by their students? Should they hearken back to the model of education developed in the early decades of this century to deal with the large influx of immigrant youngsters? At that time, educators responded to increasing cultural and linguistic diversity among their students by attempting to accelerate the assimilation into the American mainstream. Their mission was to Americanize immigrants by replacing their native language and culture with those of the United States. Educators confidently sought to fit newcomers into the American mold by teaching them the English language and literature, a sugar-coated version of American history, and a respect for the U.S.'s political system and civic life.

Although some recommend a similar approach today, it is no longer possible even to describe with confidence American culture, or to what mold educators should seek to fit all children. There is no single definition of American culture; multiple definitions have been informed by ethnic minority voices. This is particularly true along *la frontera.*

When immigrant students became shining academic stars, their success is often attributed to the values and habits of their native culture rather than their Americanization. There is some evidence that assimilation may actually inhibit academic success. Studies of Mexican immigrants, Indian immigrants, and children who escaped from Vietnam by boat all suggest that those who maintain a strong identification with their native language and culture are more likely to succeed in schools than those who readily adopt American ways.

These Students Will Change American Society

American society is not the same as it was a century ago, or even a decade ago, partly because of the different peoples who have come to our shores. Without their contributions we would not have such American icons as the Christmas tree, the log cabin, labor unions, and jazz. Jewish immigrants in the early part of this century demanded entry to college in such numbers that they transformed what had been a finishing school for the wealthy to an opportunity for individual advancement.

Those students were fortunate to have educators dedicated to their success, even if the teachers never anticipated that their efforts would have the far-reaching effect of helping to democratize higher education. Educators of that era were selected not only for their formal credentials, but for their suitability as role models for the young. The impact of an educator on the life of young people can hardly be overestimated. Education represents a link to the adult world of successful educated professionals. For children of a different culture and language especially, education has a tremendous impact; schools are their critical links to society. Without the caring guidance of educators, these youth of today will have great difficulty getting into college and becoming engineers, playwrights, or educators themselves and serving as positive contributors to our social and economic well-being.

This volume touches the many aspects of how education is meeting this challenge in *la frontera*. There are no easy answers, but this volume provides the analysis needed, a forum for dialogue that must continue and for the hope that is felt along *la frontera*.

Notes:

Population information is from United States Census Bureau reports.

For information on early twentieth century immigrants and education, see *Going to America, going to school: The Jewish immigrant public school encounter in turn-of-the-century New York City* by Stephan F. Brumberg (1986), New York: Praeger.

For further information on diversity and academic achievement, see *Understanding and meeting the challenge of student cultural diversity* by Eugene E. Garcia (1994), Boston: Houghton Mifflin; and *Handbook of research on multicultural education*, edited by James A. Banks and Cherry A. McGee Banks (1995), New York: Macmillan Publishing.

For further information on second language learning, see *Myths and misconceptions on second language learning: What every teacher needs to unlearn* by Barry McLaughlin (1992), Santa Cruz, CA: National Center for Research on Cultural Diversity and Second Language Learning; and "How long? A synthesis of research on academic achievement in a second language" by Virginia P. Collier, *TESOL Quarterly*, September 1989 Vol. 23, No. 3, pp. 509-531.

Preface

I believe that *Children of La Frontera* will be just the first in a line of many publications about binational efforts on behalf of migrant and immigrant children and their parents. It is my hope that this book will enhance the educational achievement of Mexican migrant and immigrant students and enlighten and assist, in comprehension and understanding, those educators, parents, administrators, local education agencies, community associations, researchers, and university staffs who are not aware of the differences between the processes of education in Mexico and the United States and, therefore, may now know the significance of the bicultural and bilingual potential.

I want to extend *mil gracias* to Dr. Eugene Garcia for writing the foreword that sets the framework for this book and to express my deepest appreciation for the immense effort of the contributing authors. It has been an honor and a joy to work with each of you.

For others who deserve special kudos:

To Dr. Dennis Sayers, professor of bilingual education in the Department of Teaching and Learning at the New York University's School of Education and Dr. Praxedes Martinez, Migrant Education Department, Colorado Department of Education, who gave so generously of their time in providing critical reviews.

Also, this editor wishes to "dar las gracias" to Praxedes Martinez whose idea it was to gather together and tell the world about the many current efforts in Mexico and the United States to serve migrant and immigrant children. (We salute you, Prax!)

To Gildardo Villaseñor, coordinator of the binational program for Ventura County Schools in Camarillo, CA; and Victor Manuel Velazquez Castañeda, Dirección General dé Acreditación, Incorporación, y Revalidación SEP (director, General Office of Accreditation, Incorporation Revalidation, Secretariat of Public Education), Mexico City, who provided many informational resources and documents.

To Patricia Cahape Hammer, managing editor, the ERIC Clearinghouse on Rural Education and Small Schools, for her steadfast encouragement, incredible editorial assistance, sense of humor, and humanity throughout the stages of assembling this work. She is indeed a pleasant collaborator;

To Velma Mitchell, Carla McClure, Carolyn Luzader, Mary Farley, and all the other staff members at Appalachia Educational Laboratory; I thank you warmly for your continuous efforts to make this publication a reality.

— JLF

Contributors

Victoria Andrade de Herrera holds master's degrees in elementary education (Escuela Nacional de Maestros) and geographical sciences (Escuela Normal Superior). A former middle school geography teacher and administrator (1940-1960), she is now a respected author of numerous texts, study guides, atlases, and workbooks for Mexican students (grades 1-9) on general, physical, human, and political geography; social sciences; natural sciences; mathematics; Spanish; civics; and history (most published by Trillas Publishers).

Martha Boethel is a writer and educational planning consultant. Her work includes publications on border issues, reform in mathematics and science education, rural schools, and staff development.

Jorge Botello was 13 years old and living in Okeechobee, Florida, when he wrote this essay, for which he won the Richard E. Bove Memorial Poets' and Writers' Award.

Stephanie Bressler, Ph.D., is an assistant professor of Political Science and also teaches Women's Studies at King's College, Wilkes-Barre, Pennsylvania. Dr. Bressler has researched and authored papers on Pennsylvania farmworker policy. She has also worked as an advocate for farmworkers for the past 10 years and serves on the board of Friends of Farmworkers, Inc., a legal services agency.

Carlos Carranza was living in Liberty, North Carolina, at the time he wrote his essay, "A Sacrifice," for which he received the Richard E. Bove Memorial Poets' and Writers' Award.

Margarita Calderón, Ph.D., is research scientist for Johns Hopkins University Center for Research on Education for Students Placed at Risk. She is conducting longitudinal studies on language-minority students' educational processes and contexts and on teachers' learning communities. In addition, she is a trainer and writer for *Success For All* programs.

Nancy Feyl Chavkin, Ph.D., is professor of social work, Walter Richter Institute of Social Work, Southwest Texas State University, San Marcos, Texas. She has published three books and more than 30 articles on parent/community involvement in the schools, including *Families and Schools in a Pluralistic Society* (SUNY, 1993).

Yolanda De La Cruz, Ph. D. is assistant professor of education at Arizona State University West. Currently on leave from ASU, she is working with the Children's Math Worlds project at Northwestern University. Her research interests include mathematics education and the education of Latino children.

Arlene R. Dorn began teaching in 1969 in Watsonville, California. She attended the University of the Americas in Puebla and Mexico City, Mexico, where she received her M.A. in intercultural education in 1977. She was the coordinator of the Gómez Farías Pajaro Valley Pilot Project, which eventually became the Binational Education Program. She is retired and resides with her husband in Santa Cruz, California.

Kathy Escamilla, Ph.D., is associate professor in the School of Education at the University of Colorado, Denver. She teaches graduate level classes in bilingual education and the teaching of English as a second language. She holds a Ph.D. in curriculum and the study of schooling from UCLA. She has been a bilingual classroom teacher, resource teacher, and director of bilingual/multicultural programs.

Judith LeBlanc Flores, Ph.D., has been a binational consultant, teacher, and trainer for 25 years; an associate professor instructing ESL and bilingual education graduate students for 10 years; and a presenter at TESOL, MEXTESOL, and recently at two binational educational symposiums. She is OKTESOL's past president and an ERIC/CRESS editorial board member. Her main research focus is on U.S. Hispanics.

Eugene E. Garcia, Ph.D., was born in Grand Junction, Colorado, the son of settled-out migrant farmworker parents from northwestern New Mexico, and worked in seasonal crops, harvesting sugar beets and fruits on the western slope of Colorado. He is the former director of the U.S. Department of Education's Office of Bilingual and Minority Language Affairs and is currently dean of the Graduate School of Education and professor of education and psychology at the University of California, Berkeley.

Patricia Cahape Hammer is managing editor of the ERIC Clearinghouse on Rural Education and Small Schools, where she works with authors and editors to produce publications related to the education of American Indians, Alaska Natives, Mexican Americans, and migrants, as well as outdoor education, rural education, and small schools.

Silvia Kelly, coordinator of the Geneseo Migrant Center's CAMPS (Creative Artists Migrant Program Services) and Literature programs, has worked with farmworkers for 20 years. She is the editor of a collection of poetry written by migrant workers over 15 years, *Voices of the Harvest.*

John M. Kibler is a trainer, consultant, and multicultural education specialist with the Illinois Resource Center in Des Plaines, Illinois, where he serves as an instructor in cross-cultural education, multicultural children's literature, and the foundations of language minority education. He also serves as a consulting editor for the magazine *Young*

Children and for the National Association for the Education of Young Children.

Jeri Kinser has a B.A. in Spanish and a M.A. in Spanish and English as a Second Language from Southern Illinois University. She has taught for nine years in the public school system. Two of those years were spent working in the bilingual program at Cobden Unit District #17. She currently is teaching as a graduate assistant at SIU while working on her Ph.D. in curriculum and instruction with a specialization in instructional technology.

Maribel Ledezma is an undergraduate at Stanford University, where she is studying communications and American studies. She has read her poetry and presented at migrant writing workshops and at other meetings, including the National Migrant Conference in 1995. The winner of numerous awards for her writing, she also sings and has participated in youth leadership and television video production activities.

Robert Lynch, director of the BOCES Geneseo Migrant Center, has 25 years of experience working with migrant farmworkers. He has been involved in every aspect of the Center's programs, serving all age groups, from infants to adults. He has given training workshops and other presentations to educators and other professional groups across the country.

Betty Mace-Matluck, Ph.D., is vice president of the Center for Language Minority Populations Projects at the Southwest Educational Development Laboratory in Austin, Texas. She has been with SEDL since 1977 and directs three SEDL projects, one of which focuses specifically on border issues. She has taught at both the university and public school levels.

Johnson Martin, Ph.D., is program representative for the Sexually Transmitted Disease Program of the Pennsylvania Department of Health. He has been involved in the investigation of sexually transmitted diseases in rural Pennsylvania since 1979. His work on behalf of migrant and seasonal farmworkers has resulted in the establishment of significant outreach and treatment programs for the farmworker community.

Philip L. Martin, Ph.D., is professor of Agricultural Economics at the University of California-Davis, chair of the University of California's 60-member Comparative Immigration and Integration Program, and editor of Migration News, a monthly summary of current migration developments with 1,500 readers around the world.

Robert Miller, an English teacher at Mt. Pleasant High School in San Jose, California, did his doctoral research on the Mexican educational system. Since 1978, he has been doing follow-up research on the 26 Mexican primary schools involved in the original study. He has written numerous articles and has given many speeches on education in Mexico.

Mary V. Montavon teaches junior high and high school Spanish, bilingual education, and ESL in Cobden, Illinois. She has also taught in Chicago and Guatemala City. She developed bilingual and migrant education programs for the Cobden School District. She holds a B.A. from Mundelein College in Chicago, a M. Acct. from SIU, and has completed all but her thesis for a Masters in Foreign Languages. She currently is pursuing Administrative Certification.

Christina Quintanilla was a high school student living in Immokalee, Florida, at the time she wrote her story, "Yellow Cheese and Yellow Buses," for which she received the Richard E. Bove Memorial Poets' and Writers' Award.

Harriett D. Romo, Ph.D., is associate professor of sociology at Southwest Texas State University. She has taught English to immigrant children, worked with a National Origin Desegregation Center, and studied undocumented immigration and immigrant families with children. Her book *Latino High School Graduation*, about Mexican origin youth at risk of dropping out of school, is published by the University of Texas Press (1996).

Walter G. Secada, Ph.D., is professor of curriculum and instruction at the University of Wisconsin-Madison, where he is also senior researcher in the Wisconsin Center for Education Research. His research interests include equity in education, mathematics education, bilingual education, school reform, and restructuring.

Alicia Salinas Sosa, Ph.D., is an assistant professor of early childhood education at the University of Texas at San Antonio. During her 20-year tenure at the Intercultural Development Research Association (IDRA), she directed the Desegregation Assistance Center. She has also written and developed teachers guides for children's Spanish readers, assessment instruments in Spanish, and teacher training modules, all being disseminated nationally.

Henry Stevenson-Perez, M.D., serves as a senior investigator in the National Institutes of Health. A board-certified internist and oncologist, Dr. Stevenson-Perez is widely recognized as a pioneering authority in the field of cancer immunoprevention. Dr. Stevenson-Perez served as President of the Hispanic Employee Organization of DHHS during 1994-95.

Sandra E. Trevino migrated for many years with her parents between their home base in Laredo, Texas, and Twin Falls, Idaho, beginning when she was eight years old. She graduated from high school and at the time of writing her essay, "What is a Migrant?" planned to attend Our Lady of the Lake University in San Antonio to study special education. She was a member of the Spanish National Honor Society.

Gloria L. Velásquez, Ph.D., is an award-winning writer of poetry and fiction. The first Chicana to be inducted into the University of Northern Colorado's Hall of Fame, she also won the 11th Chicano Literary Prize in fiction (University of California, Irvine). Gloria is a professor in the Foreign Languages and Literatures Department at California Polytechnic State University, San Luis Obispo.

Norma Varisco de García, Ed.D., is special assistant to the director of the Office of Bilingual Education and Minority Languages Affairs (OBEMLA) and a management official in the U.S. Department of Education (USDE). She is in charge of the overall management of the USDE/OBEMLA-Mexico SEP, Latin America, and Puerto Rico Education Initiative, and has recently written a book, *Hispanic Women: Portraits of Leadership.*

Héctor Eduardo Velasco Mondragón, M.D., serves as a professor and investigator in the Department of International Health, Division of Administrative Sciences, School of Public Health, National Institute of Public Health of Mexico. His study of access to health care among Mexican mushroom workers in Southeastern Pennsylvania was the first significant investigation of health care needs among migrant farmworkers in the country.

Gildardo Villaseñor is the director of the California Migrant Education Binational Program. Previously he taught high school English, English as a second language, and Spanish for 10 years; and was an administrator in the Oxnard school district, working in bilingual education and migrant education staff development.

Al Wright is coordinator of special projects in the Louisiana Migrant Education Program. Since 1984, he has edited the nationally distributed *MEMO (Migrant Education Messages and Outlook).* He has authored or contributed to numerous publications and papers developed by the National Association of State Directors of Migrant Education (NASDME) and the National Association of Migrant Educators (NAME).

Part I

Background: Historic and Current Conditions for Mexican Migrant and Immigrant Education

Chapter 1

Introduction

Judith LeBlanc Flores
Binational Multicultural Consultant

Patricia Cahape Hammer
ERIC Clearinghouse on Rural Education and Small Schools

In his foreword for this volume, Eugene E. Garcia uses a scholar's tools to make a thoughtful argument for improving bilingual and migrant education in the United States. He employs descriptive statistics and other research findings to tell us about the children in our schools, about the teachers who teach them, and the differences between them. He tells us plainly that we are not doing very well with these children. He reminds us of our history as a nation of immigrants and warns us about what it could mean to today's immigrant children and to our nation's future if we fail to meet the challenge of educating these young people.

Instead of using a scholar's tools, however, Garcia might have used a storyteller's tools in making his case. He could have told us the story of his own life. Born in Grand Junction, Colorado, on June 3, 1946, he is the son of settled-out migrant farmworkers from northwestern New Mexico. He, himself, worked in seasonal crops, harvesting sugar beets, cherries, apricots, peaches, apples, and pears. Garcia was one of nine children when his family became sharecroppers on one of the farms they had worked as seasonal laborers. At home, he and his family spoke Spanish. Today we call children like him and his brother and sisters *at-risk students* or *formerlies* (formerly migratory students).

Garcia did well at school. He was a leader in sports and school organizations and was a good student, graduating in the top 15 percent of his class at Grand Junction High School. But his SAT English scores were not impressive, and his academic talent was not always recognized. After being recommended by his Congressman for the U.S. Naval Academy, he was turned down because of those scores. His high school counselor told him that although he had a bright future ahead of him, he would never be a college professor.

Today, Eugene E. Garcia is the dean of the Graduate School of Education and professor of education and psychology at the University of California, Berkeley and the well-known author of books about bilingual students and their education. He is also the former director of the U.S. Department of Education's Office of Bilingual Education and Minority Language Affairs, a position to which he was appointed by President Clinton.

Garcia is only one of the formerlies whose words are included in these pages. Another, Gloria L. Velásquez, wrote the poem "Recuerdos/Memories" that appears in Spanish and English at the beginning of this volume. Her poem contrasts the living conditions she encountered as a migrant child—a *currently* (currently migratory child)—based in Johnstown, Colorado, to those she encountered as a formerly in Texas and Colorado after her father became a construction worker. She graduated from high school and went on to the University of Northern Colorado in Greeley, Colorado. It was there she lived in her first apartment with air conditioning, to which she refers in her poem. Today, she is a professor in the Foreign Languages and Literatures Department at California Polytechnic State University, San Luis Obispo, and has published and won awards for her poetry and fiction.

Keeping Garcia and Velásquez in mind, we invite you to read the words of Christina Quintanilla, Sandra E. Trevino, Carlos Carranza, Jorge Botello, and Maribel Ledezma in chapter 5. They are today's currentlies and formerlies. These young people and others like them are in U.S. schools today, and they could become the next generation of university professors and presidential appointees, here or in Mexico. As things stand now, the odds stacked against them are daunting. To succeed, they will have to be wizards of odds like Gloria Velásquez and Eugene Garcia. Or, as the writers of this volume suggest, we—the administrators, teachers, and professors—could find more ways to help them become resilient enough to endure the hard knocks that inevitably come on the way to a diploma, a trade, or a degree. We could also help them become confident enough to push back on doors closed by inappropriate evaluations, limited English proficiency, and societal prejudice. Or, we could turn our backs on them—or worse.

Forces Pushing and Pulling Mexicans to El Norte

Eugene Garcia was born in the decade following the Repatriation Program, which resulted in the deportation of 400,000 Mexican and Mexican American laborers and their families in the 1930s. Harriett Romo, in chapter 4 of this volume, describes this time in U.S. history. The immigrants deported in the 1930s had come to the United States earlier in the century, pushed out of Mexico by the forces of dispossession by land developers, social discontent, the Mexican Revolution, subsequent economic and political chaos, and finally, starvation. As Ronald Takaki (1993) explains, they were pulled toward El Norte by their dreams for a better life and by the need of U.S. industry for their labor—the same sorts of forces that had pushed and pulled European and Asian immigrants to these shores during the same period. They toiled—building railroads, working in factories, and helping create the great agricultural industry of California, Texas, and other regions of the United States. Industrialists considered them a good work force—easy to manage, hard workers for low pay. As their numbers swelled, however, they were increasingly seen as a threat to Anglo racial and cultural homogeneity. Anglo workers also began to see them as an economic threat. With the onset of the Great Depression, a clamor arose for the closing of the border, and for deportation of Mexican immigrants. By 1934, an estimated 400,000 people were deported to Mexico; over half of them were apparently U.S. citizens (Takaki, 1993). One observer in Santa Barbara, California, recalled the scene at the railroad depot: "They [the immigration officials] had boxcars and they put all the people that went in the boxcars instead of inside the trains . . . A big exodus . . . I'll never forget as long as I live" (Camarillo, 1979, p. 163).

Today's events are like echoes from that period. Disruptions in the Mexican economy—in part due to The North American Free Trade Agreement (NAFTA)—are pushing a new group of immigrants to El Norte. At this writing, the Mexican economy continues to be in deep recession, with serious shortages of jobs. At the same time, the labor force in Mexico is growing. In fact, some analysts project that the labor force in Mexico will grow by 2.1 percent annually at the beginning of the next century (Inmigrantes necesarios, July 20, 1995). What will all of these young people do, who are now entering the labor market?

Many of them will resort to what other Mexican workers have resorted to in the past—leaving their homeland and traveling to El Norte, where low-wage work awaits them. Responding to the pull of jobs from the north, by some estimates, Mexican immigration is up 10 percent (Collier, 1995). According to Hinojosa-Ojeda and Robinson (1992), the U.S. economy requires immigrants to compensate for the low growth of its workforce. By the year 2000, the U.S. work force will grow at a rate of only one percent per year, and this factor alone will stimulate the flow of the migrant stream from Mexico, which is expected to rise annually by between 110,000 to 500,000 persons.

Mexican observers are well aware of the ambivalence of American society to the influx of so many Mexican citizens to the United States. But as Mexican Ambassador to the United States Jesus Silva Herzog noted, the migratory phenomena responds to structural factors of the economies of both countries. He pointed out that Mexican immigrants are in the United States because the U.S. economy needs them and the immigrants subsidize important productive branches of U.S. agriculture, especially in California ("Illegal Mexicans Pillars of the U.S. Economy," 1995, p. A9).

Other U.S. observers have also noted the important role of Mexican immigrants and migrants in the U.S. and Mexican economies. According to Eric Schlosser (1995), by relying on poor migrants from Mexico, California growers have established a wage structure that discourages U.S. citizens from seeking farmwork. A system has evolved in which the cheap labor of Mexican migrants subsidizes California agriculture. At the same time, the migrants send money back home, which has helped to preserve rural Mexican communities that might otherwise have collapsed (Schlosser, 1995).

Impact on the Economy

At this time, most experts agree that it is impossible to gauge the size of the migrant agricultural workforce with any precision because, among other reasons, so many of the workers are illegal immigrants. By some estimates, depending on the crop, anywhere from 30 to 60 percent of migrant farmworkers are in the United States illegally (Schlosser, 1995). Philip L. Martin in chapter 2 of this volume describes what Labor Department studies have shown about the migratory workforce in the United States. He reports that today, there are about 840,000 migrants, and the typical migrant farmworker travels in a seasonal rotation between Mexico and one location in the United States. Huang (1993) reports the average life expectancy of migrant farmworkers is 49 years, and they suffer from many occupation-related and poverty-related illnesses. Infant mortality and mortality rates for children are substantially higher than the general U.S. population.

Migrants' importance to the U.S. food supply is stressed by Schlosser (1995), who reminds us that nearly every fruit and vegetable found in the diets of health-conscious consumers is still picked by hand: "nearly every head of lettuce, every bunch of grapes, every avocado, peach, and plum" (p. 82). This food comes to us inexpensively because of the labor of the parents of Christina, Sandra, Carlos, Jorge, Maribel, and others like them and, too often, because of the labor of the children themselves (Huang, 1993).

Despite the contribution they make to the nation's food supply, these families are widely reviled and depicted as welfare cheats. They are seen as a drain on the economy. However, Mexican immigrants subsidize through their low wages not only agriculture, but also parts of the garment and service industries. Immigrants also pay substantial taxes, according to Karn, Olsen, and Raffel (1993), writing about the California economy. "As a group, immigrants underuse public assistance programs, including Medi-Cal. The undocumented, in particular, live largely in the shadows, working hard, fueling the economy, paying taxes from which they cannot benefit, and fearing government interventions" (p. 2). Julian Simon, an economist at the University of Maryland and author of *The Economic Consequences of Immigration,* often speaks out against critics who charge that immigrants use more welfare services than native-born U.S. citizens. Among his arguments is the notion that immigrants lighten the Social Security load imposed by a graying U.S. population. As more native workers retire and collect Social Security, immigrants, who typically enter the country in the prime of their work lives and tax-paying years, make up the difference. According to Simon, when immigrants do use services they do so in small numbers. About five percent of legal and undocumented people use free medical care, four percent collect unemployment, and one percent use food stamps (in Rocha & Frase-Blunt, 1992, p. 20).

History has taught us, however, that hard work for low wages is no protection against bad press and, consequently, societal rebukes. As the number of Mexican immigrants increased during the first two decades of this century, they were increasingly seen as threats to Anglo economic well-being and cultural homogeneity. Today, there are widespread reports of the insecurity of the U.S. worker as corporations ship jobs overseas. Patrick Buchanan, in his 1996 bid for the Republican presidential nomination, is said to have capitalized on that insecurity by calling for construction of a trench and barbed-wire barricade all along the U.S.-Mexico border. Even NAFTA advocate President Clinton called for stricter enforcement of laws prohibiting the hiring of illegal immigrants and for the strengthening of border enforcement during his January 1996 State of the Union Address.

Cultural Politics

And, just as in the old days, defenders of Anglo cultural dominance such as Allan Bloom in *The Closing of the American Mind* (1987) and E. D. Hirsch in *Cultural Literacy: What Every American Needs to Know* (1987), urge assimilation to the European-American canon, to the exclusion of the contributions and experience of ethnic minorities. Meanwhile, Peter Brimelow in *Alien Nation* (1995) urges restrictions on immigration for cultural reasons. Brimelow warns us about fragmentation caused by the uneven distribution of various immigrant populations, to the point that the ethnic cultures concentrated in various large metropolitan areas will bear little in common with one another. And a popular radio talk show host declares that "[M]ulticulturalism is the 'tool of revenge' of many who have failed to assimilate and fit into 'mainstream American life'" (Stix, 1996, p. 22).

When the country gets into this kind of mood, it is not hard to understand how a measure like California's Proposition 187, "The Save Our State Initiative," could pass by a popular vote. Proposition 187 prohibited undocumented children from enrolling in public schools or receiving medical services, and required school and health service personnel to verify the legal status of students they suspected of being in the state illegally. They were to submit this information to local, state, and federal Immigration and Naturalization Service officials. Federal judicial authority superseded California voters, however. U.S. District Court Judge Mariana Pfaeizer rejected Proposition 187 as unconstitutional, pointing out that authority over immigration lies exclusively with the federal government (Guzmán de Acevedo, 1995).

Other federal protection allowing the continued education of immigrant children—documented or undocumented—is provided by the U.S. Supreme Court in its 1982 *Plyler v. Doe* decision. In that decision, the court found that education plays a pivotal role in maintaining the fabric of our society and maintaining our political and cultural heritage. The Court also recognized—consistent with all relevant studies—that undocumented minor children are likely to remain in the United States and, at some point, legalize their immigration status (Hiller & Leone, 1995). By protecting access to public schools, undocumented children are entitled to various programs, including bilingual education, Chapter 1, Head Start, free and reduced lunch, and others (Hunter & Howley, 1990).

So, perhaps this is where the echoes from the 1930s fade away, and we see how we have changed. The growing sentiment against Mexican immigrants led to the deportation of at least 400,000 people in the 1930s. As this book goes to press, the presidential candidate who has been most hostile in his attacks on Mexican immigration has been labeled an extremist, and he has dropped to a distant third place in the Republican primary race. The legal protections against Proposition 187 seem to be holding. But there is other evidence that our relationship to this important and growing minority group may be changing.

Implications for Schools

While the national debate goes on—about immigration, enforcing the border, and the merits of multiculturalism versus the European-American classical curriculum—teachers, teacher trainers, school administrators, and education officials have had to carry on with the practical business of schooling. In many parts of this country, that has meant the education of children who speak little or no English and who have come from Mexican schools. In some communities these children are immigrants—children whose families have moved across the Mexico-U.S. border permanently, many settling in the border region known as *la frontera*. In other U.S. communities, Mexican migrant children reside there for only parts of the school year, as they follow their parents' agricultural work. Most of these children, too, have had experience in Mexican schools. In chapter 3 of this book, Victoria Andrade de Herrera has provided a detailed description of the educational system in Mexico, a system that is far more comprehensive than most U.S. citizens realize. Although there are similarities between the two systems, there are also differences. The similarities and differences need to be better understood by teachers of binational children.

Increasingly, the migratory workforce has changed from one made up of native-born Anglo and African Americans with various home bases in the United States to a workforce that travels back and forth across *la frontera* (Martin, chapter 2). Teachers in agricultural communities all over the United States, including Michigan and other northern states, have children of these migrant farmworkers in their classrooms, children whose education is taking place in two different school systems. Teachers Mary Montavon and Jeri Kinser (chapter 14) describe such a community in Cobden, Illinois. They helped develop a successful summer program based on a philosophy that honors both Mexican and U.S. culture and language and recognizes the interdependence of the local growers and the hard-working, reliable Mexican workforce that comes there every year to help cultivate and harvest the fruits and vegetables grown in Cobden. Their program staff included two teachers from Mexico, whose work in Cobden was supported by the Mexican government. Marguerita Calderón in chapter 13 describes collaborations going on between districts on both sides of the border, in which native English speakers and native Spanish speakers learn together in both languages.

These programs represent a break from past approaches to Mexican migrant and immigrant education. In the 1920s and 1930s, Mexican children attended segregated schools in the southwest, where they received an education designed to keep them at the bottom of the socioeconomic structure. While there were exceptions, the prevailing attitude about educating the children of Mexicans was clear and openly stated: Educating future laborers in skills other than manual labor or domestic service was asking for trouble (Takaki, 1993). As for curriculum and language learning, the goal of U.S. education has typically been to assimilate immigrant children into the Anglo American classical tradition with English as the language of instruction.

Today, we remain far from having reached a consensus in U.S. society about these matters, but as Calderón (chapter 13) points out, the many benefits to the U.S. economy and culture of having a well educated and bilingual populace are becoming more widely understood as the border between Mexico and the United States opens up. Increasingly, political, academic, and business leaders are forming coalitions and associations that span the North American continent. In education, these collaborations began taking shape several years ago.

New Collaborations

Some of the collaboration taking place in education began at very high levels. In August 1990, then U.S. Secretary of Education Lauro Cavazos and his counterpart in Mexico, Ernesto Zedillo (now President of Mexico), signed a *Memorandum of Understanding on Education*. The Memorandum has been amended and renewed since 1990 to focus on teacher education, teacher exchanges, Spanish and English language instruction, technological education, joint university meetings, mathematics and science teaching, and migrant education. Norma Varisco de García and Eugene E. Garcia describe in chapter 10 the series of activities that have taken place as the result of that agreement. Also facilitated by that agreement has been a series of colloquia involving Mexican and U.S. state and local education officials from the border states that have resulted in development of a common set of goals for education in *la frontera*. These meetings and their outcomes are described in chapter 11 by Betty Mace-Matluck and Martha Boethel. Robert Miller (chapter 6) describes other activities of the Mexican government to assist in the education of Mexican migrant children and adults while they reside in the United States. Mexican consulates located in major cities all across the United States have supplies of Mexican textbooks and other materials to assist in the education of Mexican migrant and immigrant children and adults. Miller's chapter includes a list of Mexican and U.S. organizations involved in various activities, and contact information for each.

Earlier in this chapter, we used California's Proposition 187 as an example of the public expression of hostility toward Mexicans and Mexican Americans, similar to the hostility expressed in the pre-Depression and Depression eras, which eventually led to the deportation of Mexican and

U.S. citizens. But California is also the home of Arlene Dorn, Adriana Simmons, Gildardo Villaseñor, and others who made some of the first attempts to form communication links between local school systems in Mexico and in the United States. These efforts, initiated in 1976 by Dorn, resulted eventually in the formation of the California Binational Program, which in turn grew into the Migrant Education Binational Program that now involves 32 Mexican and at least 10 U.S. states in information exchanges, teacher exchanges, and other sorts of mutually beneficial arrangements. This story of individual determination and subsequent large-scale cooperation is told in chapters 8 and 9. (Other aspects of the U.S.-based Migrant Education Program are described by Al Wright in chapter 7.)

A triumph of the Binational Program and its committee members has been to develop, revise, and gain widespread adoption of the English/ Spanish language "Transfer Document for Binational Migrant Students" (see chapter 8). Despite cultural differences in decision-making styles, this document was developed and approved by governments on both sides of the border. As of August 1995, the Mexican Secretariat of Education[1] has printed over 200,000 copies of the document and distributed it to state and district offices across Mexico and to Mexican consulates in the United States. This is, in effect, a binational report card that makes it possible for Mexican migrant children returning to Mexico during the late autumn or winter months to gain entry into school. Before development of the Transfer Document, many Mexican children did not attend school in Mexico because they arrived home after the registration period. Also, in the United States they were often subjected to numerous assessments and sometimes to inappropriate placements in their classes. Development and official adoption of the Transfer Document took the persistent effort of people on both sides of the border to work out; it is an impressive example of how bureaucratic obstacles can be removed and information can be exchanged that allows for much greater educational access for children.

Another story of state-level cooperation—this time between Pennsylvania and the Mexican state of Guanajuato—relates to the need to share health information about migrant farmworkers moving back and forth between the two states. On behalf of the Binational Health Data Transfer Task Force, Edward Velasco Mondragón, Henry Stevenson Perez, and Johnson Martin describe the GUAPA Project, which could one day serve as another model for other sorts of educational and health collaborations that involve chal-

[1]The department that took the lead in adapting and disseminating The Transfer Document was the Subsecretary of Planning and Coordination, under the direction of Victor Manuel Velásquez Castañeda, director of the General Office of Accreditation, Incorporation and Revalidation.

lenges such as protecting client confidentiality and communicating cross-culturally within different organizational structures. In the context of NAFTA, a minimum standard of health care for migrant farm workers is an essential component of a binational collaboration.

There are other binational efforts underway, not described in this volume. For example:

- The MINT Project (Migrant Instructional Network for Telecommunications), started in November 1994, develops and produces live interactive instructional broadcasts for migrant students, teachers, and parents.[2]
- The Texas State Department of Education and the Secretariat of Education for the Mexican state of Nuevo León entered into a goodwill agreement in 1992 involving Laredo State University and La Universidad Autónoma de Nuevo León. Public school districts in Texas send bilingual teachers to Nuevo León for summer study in Spanish, history, mathematics, and a variety of cultural topics. Educators from Nuevo León frequently travel to Texas seeking ways to better develop oral and academic skills in English and computer-assisted instruction. Other aspects of the agreement relate to seeking ways to recognize course credits granted at both institutions, exchanging information about bilingual instruction in science, mathematics, economics, elementary teacher education, graduate level teacher education, and establishing a coordinated research agenda (U.S. Department of Education, 1995).
- The Binational Researchers Learning Community held its first conference in January 1996 at the Universidad Autónoma de Ciudad Juárez to share educational research findings. Papers presented at the conference will be available through the ERIC system late in 1996.

There are many potential benefits to forming these sorts of connections between nations. As people in administrative and policy-making positions get to know and respect one another, and as teachers share common experiences in the classroom and help each other discover ways to overcome difficulties in educating students, a network of friendships and professional exchanges based in mutual respect can grow. Such relationships make it more difficult for one group to rationalize exploiting or overtly working against the other's interests. That moves us a few steps closer to a safer, healthier, and more caring atmosphere for migrant and immigrant children and their families—one that makes loading people onto boxcars and shipping them away an unthinkable possibility.

---

[2]For more information, contact Zoe Acosta, MINT Project, Educational Management Group, 1300 17th St., Bakersfield, CA 93301-4533; telephone 805/636-4656.

Child Labor

One last time, we look back to the early years of this century in the United States. Vicky Goldsberg (1996), in her article "No Choice But Work," discusses the impact of Lewis Hine's somber, gripping photographs of the shocking working conditions of America's children in the early twentieth century. She comments, "Child labor was not exactly the optimal preparation for a good life in society." Young Sandra E. Trevino would doubtless agree (chapter 5). She tells us with vivid images about working conditions for migrant children in the 1990s.

> I arrive at five o'clock in the morning. While you are having your first dream, sweat washes my face, and I have bathed with fog in the long furrows. While you drop milk in the school's kitchen, I wish I could drink a drop of water because it seems like I never reach the end of the row. . . . While you checked exams . . . I revisited the fields, and sometimes I pulled out snakes instead of vegetables. . .
>
> Yes, I'm a migrant. I study when I can, so that someday I can stop being poor and stop crying in the fields close to the town that I never knew. And when I am in Laredo and I go to class, perhaps I'll get better grades than you my dear friend, because I am tired of being poor.

Most U.S. citizens live under the impression that the problem of child labor has been solved in the United States. However, thousands of migrant children work alongside their parents in the fields on both sides of the border. There are few legal protections for migrant children, and it is estimated that 25 percent of farm labor in the United States is performed by children (Farmworker Justice Fund, 1990). Studies show that at least one third of migrant children—some as young as 10—work on farms to help earn family incomes. Other children may not be hired laborers but they are in the fields to help their parents or simply because there is no available child care (General Accounting Office, 1992). The health of these children is at high risk from injuries resulting from various types of accidents such as falling from heights; drowning in ditches; and receiving injuries from knives, machetes, faulty equipment, and vehicles (Huang, 1993; National Rural Health Care Association, 1986). The health of migrant children is also affected by exposure to pesticides, including touching the residues, breathing the air, drinking the water, and eating the food. Children are more susceptible than adults, because they absorb more pesticides per pound of body weight and their developing nervous systems and organs are vulnerable (General Accounting Office, 1992).

In Mexico, too, families depend on the labor of children to survive. Martin's (1994) study, *Schooling in Mexico*, reports that declining real wages have made Mexican workers' and peasants' families think twice about any unconditional commitments to basic schooling for all their children. They are faced with the task of balancing the immediate need for income contributed by the labor of their children against their children's long-term need for education.

Child labor in general and migrancy in particular surely do not constitute the optimal preparation for a good life in society. Besides the health risks associated with agricultural labor and poverty, migrant children cope with multiple obstacles to educational achievement, including discontinuity in their education, social and cultural isolation, and the strenuous work they do outside of school (Strang, Carlson, & Hoppe, 1993). Prewitt-Diaz (1991) conducted a study of Puerto Rican, Mexican, and Central American migrants. In 598 interviews investigating parents' perceptions regarding the education of their children, he found four major categories of factors affecting educational performance: ecological, educational, psychological, and economical. More specifically, he found that:

- Constant adjustment to school culture is very hard academically for migrant children.
- Support for migrant children was evidenced only in schools that had bilingual teachers and bilingual paraprofessionals.
- Migrant children are placed in the position of bridge between their family and external society. They become the link between the school and the parents, and they are the grocery shoppers, babysitters, and representatives of the family in hospitals and social agencies. Thus, their power as decision makers is important.
- Migrant children are often major contributors to family earnings. "[I]n the fields when you are twelve and bring in 17 baskets of apples, you have the same worth as any other employee in the fields. You are respected for that which you produce" (p. 485). Thus, the reality of the world of work frequently competes with the world of school.

With dilemmas such as these facing migrant children, educators must look for ways to tip the balance in favor of attending school. Flores (1992) reports the extreme shortage of Hispanic high school counselors. Stephanie Bressler, in her study of Latina migrant mothers in Pennsylvania (chapter 18, this volume) concluded:

> Latina migrant mothers need the support of migrant educators to help them find ways to explore productively these new [educational] avenues for their children. There are natural alliances to be developed between educators and migrant mothers who share similar goals for their children. The concept of parental involvement should be expanded to include ways educators can empower mothers to find these avenues for

their children and negotiate the many cultural and lifestyle stumbling blocks that threaten to get in their way.

Nancy Feyl Chavkin and Alicia Salinas Sosa (chapters 19 and 20) each explore this relationship between the mutual interest of schools and parents in supporting education. Each suggests ways of identifying obstacles and organizing efforts to motivate children to stay in school and help them develop the resilience and confidence they will need to graduate. So, part of what we need to do to help children like Sandra Trevino feel cherished is to get to know their families and treat them with the respect they deserve.

But more importantly, we need to face the fact that we as a society have turned a blind eye on the social and legal structures in our market economy that tolerate and recruit children and youth, in the name of survival, to labor in the fields alongside their parents.

Challenges in the Classroom

Most of the children we have described in this chapter speak Spanish as their first language. That fact affects everything else related to their schooling, so a discussion of classroom concerns must begin with an examination of the challenge of bilingual education. Thomas and Collier (forthcoming) tracked language minority students' academic progress over time by examining the academic achievement measures used by school systems. In brief, they found that at least 7-10 years are needed for non-native English speakers with no schooling in their first language to reach age- and grade-level performance if instruction is given only in English. Students with 2-3 years of first language schooling in their home country take at least 5-7 years, and students schooled in high-quality bilingual programs in the United States require 4-7 years to reach native-speaker performance levels. These findings hold true regardless of other background variables such as socioeconomic status and home language.

Unfortunately, according to Spray, well-prepared bilingual teachers, resources, and materials are in short supply. In fact, the National Association of Bilingual Education (NABE) estimates that the United States needs 175,000 more certified bilingual teachers than are currently available (Spray, 1994, p. 3). Of the available pool, some are only conversationally proficient in a second language while others have been rushed through language courses. Many teachers in Mexico are not well prepared to teach English, either. Teachers educated in Mexico's normal schools take a four-hour English course in their last semester. Clearly, there is tremendous work to be done in developing an adequate supply of bilingual teachers even within optimum circumstances; however, in a climate that is hostile to bilingual education, the prospects for meeting the need would be less favorable.

Finally, we want to direct your attention to the chapters by John Kibler (chapter 15), Kathy Escamilla (chapter 16) and Walter G. Secada and Yolanda De La Cruz (chapter 17). Kibler provides guidance in the use of Latino children's literature in the classroom, Escamilla urges the teaching of Mexican American history within the social studies curriculum, and Secada and De La Cruz describe how to teach mathematics for understanding in the bilingual classroom. Each of these chapters discusses the cultural and linguistic frameworks necessary to make classrooms more relevant and inclusive for Mexican immigrant and migrant students.

Concluding Thoughts

According to the National Agricultural Workers Survey data collected by the U.S. Department of Labor, there are approximately 840,000 migrant farmworkers, who are mostly based in Mexico and spend part of each year in the United States. Traveling with them are 409,000 children and an additional 169,000 youths traveling to do farmwork without their parents. Martin (chapter 2) estimates that 67 percent of these workers were unauthorized at the time the survey was taken in 1989, or had been unauthorized until 1987-88. That is a large number of people.

Ricardo Insunza, deputy commissioner at the Immigration and Naturalization Service (INS), is quoted (Rocha & Frase-Blunt, May 1992) as saying, "We are now seeing more family reunification. The breadwinner who has been here for a few years sends for his family, so there are more women and children crossing the ravines at night" (p. 16). According to Insunza, the INS acknowledges that it is simply not possible to halt illegal immigrants. "There is not the will, nor the way" (p. 18). Montavon and Kinser (chapter 14) noticed the increased number of children in their rural Illinois community, which used to see mostly men return each year to work the fields and orchards.

These are the children of *la frontera* and they live here amongst us with their hard-working families. Perhaps it is time we made them feel welcome.

References

Bloom, A. D. (1987). *The closing of the American mind: How higher education has failed democracy and impoverished the souls of today's students.* New York: Simon and Schuster.

Brimelow, P. (1995). *Alien nation: Common sense about America's immigration disaster.* New York: Random House.

Camarillo, A. (1979). *Chicanos in a changing society: From Mexican pueblos to American barrios in Santa Barbara and southern California, 1848-1930.* Cambridge, MA: Harvard University Press.

American barrios in Santa Barbara and southern California, 1848-1930. Cambridge, MA: Harvard University Press.

Collier, R. (1995). NAFTA stumbles short of expectations. San Francisco Chronicle. (Republished on LatinoLink Enterprises, Inc., http://www.latinolink.com/nafecon.html).

Farmworker Justice Fund, Inc. (1990). Testimony for hearing record on "Environmental toxins and children: Exploring the risks." In Congress of the U.S. *Environmental toxins and children: Exploring the risks, Part II, Hearing held in Washington, DC before the Select Committee on Children, Youth, and Families.* Washington, DC: Government Printing Office. (ERIC Document Reproduction Service No. ED 336 178)

Flores, J. L. (1992, April). *Persisting Hispanic American college students: Characteristics that lead to baccaulaureate degree completions.* (Paper presented at the annual meeting of the American Education Research Association, San Francisco, CA). (ERIC Document Reproduction Service No. ED 345 609)

General Accounting Office. (1992). *Hired farmworkers' health and well-being at risk.* Washington, DC: Author.

Goldsberg, V. (Jan./Feb. 1996). No choice but work. *Civilization, 3*(1), 58-59.

Guzmán de Acevedo, E. (1995, 24 de Noviembre). *Rechazo de la ley anti-immigrantes.* [Rejection of the anti-immigrant law]. *El Nacional.* (Oklahoma's Spanish-English Newspaper) Viernes, 1.

Hiller, F., & Leone, B., (1995, February/March) California's Proposition 187: Moving toward racism and intolerance, *TESOL Matters, 5* (1).

Hinojosa-Ojeda, R. & Robinson, S. (1992). Labor issues in a North American free trade area. In N. Lustig, B. P. Bosworth, & R. Z. Lawrence (eds.) *North American free trade: Assessing the impact.* Washington, DC: The Brookings Institute.

Hirsch, E. D. (1987). *Cultural literacy: What every American needs to know.* Boston: Houghton Mifflin.

Huang, G. (1993). *Health problems among migrant farmworkers' children in the U.S.* Charleston, WV: ERIC Clearinghouse on Rural Education and Small Schools. (ERIC Document Reproduction Service No. ED 357 907)

Hunter, J., & Howley, C. (1990). Undocumented children in the schools: Successful strategies and policies. Charleston, WV: ERIC Clearinghouse on Rural Education and Small Schools. (ERIC Document Reproduction Service No. ED 321 962)

Ilegales mexicanos pilares de la economía de EU. [Illegal Mexicans pillars of the U.S. economy]. (1995, July 20). *Novedades, No. 19605,* Health A9.

Inmigrantes necesarios [Necessary immigrants]. (1995, July 20). *Novedades, LIX* (19605), A12.

Karn, K., Olsen, L., & Raffel, L. (1993, November). Action alert: A response to anti-immigrant proposals. *California Tomorrow,* pp. 2-3.

Martin, C. J. (1994). *Schooling in Mexico: Staying in or dropping out.* Aldershot, England: Avebury.

National Rural Health Care Association. (1986). *Occupational health of migrant and seasonal farmworkers in the United States: Report summary.* Kansas City, MO: Author. (ERIC Document Reproduction Service No. ED 292 594)

Plyler v. Doe. 457 U.S. 202, 102 S. Ct. 2382 (1982).

Prewitt-Diaz, J. O. (1991, Summer). The factors that affect the educational performance of migrant children, *Education, III* (4), 483-486.

Rocha, V. A., & Frase-Blunt, M. (May 1992). Coming to America. *Hispanic,* pp. 15-16, 18, 20.

Schlosser, E. (1995). In the strawberry fields. *The Atlantic Monthly, 276*(5), 80-108.

Simon, J. (1989). *The Economic consequences of immigration.* Cambridge, MA: Blackwell Publishers.

Spray, M. S. (1994). *Tending the border. Schools along the border: The educational implications of NAFTA.* Washington, DC: Council for Educational Development and Research (CEDaR).

Stix, G. (1996, February). The rainbow majority. *Scientific American, 274*(2), 22.

Strang, E. W., Carlson, E., & Hoppe, M. E. (1993). *Services to migrant children: Synthesis and program options for the Chapter 1 Migrant Education Program.* Prepared under contract for the U.S. Department of Education by Westat, Inc., Rockville, MD. (ERIC Document Reproduction Service No. ED 364 385)

Takaki, R. (1993). *A different mirror: A history of multicultural America.* Boston: Little, Brown, and Co.

Thomas, W. P., & Collier, V. P. (forthcoming). *Language minority student achievement and program effectiveness.* (in *Newsletter of the National Clearinghouse for Bilingual Education, 18*(5), 4-5, November, 1995.)

U.S. Department of Education. (1995). Binational Symposium II on Professional Development, U.S./Mexico [*II Simposio del Desarrolo Profesional del Maestro, México-EE.UU*]. Collaboration Initiatives, Cibeles Convention Center, Cuidad Juárez, Chihuahua, Mexico, September 14-15, Resource Book (*Compendio de acuerdos*). Washington, DC: Office of Bilingual Education and Minority Languages Affairs.

Chapter 2

Migrant Farmworkers and Their Children: What Recent Labor Department Data Show

by Philip L. Martin
Department of Agricultural Economics
University of California-Davis

This chapter reviews the population characteristics of migrant and seasonal farmworkers and their children. No current data system provides a reliable count or profile of migrant children, but a data-gathering initiative launched in 1989 to determine the effects of the Immigration Reform and Control Act on agriculture suggests that there are about 840,000 migrant farmworkers who have 409,000 children traveling with them as they do farmwork.

According to these data, the typical migrant child today shuttles between one U.S. and one Mexican residence, rather than following the crops from one U.S. residence to another. However, farmworkers and the farm labor market are changing rapidly in the face of immigration reforms, the North American Free Trade Agreement (NAFTA), and structural changes in Mexico and Latin America, making a better database on farmworkers and their children more important than ever.

Expansion of Federal Efforts to Serve Migrants

The 1960s image of a migrant farmworker depicted a hardworking White, Black, or Hispanic family who lived during the winter months in southern Florida, southern Texas, or central California. Every spring, they followed the sun northward to harvest ripening crops from New York to Michigan to Washington.

The federal government began programs in the 1960s to help migrant workers and their families to escape from "the migrant stream." In 1965, observers estimated there were 466,000 migrant farmworkers, most of whom were U.S. citizens. Many of these workers traveled across state lines with their families to harvest crops.

During the era of the civil rights movement, federal assistance was provided to overcome the reluctance of state and local governments to assist migrant workers who were in the area for only a short time. Many communities wanted migrants to depart as soon as the harvest was over. For example, 39 states in 1960 had welfare regulations that required recipients to be residents of the area from 6 months to 3 years (Migrant and Seasonal Farmworker Powerlessness, 1970-71).

During the 1970s and 1980s, federal programs for migrant workers and their families multiplied. Today the 12 major migrant and seasonal programs for farmworkers spend over $600 million annually, which is equivalent to about 10 percent of what the 1 million migrant and seasonal farmworkers earn in wages (Martin & Martin, 1994).

However, none of these federal migrant and seasonal farmworker programs has the same definition of *migrant* or *seasonal farmworker*, and many programs have expanded their definitions over time. For these reasons, there are no time-series data that allow analysts to chart the number of migrant farmworkers and their children over time. During the 1980s, when Congress expressed interest in the number and legal status of farmworkers to project the effects of immigration reform on U.S. agriculture, the data problems were described as a harvest of confusion (Martin, 1988).

What Current Labor Department Data Show

This chapter summarizes data about worker characteristics drawn from the National Agricultural Worker Survey (NAWS). The NAWS study was initiated by the U.S. Department of Labor in 1989 to address fears that immigration reforms were likely to result in farm labor shortages. Other federal databases exist: The Department of Agriculture Farm Labor Survey includes information on farmworkers and their children based on data collected from farm employers about workers they employed during a particular week, and the Department of Education's Migrant Student Record Transfer System includes data on students identified as having parents who are or were migrant farmworkers. Farm labor researchers consider the NAWS data, however, to be the best data currently available. (For reviews of other farm labor data sources, see Martin & Martin, 1994.)

NAWS data examines migrant farmworkers as a category of workers in the total farm labor force. According to the study, there are about 5 million persons employed sometime each year to work on the nation's 800,000 farms that hire labor. About 2 million of these workers help to produce crops. Crop production involves more seasonal employment peaks and troughs than livestock production, hence, most migrant and seasonal farmworkers are employed on crop farms. About half of these 2 million crop workers are employed more than one month in agriculture, but less than 10 months, which translates into about 1 million American workers depending on seasonal farm jobs for most of their annual earnings (Mines, Gabbard, & Samardick, 1993). In the absence of a single federal definition for migrant farmworkers, the NAWS study defined migrants as workers who travel 75 or more miles in search of crop work. About 42 percent of the 7,200 workers interviewed while doing crop farm jobs between 1989 and 1991 fit this definition of migrant workers. This suggests that approximately 840,000 of the nation's 2 million crop workers are migrants. Migrant and seasonal farmworkers average about $5 hourly for 1,000 hours of work, for an average income of $5,000 annually.

The NAWS study revealed that the migrant farmworkers were

- primarily Hispanics (94 percent);
- born in Mexico (80 percent);
- married, with children (52 percent);
- doing farmwork in the United States without their families (59 percent);
- mostly men (82 percent); and
- are today, or were until 1987-88, unauthorized workers (67 percent).

NAWS interviewers obtained job histories from each worker interviewed, and this enabled them to distinguish among three different groups of migrant farmworkers:

- about 280,000 followed the crops from farm to farm and often from state to state;
- about 700,000 workers shuttled into the United States from homes abroad, usually in Mexico, but then remained at one U.S. residence while they did farmwork; and
- about 140,000 of the workers first shuttled into the United States from homes abroad and then followed the crops, and are thus double counted in the first two groups.

These migrant farmworkers together are accompanied by about 409,000 children. Of the children, 373,000 traveled with their parents and did not do farmwork, while 36,000 traveled and also did farmwork. In addition, the NAWS data suggest that there are 169,000 youths, who travel at least 75 miles to do farmwork without their parents.

It should be emphasized that the data on migrant farmworkers and their children are remarkably inadequate. The data presented here could be misconstrued to suggest that there are fewer migrant children than the target populations of some of the federal programs designed to serve migrants and their families. For example, the Migrant Education Program serves the children of year-round workers employed on livestock farms (if they moved within the last 6 years) and also serves the children of workers employed in food processing plants in which there is a high turnover among the workers. Labor laws consider this last group of workers nonfarmworkers; not all migrant workers work on farms.

Other federal programs serve fewer workers than are indicated by this description. The Job Training Partnership Act (JTPA) 402 program, for example, casts a wide net to include migrant and seasonal farmworkers employed in nonfarm packinghouse and processing operations. However, JTPA limits eligibility for its services to workers legally authorized to be in the United States who are employed at least 25 days in agriculture and who obtain at least 50 percent of their earnings from farmwork, or spend 50 percent of their working time doing farmwork.

Implications for Migrant Programs

Migrant farmworkers are probably the largest needy workforce in the United States. Evidence exists that migrant children's chances for success in the U.S. economy are hurt rather than helped by their parents' occupation (National Commission on Agricultural Workers, 1992).

The situation is not likely to go away by itself, either. Labor-intensive crop production in the United States has increased at a pace faster than that at which labor-saving machines have displaced farmworkers (Martin, 1990). The value of U.S.-produced fruits and nuts, vegetables and melons, and horticultural specialties such as flowers and mushrooms reached $30 billion in 1991, 38 percent of the value of total U.S. crop sales (U.S. Department of Agriculture). To put this growing sector of U.S. agriculture in perspective, the value of only four of the hand-harvested commodities—oranges, grapes, apples, and lettuce—exceeds the value of the U.S. wheat crop.

NAFTA is unlikely to change the role of the United States as North America's fruit and salad bowl, largely because most fruits and vegetables are harvested in the fall, during the season when Mexican production is lowest (Martin, 1993). But NAFTA and economic restructuring in Mexico are changing the characteristics of migrant farmworkers and their children. Displacement and dislocation in rural Mexico, where 30 million people have an average income of less than $1,000 annually, are expected to accelerate Mexico-to-U.S. migration in the 1990s. Some of these new migrant children will likely speak Indian languages rather than Spanish.

Migrant and seasonal farmworker service providers thus may see their roles evolve into being the primary government-funded service group addressing the needs of new immigrants to the United States. In this capacity, they will be dealing with children who may not speak English or Spanish, and whose parents may not know whether they will want or be able to remain in the United States. For these reasons, migrant programs that serve migrant farmworkers' children will need flexibility to deal with an ever-changing population as we move through the last years of this century.

References

Martin, P. L. (1988). *Harvest of confusion: Migrant workers in U.S. agriculture.* Boulder, CO: Westview Press.

Martin, P. L. (1990). The outlook for agricultural labor in the 1990s. *U.C. Davis Law Review, 23*(3), 499-523.

Martin, P. L. (1993). *Trade and migration: NAFTA and agriculture.* Washington, DC: Institute for International Economics.

Martin, P. L., & Martin, D. (1994). *The endless quest: Helping America's farmworkers.* Boulder, CO: Westview Press.

Migrant and seasonal farmworker powerlessness: Hearings before the Subcommittee on Migratory Labor of the Committee on Labor and Public Welfare, Senate, 91st Cong., 1st and 2nd Sess. (1970-71). (16 volumes of hearings produced under the direction of Senator Walter Mondale)

Mines, R., Gabbard, S., & Samardick, R. (1993). *U.S. farmworkers in the post-IRCA period: Based on data from the National Agricultural Workers Survey (NAWS).* (Research Report 4). Washington, DC: U.S. Department of Labor, Office of the Assistant Secretary for Policy.

National Commission on Migrant Education. (1992). *Invisible children: A portrait of migrant education in the United States. Final report.* Washington, DC: Author. (ERIC Document Reproduction Service No. ED 348 206)

U.S. Department of Agriculture. Economic Research Service. ERS. *Economic Indicators of the Farm Sector (annual).* Washington, DC: Author.

This chapter was originally published as an ERIC Digest, EDO-RC-94-7 in November 1994.

CHAPTER 3

Education in Mexico: Historical and Contemporary Educational Systems

VICTORIA ANDRADE DE HERRARA
EDITORIAL TRILLAS, MEXICO, D.F.
(TRANSLATED BY JUDITH LEBLANC FLORES)

To meet the challenge of educating children who have recently arrived from Mexico or who are involved in a seasonal rotation between the United States and Mexico, it is important for U.S. educators to have a current and historical perspective on the education system of Mexico. The first half of this chapter describes the history and conditions of different periods in the evolution of Mexico's education system, beginning in colonial times and continuing up to the present time. Education in Mexico, like education everywhere, has undergone various reform movements as different factions have gained political power. Readers will see, however, that Mexico's system has grown steadily to include ever greater numbers of children and adults, educating them to ever higher levels.

The second half of this chapter describes the current organization of Mexican schools, which has undergone a massive restructuring since 1992. It is a complex and comprehensive system. The chapter is organized to describe its scope, beginning with preschool up through postgraduate university education.

Historical Background

Colonial Times

The development of education in Mexico during colonial times has reflected the country's political development. The Spanish conquest of 1521 markedly influenced Native educational institutions; during colonization, education was used by Spain as an instrument of domination to nurture political dependency among Natives. Throughout this period, Mexico's educational system was in the hands of the Catholic clergy. Education developed among the Natives and Mestizos within some of the religious orders, including the Dominicans, Franciscans, Augustines, and Jesuits. These religious orders acquired great ascendancy of influence in the middle and upper classes of the New Spain society (Salvat, 1974, Vol. 5; pp. 166, 167, & 174; Solana, Cardill Reyes, & Bolanos Martinez, 1982, p. 13).

The religious orders, especially the Jesuits and Dominicans, created numerous educational institutions. The Jesuits were dedicated particularly to the study of the humanities; the Dominicans, to the arts and theology (Salvat, 1974, Vol. 5 pp. 166-167).

Educational advances quickly demanded the foundation of a university and, beginning in 1526, efforts were initiated to obtain authorization from the Spanish monarchy. In 1551, with the appropriate approval, the University of Mexico became the first university of the Americas. In 1570, it acquired the title of Royal University and was given the right to use the shield of the guns of Castille and León, and, in 1579, Pope Clemente VII issued a Bull (a solemn papal letter) that changed its name to Royal and Pontifical University (Salvat, 1974, Vol. 5, p. 178).

Independence

Mexico's post-independence history is characterized by the struggle of two opposing political groups—the Centralists and the Federalists, later known as the Conservative and Liberal parties.

The Liberals sought to take away Catholic clerical control of the educational system and place it in the hands of the government. With this in mind, Liberal Vice President Gómez Farías founded in 1833 the Public Guidance for the Federal District and Federal Territories. For the first time in Mexico, public education was controlled by the government, with administration of municipal schools centralized in Mexico City. This arrangement preceded the subsequent establishment of the Education Ministry (Barbosa, 1972, p. 27; Larroyo, 1986, p. 253; Solana et al., 1982, p. 22).

These measures caused the rebellion of Conservative forces, which, headed by Antonio de Santa Anna, dismissed Gómez Farías in 1834 and impeded implementation of his project. After that, the struggle between

Liberals and Conservatives continued, further complicated by the separation of Texas in 1836 and the war with the United States in 1847 (Larroyo, 1986, p. 253: Salvat, 1974, Vol. 7, p. 251; Solana et al., 1982, p. 22).

The Reform (Reforma) Movement

Antonio de Santa Anna, a picturesque character in Mexican history, manipulated the problems between the Conservative and Liberal parties for his own gain, and ascended to the presidency on seven separate occasions. In 1844, during one of his presidencies, he named educator Manuel Baranda Minister of Justice and Public Instruction. Baranda authored the General Plan of Studies and, for the first time, teaching methods and school organizational structures were consigned to legislative norms (Larroyo, 1986, p. 251).

Once again, a comprehensive educational project was forgotten when a group of young Liberal politicians—among them Benito Juárez—rebelled and pursued a total reform of the country. In 1856, this group was able to reunite the legislators, who proclaimed a new constitution in 1857. Among the rights proclaimed in this constitution was the right to learn. In October of the same year, the Liberal president, Comonfort, informed Congress that the Normal School for Teachers had been established (Barbosa, 1972, p. 27; Solana et al., 1982, p. 23).

New conflicts impeded the development of educational institutions. The first of these conflicts was the War of Three Years (1858-1860) between Liberals and Conservatives. During this struggle, Mexico had two presidents: Zuloaga, a Conservative, and Juárez, a Liberal. During the three years that the war lasted, Juárez and his collaborators put together the Reform (Reforma) Laws, one of which established the separation of church and state, eliminating religious instruction from public education (Solana et al., 1982, p. 26).

Although the Liberals triumphed, the country enjoyed only a short period of tranquility, as Mexico was invaded by France in 1864. France wanted to create an empire to oppose the growing power of the United States, and imposed an emperor on Mexico: the Austrian Maximilian of Hapsburg. The French intervention and the reign of Maximilian (1864-1867) constituted a parenthetical period in the history of Mexican education. Although the emperor developed his Law of Public Instruction, the brevity of his government did not allow him to carry it out (Solana et al., 1982, pp. 26-27).

When Maximilian was defeated in 1867, the government of Benito Juárez once again took over the education of the country, establishing three education characteristics that continue to this day: Education in Mexico is nonreligious, free, and obligatory (Barbosa, 1972, p. 29; Larroyo, 1986, pp. 274-275; Solana et al., 1982, p. 32).

One of the first steps taken by Juárez was to proclaim in December of 1867, the Organic Law of Public Instruction in the Federal District, elaborated by Martínez de Castro, Minister of Instruction; and Gabino Barreda, a distinguished positivist. This law established the unity of the country in instruction and declared primary education free and obligatory. That same year, the Secondary School for Young Ladies, The National Preparatory School, and the Academy of Sciences and Literature were founded. Provisions also were made for studies such as medicine, law, agriculture, engineering, and fine arts in other schools. This project culminated with the Law of the Public Instruction of the Federal District, published in 1867 and modified in 1875 (Barbosa, 1972, p. 28; Larroyo, 1986, pp. 273-274; 276-277; Salvat, 1974, Vol. 8, p. 22).

Transition of the Educational Reform to Porfirioism

Beginning in 1867, and continuing through the first presidential period of Porfirio Díaz (1876-1880), Mexican leadership was heavily influenced by the doctrine of positivism. Leaders worked to apply the methods employed in the natural sciences, especially the techniques of experimentation. Ignacio Ramírez, designated in 1876 to work out the complicated question of education of the country, impressed on his work a sensible mixture of his liberal ideals and those of the positivist doctrine (Larroyo, 1986, pp. 302-303; Solana et al., 1982, Vol. 8, p. 122).

With Ramírez, education received a great boost: the spread of primary and secondary instruction was broadened; the importance of the preparation of women and of higher education were confirmed; and, for the first time, official attention was given to indigenous instruction. The work of Ramírez extended into other fields of education: he founded libraries and scholarships, fomented popular education, protected the fine arts, and fought to incorporate the indigenous population into the life of the nation (Barbosa, 1972, p. 75; Larroyo, 1986, pp. 302-303; Solana et al., 1982, p. 46).

The Porfiriato (Díaz's Government)

Ramírez collaborated with President Porfirio Díaz until an illness retired Ramírez from public life in 1877. The work that he initiated was continued, during "Porfirioism," with a brilliant generation of educators. Among the most outstanding are two ministers of public instruction, Joaquín Baranda and Justo Sierra.

During the early years of this period, education in Mexico was enriched by the contributions of two prominent educators: Enrique C. Rébsamen and Enrique Laubscher. In the state of Veracruz, these two produced the first important essays on the theory and practice of education. To demonstrate their theories, they founded in 1883 the Model School of Orizaba, and some years later, the Veracruzana Normal School of Jalapa. These institutions made Veracruz the original site of one of the most important education reforms in Mexico during the nineteenth century (Barbosa, 1972, pp. 92-93; Larroyo, 1986, pp. 313,319-326; Solana et al., 1982, pp. 55-56). Rébsamen and his students directly influenced the organization of education in 10 states, but within a few years, their "Reforma" extended over the greater part of the country. In 1901, Rébsamen was called to the capitol, where he filled the positions of the Director of Normal Instruction and the Director of the Normal School until 1904, the year of his death (Larroyo, 1986, p. 326).

At the national level, "Porfirioism" was carried out by Joaquín Baranda, minister of education. During Baranda's tenure, normal education made notable advances. He established normal schools to train professors in Guadalajara, Monterrey, Puebla, San Luis Potosí, and Colima. To further increase the supply of professors, other normal schools were founded in Victoria, Tamaulipas (1889); the capital of the country (1889); Oaxaca (1890); and Saltillo, Coahuila (1894). At the end of the century, there existed 45 normal schools in the Republic (Barbosa, 1972, p. 92; Larroyo, 1986, pp. 347-348).

Baranda was aided in his labors by Justo Sierra, an outstanding historian, philosopher, and teacher who, in 1901, became the Subsecretary of Public Instruction. Sierra was able to gain both the cooperation of educators from diverse backgrounds and the backing of all members of Congress. In January 1904, he carefully planned and established the first two kindergartens in the Federal District (Barbosa, 1972, p. 98; Larroyo, 1986, pp. 359-360).

After a brilliant collaboration with Baranda, Sierra filled various offices and, in 1905, initiated the creation of the Office of the Secretaría of Public Instruction and Fine Arts, a position he was the first to fill. After his appointment, he took charge of Primary and Normal, Preparatory, and Professional Instruction in the Federal District and territories; the Fine Arts School of Music and Declamation; the Schools of Arts and Trades, Agriculture, Commerce, and Administration. He carried out the progressive federalization of instruction without affecting the sovereignty of the states, and he insisted on the constant revision of programs and plans of study (Barbosa, 1972, pp. 101-103; Larroyo, 1986, pp. 361-362).

The creation of this Secretaría office conferred great power on Sierra, who, in turn, proposed two main objectives. First, he worked to transform primary education from instruction that simply dispenses knowledge to a system for developing in the child new forms of thinking (Barbosa, 1972, p. 108; Larroyo, 1986, p 366). Second, he aimed to establish continuity in the Mexican educational system, including higher education. To this end, he obtained the support of President Díaz and Congress and founded, in 1910, the National School of Higher Education to train professors in secondary and professional education. In the same year, he also led the effort to reorganize the National University of Mexico as a lay university, and charged the school with purposes different from those carried out during its time as a Pontificate University (Barbosa, 1972, p. 107; Larroyo, 1986, pp. 370-371).

The unification of the national educational system was advanced through a series of national assemblies designed to bring educators up to date. Sierra actively participated in all of these activities, and the last of the assemblies took place in September 1910 (Barbosa, 1971, p. 107; Larroyo, 1986, p. 370).

The following month, the Revolution exploded, led by Francisco Madero against the dictator Porfirio Díaz. In a last attempt to prolong his power, the Porfiriato (Díaz's government) produced in that same year laws that established Schools of Rudimentary Instruction, antecedents of rural schools throughout the Mexican Republic. By decree, these institutions were to teach Native people to speak, read, and write Spanish and to do basic arithmetic. When the decree was approved by the Chambers (similar to Congress), Porfirio Díaz and his cabinet presented their resignations. In June 1911, the law was put in place by the interim president, León de la Barra (Barbosa, 1972, p. 115; Larroyo, 1986, p. 401; Solana et al., 1982, p. 113).

The Post Revolutionary Period

One of the first worries of President Madero, when he came into power, was the realization of the Rural Schools Project. However, he considered it necessary to study the situation before launching a project that would have such a profound impact on the indigenous population.

Before the project even got underway, however, political upheaval once again changed the direction of the republic: on February 22, 1913, Madero was assassinated. In the chaos following the President's death, various factions tried to come into power and, consequently, progress in education was abandoned over a long period. Between May 1911 and February 1917, there were 15 different ministers of Public Instruction and Fine Arts (Barbosa, 1972, p. 116).

In 1916, Venustiano Carranza, leader of the group that obtained power, convened Congress in the city of Querétaro to produce a new Constitution. This Constitution was adopted on February 5, 1917. Article 3, dedicated to education, declared that education was to be free and nonreligious. This same stipulation that education be nonreligious applied even to private, primary, secondary, and higher education. No religious corporation, or minister of any cult, would be allowed to establish or administer schools of primary instruction (Barbosa, 1972, pp. 144-145; Larroyo, 1986, p. 147).

Under the new Constitution, education was decentralized, and the National Office of the Secretaría was eliminated. The municipalities were given responsibility for the control and organization of kindergarten and primary education. The middle schools, normal schools, preparatory, and commercial schools (among others) were placed under the control of the governments of distinct entities (included in these, the Federal District), while control of the National University of Mexico was transferred to a newly created University Department (Solana et al., 1982, pp. 149-150).

It soon became apparent that the decentralized governance plan was not functional. The municipalities lacked resources to build schools, provide furnishings, and pay teachers' salaries. Also, they had difficulty locating persons with the scholarly or pedagogical preparation necessary to carry out the task (Solana et al., 1982, pp. 151-152).

In 1920, the nation was shaken by another assassination: Carranza's. Interim president Adolfo de la Huerta named José Vasconcelos as rector of the National University, and the appointment was confirmed by the new president, Álvaro Obregón (1920-1924). Vasconcelos, a prestigious intellectual, was given broad authority to carry out a comprehensive national education program. To achieve this goal, he created a new Secretaría and succeeded in getting it approved by the Congress in September 1921. The office was called the new Secretaría of Public *Education*, not *Instruction* (as the old office was designated), to signify that the new Secretaría would work toward more than mere instruction, but instead would work to develop students' full potential (Barbosa, 1972, p. 31, 160-161; Solana et al., 1982, p. 158). During Vasconcelos' tenure in the Secretaría, he received President Obregón's full political and economic support.

In the brief period between 1921 to 1924, great emphasis was given to the fight against illiteracy, the growth of rural schools, the creation of libraries, support of arts and crafts, and artistic and scientific interchange with foreign institutes. For Vasconcelos, the educational process should not only develop the full potential of the individual, but should find a way to join the indigenous world with that of the Hispanic. Such a fusion would give birth to the *Mexican* identity and to other national identities of Latin America. Believing that Indians should not constitute a group apart, he thought they needed to mix in and participate, thus creating an integrated Mexican society. To combat illiteracy, not only of the indigenous population but of all Mexicans, intense campaigns were initiated in which specialized personnel and numerous volunteers participated (Larroyo, 1986, p. 482; Solana et al., 1982, pp. 159, 174-175).

In his support for the formation of the essential Mexican identity,

Vasconcelos patronized diverse aspects of the arts. Artists of the stature of Montenegro, Rivera, Orozco, Charlot, and Xavier Guerrero painted murals on public buildings. He also arranged for support to rehabilitate The National Symphony so that it could offer concerts to teachers in the capital and the provinces. Visits by prominent Latin American intellectuals also were promoted. All of this activity took place without neglecting the building of new schools, especially technical schools for men and women (Salvat, 1974, Vol. 9, p. 256; Solana et al., 1982, pp. 176-177).

To stimulate reading, a basic element in people becoming self-taught, classic literature of every era was published, along with teacher guides. These works, sold at very low prices so the people could buy them, were in great demand. During his management, Vasconcelos founded 671 permanent libraries and 21 circulating libraries, thus increasing access to books for people in the provinces (Solana et al., 1982, pp. 179-180).

Rural education, too, received attention and support from a Department of Indigenous Culture, which had the authority to implement its plans. By 1923, basic organizational structures for the establishment and functioning of rural schools were in place, and missionary teachers were selected and charged with equipping local primary schools and delivering primary instruction in areas with small or remote populations. These schools began providing Spanish language instruction and advising, supporting, and orienting the rural populations on social and economic questions. Students cooperated in building school furniture, buildings, and annexes for the learning of trades and updated agricultural practices and for the practice of sports. These schools, apart from being educational centers, soon became places of consultation for everyone in the community, and the schools were renamed *Village Houses*. In 1924, after a tremendous output, Vasconcelos left the Secretaría. At that time, more that 1,000 Village Houses were functioning (Aguilar, 1988; Barbosa, 1972, pp. 164-166; Larroyo, 1986, pp. 404-405; Solana et al., p. 482).

The transfer of power from President Obregón to President Calles was peaceful. Calles had worked as a teacher and favored the springing up of diverse educational institutions to benefit various popular groups. In 1925, the Department of Indigenous Culture changed its name to the Department of Rural Schools, Outside Primary Schools, and Indigenous Cultural Incorporation. The Village Houses were once again called rural schools. Among the purposes of this Department was to develop individuals' abilities to better the conditions of their own lives. Therefore, officials recommended that teachers instruct more through experience than through classroom lectures. Calles also considered it a necessity that each region have its own special program to meet its own needs. As a basis for the participation of the indigenous population, the continuing importance of instruction in

Spanish was conceded but with the stipulation that all grades be part of the instruction (Larroyo, 1986, p. 400).

It is notable that, while the purposes of education remained the same as that stated by preceding governments, Calles increased the budget for rural education and initiated the construction of appropriate buildings. For these new schools, he provided furnishings and large parcels of land for regional crops, hen houses, rabbit hutches, and bee hives (Larroyo, 1986, pp. 405-406, 408).

Calles' presidency (1924-1928) was characterized by his determination to have education reach all the great population centers, both urban and rural. In 1926, cultural missions were initiated and charged with disseminating hygiene practices, giving vaccinations, instructing teachers in rural home medicine and first aid, organizing cottage and regional industries, and giving classes in horticulture, zoology, and rural construction (Barbosa, 1972, p. 181; Larroyo, 1986, pp. 407-409). By 1928, there were more than 5,000 rural schools, 206 urban schools, and 38 kindergartens. During the same period, normal school instruction was intensified. The National School for Teachers, founded in 1924, gained prestige when renowned teachers were invited to teach there (Larroyo, 1986, 484-485).

However, during Calles' presidency, there were constant conflicts in Mexico's capitol between the National University and the Secretaría of Education. The Secretaría of Education struggled for lay instruction; the University pushed to allow for religious control of instruction. To reduce the University's strength, since it controlled the 5 years of preparatory school, Subsecretary Moisés Sáenz separated out from the University responsibility for the first 3 years of preparatory school and with these formed secondary (middle school) education, dependent on the Secretaría of Education (Barbosa, 1972, pp. 17, 177).

Before the end of Calles' term, Obregón tried to get himself reelected but was assassinated in 1928. A provisional president, Portes Gil, and two others filled the period. Conflicts intensified between the authorities of education and those of the universities and, after a student strike, supported by various sectors of the population, the National University obtained its autonomy on July 10, 1929 (Larroyo, 1986, p. 438; Solana et al., 1982, p. 257).

In December 1933, during the Regular Convention of the National Revolutionary Party (PNR), delegates Froylán C. Manjarrez and Alberto Bremauntz proposed a modification to Article 3, replacing the word *lay* with the word *socialist*. At this time, the Secretary of Education and member of the PNR, Narciso Bassols, drew up the new Article that, upon being publicized, provoked a controversy that obligated Bassols to resign in May 1934 (Solana et al., 1982, pp. 267-269).

Notwithstanding strong opposition, the new article was approved by the House Chamber and came into effect on December 1 of that same year, the date that Lázaro Cárdenas occupied the presidency. The text of the Article was as follows:

> Article 3. The education that the State imparts will be socialist and furthermore will exclude all religious doctrine, will combat fanaticism and prejudice, for which the school will organize its instruction and activities in a way that permits the creation of a rational and an accurate concept of the universe and a social life within its youth. Only the government—Federation, State, Municipality—will give primary, secondary, and normal education. Authorization to private schools who wish to give instruction in any of the three previously mentioned must be in accord with the following norms: ...In each virtue, the religious corporations, the ministers of the cults,...will not intervene in any form in primary, secondary or normal schools, nor will they be supported economically (Barbosa, 1972, p. 213); Larroyo, 1986, pp. 492-493; Solana et al., 1982, pp. 274-275).

To plan the new educational curriculum, the Institute of Socialist Orientation was created in 1935 and put in charge of carrying out the new plans, programs, and texts from the preschool level to the professional level. Other responsibilities of this Institute included spreading socialist orientation among the magistrates, doing away with fanaticism, eliminating illiteracy, and preparing teachers to spread culture in indigenous centers (Solana et al., 1982, p. 276).

To improve agricultural methods and organize collective production systems, the Institute designed special courses to lift workers and the rural population from the primary level of instruction up through the highest levels of professional and cultural technology. Assimilation brigades and centers for indigenous education were created. The number of rural schools was increased by 2,200 (Solana et al., 1982, pp. 276-277).

The part of the plan that called for preparation of teachers to spread culture failed. Teachers protested the burden of developing multiple social activities such as organizing assemblies, clubs, committee organizations, and commissions to solicit public services in addition to developing workshops to guide cooperative production. Add to this list fulfilling the academic subject programs, and it is easy to deduce that teaching became an unpopular profession, increasingly so after numerous rural teachers were attacked physically by those opposed to this type of education (Solana et al., 1982, pp. 281, 287).

One of the positive initiatives of the Cárdenas period was the creation in 1935 of the National Polytechnic Institute (IPN), one of the most important educational institutions in the country. Initially geared to agricultural and industrial preparation, today it embraces all disciplines (Cooms, 1991, p. 91).

In 1936, the Department of Indigenous Matters, the University of the Laborer, and the Institute for the Preparation of Administration of Secondary (Middle School) Instruction were created; in 1942, these were transformed into the Normal Superior School. The Department of Artistic and Historic Monuments was converted into the Institute of Anthropology and History. Distinguished Spanish intellectual refugees in Mexico were retained, due to the internal struggle in Spain (1936-1939). For the orphaned children of the Spanish war, the Boarding School of Spain-Mexico was founded in Michoacán (Barbosa, 1972, pp. 224-225; Larroyo, 1986 p. 494; Solana et al., pp. 323-324).

After the Cárdenas period, subsequent governments modified plans and programs until, gradually, the socialist features disappeared. Cárdenas' successor, President Avila Camacho, appointed Torres Bodet, a distinguished intellectual, to the position of Minister of Education. Bodet prepared, without any publicity, a modification of Article 3. President Camacho sent the modification to Congress in December 1945. It was approved by the two Chambers and by the legislators of the Mexican states and was published in the Official Diary, December 30, 1946 (Barbosa, 1972, pp. 236-237; Solana et al., 1982, pp. 323-324).

The text of the Article, after the reform of 1946, read as follows:

> The education given by the state-federation, states, or municipalities, will develop harmoniously all the faculties of the human being and will nurture in this being at the same time the love of Country and the consciousness of international solidarity, in independence and in justice.
>
> I. Guaranteed by Article 24, the freedom of beliefs is the criterion that will guide education, which will maintain itself completely apart from any religious doctrine and base itself on the results of scientific progress, thus fighting against ignorance and its effects, fanaticism and prejudice (Political Constitution of the United States of Mexico with Reforms and Additions, 1969).

In each of the following presidential periods, education underwent modifications—some of little consequence; others, of great scope. During the period of President Alemán (1946-1952), the following institutions were created: the National Institute of Fine Arts (1946), the Indigenous Institute (1948), the National Institute of Youth (1950), and the National Autonomous University of Mexico City was constructed (1952), with various branches throughout Mexico City. These branches included the

Teaching Institute and Administrative Research and Services; Physical Education; Spectacle Sports; and Residential, Parks, and Horticultural Nurseries. As of 1995, this University enrolls more that 100,000 students. (Larroyo, 1986, pp. 534-535, 548; Solana et al., 1982, pp. 344-346).

Alemán was succeeded by Ruiz Cortines (1942-1958), who was succeeded by López Mateos (1958-1964), who again appointed Torres Bodet as Minister of Education. Bodet took the position with reserved gratitude, recounting his accomplishments during the Camacho administration.

In 1960, Torres Bodet presented his Plan of Eleven Years, which had as its principal end the solution to the growing demand for national quality primary education. Meeting the demand required the construction of new classrooms, rehabilitation of the existing ones, and teacher preparation. Although Bodet's work was difficult, upon handing over the Secretaría to his successor, in 1964, he considered that his plan had been 83 percent completed in the urban areas and 62 percent completed in rural areas (Larroyo, 1986, pp. 546-547; Solana et al., 1982, pp. 369-371).

In respect to secondary education, the National Technical Council of Education (reformed in 1958) revised and organized the plans and programs of study. The Council reduced the number of academic hours to 22 weeks and added 14 hours of technological activities weekly so that students who felt obligated to abandon their studies (a frequent situation in the country) could count on a basic preparation for a life of work (Barbosa, 1972, p. 36; Larroyo, 1986, p. 380).

A measure received with enthusiasm by persons of scarce economic resources was the 1958 creation of the National Commission of Free Text Books for Elementary Schools. From 1960 to 1964, the Commission distributed 107,155,755 books and workbooks and 494,255 teachers' manuals. This measure sought to make a primary education truly free by making both instruction and books available at no cost to families. From 1964 on, the Secretary of Education continued producing and distributing free texts in primary schools across the country (Larroyo, 1986, pp. 547-548; Solana et al., 1982, p. 367).

In 1973, during the presidency of Luis Echeverría, a large select group of teachers and specialists from diverse fields gathered in Chetumal and approved a plan of studies for basic secondary education, based on Article 25, Section II of the Federal Law of Education. The new plan called for two basic areas of study: (1) Social Sciences (including history, economics, social geography, and civics) and (2) Natural Sciences (including physics, chemistry, biology, and physical geography) (Agreement 16 363 of Chetumal, August 31, 1974).

Several sectors who favored the study of individual academic disciplines protested energetically. After many meetings of teachers and parents, it was agreed that the director of each school would decide if the curriculum would be presented by content areas or by academic disciplines. In the end, about half of all secondary schools worked with content areas and the other half with academic disciplines. These arrangements remained in place until 1992, the year that the present reform came into effect as proposed by ex-president Salinas de Gortari (1988-1994).

In January 1991, the Secretary of Education, Manuel Bartlett-Díaz, installed a National Commission for Consultation on the Modernization of Education. Community, local, regional, state, and national meetings were held over 3 months in which teachers, parents, researchers, experts, representatives of social sectors, and authorities participated. More than 65,000 papers were given. The Program for Educational Modernization was derived from this study. It is the foundation document for initiating a comprehensive change of plans and programs of basic education of the country (Program for the Educational Modernization 1989-1994).

In 1990 the Program was field tested in a limited number of preschool education, primary, and secondary (junior high) schools. The analysis of the obtained results and the ideas contributed by teachers and educational authorities guided the elaboration of a document titled *National Agreement for the Modernization of Basic Education (ANMEB)*, signed May 18, 1992.

To carry out this comprehensive plan to modernize Mexico's schools, the Congress modified two Constitutional Articles—the 30th and 3lst—and approved a General Law of Education, enacted in July 1993 (hereafter referred to as the Articles and the Law). With the *National Agreement*, the last stage of the reorganization of plans and programs of study was initiated (Political Constitution of the United States of Mexico, Editorial Trillas, 1994 Edition; Federal Law of Education, Daily Office of the Federation, July 13, 1993).

After publication of the first plans and programs in 1993, the Council proceeded to develop its first series of free textbooks for preschool and primary instruction, didactic guides, and supplementary materials for teachers.

Legal Basis of the Present Educational System

The present structure of the Mexican Educational System is based on (1) Articles 30 and 31 of the Constitution, (2) the *National Agreement for the Modernization of Basic Education (ANMEB)*, and (3) the General Law of Education. Each of these components is described in this section.

Constitutional Articles 30 and 31

Article 30. Every individual has the right to receive an education. The government—Federation, States, and Municipalities—will impart

> preschool, primary, and secondary education. Primary and secondary education are obligatory.
>
> I. Guaranteed by Article 24 on liberty of thought, said education will be lay and, because of that, it will remain completely apart from any religious doctrine.
>
> III. . . . [t]he Federal Executive will determine the plans and programs of study for primary, secondary, and normal education for the entire Republic....
>
> IV. All the education that the state imparts will be free.
>
> VI. Private schools will be able to impart education in all of its types and modalities. . . .[t]he State will grant and decline recognition of official value on the studies carried out in private schools.
>
> VII. The Universities and the other institutions of higher education upon which the law bestows autonomy, will have the authority and the responsibility of governing themselves, and will realize their purposes to educate, investigate, and diffuse culture in accordance with the principles of this article, respecting the liberty of professorial appointments, research, and the free examination and discussion of ideas....

Please note that this Article

- guarantees the right of all individuals—regardless of age, nationality, or social condition—to a free education, provided by the state;
- establishes both primary *and* secondary (junior high) as parts of basic instruction; unlike previous law, which stipulated only preschool and primary levels (Official Diary of the Federation, March 5, 1993; Political Constitution of the United States of Mexico, Editorial Trillas, 10th Edition, 1994, pages 10 and 11);
- assigns to the Federal Executive (through the Secretaría of Education) the authority to determine the program of study for basic and normal education while allowing states some latitude, as long as their plans conform to the basic criterion established by the Federation; and
- allows private schools to carry out education, the only requirement being that they obtain the necessary authorization from the State.

Another constitutional article modified by the Union Congress was the 31st, reproduced in part below.

> *Article 31.* Obligations of all Mexican citizens to assure that their children or pupils attend public or private schools, in order to obtain

primary and secondary education and to take an active part in the military, according to the terms established by law.

Article 31 institutes the responsibility of parents to endeavor to get for their children basic education to such an extent that their obligation does not stop until the pupil finishes secondary education. This requirement is important in Mexico, because numerous parents of scarce economic resources abstain from sending their children to school and obligate them to work. At present, these parents are outside the law (Political Constitution of the United States of Mexico, Trillas Editorial, Tenth Edition, 1994, p. 55).

National Agreement for the Modernization of Basic Education (ANMEB)

The ANMEB was signed on May 18, 1992, by Ernesto Zedillo, then Minister of Education (now President of the country). It represents the agreement of various interest groups within the country to reach common objectives through federal education and to share among the federation and the states the technical, administrative, and financial responsibilities. It is, furthermore, an instrument of planning that requires a restructuring of the educational system and diverse reforms in the organization of the office of Secretaría of Public Education (SEP, *National Agreement for the Modernization of Basic Education*, 1992).

This Agreement contains three watershed changes:

1. decentralization of the educational system,
2. reformulation of content and educational materials, and
3. reevaluation of the teaching function.

Each of these changes is discussed below.

Decentralization of the educational system. As a first step toward decentralization of the federal educational system, Zedillo transferred to the state governments the administration of preschool education and primary (including indigenous education), secondary (junior high) school, normal, and special institutions. This includes the management of around 100,000 real estate properties with furnishings, 513,000 teaching posts, 115,000 administrative posts, 2.9 million class hours, and 13.5 million students (SEP, General Management of Information, Executive Report 1992, p. 131).

This decentralization, accomplished with great effort, came up against a lack of understanding and the resistance of some local educational authorities. These problems, fortunately, were overcome. The agreement established several sets of obligations:

Obligations of the Federation—

- to carry out Article 30 of the Constitution,
- to expedite general standards of education,
- to formulate plans and programs, and
- to evaluate the educational system.

Obligations of the States—

- to direct state schools;
- to assume responsibility for the technical, administrative, and financial aspects;
- to form collegiate/professional councils; and
- to propose regional criteria.

Obligations of the Municipalities—

- to create municipal education councils, and
- to maintain and equip schools.

Obligations of the federation and state teams—

- to recognize the National Syndicate of Educational Laborers (SNTE) as officials of labor relations for the teachers association;
- to stimulate social participation;
- to assign greater resources to the most needy entities and regions;
- to strengthen the capacity of the teacher, parent, and student organizations; and
- to create school educational councils.

Reformulation of educational content and materials. To carry out the second watershed change of the *National Agreement*, consultation and debate forums were conducted during the 1992-93 school year. The purpose of the forums was to solicit input to optimize planning for new programs of study and for textbooks. Adjustments were made to the requirements at the primary and secondary levels for instruction by content areas versus instruction by academic disciplines (SEP, General Management of Information, Executive Report 1993, p. 134).

Among these changes, the most significant include

- reform of educational content and curriculum through the total renovation of plans and programs of study and textbooks;
- application of a new preschool educational program;
- application of a new emergent primary education program;
- increase in instructional hours in mathematics and Spanish at both primary and secondary levels;
- discontinuation of the content areas of instruction approach in social sciences, and adoption of the study of geography, history, civics, and related but independent disciplines at the primary and secondary (junior high) school levels;
- continuation of the content area of natural sciences at the primary level

but adoption of the discipline approach to physics, chemistry, and biology at the secondary (junior high) level.

- design of a new school calendar that guarantees 200 days of classes during the school year;
- renovation of methods and processes of instruction;
- articulation of the distinct educational levels;
- updating of educational processes in accordance with scientific and technological advances; and
- reaching agreement with the Secretary of Communications and Transport and establishing an impetus for long-distance, televised learning through the use of satellite communication and parabolical antennas (SEP, Executive Report, 1993).

Reevaluation of the teaching function. The economic situation of teachers had deteriorated over the years to the point that, in some municipalities, their salaries were only a little above minimum wage. This situation frequently obligated teachers to meet their financial needs by taking other jobs and neglecting their students. Other teachers simply abandoned the teaching profession (SEP, Executive Report, 1993, p. 134).

To alleviate teachers' financial distress and to respond to their requests for professional development, several actions were taken: (Advances in Educational Modernization, May, 1994, p. 16; Executive Report, 1993, p. 134).

- implementation of a system for teacher training in each state;
- reform of entrance requirements to a normal school program, such that the certificate of preparatory (equivalent to a [U.S.] high school diploma) is required;
- application of a modernized educational program;
- improvement in teachers' salaries, as of May 1993, to the tune of a 70 percent increase;
- initiation of a Teacher Training Career program to stimulate teacher academic improvement, organized as a career ladder that permits teachers to increase their level of income according to evaluation criteria such as length of service, academic level, upgraded training, preparation, and professional development (80 percent of all teachers have participated);
- endowments to school book collections to support the performance of the staff; and
- implementation of a special program to promote the development of housing for teachers.

The General Law of Education. The General Law of Education came into effect July 14, 1993, replacing the old Federal Law of Education. The new law clearly specifies the rights and obligations of all educational agencies (Official Diary of the Federation of July 13, 1993).

Some of the rights and obligations it contains are outlined below.

- The new law provides support for Article 30's guarantee of a free, secular, basic education for all Mexicans as an obligation of the government.
- With regard to the federalization of education, the law establishes the norms for relations between the federation and the states and municipalities. It confers on the states the responsibility for the technical, administrative, and financial aspects of its educational institutions, without losing sight of the objectives of federal education. This measure permits strengthening of national unity without weakening regional developments. To support regional development, educational services are set up that are responsive to the needs and characteristics of each region.
- In view of the fact that the quality of the educational process is one of the principal purposes, the school calendar is extended to 200 school days. The Law also confirms the right of parents to be informed periodically about the level of progress of their children.
- The law recognizes the experience of some persons on the basis of their knowledge, abilities, and skills, thus giving official certification if they meet the evaluation standards.
- The law broadens the social participation in education by supporting the role of parents in the educational process, creating school advisory boards, seeking more involvement of various communication mediums, and inviting society to participate in the production of free textbooks.

Present Structure of the Educational System

Education in Mexico comprises the following educational stages: basic preschool, primary, secondary (junior high), prep school, higher education, and postgraduate (Federal Law of Education, Official Diary of the Federation of July 13, 1993; SEP, Mexico, Advances of the Educational Modernization, May, 1994). Each level is described in this section.

Basic Education

Basic Education comprises initial, preschool, primary, secondary, and special education. In addition, it includes physical, artistic, and cultural education.

Initial Education

The needs of approximately 9 million children under the age of 4 and their mothers (increasing numbers of whom are employed) in urban, rural, and indigenous communities spawned the creation of a new type of informal schooling. These new "schools" pursue two objectives: to empower mothers in the care and attention of their children and to help mothers adapt new parenting methods to their home environments through diverse activities.

This initial education is dedicated to children age 45 days to 3 years. It is imparted in the Centers of Infantile Development (CENDI) (created through a constitutional mandate) in federal, state, dependency, and private institutions. In 1992, 142,000 infants attended; however, the enormous demand would have required a supply of up to 216,000 more slots.

The programs, support materials, and educational resources for infants and their parents are designed to prepare children for preschool education. To this end, the curriculum has been infused with content about ecology, hygiene habits, and nutrition, of great importance especially in the rural and indigenous communities. Taking into account the importance of parental participation, content that encourages attentiveness to infants has been included in the adult education programs.

In addition to stimulating children's distinct abilities, the suggested methods nurture expressiveness, creativity, and artistic sensibility. For older infants, didactic packages tied to preschool education have been produced.

At present, to broaden participation, efforts are underway to solicit participation of various communications media to help promote public awareness. Other efforts are underway to obtain the cooperation of those international organizations interested in the well-being of infants (SEP, Performance Report, 1993).

Preschool Education

In Mexico, public preschool education consists of 2 years of instruction and constitutes the first contact of the child with formal education. To enter kindergarten, a child must have reached his or her fourth birthday. In many private kindergartens, where a foreign language is taught along with the native language, preschool education takes 3 years. During the last year, called pre-primary, children alternate between languages and learn elements of reading and writing in both. In the 1993-94 school year, 2.9 million children were enrolled in Mexico's preschool education program. They were taught by over 116,000 teachers in over 52,000 schools.

The content of the new preschool program of studies is taught in relation to the child's natural and social environment and seeks to tie this educational stage to what comes later. With this objective, the proposed activities emphasize mathematics, oral and written language, artistic sensibility, nature study, and development of psycho-motor abilities (SEP, Fundamentals of the Theoretical-Methodology of the Preschool Educational Program, 1992, pp. 11-23).

Following the first year of implementation, an evaluation was carried out in 19 states of the Republic. The results provided useful information in revising the content of the pedagogical guides used during the 1992-93 school year. Approximately 687,000 copies of the program were distributed to teachers (SEP, Performance Report, 1993).

Examples of program materials include a book for children, *My Work Notebook (Mi Cuaderno de Trabajo)*; didactic packages integrated with games of primary graphics; modules about musical instruments; cassette tapes; a music book; and other material that stimulates creativity through simple crafts. Together, the material is designed to support the physical, affective, intellectual, and social development of students (SEP, Performance Report, 1993, 287).

In 1992, an innovative information database and computer literacy program was established in 141 kindergartens in the Federal District. After 2 years of experience, this effort to address an aspect of education that had lagged behind was considered successful; in 1994, 178 Micro-SEP computers were installed and software manuals distributed, which would benefit more than 32,000 students. (SEP, Office of General Information, Performance Report, 1993, 288).

One of the concerns of the Secretaría of Public Education has been the integration of isolated indigenous groups, some of whom have resisted abandoning their traditional ways of life. The Secretaría initiated the teaching of Spanish as a national language in the preschool groups without displacing the distinct Native languages and traditional customs. The basic elements of Spanish are easily assimilated by children of this age (SEP, Performance Report, 1993, 287).

For this task, bilingual teachers were counted on, most of whom were Natives of the indigenous communities. These mentors received a *Manual for the Indigenous Teacher* and were prepared through special courses. The effectiveness of the *Manual* was evaluated in the states of Jalisco, Michoácan, and Puebla (The Office of General Information, Performance Report, 1993, 288).

Rural areas also received special materials. In addition to previous preparation, teachers received 5,876 work guides and didactic packages for 59,114 students (The Office of General Information. Performance Report, 1993, p. 288).

One of the commitments of the Secretaría of Public Education in this national education reform effort is to support the professional development of teachers. In 1993, 126,911 teachers attended training workshops, seminars, and a course on Preschool Teaching-Learning methodology carried out through the General Project of Teaching Empowerment (Office of General Information, Performance Report, pp. 288-290).

Themes covered in the preschool course included fundamentals of technique and methods in preschool education; early childhood development in the affective, social, intellectual, and physical domains; program organization; and the social function of the school.

Primary Education

Until recently, basic and primary education were synonymous in Mexico. Primary school, divided into lower (first, second, and third years) and higher (fifth and sixth) grades constituted the base of the educational system. In many communities across the country, it was the only education to which inhabitants had access.

Today, primary school continues to carry out its important role as the bridge between preschool and secondary. During the 1993-94 school year, nearly 14.5 million students were taught by over 488,000 teachers in more than 85,000 Mexican primary schools.

Among main goals of the plan of studies for primary students are

- to strengthen reading, writing, and oral expression—intellectual abilities considered basic to the development of permanent learning and communication capacities;
- to learn mathematical concepts and apply them to problems of everyday life;
- to obtain basic knowledge needed to comprehend natural phenomena, especially the relationship of hygiene and health care, protection of the environment, and rational use of natural resources;
- to acquire fundamental knowledge of history and geography, thus gaining an understanding of other countries and of Mexico in particular;
- to acquire an appreciation of the students' rights and responsibilities and to practice these values in their relations with others;
- to appreciate and enjoy music, painting, dance, literature, and other artistic achievements of humanity; and
- to enjoy physical exercise and sports.

The contents outlined above are considered fundamental to the development of the whole student. Teachers are encouraged to make sure that, along with these necessary abilities for permanent learning, the acquisition of knowledge is associated with the exercise of intellectual abilities and meditation (SEP, Plan and Programs of Study 1993, Elementary, p. 14).

For the 1993-94 school year, new plans and programs of study were designed and implemented in first, third, and fifth grades. These changes necessitated the development of new materials and free textbooks. Specialists were invited to compete to rewrite textbooks. New curriculum has now been implemented in all six grades.

The development of the new plan requires an annual calendar of 200 working days and 4-hour class days, which translates into 800 annual hours—150 hours more than previous cycles. The distribution of instructional time is shown in Table 1 (SEP, Plan and Programs of Study 1993, p. 14).

Notice that beginning in the first grade, special attention is given to Spanish (45 percent of class time), and mathematics (30 percent). In these

Table 1
Distribution of Work Time (1993 Plan)
First and Second Grades

Subject	Weekly hours	Annual hours
Spanish	9	360
Mathematics	6	240
Knowledge of the Environment (Natural Sciences, History, Geography, Civic Education)	3	120
Artistic Education	1	40
Physical Education	1	40
Totals	20	800

Source: SEP Plan and programs of study 1993, p. 14

two grades, under the rubric of Knowledge of the Environment, the natural sciences, history, geography, and civic education are integrated. The last three subjects are an integrated study of the community, municipality, and political entity where the students live.

In third, fourth, fifth, and sixth grades, Spanish and mathematics continue to receive the most attention, as shown in Table 2. The focus of earlier Spanish programs was the study of grammatical structure and linguistic forms. The central purpose of the new programs is the development of the communication capacity in speaking and writing (SEP, Plan and Programs of Study 1993, Elementary, pp. 14 and 15).

The mathematics program develops the capacity to recognize, plan, and solve problems; anticipate and verify results; estimate results of computation, and measure and use measurement design and computational instruments (SEP, Plan and programs of study 1993, Elementary, p. 52).

The contents of the natural sciences are grouped in five thematic axes: living beings; the human body and health; the environment and its protection; matter, energy and change; and science, technology, and society. From third grade on, 3 hours a week are set aside for the natural sciences because of their importance in the preservation of health and the protection of natural resources and the environment (SEP, Plan and Programs of Study 1993, Elementary, p. 74).

An important modification was the development of an integrated social sciences unit, which replaced fragmented geography, history, and civics

Table 2
Distribution of Work Time (1993 Plan)
Third to Sixth Grades

Subject	Weekly hours	Annual hours
Spanish	6	240
Mathematics	5	200
Natural Sciences	3	120
History	1.5	60
Geography	1.5	60
Civic Education	1	40
Artistic Education	1	40
Physical Education	1	40
Totals	20	800

Source: SEP Plan and programs of study 1993

lessons taught previously (SEP, Plan and programs of study 1993, Elementary, pp. 91-140).

For the 1993-94 academic year, the new Program for Updating Teachers consisted of four courses addressing problems in teaching Spanish, mathematics, and history, and three courses about classroom planning (SEP, Office of General Information, Chapter on Education, p. 133).

In the school period that began in September 1993, primary school students and teachers received more than 113 million books, state monographs, and teacher guides. Of these, nearly 46 million were free textbooks.

A Program of Environmental Protection was developed in the 1993-94 school year in Mexico City as an extracurricular activity. Its purpose was to create an awareness in students of the important role they could play in reducing contamination in various cities of the country, especially in Mexico City, Guadalajara, and Monterrey.

The literacy services in the indigenous communities focus on reading and writing in Spanish, arithmetic elements, and basic Mexican history and geography. These services are offered to children and adults who request them. Outstanding students who wish to continue their studies are given economic help. The literacy campaigns have helped lower illiteracy, which currently stands at about 8 percent of the population (SEP, Office of General Information, Chapter on Education, p. 138).

In coordination with specialists in 20 indigenous languages and dialects, books were prepared for first- and second-grade instruction in reading and writing in indigenous languages. Content was tailored to match specific regional conditions. At the same time, a support manual on the educational process of indigenous primary schooling was distributed to teachers. This manual was based on test programs conducted in the states of Chiapas, Chihuahua, Hidalgo, and Morelos. Approximately 152,000 copies were used for instruction in Spanish; 101,000 in indigenous languages (SEP, Office of General Information, Performance Report, p. 289).

To serve populations with special needs, the Primary Program for Migrant Children was developed to benefit 10,000 children of migrant agricultural laborers. These students migrate within 14 states of the Republic. [See chapters 6 and 8 for more information about programs sponsored by the Mexican Secretaría of Public Education that serve migrant students who travel into the United States.]

Secondary (Junior High) Education

In contrast to primary, the secondary (middle school) level occupied a place of little importance in earlier eras. Although the 1865 Law of Instruction includes language about secondary education, organized on the style of the French lyceums of that era (covered in 7 or 8 years), it was not until 1925, after two presidential decrees, that the secondary school in Mexico was born (Larroyo, 1986, 461-462).

The 1993 reform resulting from Article 30 of the Constitution conferred great importance on secondary education by including it as an obligatory component in a basic education in Mexico. That reform created for the government an obligation to increase the number of secondary schools available to serve those students who, upon finishing primary school, acquire the right and obligation to go on to secondary education through the ninth grade (SEP, Program for Educational Modernization 1989-1994, p. 46).

The decentralization of the educational system meant that the states provided for 81.2 percent of the demand for secondary education; the Federation, 10.5 percent; and private schools, 8.2 percent (SEP, Education, p. 133).

During the 1993-94 school year, student enrollment stood at 4,311,800, indicating that many students passing out of primary school did not enter middle school. Even though the enrollment in middle school registered a growth of 1 percent that year, educational authorities are adopting measures to better publicize this service. Among other strategies, groups of teachers visit primary schools to inform sixth-grade students and their parents about the importance and obligation of continuing their studies (SEP, Education, pp. 133-134).

As in primary school, the program of study emphasizes Spanish instruction, which receives 5 class hours weekly at all three grade levels. The program consists of four axes: spoken language, written language, literary recreation, and reflection on the language (SEP, Plan and Programs of Study 1993, Secondary p. 20).

Mathematics, too, receives 5 weekly class hours. The themes of the program are grouped in five areas: arithmetic; algebra; geometry; probability; and, in ninth grade, trigonometry (SEP, Plan and Programs of Study 1993, Secondary, p. 37).

Sketch of the Subjects of the Three Grades of Secondary Education and Number of Weekly Hours

Subjects	first (7th grade)	second (8th grade)	third (9th grade)
Spanish	5 hours	5 hours	5 hours
Mathematics	5 hours	5 hours	5 hours
World History	3 hours	3 hours	
History of Mexico			3 hours
General Geography	3 hours		
Geography of Mexico		2 hours	
Educ. Orientation			3 hours
Civics	3 hours	2 hours	
Elective Subject			3 hours
Biology	3 hours	2 hours	3 hours
Intro to Physics & Chemistry	3 hours		
Physics		3 hours	3 hours
Chemistry		3 hours	3 hours
Foreign Language	3 hours	3 hours	3 hours

Developmental Activities

Artistic Expression & Appreciation	2 hours	2 hours	2 hours
Physical Education	2 hours	2 hours	2 hours
Technological Education	3 hours	3 hours	3 hours

Source: SEP, Plan and Programs of Study 1993, Secondary, p. 16

In previous years, the natural sciences course consisted of the rudiments of biology, physics, chemistry, and physical geography. Two courses now have been established for each of those disciplines. Introductory physics and chemistry courses tie in the natural sciences of the first year of secondary (7th grade) with physics and chemistry courses in the second (8th grade) and third (9th grade) years (SEP, Plan and Programs of Study 1993, Secondary [Middle School], p. 13).

Under the old program, social sciences integrated history, geography, and civics. In the current plan, these disciplines are studied separately. (SEP, Plan and Programs of Study , 1993, Secondary, p. 14).

With regard to foreign language studies, only two are offered at the secondary level: English, preferred by the majority of schools for obvious reasons, and French. Three hours weekly are dedicated to these languages in public schools. Some of the purposes for studying a foreign language include

- development of an attitude of respect for the ideas of others,
- appreciation for one's own culture, and
- the acquisition of linguistic basics that allow students who go on to higher education the choice of advancing in their knowledge and command another language (SEP, Plan and Programs of Study 1993, p. 133).

Developmental activities in the secondary program consist of artistic expression and appreciation (music, drawing, and painting), physical education (sports and gymnasium), and technological education. The latter consists of diverse activities from which each school may select in accordance with the region in which it is located (SEP, Plan and Programs of Study 1993, Secondary [Middle School], p. 14.)

As in the lower levels of schooling, the modification of the secondary education program called for the development and publication of new texts. One difference from the primary program is that the secondary texts are not free. These texts are produced by private publishing houses. The authors write their works according to the programs put forth by the Secretaría of Public Education (SEP). The texts are then revised by a Findings Commission that takes into consideration accuracy, currentness, and the efficacy of the teaching-learning processes employed.

The approved books appear in the SEP catalog. The teachers select one or more texts. To acquaint educators with the new texts, SEP acquired 800,000 books of each subject from publishers and gave them to the teachers of seventh and eighth grades. In addition, each teacher received a didactic guide to the materials in his or her specialty (SEP, Education, p. 134).

In the 1993-94 school year, the Introduction to Computers in Basic Education program was initiated. Five computer centers were set up in secondary schools (SEP, Education, p. 134).

Other new measures recently implemented include remedial summer courses; standardized exams for students who failed one to three subjects; and scholarships for students in rural communities.

Special and Private Schools

The majority of private Mexican schools must comply with the same established programs as the public ones do. Those that teach with a foreign language must dedicate extra hours to that language apart from the obligatory hours of the official school program. Some solve the problem with additional afternoon hours; others, within the regular hours, teach some classroom subjects in the foreign language and others in Spanish (Information supplied by Professor Homero Sánchez Nájera, Inspector General of Secondary Education of the SEP).

Other private schools, such as el Colegio Americano (The American School), Liceo Francés (the French Lyceum), Colegio Alemán (German School), Colegio Suizo (Swiss School), Colegio Irlandés (Irish School), Colegio Japonés (Japanese School), and many others are governed by bicultural agreements that allow these schools to deliver instruction in accordance with the educational programs of the sponsoring country. Mexican students who plan to continue their studies in other countries can attend these schools. The certificates issued by these schools are valid in Mexico (information supplied by professor Homero Sánchez Nájera, Inspector General of Secondary Education, SEP).

Students who divide their time between Mexico and another country are advised to continue their studies in one of the aforementioned schools, because the official Mexican schools accept students from other countries only when the courses taken are recognized and the students take the exams that otherwise correspond to these courses.

Media Superior (Preparatory) Education

Students who complete their secondary education may continue their studies in one of numerous preparatory schools in Mexico. Some of these are under the direction of the SEP, and others are directed by the Universidad Nacional Autónoma de México (UNAM) [The National Autonomous University of Mexico]. The Instituto Politécnico Nacional (IPN) [The National Polytechnical Institute] relies on Technical Schools, equivalent to the middle schools, and along with Centros de Estudios Científicos, Tecnológicos e Industriales de Servicio (CETIS) [Centers of Scientific Studies, Technologies and Manufacturing Service], equivalent to the preparatories. The IPN studies are incorporated to SEP.

In the college preparatory school, programs vary between 2 and 3 years in duration. In almost all institutions of this type that function in Mexico City, courses taken during the first 2 years are the same for all students. In the third year, students must decide if they wish to continue with university studies or technical studies, and in accordance with the choice made, they receive a list of required subjects and electives (UNAM, Plan of Studies, 1989).

In the majority of preparatory schools, students select from the following four areas: physical-mathematics, chemical-biological, economic-administrative, and humanities. Each area prepares students for a number of professions and specialties. For example, corresponding to the area of Physical-Mathematics are professions such as physicist, astronomer, mathematician, engineer, and actuary.

SEP's registries report that in the 1992-93 school year, 1.77 million students were taught by 115,343 teachers in 4,812 preparatory schools. The following year saw an increase in enrollment of 60,000 students (SEP, Education, pp. 134-135).

The growth in enrollment was due, in part, to the creation of 128 new schools, especially in the science-related fields. Sixteen new vocational programs have been started in the areas of broadcasting, land and cattle management, administration, rural accounting, development of livestock farming, horticulture, hospital maintenance, hotel management, restaurants, and tourism. This growth is also due to targeted efforts to better inform secondary school graduates including promotional campaigns conducted through various communication media and orientation programs carried out by the National System of Educational Orientation (SEP, Education, p. 135).

The expansion system, which allows workers to finish their studies in a profession, served 19.7 percent more students in 1993-94 than in the preceding cycle. This growth may be due to the restructuring of the National Commission for Planning and Programming of Preparatory Education. This restructuring was done to integrate these programs with the National Commission for the Planning of Higher Education. Plans and programs of study were modified through consultation with different social sectors, and include the contributions of specialists from diverse fields of knowledge. During the 1992-93 school year, by means of a modular system of curriculum development, 119 plans and 1,499 programs of study were developed; of those, 69 plans and the entire number of programs of study are functioning (SEP, Education, p. 135).

Higher Education

In the higher education system (SES), there exists major differences among the public universities of the capital and those of the states, and between the leading and private universities. These differences relate to means, quality of facilities and faculties, and prospects for development and expansion.

Higher education is divided into three principal subsystems:

- 36 public universities with 64 percent of the total enrollment at the level of baccalaureate degree (1989 figures) (most enjoy administrative autonomy);
- a national network of 87 regional technological institutes, with 15 percent of the total enrollment (most operate under SEP controls);
- 35 private universities of diverse means and quality, as well as approximately 120 small institutions with programs of remedial studies. This last group represents 16 percent of the total enrollment. Some universities are autonomous, while others depend on SEP (Cooms in SEP and Foundation for Economic Culture, 1991 p. 25).

After the seventies, the higher education system began decentralizing until, presently, almost all Mexican states have state universities and many have technological institutes. This decentralization has resulted in an increased SES enrollment outside of Mexico City. Previously, 70 percent of the students enrolled in universities in Mexico City. Recent statistics show that, although the number of students has grown in Mexico City, the proportion in relation to the rest of the country has diminished by about 24 percent (Cooms, 1991, pp. 25-26).

Some of the universities and technological institutes have acquired considerable prestige. The Universities of Guadalajara, Jalisco, and the Technological Institute of Monterrey in Nuevo León attract ever-increasing numbers of students from the rest of Mexico and from various U.S. and Central American locations.

SEP has jurisdiction over all other levels of education, including planning and budgeting. The Subsecretary of Higher Education and Scientific Investigation and the General Director of Higher Education handle relations with the universities. The Subsecretary of Research and Technological Education controls the system of public technological institutions (Cooms, 1991, p. 27).

Since 1929, The National Autonomous University of Mexico (UNAM) has been independent in developing its plans and programs of study, and in deciding its budget distribution. The annual student fees are symbolic (20 Mexican pesos) and, despite various attempts to increase them, student protests supported by some political groups have stopped the adoption of increases, more needed as each year passes. The government subsidy represents a major portion of the monies coming into UNAM. This subsidy is increased by private donations. Many universities throughout Mexico follow UNAM's model; others have created their own systems.

Among the public universities, the Universidad Autónoma Metropolitana (UAM) [The Autonomous Metropolitan University] located in Mexico City has a special place. The UAM is organized academically by departments, different from the UNAM, organized by schools in the Spanish and French style. The UAM was planned by a group of the most severe critics of the UNAM, who proposed to create an institution inspired by the organization of the universities of the United States and the United Kingdom. The UAM enrolls about 50,000 students, and has a large, full-time faculty who teach and conduct research activities in undergraduate and graduate programs (Cooms, 1991, p. 28).

Mexico also has numerous private and technological universities. Some universities follow the model of the UNAM; others, that of the UAM. Various universities stand out for the quality of their teaching, including the Iberoamericana, Panamericana, Anáhuac, and LaSalle, among others. El Instituto Tecnológico Autónomo de México (ITAM) [The Autonomous Technological Institute of Mexico], one of the most prestigious in the country, is financed by the students' college fees and by private contributions. Nevertheless, in Mexico, there does not exist an effective system of scientific research at the university level. Of the 400 universities in existence, only 40 carry out investigative research.

To enter into the university, students must have finished preparatory school with a bachillerato (preparatory or high school diploma). Many of the private universities have their own preparatory schools; students in these schools do not have to pass entrance exams if they continue their studies in the same university. Due to a student strike, the students of the public preparatories no longer present exams of admission to the UNAM. On the other hand, the entrance exam is required in the private universities that do not have preparatory programs (Cooms, 1991, p. 29).

In contrast to the UAM, where a large number of teachers work full-time, only 25 percent of teachers employed by the UNAM devote all their time to teaching. This is because many of the teachers are highly accomplished scholars who devote a great part of their time to their professions. In private universities, the majority of the professors works on an hourly basis (Cooms, 1991, p. 29).

Technological Education

In 1958, when the Subsecretary of Higher Technical Education was put in charge of the coordination and development of technological education in Mexico, two areas of activities were designated: (1) to direct the Instituto Politécnico Nacional (IPN) [The National Polytechnic Institution] as an institution of a higher academic level and (2) to direct other technological institutions, among them the technical secondary schools, the Centers of Scientific and Technological Studies, and the Regional Technological Institutes. This subsecretary has changed names with each presidential administration; currently the office is called the Subsecretary of Technical Studies, under the Secretary of Public Education (SEP, 1995).

The IPN endeavors to form professionals in technical careers that are needed for Mexico's development. Divided into cycles, these consist of complete teaching of the careers that they attempt, from prep school to professional to postgraduate work (Solana et al., 1982, p. 480).

The unique four-level Mexican system of technological education consists of schools that have varying levels of preparatory and higher education, ascending to the National Polytechnic Institute (IPN), which takes in a net of 87 smaller technological institutes (Cooms, 1991, p. 91).

As mentioned earlier, the IPN was founded by President Cárdenas in 1935. Its establishment responded to the President's call for an institution dedicated primarily to teaching technical and scientific subject matter that would have practical application to the needs of a country in development. At the onset, notable differences existed between the IPN's plans of study and those of the UNAM, but the diversification of the plans of study of both institutions has narrowed the differences. The IPN has broadened its scope into areas such as medicine, economics, social sciences, and administration and offers doctoral degrees in many fields, which were in the past exclusively the UNAM's domain. The UNAM, in turn, has entered some technological areas (Cooms, 1991, pp. 91-92; Solana et al., 1982, p. 480).

Postgraduate

Postgraduate education consists of specialization studies and master's and doctorate degree programs. These can be accomplished in the UNAM, the UAM, the IPN, and in various private universities.

More than 55,000 students were enrolled in these programs in 1993-94. During this period, 199 plans and programs of study were brought up to date, of which 94 correspond to the university area and 105 to the technological area. The UNAM started the university postgraduate system, with eight integrated programs. For its part, the IPN created the doctorate in Metallurgy and Materials and the specialization in Thermal Engineering (SEP, Education, p. 137).

An important institution supporting postgraduate study is in the Consejo Nacional de Ciencia y Tecnología (CONACYT) [The National Council of Science and Technology], which stimulates research through scholarship programs. In 1993, it gave approximately 650 scholarships, representing a 30 percent increase from the previous year. The educational sector, in turn, granted 3,555 scholarships to carry out postgraduate studies in national institutions and 649 for studies in foreign countries (SEP, Education, p. 142).

Normal Education

All the information contained in this section was obtained in direct consultation with students and teachers of the Escuela Nacional de Mae-

stros (The Normal School of Teachers), the magisterial profession, and with the scholarship holders of the Universidad de las Américas (The University of the Americas).

Normal education has undergone numerous reforms throughout the political history of the country and, despite its importance, has received less support than other professions. Thanks to the decentralization of education, the whole country now has normal schools.

The basic teaching profession is studied in Mexico in the Escuela Nacional de Maestros (the National School of Teachers), in the state normal schools, and in some Mexican private schools. In the first years after the foundation of the National School of Teachers, so little importance was given to the career of *professor* that only a middle school certification was sufficient to enroll in this institution and, after 3 years of studies, students received the title of Professor of Elementary Instruction.

At present, to enroll in the same school, the bachillerato is required (graduation from preparatory school). The studies last 4 years and, after an intense student teaching experience with primary groups beginning in the fourth semester, the degree of Licenciatura (Baccalaureate) in primary education is obtained.

Students who obtain the Licenciatura are certified to receive appointments as teachers of primary instruction. If they wish to aim higher, they can enroll in the Escuela Normal Superior (Higher Normal School) or the Universidad Pedagógica (the Pedagogic University). In the Normal Superior institutes, specialties are offered such as Spanish, mathematics, natural sciences, social science, and foreign language. Graduates of this institution acquire the degree of Licenciatura (Baccalaureate) in secondary education and fill secondary teaching posts throughout Mexico. The studies in the Pedagogical University are designed to result in a master's or doctorate degree.

Since 1992, as an incentive to improve teaching, the Educational Modernization Agreement established a plan for the reevaluation of teachers in front of their peers at all the instructional grade levels. The teachers attend the Centers of Teacher Modernization and, if they complete the stringent requirements, obtain an annual economic benefit. The Secretary of Public Education, in cooperation with the Bank of Mexico, grants to distinguished teachers scholarships to obtain the master's or doctorate degrees in education. Scholarship holders, apart from having obtained a superior grade-point average, must take an admission exam at the university of their choice.

The National Agreement for the Modernization of Basic Education (ANMEB), established in May 1992, states that responsibility for material and personnel resources needed to provide normal education and teacher training services would be transferred from the federal government to the states (SEP, Education, p. 136).

Adult Education

In Mexico, adult education is fundamental. According to the 1990 census, 12.4 percent of Mexicans could not read or write. Adult education is the charge of the National Institute for the Education of Adults (INEA). This Institute develops activities related to illiteracy, primary and secondary education, and work requirements for Mexicans older than 15 who have never gone to school or who did not finish their basic education (SEP, Education, p. 137).

During the 1993-94 school year, the INEA taught 1.13 million adults to read, of whom 8.3 percent were indigenous persons; 73.7 percent were rural inhabitants, and 18 percent were urban inhabitants. To extend the coverage, two systems were used: (1) a radio literacy service transmitted radio programs at fixed times and repeated them during the day; and (2) study groups were formed and provided with audiocassettes and cassette players. To help adults exercise reading and writing skills, workshops were conducted that produced diverse types of materials (SEP, Education, p. 138).

Primary and secondary classes for adults were attended by approximately 1.56 million people, of whom 70 percent had some previous primary schooling and 30 percent had some middle schooling. Through an agreement to promote adult education in industries of the private sector of goods and services, 400,000 workers were included in the primary and secondary school program. Taking into consideration the special needs of these groups, appropriate educational materials and texts were adopted. Materials developed for adults in rural areas comprise six state biographies, 26 regional monographs, and 22 books of history (SEP, Education, p. 138).

Summary

The decentralization process will continue as each state plans and carries out its own particular educational programs to meet state and local needs. The states are allowed latitude as long as they conform to basic criteria established at the Federal level. SEP specifies standards and values, thereby controlling i.e., the national character of Mexico's educational system. The state Secretaries of Education, school administrators, professors, teachers, and others will need time to adjust to a more autonomous system in contrast to Mexico's highly regulated and centralized educational system of previous years.

Bibliography

[Some of the sources cited below are documents created for administrative use. Most are available through the Secretaría de Educación Pública in Mexico City. For more information about sources, contact the author through her publisher, Editorial Trillas in Mexico City.]

Advances de la Modernización Educativa. 1994, Mayo. [Advances in Educational Modernization]. México, DF: Secretaría de Educación Pública (SEP).

Aguilar, P. H. (1988). *La Educación Rural en México* [Rural education in Mexico]. México, DF: Secretaría de Educación Pública.

Annuales de Estadísticas de UNESCO [Statistical Annuals of UNESCO]. 1989.

Barbosa, H. A. (1972). *Cien Años en la educación de México.* [One hundred years of education in Mexico]. México, DF: Editorial Pax.

Brunner, J. J. (1990). *Educación superior en America Látina: Cambios y desafíos* [Higher education in Latin America: Changes and challenges]. Santiago, Chile: Fondo de Cultura Económica.

Constitución política de los Estados Unidos Mexicanos, edición décima [Political Constitution of the United States of Mexico, 10th edition]. (1994). México, DF: Editorial Trillas.

Convocatoria al concurso para la renovación de los libros de textos gratuitos de educación primária (1993-1994) [Summons to the Competition for the Renovation of the Free Educational Text Books for Elementary, 1993-94]. México, DF: Secretaría de Educación Pública.

Cooms, P. H. (1991). *Estratégia para mejorar la calidad de la educación de México* [Strategies for bettering the quality of education in Mexico]. México, DF: Secretaría de Educación Pública, Fondo de Cultura Económica.

Dirección General de Información, Capítulo Educación [General Management of Information, Chapter on Education]. (1992). México, DF: Secretaría de Educación Pública.

Dirección General de Información, Informe de Ejecución [General Management of Information, Executive Report]. (1993). México, DF: Secretaría de Educación Pública.

Dirección General de Planeación, Programación y Presupuesto, *El XI Censo General de Población y Vivienda* [General Management of Planning, Programming, and Budget, The XI General Population and Housing Census]. México, DF: Secretaría de Educación Pública.

Estadística básica del sistema educativa. Fin de cursos [Basic statistics of the national educational system. End of courses]. (1992-1993). México, DF: Secretaría de Educación Pública.

Fundamentos Teórico-Metodológicos del Programa Preescolar (1992). [Theoretical-Methodological Fundamentals of Preschool Education]. México, DF: Secretaría de Educación Pública.

Guerra, R. (1978). *Systems of Higher Education: Mexico.* International Council for the Development of Education.

Informes Annuales [Annual Reports], (1992-1993). (1993-1994). México, DF: Secretaría de Educación Pública.

La Federación de Educación, Diario oficial de la federación, 5 de marzo de 1993. [The Federation of Education, Official Diary of the Federation, March 5, 1993.] Mexico, DF: Secretaría de Educación Pública.

La Federación de Educación, Diario oficial de la federación, 13 de julio de 1993. [The Federation of Education, Official Diary of the Federation, July 13, 1993.]

Larroyo, F. (1986). *Historia comparada de la educación en México.* [Comparative History of education in Mexico.] Mexico, D.F.: Editorial Porrua.

México: Advances de la Modernización Educativa, 1989-1994. [Mexico: Advances in Educational Modernization, 1989-1994]. México, DF: Secretaría de Educación Pública.

Nájera, H. S. *Inspector General de la Secundaría, de la SEP. Datos proporcionados.* [Inspector General of Middle School Education, of SEP. Information supplied through interviews.]

Plan y programas de estudio, 1993. PRIMÁRIA. Educación Básica. [Plan and programs of study, 1993. Elementary school. Basic education.] México, DF: Secretaría de Educación Pública.

Plan y programas de Estudio, 1993. Secondária. Educación Básica. [Plan and programs of study, 1993. Middle School. Basic education.] México, DF: Secretaría de Educación Pública.

Poder Ejecutive Federal. (1989). [Federal Executive Power]. México, DF: Secretaría de Educación Pública.

Programa para la Modernización Educativa. [Program for Educational Modernization]. 1989-1994. México, DF: Secretaría de Educación Pública.

Salvat. (1974). *Historia de México en 11 tomos.* [History of Mexico in 11 Volumes]. México, DF: Author.

Solana, F., Cardill Reyes, R., & Bolanos Martinez, R. (1982). *Historia de la educación pública en México.* [History of Public Education in Mexico]. México, DF: Fondo de Cultura Económica.

CHAPTER 4

The Newest "Outsiders": Educating Mexican Migrant and Immigrant Youth

HARRIETT D. ROMO
SOUTHWEST TEXAS STATE UNIVERSITY

This chapter discusses the important characteristics of the secondary school Mexican immigrant population and how schools can meet the educational and affective needs of those students. Over the past decade the Mexican immigrant population has grown considerably. Forty percent of the 2.3 million limited-English-proficient (LEP) students attending public schools in the United States are of Mexican origin. The vast majority of those students live in Texas and California. Yet, few school districts have changed their policies to meet the immigrant students' special needs. A brief history of the Mexican experience in U.S. schools is presented in this chapter to demonstrate the social, cultural, and political context of schooling that has affected Mexican immigrant student achievement. The chapter also includes case studies drawn from field research conducted by the author over a span of 12 years of work with immigrant families. The experiences of these families demonstrate how human capital, i.e., the language and academic skills that students bring with them to the schools, as well as the organization of schooling, influences achievement. An overview of programs serving immigrant high school students and recommendations regarding effective strategies for educating these students are also presented.

Historical and Social Circumstances

The historical circumstances of Mexican immigration to the United States have had a profound impact on the ability of Mexican children to take advantage of schooling. This brief history illustrates how the immigration experience has affected access to education in the United States.

Mexican immigration to the United States and movement back and forth across the United States/Mexico border has a long history. During the early nineteenth century and into the years prior to the Mexican American War, authorities took surprisingly little notice of this movement.

Frontier contact between Anglos and Mexicans began with the opening of the Santa Fe Trail in the 1820s. Contact increased significantly with the offer of free land in the Mexican state of Texas to those who could bring in immigrant families from the United States (McComb, 1989, pp. 34-36). Anglo settlers also migrated into the Mexican borderlands as farmers, ranchers, and prospectors in search of gold and silver. Conflict occurred between the United States and Mexico over the control of the Southwest and resulted in the Mexican American War of 1846-1848.

Prior to 1848, what education there was in the U.S. Southwest—and there was little—occurred under the auspices of the church, or in the home, or abroad if a family were wealthy (Moquin & Van Doren, 1971, p. 191).

The end result of the brutal Mexican American War was that Mexico ceded most of the Southwest to the United States with the Treaty of Guadalupe Hidalgo in 1848 and then the Gadsden Purchase of 1853. The Treaty of Guadalupe Hidalgo gave Mexicans residing in those areas the options of becoming American citizens or remaining Mexican citizens and guaranteed the protection of their religion and property rights (Hraba, 1994, pp. 248-255; Moquin & Van Doren, 1971). However, with the discovery of gold in California and with U.S. courts seldom recognizing Spanish land grants, Anglo capitalism and culture eventually dominated the region (Montejano, 1987; Rosenbaum, 1981; McWilliams, 1968).

Almost overnight, people of Mexican descent became an ethnic minority. Tensions between Anglos and Mexicans increased as the groups clashed over language, religion, food, work habits, racial prejudices, and expropriation and takeover of land (Montejano, 1987; Rosenbaum, 1981). Although a public school system was brought to the Southwest in 1848, the education of children was not a priority during these times and was a luxury even for those families who could afford private teachers or boarding schools.

Mexican workers, with their history of labor in farming, ranching, and mining in both Mexico and the borderlands, supplied the bulk of the unskilled labor force in the Southwest. Throughout the first half of the twentieth century, labor bosses brought gangs of Mexican laborers to growers to meet their labor needs in agriculture. In southern Texas, border guards also acted as labor agents (Foley, 1988). Few Anglos were concerned about the education of the children of those workers, and exploitation and discrimination against Mexican workers were common (Acuna, 1981). The Mexican workers frequently worked together at migratory jobs and as part of recruited labor gangs, and, as a result, were isolated from workers of different ethnic backgrounds and from many of the assimilative mechanisms in the Southwest (McWilliams, 1968). When their labor was needed, they were recruited and hired at low wages; in bad economic times, they were seen as taking jobs of U.S. workers and deported. During the Great Depression, when labor demands fell off and the labor supply in the Southwest went up as U.S. migrants arrived from the dust bowl, some 500,000 Mexicans—many of them born in the United States—and U.S. citizens were repatriated to Mexico (McLemore & Romo, 1985; Romo, 1983, pp.164-165). In the 1950s, over a million Mexicans were again deported in Operation Wetback (Steiner, 1969, p. 128).

The lack of educational opportunity was compounded by the low socioeconomic status of Mexican workers. As low wage laborers and farmworkers, few Mexican families accumulated the resources necessary to prepare themselves for white-collar occupations and send their children to good schools. Migratory agricultural work often precluded the adequate education of their children. Children of migrant workers attended poorly equipped schools and often missed school to work in the fields to help their parents or to take on other family responsibilities while their parents worked. Migrant children whose families followed the various crop harvests moved from school to school on the migrant trail. Children who attended classes for only a portion of the school year, year after year, often fell behind. The large landowners, especially the big growers and railroads, and public officials had little interest in supporting schools for Mexican children. They wanted workers who would work for low wages, not an educated workforce. The wealthy parents sent their children to private schools so they had little interest in spending their taxes on better public schools for laborers' children (Barnes, 1971). In many school districts in Texas and California, Mexican children were segregated in "Mexican schools." The courts permitted English language difficulties to justify segregation despite clear evidence that school officials used the linguistic rationale as a pretext for segregating Mexican Americans from Anglos. In some cases, school districts refused to allow Mexican students to attend Anglo schools even when the Mexican students spoke no Spanish (Martinez, 1994). The pattern of poor school performance among Mexican American students was prevalent (San Miguel, 1987, p. 104). As Mexican students moved through the U.S. school system, if they did not drop out completely, their level of educational attainment declined compared to the achievement of Anglo students. Differences were reflected in comparative drop-out rates and percentages of the respective groups that graduated from high school and college.

Court Action Affecting Immigrant Children

Over the past 30 years, several significant court cases have addressed the lack of educational opportunities for Mexican immigrant children. The 1974 *Lau v. Nichols* case, based on the experiences of Chinese immigrant students in California, applied to Mexican immigrant and other limited-English-proficient students throughout the United States. The *Lau* decision determined that the failure of the San Francisco school system to provide English language instruction to Chinese students who did not speak English denied those students a meaningful opportunity to participate in the public educational program. The court reasoned that merely providing the same facilities, textbooks, teachers, and curriculum for students who did not understand English was not equal treatment. The court ruled that when the schools provided only regular English language instruction for limited-English-speaking students, those students were effectively shut out from any meaningful education. The court decision did not specify how the school district was to meet the special needs of these children. The decision (*Lau v. Nichols*, 1974) read "Teaching English to the students of Chinese ancestry who do not speak the language is one choice. Giving instruction to this group in Chinese is another. There may be others."

The interpretive guidelines for the *Lau* decision published by the Office for Civil Rights of the U.S. Department of Health, Education, and Welfare (1970) clearly indicated that "school districts had to take affirmative steps to rectify the language deficiency in order to open their instructional program" to immigrant students. The guidelines were issued to clarify the government's position in Title VI of the Civil Rights Act of 1964 (45 CFR, pt. 80) that provided that "no recipient of federal funds may provide services, aid, or other benefits to an individual which is different or is provided in a different manner from that provided to others under the program; or restrict an individual in any way from the advantages enjoyed by others receiving service, aid, or benefit under the program." The *Lau v. Nichols* decision required schools to "open up instruction" so that students from families in which English was not the spoken language could benefit.

In the summer of 1975, the Office for Civil Rights (U.S. Department of Health, Education, and Welfare) offered specific remedies to eliminate past educational practices ruled unlawful under the *Lau v. Nichols* decision. Those remedies included identifying the students' primary or home language, diagnosing the students' educational needs, and selecting a program appropriate for the students. The remedies specified that secondary students could receive instruction in subject matter in the native language and receive English as a second language (ESL) as a class component or they could receive required and elective subjects in the native language and bridge into English, learning English in a natural setting. The regulations also allowed secondary students to receive high-intensity language training in English until they could operate successfully in school in English and then bridge into the school program for all other students. While recognizing that programmatic approaches would vary from school district to school district, the *Lau* remedies recommended bilingual education as the best way to provide special aid to limited-English-proficient students.

The use of bilingual education in public schools provoked bitter political disputes throughout the 1960s and 1970s (Spring, 1991). Debates over ESL approaches versus bilingual instruction raged in the 1980s. Opponents of bilingual education argued that the programs were not successful. Some claimed that bilingual education was a self-interested and political tactic of Hispanic leaders and that the programs "blocked the integration of minority children into mainstream society" (Porter, 1990).

Supporters of bilingual education argued that children learned best in a language they could understand (Hakuta & Gould, 1987). They wanted immigrant students to function in the majority culture and at the same time maintain the traditions of their own culture. Kenji Hakuta (1986) wrote a respected and scholarly book, *Mirror of Language*, about the bilingual debate concluding that all students in the United States should be bilingual. He argued that speakers of immigrant languages should be seen as "holders of a valuable natural resource to be developed." He pointed out that the success of pluralism in the United States depended on the success of such bilingual programs. Research over time has provided strong evidence that advanced bilingualism promotes academic achievement (Bankston & Zhou, 1995; Cazden & Snow, 1990; Matute-Bianchi, 1986; Baker & Kanter, 1981).

The intent of the *Lau v. Nichols* decision was clearly to include immigrant children in the educational system by providing special English language instruction and bridging into the academic curriculum. Still, the education of Mexican immigrant students has remained controversial. In another case that went all the way to the U.S. Supreme Court (*Plyler v. Doe, 1982)*, one Texas school district attempted to exclude Mexican immigrant students from public school altogether.

The Courts and Undocumented Immigrant Children

In the *Plyler v. Doe* case, a Texas school district attempted to deny local school district funds for the education of undocumented children and, thus, deny free public education to such children. By a 5-4 vote, the U.S. Supreme Court struck down the statute as violating equal protection, arguing that the equal protection clause was intended to cover any person physically within a state's borders, regardless of the legality of his/her presence. The Court argued that while public education was not a right guaranteed by the U.S. Constitution, it was certainly more important than other social welfare benefits. Denying children an education would make them illiterate and would prevent them from advancing on their individual merit and becoming useful members of U.S. society. The Court also rejected the argument of the attorneys for Texas who claimed that undocumented children were less likely than other children to remain within the state and put their education to use there. The Court found nothing in the record to suggest that this was true (Emanuel, 1983).

The issue resurfaced in the 1990s. In November of 1994, the voters of California passed Proposition 187—"Illegal Aliens, Ineligibility for Public Services Verification and Reporting Initiative Statute." This initiative made undocumented immigrants ineligible for public school education at elementary, secondary, and postsecondary levels. It required various state and local agencies to report persons *suspected* of being illegal aliens to the Immigration and Naturalization Service. Opponents of this Proposition argued that it was not constitutional and that it was contrary to the 1982 U.S. Supreme Court ruling in *Plyler v. Doe*. Some argued that Proposition 187 violated parents' due process, because families were not given the right to contest being reported as "suspected" illegal aliens. Others argued that the reporting requirement of Proposition 187 might encourage discrimination based on race, color, or national origin. The implementation provisions of Proposition 187 also appeared to violate the restrictions of obtaining personal information about a student without prior consent of the parent. Educators argued that the proposition imposed a law enforcement function on schools that would adversely affect the learning environment for all children. The supporters of Proposition 187 claimed that the ultimate objective of the initiative was to curtail undocumented immigration by making the process of immigration less attractive. Those who opposed the proposition argued that depriving immigrant children of education was not likely to cause them to return to their countries of origin. It was more likely to cause them to become further marginalized from educational access than they already were.

The *Plyler v. Doe* case and the California Proposition 187 indicated that the public mood in Texas and California did not support the assimilation of immigrant children.

Increased Immigration and Demands on U.S. Schools

Despite the negative climate, increasing numbers of immigrant students—with or without their families—have entered the United States in search of the advantages associated with life and work in this country (Massey, 1985; 1986). According to the U. S. Department of Education, there were 2.31 million limited-English-proficient students in public elementary and secondary schools in the 1991-92 school year. That figure represented a 70 percent increase since 1984. Almost three out of four LEP students spoke Spanish as their native language. Of the Spanish speakers at all grade levels, 40 percent were born in Mexico (U.S. Department of Education, 1993).

Increases in both legal and illegal immigration to the United States in the 1970s and 1980s, together with increases in the proportion of immigrants coming from Latino and Asian countries, has generated renewed interest in the impact of immigration on schools (Passel, 1985; 1986; Massey, 1981). One result of this concern has been heightened immigration restrictions. The 1986 Immigration Reform and Control Act (IRCA) has been referred to as the "most sweeping revision of the nation's immigration laws since 1965" (Goodis, 1986).

With increasing immigration, the public education of immigrant students is of particular concern because the schools have historically been the key institution responsible for integrating immigrants and their children into the larger society. Interestingly, little of the literature on the impact of immigration has focused specifically on education. Most studies have addressed the complexity of counting undocumented immigrants, immigrants' impact on the U.S. workforce, their use of health and social services, and the effects of changes in the immigration laws on immigrant flows to the United States.

Many of the analyses of the 1986 immigration reforms suggested that immigration restrictions did not substantially lessen the influx of immigrant students. Through a general amnesty provision for those able to demonstrate continuous residence in the United States after January 1, 1982, IRCA allowed about 1.7 million persons immediately to apply for legalization. Experts estimated that 87 percent of those applying for the general amnesty were Mexican (Hoefer, 1989). Massey, Donato, and Liang (1990) found that as the immigrants obtained legal status they were more likely to send children to public schools in the United States. Thus, the use of public school services was expected to significantly increase as a result of the amnesty provision. Massey and his colleagues estimated that 5 years after legalization, some 42 percent of all amnesty recipients would enroll children in U.S. public schools. Given that the number of amnesty recipients was in the millions once family members were included and that those qualifying for amnesty were highly concentrated in California (55 percent) and Texas (18 percent), the enrollment of Mexican immigrant children in public schools was expected to increase sharply in those states (Massey, Donato, & Liang, 1990, p. 207).

Several other factors about immigration added to the school-age population in the 1990s. Increased *legal* immigrant quotas added more to the growing numbers of school-age children and youth. During the 1980s, almost 600,000 immigrants each year were granted lawful permanent residence in the United States (Bean, Edmonston, & Passel, 1990). In 1990 alone, the United States legally admitted 1.5 million immigrants, exceeding the record high set in 1907 of nearly 1.3 million (Donato, 1993). Moreover, a growing number of these legal immigrants were young adults in the prime of their childbearing years, many of whom would require day care and education for their children. The family reunification components of immigration legislation also gave priority to children of immigrants already in the United States (Cafferty, Chiswick, Greeley, & Sullivan, 1984). The 1990 Immigration Reform Act left virtually intact the family unification provisions of previous law and provided for legalization of sizable numbers of family members of persons previously legalized under IRCA (Bean & Fix, 1992). In addition to increases in *legal immigration* of young Mexicans, *undocumented migration* among Mexican women and children increased to even higher levels than those preceding the passage of the Immigration Reform and Control Act (Bean, Espenshade, White, & Dymoski, 1990).

Since 1990, twice as many people have come to the United States each year than arrived during the "Great Immigration" of European immigrants a century ago (Macionis, 1996). In some cities the impact of immigration has already been proportionately greater. In Los Angeles, San Francisco, Dallas, Houston, and Miami, foreign-born residents now make up between a fifth and a third of the total population (Valdez, DaVanzo, Vernez, & Wade, 1993). These immigrants make their largest service demands on education (Vernez, 1994). Immigrants' concentration in urban centers and their relatively high fertility rates add to the pressures on American public schools. A contemporary portrait of immigration patterns shows that the recent flows of immigrants have relatively low levels of education. This increases the challenge to schools to educate immigrant children who speak little English and arrive with differing levels of sophistication (Portes & Rumbaut, 1990).

The ability of the immigrant population to participate in the United States as future citizens depends on the quality of the instruction and training that their children receive and the measures taken to promote their integration into U.S. society. Low levels of education command low wages and lead to greater employment instability that may last over the duration of the immigrant's working life in the United States (Vernez, 1993). Uneven access to preschool programs and low expectations of those Mexican immigrant students who do attend school perpetuate the low educational attainments of large numbers of second- and third-generation Mexican Americans (Chapa, 1990).

Mexican immigrant children will play an important role in the United States as the total U.S. citizen population ages and the working population contracts in the coming years (Cafferty, Chiswick, Greeley, & Sullivan, 1984). As the restrictive immigration policies begin to have an impact, the United States has several recourses for meeting the need for skilled workers. To succeed without bringing in new immigrant labor, our schools will have to assure that all youth residing in the United States are well educated and trained.

Immigration and Educational Policy

The approaches regarding the education of immigrants range from assimilationist to exclusionist, reflecting different perceptions of how society should be structured. Prior to 1965, immigration was regulated by the 1924 Quota Act, which determined the national groups allowed to immigrate based on the percentage of the national groups already in the United States. The act was passed during a period of extreme racism in the United States, and the clearly stated purpose of the act was to limit immigration of non-White populations. During this time of primarily White immigration, U.S. educational policy was assimilationist. The mission of the schools was to "Americanize" immigrant children. Jane Addams, speaking of public education, claimed, "The public schools in the immigrant colonies deserve all the praise as Americanizing agencies which can be bestowed upon them" (Addams, 1910). The immigrant education programs of the 1920s emphasized the teaching of English and the American way of life, including pledging allegiance to the flag, eating American foods, and the superiority of the United States' form of government (Glazer, 1985).

The educational response to immigration since 1965 has been quite different. Post-1965 immigration has been largely Asian and Hispanic rather than European in origin. According to Reimers (1985), the Western Hemisphere ceiling on immigrants debated in 1968 was a clear desire for restricting Hispanics, Black English-speaking and Creole-speaking West Indians, and other Caribbean and Latin American peoples. In the 1970s, much of the public and political concern over immigration centered on Hispanics who entered in growing numbers after 1965. In 1974, *U.S. News and World Report* wrote about the "newest Americans," claiming that the United States was experiencing "a second Spanish invasion."

The United States' response to the question of how to educate the children of these recent immigrants has been complicated by court decisions and political divisions. Public support and funding for bilingual education have emphasized the early elementary grade levels, especially kindergarten through third grade (San Miguel, 1987). In 1992, only 22 states (43 percent) provided state funds designed specifically for instructional services to limited-English-proficient students. Only 17 percent of the schools offering services offered intensive LEP services that included significant native language use (U.S. Department of Education, 1993).

Most middle school and secondary bilingual programs offer only a few core subjects of reading, writing, and basic math, and few high schools offer an expansive course offering or college preparatory courses in the bilingual track. Plus, a shortage of certified bilingual teachers in many secondary school subject areas adds to the difficulty of implementing effective secondary level bilingual programs. In 1992, about 80 percent of all districts reported having "some" to "a lot" of difficulty recruiting bilingual teachers of Spanish and other languages. Over half (53 percent) reported having the same difficulty hiring English-as-a-second-language (ESL) teachers. Only 10 percent of the teachers of LEP students were certified in bilingual education and 8 percent in ESL instruction (U.S. Department of Education, 1993).

Complicating program choices is the reality that the educational backgrounds of Mexican immigrant adolescents vary considerably. Upon arrival, some adolescents have attended *Secundaria* in Mexico (approximately 7th-9th grade in the United States), giving them a comparatively strong educational background. Many others, however, have attended only a few years of *Primaria* (grades 1-6), while still others have never enrolled in school in Mexico. This latter group of adolescents have few literacy skills. The need to learn English characterizes most new Mexican immigrants, but it is a skill that most seek willingly.

Case Studies

As discussed earlier, the Mexican immigrant population in the United States is extremely heterogeneous. Immigrants can be temporary migrants, border commuter migrants, long-distance migrants who stay for several years at a time, legal migrants who may or may not return to their country of origin, permanent legal residents who have decided to remain in the United States, or undocumented immigrants who entered the United States clandestinely.

The following case studies show how inadequate educational programs, lack of counseling support, and insufficient vocational training leave immigrant students with less than adequate skills. Earning enough to be self-sufficient or to improve the lives of their children is difficult without a good education.

Information about these families has been collected from field work within an immigrant community in Texas over the past 15 years. Through several research projects, the author followed a small number of immigrant families longitudinally from the time they first arrived in the United States until their children left the U.S. school system. While there have been considerable improvements in the education of immigrant children, especially at the elementary school level, the failures of the school systems in meeting the needs of many youth are cumulative and result in severe educational disadvantages. The following case studies illustrate how this occurs.

The Gómez Family

Sra. Gómez was married in Mexico at age 12 and had 15 children. Three of her oldest sons worked in the United States for several years and earned the money to bring the rest of the family to the United States. Although Sra. Gómez did not want to leave her home in Mexico, she felt the younger children would have better opportunities in the United States. Neither she nor her husband ever attended school and did not read or write. When the Gómez family came to the United States, they had seven children living at home. Oton was 16. He had arrived 3 years earlier and went immediately to work with his brothers helping to earn the money to bring his parents. He did not enroll in school. Another 14-year-old son also went to work instead of enrolling in school. A 13-year-old daughter was placed by the school district in a class for the mentally retarded. An 11-year-old was enrolled in a fourth-grade class and began having disciplinary problems at school because he did not understand his English-speaking teachers. The 9-year-old was placed in a second-grade class and was considered for grade retention at the end of the year but was passed on to the third grade. The 6-year-old was placed in a full bilingual program and was doing well at the end of the year. A 5-year-old was not enrolled in school because the family felt he was too young.

At one interview in her apartment, Sra. Gómez told the author she suffered from migraine headaches and felt anxious and depressed. She explained in Spanish, "First a problem with one, then a problem with another. And when I need help there is no help here, all the problems come together. I wish I could die. I don't have any other desire for myself, nothing else. If it weren't for them, it would be better if I would die. I came here, but I am worse off than in my home in my own land. Here because I don't know how to read, I don't know how to write, I can't do much here. I get a terrible headache, my whole chest hurts, I feel the pain will never go away." (Interview 6/83)

She seldom left her apartment. The youngest children were bused across town to a predominantly Anglo school, and without a car or a telephone she worried about them constantly. She attended a school meeting when the author accompanied her, but never spoke up. She talked afterward with bilingual staff and urged them to take care of her children. Her children told her about problems with teachers and other children.

The family remained in the United States and the mother and children qualified for legal residency under the amnesty provision of the 1986 Immigration Reform Control Act. Only one of her children, the ll-year-old, graduated from high school. He got a job working in construction with his older brother. The 9-year-old, Enrique, learned English well and won achievement awards at his school in the 7th grade. When Enrique was in 9th grade, the parents joined the citrus crop migrant stream and the father was injured in the fields. Enrique dropped out of school to help support his parents. In his job at a restaurant, he earned $4.35 per hour, about the same as the brother with the high school diploma in his construction job. He argued that the restaurant job was better because he worked in air-conditioning and did not get dirty.

During the time the Gómez children were attending school, anti-immigrant sentiment around immigration reform spilled over into the school. One of the boys was involved in a fight at the high school campus when other students called him "wetback." He was expelled for several days for fighting. He explained:

> When I was in school it was basically all Hispanics were together and all the Whites were together.... If you saw a Hispanic you couldn't talk to him. They would call them wetbacks. That would hurt me. I would get into a fight. I did not like to be called a wetback. (Interview 2/93)

Commentary. This case study brings up several dilemmas facing a great many immigrant students. One is the choice of staying in school or working to help the family. Despite being good students, economic pressures frequently cause immigrant youth to leave school.

The two girls in the family had less success in school than the boys. The parents took the mentally retarded daughter out of school because peers teased her and they worried about her safety at school. The other daughter dropped out of school and started a family. She found a job with her brother at the restaurant.

With proper programs, immigrant students can overcome tremendous obstacles and succeed in school. Despite entering U.S. schools with no

English or academic skills, two of these children learned sufficient English to do well in school. One, who was in a partial bilingual program, managed to earn a high school diploma. The other, who received full bilingual instruction in first through sixth grade, earned awards for his scholarship. The award-winning student was unable to continue in school because of his family's lack of economic resources. His counselors could only offer him encouragement to remain in school; they offered no programs to allow him to work part-time and continue in school. The counselor did not try to work with his family to convince them to support their son's academic efforts.

When students arrive and enroll in U.S. schools at young ages, their opportunities for success are greater. The older sons, who never enrolled in U.S. schools, continued to work in landscaping and construction jobs. They learned basic English at their worksites, but, because they worked primarily with other Mexican workers and lived in predominantly Mexican neighborhoods, they found few opportunities to gain advanced English or other acculturation skills. One of the brothers had an opportunity to move up in his job as manager, but because he could not read or write, he was unable to go beyond the rank of job supervisor.

The role of family is obvious in this case. These parents lacked literacy and English skills and could not intervene for their children when they experienced problems at school. The mother struggled with her own mental health problems associated with immigration and had little energy left to encourage her children. The obligations of the older youth to help support the family, especially in times of economic or family crisis, remained strong values in immigrant families. The older sons worked to bring the other family members to the United States, and the younger sons and daughters were expected to do their share to support the family, even at the expense of school.

Although at least two of these youth demonstrated the ability to succeed academically in school, the parents and older siblings were unable to give them the information or resources needed to complete high school or go to college. The son working in the restaurant was able to use his bilingual skills to his advantage. Yet, when the younger brothers and sisters compared the high school graduate with his brothers, they did not see that the diploma paid off in a job advantage. They saw little incentive to remain in school and struggle with peers and English-speaking teachers.

The family experienced negative repercussions from the *Plyler v. Doe* ruling and the desegregation efforts of the school district. The children were called *wetbacks* and were bused across town to desegregate predominantly Anglo schools. The demands of living in a community where their presence was not valued, but rather disparaged, had an effect on the children and the parents. A strong family network helped counter some of these negative effects, but the obligations to family came at the cost of staying in school.

The Juárez Family

The grandfather and father in the Juárez family had a long history of working as migrant workers in the United States before Sr. Juárez brought his wife and six children to join him. Both men had spent long periods in the United States without their families and sent the majority of their earnings to Mexico to support their children. None of the adults in the family had attended school.

The family crossed into the United States without immigration documents and, with the help of other family members already living in the United States, found low-cost housing in a predominantly African American neighborhood. The oldest child, a 13-year-old daughter, had attended a few years of school in Mexico but spoke no English. She was placed in a fifth-grade classroom in a school that offered no bilingual education. The 11- and 9-year-old daughters were both placed in the third grade and bused across town to a predominantly Anglo school. They received pull-out bilingual instruction together with other immigrant students for two periods in the morning and then returned to an English-speaking teacher for the remainder of the day. The 7-year-old boy began school in first grade with a bilingual teacher. The 4-year-old was enrolled in a preschool program also with a bilingual teacher. A 3-year-old remained at home. Two other children were born in the United States within the first three years of the family's arrival. Those children were automatically U.S. citizens.

Urban renewal forced the family to move to the Mexican barrio across town about a year after their arrival. The move meant that the children had to change schools. Several months later, they moved a third time in the same area to try to find better housing. Sra. Juárez found out about a housing program that allowed the family to purchase a house owned by a federal Housing and Urban Development program because of foreclosure. The family moved again, this time across town, which required another school change for all of the children.

The father was picked up at his construction work site and deported by the U.S. Immigration and Naturalization Service. The family had to borrow money from relatives to cross the father back into the United States. The mother began working as a hotel maid to help pay expenses. The father and sometimes the older girls assumed responsibility for caring for the youngest children while the mother worked. Although both parents wanted their children to do well at school and did not like for them to miss classes, the daughters had to miss school to help out when the father could not care for the babies.

The oldest daughter was much more mature physically than the other fifth graders, who were about two years younger than she. The teacher considered passing her to the seventh grade at the end of the first year of school, but decided not to do so because she had not mastered English well enough. The teacher promoted her to sixth grade. The 11-year-old was embarrassed to try to speak English and received several notes home complaining of a poor attitude and refusal to do work. Her teacher recommended that she repeat the third grade. The mother requested that the child be transferred to a bilingual classroom. This required that she be transferred to a different school. The school arranged for both sisters to be transferred and their achievement and behavior improved. The 9-year-old made the "second honor roll," achieving mostly B grades. The first-grade child was identified as "gifted and talented" and brought home positive school reports. The mother worried about the preschool child because he seemed to be having a difficult time remembering Spanish, but he got good reports from the school.

Ten years later, the oldest daughter had dropped out of school at the seventh grade. She had learned basic English skills and worked in a fast food restaurant with other Mexican workers. She had two children. The daughter who had the disciplinary problems earned a high school diploma, but was not allowed to participate in the graduation ceremonies because she was pregnant at the time. She married, had her child, and worked with her mother cleaning office buildings at night. The honor roll student dropped out of school in 10th grade and got pregnant. She had her baby and attempted to return to school but, with work and child-care problems, dropped out again. The "gifted-and-talented" son became involved in gang activities, was expelled for fighting and truancy, and stopped attending school in the seventh grade. He tried to enroll in an alternative school to make up credits, but transportation problems and lack of motivation caused him to miss too many days of classes to continue. The three youngest children continued in school. The child who had begun in preschool could not communicate well in Spanish. The younger girls were doing average academic work but had been harassed by peers, causing the family to change their telephone to an unlisted number.

The parents struggled financially but managed to keep their house payments current with the help of their daughters' earnings. Both parents were disappointed that only one of their children had earned a high school diploma.

Commentary. The oldest daughter faced problems common to immigrant students who arrive in their early teens with little previous schooling. The school placed her with younger students because of her low level of skills in academic areas, but she was physically much more mature than her classmates. She left school as soon as she had learned basic English skills.

Her parents relied on her to translate for them and deal with paperwork in English.

The daughter who received negative notes from her teacher explained that she did not understand the work and, therefore, could not do what her teacher expected. The teacher did not know the capabilities of this student and did not understand the difficulties that a student who spoke no English and had little previous schooling might encounter in her classroom. When this child was placed with a bilingual teacher, she was able to complete her work and went on to earn the credits for her diploma.

The two children who did well in school, one making the honor roll and the other, identified as "gifted and talented," did well in the elementary grades, but had difficulties when they reached middle school and high school. The boy became involved in gang fights that caused him to be expelled from school. Gang members often harassed immigrant students in his neighborhood. The girl got pregnant and struggled with child-care problems when she attempted to return to school. The parents could not intervene for their children at the upper grade levels and could not control the negative peer influences.

Although this family was not migrating because of agricultural work, their frequent moves within the city because of housing problems resulted in disruptions in the children's schooling. The access to bilingual teachers and instruction varied from school to school and grade level to grade level. Although several of these immigrant students demonstrated exceptional potential in the early grades, they encountered numerous problems at the secondary levels. Their schools lacked programs to help them make a successful transition from elementary to secondary school. Their parents, without English and literacy skills, could not act as advocates for their children in the school context.

Analysis of the Cases

These children and their families, like many other immigrants, remained in the United States and now have legal resident status and families of their own. Their children are U.S. citizens. The opportunities to work with these youth in our public schools is a short-term investment. In the long run, we will have made a good investment if they are able to find better jobs and can provide solid family support for their children.

These cases demonstrate that many immigrant children began school in the United States with the ability to achieve and with high motivation. As these immigrant children moved through the U.S. school system, the programs and supports they needed were missing.

At the secondary level, school-related violence, in some cases reflecting anti-immigrant sentiments, affected immigrant students. The gangs who harassed several of these students targeted immigrant youth. The schools refused responsibility, claiming that the fights occurred outside of school.

When family needs pressured students to leave school, there were no work-study programs to allow the students to earn money and continue their education. Frequent school changes also contributed to ultimate school dropout.

After the students dropped out of public school, there were few programs to allow them to continue their education. The alternative schools did little to help the isolation and lack of achievement that immigrant youth often experience. These schools placed truant students together with students who had more serious disciplinary problems. The alternative school's location also created transportation problems.

Emotional and financial stress associated with extreme poverty (poor housing; mobility; the need for adolescents to help their families financially; unemployment; and, when employed, long work hours that left parents little time to supervise their children) affected both families.

The schools cannot resolve all the problems facing immigrant students. However, the schools must do a better job of educating immigrant youth if we expect them to provide financially for their own families later on. The schools must invest in these youth if we want to alleviate some of the same problems in the second and third generations of immigrant families. The social and economic consequence of not educating these students is their entry into the labor market without job skills. They leave school early at a time when unskilled jobs are sharply on the decline and when workers require at least a high school education from the very beginning of their work lives. Their inability to adapt to U.S. labor market demands and to provide adequately for their families will affect all of us. The consequence of neglecting their education is to perpetuate an underclass of immigrants and their children.

Program Types

What are the program options? What can secondary schools do to improve the achievement of immigrant students? The following overview of programs looks at strengths and weaknesses of the various options. Bilingual programs are available at the elementary level when there are large numbers of immigrant students and, in some states, such as Texas and California, such programs are mandatory. Once immigrant students reach the middle school and high school level, however, the program offerings at their schools frequently do not meet their needs. Some secondary schools have offered no special programs for immigrant/migrant students. A high percentage of students drop out before reaching the middle school because instructional support services and counseling are not available (Dryfoos, 1990).

When secondary schools have established programs, they have tended to be either intensive English-for-speakers-of-other-languages (ESOL) classes; bilingual programs that teach subject courses in the students' native language as they learn English; or newcomers' schools, which try to address the cultural and academic adjustments of immigrant students. Quality of instruction is hampered in each of these programs by the students' varying levels of academic skills and English proficiency and a curriculum that usually does not parallel that provided to English-speaking students. Each program approach has strengths and weaknesses.

ESOL classes. These classes are typically found in schools that enroll students whose native languages vary widely. ESOL tends to focus on goals that are immediately useful to, and appreciated by, students; this feature constitutes both a strength and a shortcoming. Immigrant students and their parents have a strong desire to learn English for its economic utility—opening up more and better job opportunities in the United States (Romo, 1984). Immigrants are, therefore, eager to participate in ESOL classes. The disadvantage of ESOL programs is that they tend to emphasize oral language and do not cultivate students' reading and writing skills, more specific academic needs (such as specialized high school courses), or critical thinking.

Bilingual programs. These programs teach academic concepts in a student's strongest language while simultaneously teaching English language skills. The catch for adolescent immigrants is that bilingual programming is more comprehensive in elementary schools (San Miguel, 1987). As a result, most secondary bilingual programs are limited to the core subjects of reading, writing, and basic math. The shortage of certified bilingual faculty to teach specialized subjects at the high school level means that, no matter how great the need, providing expansive course offerings in the bilingual track is very difficult.

Newcomers' programs. These programs provide a series of transition courses, allowing recent immigrants to learn about American culture and to receive counseling on adjustment problems. They teach English language skills that will help students make the transition into the regular school program. The programs facilitate adjustment, but being grouped with other newcomers cannot by itself give immigrant students access to mainstream activities and social groups.

A common feature of each of these programs is that they tend to segregate immigrant students from their English-speaking peers and track them away from academic or college-prep courses. This tendency is particularly objectionable in the case of gifted immigrant high school students. Those students, most particularly, need a broad-based program of intellectual challenge and cultural enrichment. Special attention should be provided in areas that will help these students graduate from high school, attain high scores in examinations, enroll in 4-year colleges and universities, and attain advanced college degrees.

Characteristics of Good Practice

Investing in the education of immigrant children is the best way to assure that youth become productive citizens. Education involves teaching skills, but it also involves the transmission of the adult culture of a society to the young. It is the process of selecting the most significant parts of our cultural heritage, including skills, knowledge, attitudes, and values, then teaching them to the next generation. If the immigrant youth have opportunities to socialize with English-speaking American youth, some social information—such as conversational English, ways of interacting with others, and good taste—will be absorbed without formal instruction. Recent studies have suggested, however, that the options of assimilation are less clear-cut for Mexican immigrant children, compared to those of earlier European immigrant groups. Mexican immigrant children may not have the opportunity to gain access to White middle-class society, no matter how acculturated they become. Portes and Zhou (1993) suggest that the deterioration of public schools in urban areas and the adversarial culture of many minority youth in inner cities contribute to an environment with fewer incentives and opportunities for second-generation immigrant children to get ahead. Without a good education and the exposure to American society that comes with attending school, immigrant children will continue to experience subordination and disadvantage and remain segregated in their ethnic communities (Hraba, 1994; Hirshman, 1994). If we expect Mexican immigrant youth to fully participate in U.S. society, they must be given the opportunity to gain strong academic skills and be exposed to the values that make this society distinct (Hurn, 1993).

The United States is not alone in struggling with policy issues related to the education of immigrant youth. European countries have worked together through the United Nations Education, Scientific, and Cultural Organization (UNESCO) (1986, 1988, 1989) to study these issues and have made numerous recommendations. In the United States, the work of Carter and Chatfield (1986); Garcia (1994); Lucas, Henze, and Donato (1990); Moran and Hakuta (1995); and Olsen and Dowell (1989) reports the positive characteristics of programs that effectively meet the needs of Mexican immigrant students. Such characteristics include many that describe good schools in general (e.g., high expectations for academic achievement for all students, high levels of parental involvement, and strong instructional and organizational leadership). Other important characteristics discussed below are effective with this population.

Valuing the students' home languages and cultures. Problems of cultural identity underlie many difficulties of immigrant students. This inevitably occurs when immigrant students enter U.S. schools where learning English and socialization are emphasized. Reactions sometimes include an attitude of failure, rejection and hostility toward school, delinquency, and social and family problems. Often these issues are intensified for second-generation immigrant youth whose parents are determined to preserve cultural or religious traditions that mean little to their U.S.-schooled children. Helping these students to maintain a positive link with their culture of origin is the most appropriate way to provide a good education and a strong value for U.S. society. This can include incorporating the home culture into the classroom, including materials on the culture, building on the home language in instruction, and observing the values and norms of the home culture while teaching the majority culture norms.

Adequate assessment of language proficiency and academic needs. One of the most troublesome practices for new immigrants is the use of standardized testing (Valencia & Aburto, 1991). A basic principle of testing immigrant students is that assessment should be embedded in teaching and learning and should be used to inform more skillful and adaptive teaching that leads to greater student success, not to sort students into low-level classes.

Language assessment can help schools identify the immigrant students in their schools and recruit them to the programs that can best meet their needs. However, the availability of adequate tests for language-minority students remains a problem (Masahiko & Ovando, 1995). The most common methods used by schools to determine a student's English-language proficiency are tests of oral proficiency in English that primarily test vocabulary, grammar, and ability to produce basic English sentences. Few tests assess students' reading and writing skills. Many schools also use a home language survey that asks students to report the language most often used in their homes, the language they first learned, and the students' dominant language. Whether formal tests or informal teacher assessments are used, to best meet the students' needs, a district should determine students' proficiency in their native languages and their academic achievement in the native language as well as in English.

Standardized tests in English cannot provide an accurate assessment of the skills of immigrant students who are learning a new language, adjusting to a new culture, and dealing with traumas of immigration. These students may need more than the usual 9 months to achieve a grade level's worth of learning as measured on standardized tests (Stevens & Wood, 1992, p. 97). Secondary school programs also need a sound way of sending achievement information with migrant students when they move from school to school. Schools must be able to document assessment results, courses taken, and courses recommended, as well as partial and complete credits awarded for work completed. This information is essential if school staff are to meet the educational needs of the secondary migrant student.

School leadership that makes immigrant and migrant students a priority. When teachers and counselors have negative feelings about immigrant students, those feelings tend to be reflected in their expectations of the immigrant pupils. The controversies over court cases, such as *Lau v. Nichols* and *Plyler v. Doe*, and the debates surrounding bilingual education spill over into the classroom and school interactions. Many of the conditions affecting the immigrant students' integration in the schools, such as educational guidance given to them and teachers' attitudes toward them, result from the overall school attitude and staff behaviors towards immigrant students. Successful teachers have high expectations of immigrant students and confidence in their ability to teach all students. Making these students a priority means offering special programs to meet their distinct needs. One successful program in Colorado provided health education and counseling at the school site during school family nights and in homes on other nights (Migrant Education Health Program, 1992). After these sessions, staff made sure that needed follow-up was provided. A program in Indiana provided summer school programs that included clubs, school enrichment activities, junior leader programs, and educational trips to enhance the quality of life for migrant students (Pilat, 1992). These programs provided strong academic programs and opportunities for caring adults to interact with immigrant youth.

Outreach and communication in the parents' home language. Illiterate mothers, and undereducated parents in general, frequently come up against difficulties that undermine their own self-respect. These parents are often dependent upon their children to navigate the schools and learn the language of the host country. A strong factor in the immigrant child's school success is the educational level of the immigrant parents, especially the mother. Overall, teachers report that parents of immigrant students are substantially less involved in school functions or as school volunteers than parents of nonimmigrant students. Involvement of parents of immigrant students is highest in elementary schools. A good program will recognize the family's vital role in a child's education and encourage parents to participate. This will often require providing information in a language the parent understands and working with a wide range of parental education levels, including those who cannot read or write or even sign their names. It may also involve recognizing that many immigrant youth do not have parents who can become involved in their schooling. Many of the decisions that parents would normally help youth make become the responsibility of immigrant adolescents when they live with siblings or unrelated adults instead of their biological parents. Parents may have remained in the sending country or may have followed the migrant stream, leaving older children behind to attend school. In focus group meetings that the author conducted with immigrant students, one high school student explained that her parents attended activities at the primary school with her younger brothers and sisters, but at the high school level there were no activities they felt comfortable participating in because of their poor English skills. Since she was the oldest child and knew some English, she was expected to resolve her own school problems and help her parents resolve those of her younger siblings. Other adolescents reported that they lived with older brothers and sisters or relatives and had no parents to become involved in their education. School staff must be sensitive to these immigrant family structures and accommodate them in their outreach efforts.

Staff development to help teachers and other staff serve immigrant students more effectively. The influence of racism and experiences of segregation and discrimination at school are decisive educational barriers for immigrant students. Mexican immigrant students are more likely to attend segregated schools today than they were in the 1950s when the Brown decision desegregated schools (Garcia, 1992). Whether they attend all Hispanic schools or ethnically mixed schools, immigrant students are easily identifiable and are often the targets of racism at school. Their experiences with discrimination are often reflected in their general feelings of satisfaction or dissatisfaction with school. Students who have experienced racism from peers or negative attitudes from teachers are less motivated to go to school than students who have not suffered in this way. Teachers and counselors need to be aware of the effects of negative attitudes and should have skills to help students mediate these situations.

Instruction based on previous educational experience. Studies have shown that certain problems of adaptation of immigrant children are closely related to age of arrival and length of residence in the host country. Language difficulties, interrupted education, the conditions under which immigration has taken place, plus lack of previous school experience all affect immigrant students' school achievement. Knowledge of the English language remains one of the major educational problems of immigrant students in the United States. Although the situation improves with time, this problem particularly affects children who enroll in U.S. schools at older ages (Cummins, 1981). Cummins' work suggests that it takes immigrant students at least 6 years to get sufficient command of English to do strong academic work in that language. Pre-high school experience is an essential factor in increasing immigrant students' high school success. Immigrant students who arrive at older ages without previous school experiences are definitely at a disadvantage, both socially and academically. Both the primary schools and the secondary schools must have remedial programs in place for older students who enroll without appropriate grade-level skills. In most situations, U.S. high school teachers are not prepared to deal with adolescent students who cannot read in Spanish or English and do not know the alphabet. Teachers will need special training to teach basic literacy skills to young adults.

Scheduling that includes immigrant students in classes with English-speaking students. Programs that track all low-achieving students together deprive those students of the most interesting classes and the most talented teachers. Because many of the newest immigrant parents are poorly educated or lack English skills, they are likely to be tracked into the lowest level classes. A good educational program will attempt to integrate immigrant children with high-achieving students in at least some of their classes.

Placement decisions made with adequate assessment and consultation. School staff need adequate assessment tools to determine language proficiency and academic achievement levels of immigrant students in order to place them in appropriate classes. Problems of academic performance of new arrivals who know little English should not be confused with the achievement problems of second-generation immigrants who have mastered English but lack strong reading, writing, or math skills. Mexican immigrant students have too often been viewed as lacking intellectual ability instead of lacking English proficiency. IQ tests, standardized tests, and more recently competency tests have been greatly misused with language-minority students, channeling them into low-level classes, labeling them as mentally retarded, and discouraging them from higher education. Effective programs recognize the wide range of language proficiencies and academic skills among immigrant students and address those needs accordingly. Schools should maintain achievement data on immigrant students and compare their achievement with that of the general student population so that their programs for immigrant students can be improved when necessary. They should also maintain follow-up achievement data for former immigrant students, so that they can see how these students perform over time.

Programs that address multicultural concerns (both social and academic). Effective programs for immigrant students recognize that individuals cannot change their culture without losing their identity. Immigrant students should not be faced with a choice between assimilating in order to do well at school and rejecting their own culture, which often leads to failure in school (Manaster, 1992). The Manaster study found that successful students were more stably acculturated, had a clearer sense of themselves, had higher occupational aspirations, and desired stable, responsible jobs. The students' cultures must be incorporated in the learning environment to help them make that positive transition. Teaching must take into account our increasingly complex understanding of U.S. culture as a multicultural reality (Fishkin, 1995). In the Southwest, U.S. culture has evolved in common with Mexican culture, and this multiculturalism provides an interesting and healthy base for high school curriculum.

Transitions from School to Work: Postsecondary and Vocational Programs

Although most jobs that offer the prospect of upward mobility require graduation from high school, the transition from school to work precedes high school graduation for many Mexican immigrant students. Many enter school late in a school year and withdraw early in order to migrate with their families. Others drop out of school, but try to return when their lives are more stable. A successful schooling experience for migrant students demands that teachers, counselors, and administrators have sensitivity and understanding of the mobile life of migrant students and their families. Flexible instructional programming that allows students to "stop out" of school to work or take care of family responsibilities, and then allows them to return and pick up their academic work without penalties, is essential for immigrant student success. Multiple "second-chance" opportunities for education and training at worksites, community centers, churches, and school sites should be available. This flexibility also demands that these projects coordinate their instructional programs.

Flexible options, along with programs and services to combat high dropout rates, are essential at the secondary level. The Migrant Attrition Project estimates a 45 percent national dropout rate for migrant students. Conditions leading to early school leaving are (1) over-age grade placement, (2) poverty, (3) interrupted school attendance, (4) inconsistent record keeping, and (5) limited English proficiency (Salerno, 1991).

Counseling that encourages academically successful immigrant youth to consider 4-year college and community college vocational options is also important. Several programs have been successful in this area. The

University of Texas at Austin (1994) Migrant Student Program provides information on course materials and services available for migrant students. The program focuses on courses that meet the high school graduation requirements. Students can work on the courses at their own pace at any location and earn high school credit through correspondence courses, examination, or having the university where the student enrolls grade the courses. The university program offers explanation for the instruction and helps with course work through an 800 telephone number. The university trains tutors, teachers, and administrators; and provides student progress reports and follow-up services. The program includes visits to the campus and assistance to students in preparing for the exam the students must pass to graduate from high school and to enroll in college. Other programs, such as the International High School, a collaborative curriculum project developed by New York colleges and public schools, and special summer programs, such as Upward Bound, that bring immigrant high school students to college campuses for tutoring and college orientation, help bridge the gap between high school graduation requirements and college entry expectations.

Other provisions that have helped keep immigrant students in school include coordinated social services, counseling, tutoring, enrichment activities, health service referrals, and job training and placement. Self-paced curriculum, workplace English and literacy instruction, and evening school classes help ensure that Mexican immigrant students have access to programs that allow them to continue learning skills needed for decent employment (Neubert & Leak, 1990). Initiatives that lead to associate degrees (or to other certification from community or technical colleges) are important options for many immigrant students. Knowledge of career options, program quality, support services, interagency coordination, and family influence must be considered as educators help immigrant students plan vocational training (Imel, 1989).

Conclusion

The UNESCO discussions on the education of immigrant children urged that we move beyond the stereotyped thinking of immigrants as problems. Instead we should think of immigrants as individuals trying to make a better life for themselves and their families. They come with human problems, and they are diverse. They are not all poor. They come for economic, personal, and social reasons. Some are unskilled and some are highly skilled; many will make significant contributions to our country. Investing in the education of immigrant children is the best way to assure that these youth are productive future citizens.

Immigration continues to make many demands of our public schools even in times of major and sustained fiscal difficulties at all levels. As we deal with immigrant students from non-European backgrounds, the cultural ethnocentrism and assimilation roles of our schools are being questioned. We are being called upon to deal with diversity and complex social relations in our schools. The majority of the financial responsibility for educating immigrant students is located at the state and local level where people have the greatest vested interest in their schools. While it is not unreasonable to expect the federal government, the unit of government that makes decisions about immigration policy, to bear the responsibility to cover some, if not all, of the costs of educating immigrant children, the implementation of adequate programs will remain the responsibility of local school districts. Despite the immediate costs, the education of immigrant youth is an investment in the future of our communities.

California, Texas, and the rest of the United States are not alone in struggling with the predicament of how to deal with immigrant youth. Most industrialized nations are dealing with similar issues. What we are experiencing in the United States is part of a global phenomenon. The question of how to educate immigrant students is not one that can be addressed simply with reforms in immigration laws. The immigrant children who will be enrolling in our schools in most urban areas in the next 5 years are already born and residing in our communities. Programs must be in place when they arrive in our classrooms.

To make the transition from "outsiders" to respected members of the U.S. workforce and society, immigrant youth must acquire cultural and technical skills through formal education. Cummins (1986), Brice-Heath (1986), Ogbu (1987), and Trueba (1987) have suggested that the schooling of immigrant children must be understood within the broader context of society's treatment of these students and their families in and out of schools. No quick fix is likely, under present social and schooling conditions. There is no single attribute that is the only variable of importance in the education of immigrant youth. A more comprehensive view, one that includes an understanding of the relationship between home and school and one that integrates students' values, beliefs, histories, and experiences into the educational strategies employed, is essential for the educational success of Mexican immigrant students.

All trends suggest that immigrant students in our high schools will remain here as long-term U.S. residents and may eventually become citizens (Borjas, Freeman, & Lang, 1991). The longer these students reside in the United States, the more likely we will see their inclusion in terms of occupation, residence, and intermarriage. We must also consider today's students' children and grandchildren as they form their own families and begin to pass educational advantage on to their descendants (Featherman &

Hauser, 1978). Unless our public schools serve these immigrant youth well, there will be a mismatch of the skills of young and poor immigrant residents and the educational requirements of the growing and better-paying jobs (Stolzenberg, 1990). There will also be a mismatch of their skills to participate as informed and active citizens and to meet the demands of democracy in an increasingly diverse United States.

References

Addams, J. (1910). *Twenty years at Hull House* (4th Printing, 1961). New York: Macmillan.

Acuna, R. (1981). *Occupied America: A history of Chicanos* (2nd ed). New York: Harper & Row.

Baker, K., & de Kanter, A. (1981). *Effectiveness of bilingual education: A review of the literature.* Washington, DC: U.S. Department of Education, Office of Planning, Budget, and Evaluation.

Bankston, III, C. L., & Zhou, M. (1995). Effects of minority-language literacy on the academic achievement of Vietnamese youths in New Orleans. *Sociology of Education, 68*, 1-17.

Barnes, P. (1971, June). The great American land grab. *The New Republic, 164*, 19-24.

Bean, F. D., Edmonston, B., & Passel, J.S. (1990). *Undocumented migration to the United States: IRCA and the experience of the 1980s.* Los Angeles and Washington, DC: The Rand Corporation and The Urban Institute.

Bean, F. D., Espenshade, T., White, M., & Dymoski, R. (1990). Post-IRCA changes in the volume and flow of Undocumented Migration to the United States. In F. Bean, B. Edmonston, and J. Passel (Eds.), *Undocumented migration to the United States: IRCA and the experience of the 1980s* (pp. 111-158). Washington, DC: The Urban Institute Press.

Bean, F. D., & Fix, M. (1992). The significance of recent immigration policy reforms in the United States. In G. Freeman and J. Jupp (Eds.), *Nations of immigrants: Australia and the United States in a changing world* (pp. 41-55). New York and Sydney: Oxford University Press.

Borjas, G., Freeman, R., & Lang, K. (1991). Undocumented Mexican-born workers in the U.S.: How many, how permanent? In J. Abowd and R. Freeman (Eds.), *Immigration, trade, and the labor market* (pp. 77-100). Chicago: University of Chicago Press.

Brice-Heath, S. (1986). Sociocultural contexts of language development. In (n.a.) *Beyond language: Social and cultural factors in schooling language minority students* (pp. 197-230). Los Angeles, California: California State University, Evaluation, Dissemination, and Assessment Center.

Cafferty, P. San Juan, Chiswick, B. R., Greeley, A. M., & Sullivan, T. A. (1984). *The dilemma of American immigration: Beyond the golden door.* New Brunswick, NJ: Transaction Books.

California Proposition 187. (November, 1994). Illegal Aliens, Ineligibility for Public Services Verification and Reporting Initiative Statute.

Carter, T., & Chatfield, M. (1986). Effective bilingual schools: Implications for policy and practice. *American Journal of Education, 95*, 200-232.

Cazden, C., & Snow, C. E. (1990). English plus: Issues in bilingual education, Preface. *Annals of the American Academy of Political and Social Science, 508*, 9-11.

Chapa, J. (1990). The myth of Hispanic progress. *Journal of Hispanic Policy, 4*, 3-18.

Cummins, J. (1986). Empowering minority students: A framework for intervention. *Harvard Educational Review, 56*(1), 18-35.

Cummins, J. (1981). The role of primary language development in promoting education success for language minority students. In *Schooling and language minority students: A theoretical framework* (pp. 16,23-28). Los Angeles: California State Department of Education, National Evaluation, Dissemination and Assessment Center.

Donato, K. M. (1993). *U.S. policy and Mexican migration to the United States, 1942-92.* Paper presented at the annual meeting of the American Sociological Association in Pittsburgh, PA: revised for Second Binational Conference on Mexico-U.S. Migration, sponsored by the Latin American Studies Department at the University of Chicago.

Dryfoos, J. G. (1990). *Adolescents at risk: Prevalence and prevention.* New York: Oxford University Press.

Emanuel, S. (1983). *Constitutional law.* New York: Emanuel Law Outlines, Inc.

Featherman, D., & Hauser, R. (1978). *Opportunity and change.* New York: Academic Press.

Fishkin, S. F. (1995, March 10). The multiculturalism of 'Traditional' culture. *The Chronicle of Higher Education, Point of View, A48.*

Foley, D. E. (1988). *From peones to politicos: Class and ethnicity in a South Texas town, 1900-1987 (Rev. ed.).* Austin: University of Texas Press.

Garcia, E. (1994). *Understanding the needs of LEP students.* Boston: Houghton Mifflin.

Garcia E. (1992). Hispanic children: Theoretical, empirical, and related policy issues. *Educational Psychology Review, 4*(1), 69-93.

Glazer, N. (1985). Immigrants and education. In N. Glazer (Ed.), *Clamor at the gates: The new American immigration* (pp. 213-41). San Francisco: Institute for Contemporary Affairs.

Goodis, T. A. (1986). *A layman's guide to 1986 U.S. immigration reform: Impacts of immigration in California policy.* (Discussion Paper PDS-86-4). Washington, DC: Urban Institute.

Hakuta, K. (1986). *Mirror of language: The debate on bilingualism.* New York: Basic Books.

Hakuta, K., & Gould, L. J. (1987). Synthesis of research on bilingual education. *Education Leadership, 44*(6), 38-44.

Hirshman, C. (1994). Problems and prospects of studying immigrant adaptation from the 1990 population census: From generational comparisons to the process of "becoming American." *International Migration Review, 28(Special Issue)*, 690-713.

Hoefer, M. D. (1989, March 29). *Characteristics of aliens legalizing under IRCA.* Paper presented at the annual meeting of the Population Association of America, Baltimore, MD.

Hraba, J. (1994). *American ethnicity (2nd edition).* Itasca, IL: F. E. Peacock Publishers.

Hurn, C. J. (1993). *The limits and possibilities of schooling.* Boston: Allyn and Bacon.

Imel, S. (1989). The New Workforce (Trends and Issues Alerts). Columbus, OH: ERIC Clearinghouse on Adult, Career, and Vocational Education. (ERIC Document Reproduction Service No. ED 312 412)

Lau v. Nichols, 414 U. S. 563 (1974).

Lucas, T., Henze, R., & Donato, R. (1990). Promoting the success of Latino language-minority students: An exploratory study of six high schools. *Harvard Educational Review, 60*(3), 315-339.

Macionis, J. (1996). *Society: The basics.* Englewood Cliffs, NJ: Simon & Schuster.

Manaster, G. (1992). Mexican American migrant students' academic success: Sociological and psychological acculturation. *Adolescence, 27*(105), 123-136.

Martinez, G. A. (1994, Spring). Legal indeterminacy, judicial discretion and the Mexican American litigation experience: 1930-1980. *U.C. Davis Law Review, 27*(3), 555-618.

Masahiko, M., & Ovando, C. J. (1995). Language issues in multicultural contexts. In J. A. Banks and C. A. McGee Banks (Eds)., *Handbook of research on multicultural education* (pp. 427-444). New York: Macmillan Publishing.

Massey, D. S. (1981). Dimensions of the new immigration to the United States and the prospects for assimilation. *Annual Review of Sociology, 7*, 57-85.

Massey, D. S. (1985). The settlement process among Mexican migrants to the United States: New methods and findings. In D. Levine, K. Hill, and R. Warren (Eds.), *Immigration statistics: A story of neglect* (pp. 255-292). Washington, DC: National Academy Press.

Massey, D. S. (1986). Settlement of American migrants in the U.S. *American Sociological Review, 51*, 670-684.

Massey, D. S., Donato, K. M., & Liang, Z. (1990). Effects of the Immigration Reform and Control Act of 1986: Preliminary data from Mexico. In F. D. Bean, B. Edmonston, and J. S. Passel (Eds.), *Undocumented migration to the United States: IRCA and the experience of the 1980s* (pp. 183-210). Washington, DC: Urban Institute Press.

Matute-Bianchi, M. E. (1986). Ethnic identities and patterns of school success and failure among Mexican-descent and Japanese-American students in a California high school: An ethnographic analysis. *American Journal of Education, 95*, 233-55.

McComb, D. G. (1989). *Texas: A modern history.* Austin: University of Texas Press.

McLemore, S. D., & Romo, R. (1985). The origins and development of the Mexican American people. In R. O. De La Garza, F. D. Bean, C. M. Bonjean, R. Romo, and R. Alvarez (Eds.), *The Mexican American experience: An interdisciplinary anthropology* (pp. 3-32). Austin: University of Texas Press.

McWilliams, C. (1968). *North from Mexico: The Spanish-speaking people of the United States.* New York: Greenwood Press, Inc.

Migrant Education Health Program. (1992). Final Report, Colorado State Dept. of Health, Denver. (ERIC Document Reproduction Service No. ED 363 465)

Montejano, D. (1987). *Anglos and Mexicans in the making of Texas, 1836-1986.* Austin: University of Texas Press.

Moran, C. E., & Hakuta, K. (1995). Bilingual education: Broadening research perspectives. In J. A. Banks and C. A. McGee Banks (Eds.), *Handbook of research on multicultural education* (pp. 445-462). New York: Macmillan Publishing USA.

Moquin, W., & Van Doren, C. (Eds.). (1971). *A documentary history of the Mexican Americans.* New York: Praeger Publishers.

Neubert L. E., & Leak, D. A. (1990). Serving urban youth with special needs in vocational education: Issues and strategies for change. *TASPP Bulletin*, pp. 1-3 (ERIC Document Reproduction Service No. ED 326 695)

Ogbu, J. U. (1987). Variability in minority school performance: A problem in search of an explanation. *Anthropology and Education Quarterly, 18*, 312-334.

Olsen , L. & Dowell, C. (1989). *Bridges: Promising programs for the education of immigrant children.* San Francisco, CA: California Tomorrow. (ERIC Document Reproduction Service No. ED 314 544)

Passel, J. S. (1985). Undocumented immigrants: How many? In *Proceedings of the Social Statistics Section of the American Statistical Association, 1985* (pp. 65-71). Washington, DC: American Statistical Association.

Passel, J. S. (1986). Undocumented immigration. *Annals, American Academy for Political and Social Sciences*, 487, 181-200.

Pilat, M. (1992). *4-H youth programs: Enhancing the quality of life*. (ERIC Document Reproduction Service No. ED 359 449)

Plyler v. Doe, 457 U. S. 202 (1982).

Porter, R. P. (1990). *Forked tongue: The politics of bilingual education.* New York: Basic Books.

Portes, A., & Rumbaut, R. (1990). *Immigrant America: A portrait.* Berkeley: University of California Press.

Portes, A., & Zhou, M. (1993). The new second generation: Segmented assimilation and its variants. *Annuals of the American Academy of Political and Social Sciences*, 530, 74-96.

Reimers, D. M. (1985). *Still the golden door: The third world comes to America.* New York: Columbia University Press.

Romo, H. (1984). The Mexican origin population's differing perceptions of their children's schooling. In R. Garza, F. Bean, C. Bonjean, R. Romo, and R. Alvarez (Eds.), *The Mexican American experience: An interdisciplinary anthology* (pp. 635-650). Austin: University of Texas Press.

Romo, R. (1983). *East Los Angeles: History of a barrio.* Austin: University of Texas Press.

Rosenbaum, R. J. (1981). *Mexicano resistance in the Southwest.* Austin: University of Texas Press.

Salerno, A. (1991). Migrant students who leave school early: Strategies for retrieval. ERIC Digest. (ERIC Document Reproduction Service No. ED 335 179)

San Miguel, Jr., G. (1987). *Let all of them take heed; Mexican Americans and the campaign for educational equality in Texas, 1910-1981.* Austin: University of Texas Press.

Spring, J. (1991). *American education: An introduction to social and political aspects.* New York: Longman.

Steiner, S. (1969). *La Raza: The Mexican Americans.* New York: Harper & Row.

Stevens, E., Jr., & Wood, G. H. (1992). *Justice, ideology, and education: An introduction to the social foundations of education (2nd ed.).* New York: Mc Graw-Hill.

Stolzenberg, R. M. (1990). Ethnicity, geography and occupational achievement of Hispanic men in the United States. *American Sociological Review, 55,* 143-154.

Title VI of the Civil Rights Act of 1964 and the Departmental Regulation (45 CFR Part 80).

Trueba, H. (1987). *Success or failure? Learning and the language minority student.* Cambridge: Newbury House.

UNESCO. (1988, December). *Annotated bibliography: Education of immigrants.* Paris: Author.

UNESCO. (1989, April). *The socio-educational situation of the children of migrants.* Paris: Author.

UNESCO. (1986, October). *Programme of exchanges between educators of migrant workers in the host countries and educators in the countries of origin.* Paris: Author.

UNESCO. (1989). Meeting of specialists on the socio-cultural and linguistic integration of the children of migrant and former migrant workers. Yugoslavia: Author.

University of Texas at Austin. (1994). *Migrant student program receiving school guide.* (ERIC Document Reproduction Service No. ED 352 234)
U. S. Department of Education. (1993). Descriptive study of services to limited English proficient students (provided for the 1993 reauthorization of the federal elementary and secondary education programs). Washington, DC: Office of the Under Secretary.
U. S. Department of Health, Education, and Welfare. Office of the Secretary. (1970, May 25). Memorandum from J. Stanley Pottinger to school districts with more than five percent national origin-minority group children. *Identification of discrimination and denial of services on the basis of national origin.* Washington, D. C.
U. S. Department of Health, Education, and Welfare. Office for Civil Rights (1975, Summer). *Task force findings specifying remedies available for eliminating past educational practices ruled unlawful under* Lau v. Nichols. Washington, DC: Office of the Secretary.
U. S. Immigration Reform and Control Act of 1986 (IRCA).
U.S. News and World Report. (1974, July 8). The newest Americans: The second "Spanish invasion," 34-36.
Valdez, R. B., DaVanzo, J., Vernez, G., & Wade, M. (1993 June). Immigration: Getting the facts. (RAND Issue Paper, No. 1). Los Angeles: The RAND Corporation.
Valencia, R. R., & Aburto, S. (1991). The uses and abuses of educational testing: Chicanos as a case in point. In R. R. Valencia (Ed.), *Chicano school failure and success: Research and policy agendas for the 1990s* (pp. 203-251). New York: The Falmer Press.
Vernez, G. (1993). *Mexican labor in California's economy: From rapid growth to likely stability.* Palo Alto, CA: Stanford Press.
Vernez, G. (1994). *Undocumented immigration: An irritant or significant problem in U.S.-Mexico relations?* (Labor & Population Program, Reprint Series 94-18). Los Angeles: RAND Corporation.

Chapter 5

Stories and Poems by Migrant Writers

Compiled by Silvia Kelly and Robert Lynch
BOCES Geneseo Migrant Center

The following stories and poems were written by Mexican and Mexican American migrants working in Texas, Florida, and North Carolina. They tell of life in the camps, work in the fields, difficulties in adjusting to new schools and a new language, love for their families, anger over the actions of authorities, and their hopes for the future. Most of the authors were junior high or high school students when they wrote these award-winning personal narratives and poems. (See the Contributors section for information about individual authors).

Yellow Cheese and Yellow Buses

Christina Quintanilla

A two-and-a-half-day journey among a family of five adults and eight children, cramped in the back of a pickup truck, brought me across the Mexican border to the United States. For an eight-year old, it seemed an entire lifetime. The irony was that everyone was depending on the driving experience of my cousin—a sophomore in high school. Only now do I see the risk we all took the moment we got in the truck to leave Reynosa, Mexico, to come to Farm Worker Village in Immokalee, Florida.

Upon entering school, I had to face the fact that I didn't know anyone! Eating lunch at school such as yellow cheese and hamburgers, along with milk, no uniforms to wear, yellow buses and air conditioning didn't seem right. The confusion I felt was dreadful.

Another difficulty was accepting a "dumb" status among my classmates. I was the new kid, a foreigner, and not considered a good student even though I used to be the best student in Mexico. I knew I hadn't become stupid on the way to Florida. I pulled myself together, and not only mastered English in seven months, but went on to become one of the top students in Immokalee High School.

Now I plan to take the next step and go on to college. Since children are the future of the country, I want to make an impact on their lives by becoming a pediatrician.

What is a Migrant?

Sandra E. Trevino

I am not a number, a statistic, nor an illegal. I am a person with feelings. Yes, I have feelings, and many.

"Why?" perhaps you ask.

I have worked and greatly suffered. You know, it is not easy being a migrant.

Sometimes my friends ask me how it feels to be a migrant. Great! To leave school early, to enroll late, have a tutor, take night classes, Saturday classes, and sometimes correspondence classes. Great! I want to be a migrant.

No, my dear friend, I do not arrive late. I arrive at five o'clock in the morning. While you are having your first dream, sweat washes my face, and I have bathed with fog in the long furrows. While you drop milk in the school's kitchen, I wish I could drink a drop of water because it seems like I never reach the end of the row.

You say that you are bored with school, that you are tired of writing. Here I do not get bored, I do not have time., Yes I get tired, my back hurts from bending over; and at the end of the day, I feel that I will not be able to straighten up.

Yesterday, they took my mother to the hospital. They said she had a sun stroke. Poor thing, she did not stop working until she fainted. Last year, my brother had a car accident, and we had to spend all that we had earned on doctor bills. Later, our truck broke down, and to make matters worse, we could not work because it rained all month.

No, my friend, it is not all "fun." I have struggled so much. Yes, I am a "migrant" and I am not ashamed of it. However, I do not wish this on anyone.

My teacher asked me, "Where were you? Did you take a long vacation, or what?"

I answered, "Yes, I went to California, but not to visit Disneyland. I went to Montana, but not to ski. Also, I went to Ohio, but I could not go to the State Fair there. I have traveled all over the United States, but I have not seen anything, only farms."

While you checked exams and gave zeros as usual, I revisited the fields, and sometimes I pulled out snakes instead of vegetables. While you had an "off" period and ate your taquitos, I also ate my cold egg and bean taquitos, not for pleasure, but because of necessity. While you had your vacations, I also traveled, but I couldn't see anything from the truck's bed, traveling heaven knows where, in search of work.

Yes, I'm a migrant. I study when I can, so that someday I can stop being poor and stop crying in the fields close to the town that I never knew. And when I am in Laredo and I go to class, perhaps I'll get better grades than you my dear friend, because I am tired of being poor.

You want to be a "migrant"? I invite you to come with me for a year.

A Sacrifice

Carlos Carranza

When someone makes a sacrifice, that person gives up something he really values to achieve something even more important. Many people make sacrifices for different reasons. A young person may sacrifice spending time with his friends so he can work to make money for a car. Some people sacrifice having things like a television or telephone so they will have money for food. My father made a great sacrifice so he could provide a better way for his family.

My father sacrificed his lifestyle and his childhood for his family. In 1983 my father made a decision to come to America. He left Mexico and went to Texas to get a job. He worked every day as a delivery man for a tortilla store. Next he managed a floral shop. Every week he sent money to us in Mexico so we would have food and clothes. For three years, my dad worked all over the United States in any job he could find. We did not see him during this time. We continued to attend school while our mother worked washing clothes and cleaning houses for people.

In 1988, our family was reunited when we moved to Liberty, North Carolina. My dad was the only member of our family who could speak English. It was his dream that his family learn to speak English and live in America. We began school while he worked on a pig farm to support us. Living conditions were not ideal. In 1989 my family moved to Asheboro so my dad could work on a dairy farm. Once again, problems prompted us to move to our present home at Williams Dairy.

Finally my father's sacrifice paid off. Our family is together and working on a dairy farm. My brother and sisters attend good schools and speak English well. Since coming here, my sister Diana was born, and we all love her so much. I am proud of my dad for the sacrifices and hardship he endured so we could have better lives.

Migrant Dropouts

Jorge Botello

In my essay, I'm going to be expressing my feelings about a subject so important it is hard to miss: migrant teenagers dropping out of school because we are forced to work in the field with our parents. We must also migrate up and down the migrant stream, missing a lot of school.

For most people, dropping out of school is good for them because they think school is just a waste of time. However, in my opinion, I think school is a very important part of your life. I'm not just saying this because I want to win the contest. I'm saying this because I feel very bad for people that can't make a good living or get a good job because they didn't finish school.

Migrant students that are dropping out don't realize that they're making a big mistake. They just don't realize it because they're young. I can understand that any youngster that is still in school can be very stupid and make mistakes, but in this case, big-time mistakes. You see, if everybody starts dropping out of school, there will be no future for us. Now, the way I see it, we are the future, regardless of our lifestyle. What we do will probably end up hurting someone or something in the future.

Now, this is me talking! Since I was in kindergarten, I've had a dream. That dream for me has been very challenging. My dream is to become successful, regardless of my migrant life style. So far, I have been successful, because I haven't lost faith in my dream and I haven't dropped out of school. For me, school is the best thing that has ever happened to me. Why? Because school has given me a chance to learn more about my past, my history, my future, practically everything. All this has happened because I haven't lost faith in others or myself.

This is to all the dropouts: Whether you are migrant or not, if you dropped out years ago and you don't think you can come back to school, give it one more chance! Think again! There is such a thing as starting over. It's never too late to correct your mistakes. I know it feels bad when you fail at something, but life is like a carnival ride: Sometimes you ride the carnival rides perfectly, and sometimes you come against a very tough obstacle and you just feel like backing down. Well, don't!

Most people would probably ride this tough obstacle many times until it hit them, and they said to themselves, "Hey! I did it. I actually succeeded!" The major reason is because that person didn't quit—they knew that every time that they would go for a ride, they were going to fall off the ride sometime. But, they know that if they keep trying, they will succeed. The point is, they didn't let their failure get the best of them.

I'm 13 years old in the 7th grade, and I have 4.0 GPA. I always enroll in school late, but I always manage to keep my grades up. Being a migrant student doesn't mean we are quitters. It's a challenge to me to enroll in school late and still be at the top of the class. So, to all the dropout migrant students, give it another chance, because your education can be a very bright future for you.

Migrant Me

Burning Hands
Calloused by the espiga1
Hurting Back
Damaged by the cucumber
Blind Eyes
From seeing the sun
    to count the hours.

—Maribel Ledezma, April 1994

La Migra in Manteca

My sister Rosa remembers—
I wasn't there.
I was sitting in a hot car—
It was six thirty A.M.
The sun was rising
The flies were dancing among
    the pesticides,
The grapes were wet.
And hay venía la migra[2]. . .

"Keep walking!" my Mom said.
A paisano[3] fell before Rosa's eyes
    and rolled under the vines.
And she stopped.
"Keep walking," Mom said urgently.
The migra threw a light onto them.
And the paisanos would fall and roll.
Just another morning
    in the field.
(Is the dirt where they want us?)

—Maribel Ledezma, April 1994

---

[1]thorns
[2]And there came the border patrol . . .
[3]Fellow Mexican

Fiesta in the Labor Camp

The sun sets at seven.
The music comes in with the moon.
It fills the campo.[4]
Los chicos van por el parque,[5]
    cruising, checkando las girls.
Se oyen las novelas[6] in the houses—
    María Mercedes, Corazón Salvaje,[7] Crystal—
I heard them all.
Los hombres[8] gather by a compadres[9] truck—
It broke down en el fil,[10]
Juntos la componen—
Para eso son los compadres.[11]
Las mujeres hablan[12] at the clothesline.
Tendiendo la clothes del trabajo.
    "Oyó usted de la señora de 12-A" pregunta una.
    "No, que pasó?" contesta mamá.[13]
And the young girls play at their ankles,
    making meals on plastic plates
    from weenies and grapes—
    before the boycott of '88—

---

[4]camp

[5]The boys go through the park

[6]You can hear the soap operas

[7]Wild Heart

[8]The men

[9]friend's

[10]in the field

[11]Together they fix it—
That's what friends are for.

[12]The women talk

[13]Hanging out the work clothes.
"Did you hear about the woman of 12-A?" one of them asks.
"No, what happened?" answers mama.

I learned early to be una esposa buena.[14]
Y las muchachas se pintan.[15]
They go out to the parque
Where the boys have parked.
Oyen Los Bukis, y a veces
  Los Invasores.
Allí se juntan y hablan
de sus días en el fil.[16]

La fiesta en el campo se
acaba a las ten.[17]
At ten, you go inside.
Porque tomorrow—"a jalarle . . .
Tenemos que comer."
Pero a las siete again
Fiesta en el campo.[18]

—Maribel Ledezma

---

[14]A good wife

[15]And the girls put on makeup.

[16]They listen to the Bookies, and at times
The Invaders.
There they get together and talk
about their days in the field.

[17]The celebration in the camp is over at ten.

[18]Because tomorrow—"you give it all you've got . . .
We have to eat.
But at 7:00 again
Celebration in the labor camp.

Corazón

We do not have much—
    My parents say—
But we have corazón[19]
And we have each other.

You see, Hijita,[20] we came here with nothing.
Not a penny to our names.
Between your Father and I,
We created the "poverty line."
And even still, we had each other.

I know that it is hard
For you and your brothers and sisters.
You do not wear the clothes,
You do not own the homes,
Never had the Cabbage Patch dolls,
The He-Man's, the hot rods.
But you are still ours
And we have each other.

You see, God made a people,
In the south,
With tough skin
And soft hearts
    To give each other.

We have tried, Hijita,
To give you all.
We may not have much
But we have each other.

—Maribel Ledezma
April 1994

---

[19]heart
[20]My little daughter

Part II
Federal and State Programs

Chapter 6

Mexico's Role in U.S. Education: a Well-Kept Secret

Robert Miller
East Side Union High School District
San Jose, California

Even as the debate on the North American Free Trade Agreement continues, Mexico and the United States have reached a number of agreements designed to improve the literacy and the schooling of Mexican immigrants in the United States. Mr. Miller provides the details.

The North American Free Trade Agreement has sparked a national political discussion. Politicians, special interest groups, labor unions, and think tanks on both sides of the U.S./Mexican border have publicly debated and are still debating the merits of this agreement. Even as the debate continues, Mexico and the United States have reached a number of agreements concerning education. These agreements are designed to improve the literacy and the schooling of Mexican immigrants in the United States, and they involve national, state, and local governments and even private agencies.

On the U.S. side of the border, agreements have been made with individual school districts, Mexican American organizations, programs for migrant education, state departments of education, universities, and the U.S. Department of Education. At the outset the agreements usually involve relatively small numbers of individuals, so they do not receive widespread media attention, even in national publications dedicated to education. However, when we examine these programs together, we see that the Mexican government has a substantial presence in educational programs in many parts of the United States.

Since there is no office or clearinghouse that lists all the Mexican programs in the United States, the first step in creating awareness of these programs is simply to describe the ones currently in operation. A word of caution is in order, however. The range of programs offered by the Mexican government is continuing to expand, so this report is not exhaustive in its coverage. I will focus here on educational agreements and programs between Mexico and the United States at the national, state, and local levels that have been in existence since at least 1993. In addition, I will discuss agreements with private agencies.

National Projects

The educational agreements between Mexico and the United States came about as a result of a long and complicated process. The Echeverría Administration in Mexico (1970-76) made attempts to meet with Mexican American leaders to strengthen ties with Mexico, but differences among the organizations in the United States prevented any institutional relationship from developing. President José López Portillo (1976-82) did meet with Mexican American organizations, and this meeting started the work in the United States (Riding, 1989).[1]

Things got off to a slow start. In 1980, the Association of Mexican American Educators held a conference in Mexico City. The plan was for Mexican teachers to share their experiences with teachers from the United States. The few Mexican teachers who attended the conference, however, were outnumbered by officials from the Ministry of Education.

---

[1]In the past, Mexico has been reluctant to share information about its education system. In June 1978, after the Mexican Ministry of Education failed to respond to my written requests for permission to conduct a study of the teaching of reading and writing in Mexican public schools, I went in person to request permission. I received assurances that the ministry staff would help me with the study, which was to begin at the start of the new school year in September. I also toured the textbook commission facility. When I returned in September, officials from the Consejo Técnico de la Educación (Technical Advisement on Education Office) interrogated me about the purpose of my study. For three days, I answered questions. At the end of October, I received permission to do the study. Official orders came, and I presented information about my study at each school. Officials were still reluctant to share "official" information.

But soon, the process began to gather momentum. Under the leadership of Graciela Orozco and, later, of Roberto López, both of whom worked for the Ministry of Education, the number of programs with the United States increased. Mexican teachers went to Los Angeles and Louisiana, training programs were held for bilingual teachers from the Los Angeles area, bilingual programs in San Jose (California) used Mexican textbooks, and Mexican officials became visiting scholars in the United States. The Office of International Relations in the Ministry of Education was in charge of these programs (Miller, 1991).

Program for Mexican Communities Abroad. In February 1990, Mexican President Carlos Salinas created the Program for Mexican Communities Abroad. The program promotes and runs joint projects linking U.S. communities of Mexican origin to Mexico. Mexican consulates throughout the United States administer the program and are establishing nonprofit Mexican cultural institutes. At this writing, such institutes exist in 13 U.S. cities. The objectives of these programs are to promote business, tourism, culture, exhibits and artistic events, academic exchanges, scholarships, training for bilingual teachers, adult education programs, migrant education, medical insurance for Mexican workers in the United States, sports, and housing.

Each month, the list of projects related to education grows. Currently, the program supplies Mexican textbooks for use in preschools and elementary schools. In addition, literacy and adult education materials are being sent to U.S. cities and states, including Dallas and Brownsville, Texas; Chicago; Philadelphia; the state of Michigan; and Fresno, San Francisco, Sacramento, and Los Angeles, California. In Madera County, California, textbooks in Mixtec are helping Mixtec farmworkers to become literate (Orozco, 1992). In 1990, the Mexican Ministry of Education sent 26 Mexican teachers to work for two years in bilingual programs in Chicago. As of September 1993, 21 teachers were still there, and there are plans to increase this number (Education Section, 1993a).

Mexican educators were also present at the annual conferences of the National Association for Bilingual Education. At the 1991 conference, Mexican educators spoke on theories of bilingual education, and at the 1992 conference, they spoke on a new program of modernization and on aspects of teaching Spanish (Education Section, 1991). The same themes were repeated at the conferences of the California Association for Bilingual Education. During the 1993 conference 40 specialists from 25 Mexican educational institutions organized displays and presented workshops on education in Mexico. Mexican educators also participated in the 1992 and 1993 conferences held by the Texas Association for Bilingual Education (Education Section, 1992; 1993b).

The Program for Mexican Communities Abroad has developed a catalog containing descriptions of courses in 11 Mexican universities in Baja California, Guadalajara, Guanajuato, Morelos, Puebla, Querétaro, Sinaloa, and Mexico City. In addition, a program sponsored by the Ministry of Education is listed. In these programs, U.S. bilingual teachers can learn about the Mexican methodology for teaching subjects at the primary level (see "Contact Information" at the end of this chapter to write for catalog).

The Mexican foreign service, La Secretaría de Relaciones Exteriores, is the umbrella organization that coordinates the services of the various Mexican programs in the United States. However, the programs have no central organization in the United States, and the lack of such organization leads to some duplication of effort. Indeed, most people are not aware of the many activities in which the Mexican education establishment is involved in the United States.

Memorandum of Understanding. On August 17, 1990, U.S. Secretary of Education Lauro Cavazos and Mexican Secretary of Public Education Manuel Bartlett-Díaz signed a "Memorandum of Understanding," establishing closer U.S.-Mexican ties on education issues and programs. The agreement was to remain in effect until the end of 1991, with an automatic provision for successive two-year extensions.

The original agreement included a stipulation for holding a border conference in October 1991 to discuss the teaching of English in Mexico and of Spanish in the United States, as well as teacher exchanges, migrant education, educational administration, educational research and innovation, and the improvement of intercultural understanding. The conference was held, and it focused on technological education, teacher education, and professional development in the field of education. More than 500 people attended, with each border state sending a delegation.

The activities set in motion by an annex to the agreement for 1992-93 included: (1) exchanges of professors and researchers, (2) an examination of ways to decrease dropout rates, (3) open education programs for Mexicans living in the United States, (4) summer courses in Mexico, (5) help for migrant students, (6) joint efforts in environmental education, (7) linking U.S. and Mexican universities, (8) improving technical education in both countries, and (9) sending Mexican teachers to study in U.S. educational institutions (U.S. Department of Education, 1991).

On June 21, 1993, the Mexican and U.S. secretaries of education met again and signed another annex to the agreement. In October 1993 they met once more, though progress on a national level was limited because 1994 was the final year of the Mexican president's term, and he could not run for office again. Moreover, there had been a major change in leadership at the Ministry of Education.

U.S.-Mexico Commission for Educational and Cultural Exchange. Before 1990, Fulbright grants were administered by a foreign service officer at the U.S. Embassy in Mexico City. But no formal mechanism existed for supporting and expanding educational and cultural exchanges between Mexico and the United States, though the United States had such agreements with 40 other nations.

In November 1990, Presidents Bush and Salinas signed an agreement to create the U.S.-Mexico Commission for Educational and Cultural Exchange. The entire Fulbright budget devoted to Mexico—a total of just $2 million—became the first year's budget for the new organization. Mexico agreed to contribute $1 million as well. A 10-member board of directors was named jointly by the Mexican foreign secretary and the U.S. ambassador; six of the 10 came from the private sector. Carlos Ornelas became the first executive director of the commission.

More than 150 grants were awarded during the first year of the new agreement. In addition to the Fulbright funds, the commission has received pledges that total $1 million from the Rockefeller Foundation, the Mexican National Council for Culture and the Arts, and the Bancomer Cultural Foundation for nonacademic cultural exchanges in such diverse fields as dance, translation, and library management. Research proposals in cultural scholarship will be funded, as will support for conferences on a broad array of cultural themes. Currently, there is a Fulbright exchange program for secondary and community college teachers. Under this program a U.S. educator works in Mexico for 6 weeks, and a Mexican teacher comes to the United States for 6 weeks. A proposal to expand this program to a full semester is now under consideration at this writing.

State and District Projects

According to the Mexican foreign service, 40 percent of Mexicans living in the United States reside in California. This situation, coupled with the fact that Los Angeles is the second-largest Spanish-speaking city in the world, provides the rationale for the involvement of the state of California and a number of its school districts in projects with Mexico.

Binational Project. In 1982, the Binational Project between Michoacán and California began. The project simplifies the movement of Mexican migrants from the Mexican state of Michoacán to California. At the start of this project, many discussions seemed to be taking place in a vacuum, because research on the educational and social plight of international migrant children was scarce. In 1984, Deborah Mounts of the California State Department of Education received funding for a project that tracked students who spent part of the year in French Camp, California, and the rest of the year in Villa Mendoza and Acuitzeramo, Michaocán, Mexico. Her study was based on observations, teacher questionnaires, and family portraits. Mount's findings in terms of education were enlightening (Mounts, 1986). The migrants followed traditional patterns that did not change from year to year. They spent an equivalent number of days in each country (184 in Mexico and 181 in the United States), with an equivalent number of potential school days (142 days in the United States and 140 days in Mexico). The school days in the United States were divided between summer school (46 days) and regular school (96 days). Each time the students moved from Mexico to the United States or from the United States to Mexico, they had to take placement tests, integrate themselves into an ongoing program, become accustomed to new texts, and learn to function with new teachers and classmates. Students tended to be placed in classes and programs below their ability levels.

In 1986, the Binational Program introduced the "binational transfer document" to help correct this problem. Since then the project has expanded to include eight Mexican states and Arizona, California, Colorado, Michigan, New Mexico, Oregon, Pennsylvania, Texas, and Washington. To register at participating schools, a student must have a birth certificate and a transfer document validated with the binational seal. Students with proper documentation are accepted at any time of the year in the Mexican schools and are placed at the same grade level as in the U.S. school they last attended. No examinations are required. If a student does not have proper documentation, then an initial assessment is administered in local offices rather than at the state level. The transfer document also carries a student's grades.

Efforts in Los Angeles. On June 26, 1991, a binational conference on literacy and adult education was held in Los Angeles. The purpose of the conference was to help the Los Angeles Unified School District study the problems and educational needs of the students of Mexican origin that it serves. This conference focused on teaching skills, materials, evaluation, staff training, and the problems faced by literacy programs. A series of reports and several proposals for interinstitutional collaboration emerged from the discussions. Mexico sent representatives from the Regional Center of Adult Education and Literacy for Latin America (CREFAL), the National Institute for Adult Education (INEA), the Education Investigations Department of the Polytechnical Institute, the Northern Border College of Mexico, the Chihuahua Center for Education Studies, the Iberoamerican University (Mexico City), and the National Pedagogic University ("Conference on Literacy," 1991).

A group formed in 1992—consisting of representatives from the state departments of adult education in California, Texas, Arizona, Nevada, and New Mexico, plus representatives from the INEA—has also held meetings. The goal of the group, which calls itself Educación Sin Fronteras, is to look at Mexican concepts of education and to try to adapt these to the education of adults of Mexican origin living in the United States. Currently, the program is waiting to be funded.

In August of 1993, the Mexican secretary of education signed an agreement with the Los Angeles Unified School District to provide Mexican teachers the facility to work in bilingual classrooms in Los Angeles. The teachers will return to Mexico after working for 2 years in Los Angeles.

Private Agencies

One Stop Immigration. This is a community-based nonprofit organization that was formed in 1972. In 1975, One Stop Immigration was incorporated and began to work on legalization and immigration issues with major funding from the city of Los Angeles. In 1987, the group applied to the state department of education for permission to offer classes in history and in English as a second language (ESL) in order to prepare people for the federal amnesty program. However, the fact that many of the students were illiterate in Spanish meant that the educational program had to be expanded beyond its original scope.

During April 1990, the National Institute for Adult Education (INEA) provided training for staff members of One Stop Immigration. In August 1990, Mexico shipped seven trailer loads of INEA materials to Los Angeles (153,715 elementary and secondary books for use with adults). Teachers Martha Yolanda Ochoa, Miguel Angel Casao, Humberto Jiménez, and José Malagán came from Mexico to teach the staff members to use the materials. Since 1988, One Stop has served more than 87,000 people.

In August 1992, some 9,000 people attended One Stop schools in 21 service centers located throughout California. After completing the *primaria* or *secundaria* program, people can apply to take a test that will earn them a Mexican primary or secondary education certificate, which is sent from Mexico City. Currently, some 3,000 people are enrolled in the *primaria* program. And there are about 30 smaller agencies in the Los Angeles area that use the Mexican materials (Flores, 1992).

On July 21, 1992, I visited the One Stop Immigration Center in Oakland, California. The center teaches four levels of ESL, literacy in Spanish, and the *primaria* and *secundaria* curriculum. There are about 92 students in the program—five in the Spanish literacy program, 30 in the *primaria* and *secundaria* programs, and the rest in ESL classes. Classes for the *primaria* and the secundaria meet two nights a week for 3 hours each. One evening, the subjects are Spanish and math; the other, they are natural science and social science. Each evening, students finish one lesson in each of the two subjects. When they finish all the lessons in the books, they take tests provided by the Mexican Ministry of Education.

The teachers in the program are certified by the U.S. Immigration and Naturalization Service, but they do not have teaching credentials from the state of California. When I visited in the summer of 1992, the teachers were working without pay because of California's budget problems. They hoped to receive a paycheck on September 15—three months from the date of my visit.

PROFMEX. In 1981, nine U.S. universities in the Southwest (University of Texas, Austin; University of Texas, El Paso; University of New Mexico; New Mexico State University; University of Arizona; Arizona State University; San Diego State University; UCLA; and Stanford University) formed PROFMEX to find mechanisms to enhance communication and collaboration among researchers working on contemporary issues in U.S.-Mexican relations. PROFMEX was joined by ANUIES (Asociación Nacional de Universidades e Institutos de Educación Superior), and together the two organizations sponsor research, hold meetings, print a monograph series, print a newsletter, and offer advice on border issues. Since 1992 PROFMEX membership has included more than 70 institutions in the United States, Mexico, and Canada.

Recently, the Centre for International Studies, based at the University of Toronto, also joined PROFMEX. Though this organization focuses on a broad range of Mexican-U.S. topics, education is a major focus. In 1988, PROFMEX and ANUIES held a joint conference on education that focused on the content of Mexican textbooks. In November 1992, the seventh PROFMEX/ANUIES symposium was held in Cancún, Mexico. Education and Human Resources was one of the six panel topics.

In 1992, PROFMEXIS, a computer network, was established with the support of the Ford Foundation. PROFMEXIS gives network users customized E-mail communication, database access, and a file-transfer capability. The communications center in Mexico is the Centro de Tecnología e Información, with the database and communication facilities provided by the University of Mexico. The permanent home for the database in the United States will be at the Austin campus of the University of Texas. Through this system, scholars will have customized access to the holdings of major research libraries and to a variety of public databases in the social and natural sciences.

Perhaps the most important undertaking of PROFMEX has been the summary of research published in both languages. It is printed by the Center for U.S.-Mexican Studies at the University of California, San

Diego, and by el Colegio de la Frontera Norte, Tijuana, Baja California. The 1987 edition contained 1,231 research projects, of which 51 were in the field of education.

Implications

The border between the United States and Mexico is never wider than a river, and there are large Spanish-speaking communities on both sides of that river. Because of socioeconomic conditions, Mexicans in the United States, as a group, are not very prosperous. This has been recognized by the government and by private agencies. A truly international effort to improve the conditions of Mexicans living in the United States is now under way.

Pursuing family literacy has been shown to be an effective way of educating this group. The use of Mexican textbooks and the incentive of a Mexican diploma—coupled with mutual attempts to understand education in both countries—are paying off. As education becomes more important to the family, the economic level of the family will rise, and the younger children will stay in school longer. In addition, U.S. educators are learning from their Mexican counterparts how to handle the unique strengths of the Mexican students. The prospects are encouraging.

There is no question that the projects and programs listed above are important. However, they have developed in piecemeal fashion. The information I have presented here must be constantly updated and disseminated to the education community so that awareness of the role of Mexican educational materials and programs in the United States will expand.

Contact Information: Selected Programs

Binational Program

Collaboration and communication (including a Binational Transfer Document, teacher exchanges and shared materials, presentations, and Spanish language classes) between migrant education program administrators in the U.S. states of Arizona, California, Colorado, Michigan, New Mexico, Oregon, Pennsylvania, Texas, and Washington with administrators from the Mexican states of Baja California Norte, Chihuahua, Guanajuato, Jalisco, Mexico, Michoacán, Sonora, and Zacatecas, and others.

Contact: Gil Villaseñor, Coordinator, Binational Program,
Ventura County Superintendent of Schools Office,
5189 Verdugo Way, Camarilla, CA 93012; telephone 805/383-1924 or 800/451-9697; fax 805/383-6973.

Council for International Exchange of Scholars (CIES)

The U.S. Lecturer Program is for U.S. scholars to teach at universities in the American Republics. Grants are usually awarded for 3-9 months. Many include research as well as lecturing. Openings are announced annually by CIES.

The U.S. Regional Researcher Program provides 3-6 month grants for senior (post-doctoral) scholars to conduct research in any field in any American Republic.

The Scholar-in-Residence Program provides grants to scholars from the American Republics area to lecture at U.S. universities for one semester or one academic year.

3400 International Drive, N.W., Ste. M-500
Washington, DC 20008-3097; telephone 202/686-4000

Institute of International Education (IIE)

U.S. Student Program offers U.S. students the opportunity for up to one academic year of post-graduate study or research in the American Republics. Applicants must have an undergraduate or equivalent degree before the start of the grant, but cannot have a doctorate.

809 United Nations Plaza
New York, NY 10017; telephone 212/883-8200

Inter-Hemispheric Education Resource Center

Publisher of information about cross-border organizations in Mexico and the United States, including a directory, *Cross Border Links*, and a periodical, *Border Lines*.

P O Box 4506, Albuquerque, NM 87196;
WWW: http://lib.nmsu.edu/subject/bord/bordline
phone: 505/842-8288
E-mail: resourcectr@igc.apc.org

International Relations Department

Provides access to people in the government, letters of introduction, UNESCO library

Lic. Gustavo Ramirez
Dirección General de Relaciones Internacionales Educación Bilingue
Av. Presidente Masarik No. 526 1er Piso
Col. Polanco
Mexico, D.F. 11560 Mexico

Latin American Scholarship Program of American Universities (LASPAU)

Fulbright/LASPAU Faculty Development Program: Faculty development grants awarded to faculty members of participating American Republics universities for advanced study in the U.S. Grants provide English

language training as necessary and maintenance through completion of master's, Ph.D., or nondegree programs.
25 Mt. Auburn Street
Cambridge, MA 02138; telephone 617/495-5255

One Stop Immigration and Educational Center

Assistance in gaining legal status and citizenship, including literacy, ESL, and citizenship classes.
Contact: Martha Sanchez, 3600 Whittier Blvd.,
Los Angeles, CA 90023; telephone 213/268-8472

PROFMEX - The Consortium for Research on Mexico

Research, conferences, literature on Mexico computer data banks in United States and Mexico
WWW: http://profmexis.sar.net
Contact: Robert Gibson
phone: 310/206-8500 / 825-0870
fax: 310/825-8421 / 206-3555
E-mail: Gibson@others.sscnet.ucla.edu

Program for Mexican Communities Abroad

La Paloma newsletter, list of courses in Mexican Universities
Homero 213-13, Col. Chapultepec Morales
C.P. 11570 Mexico, D.F. Mexico
(To subscribe to *La Paloma*)
Apartado Postal 105-234 Polanco
CP 11581 Mexico, DF Mexico

Teachers in LA

Sr. Pescado was in charge of the consulate in L.A. He organized a program for teachers to work in L.A. My contact is his assistant.
Lic. Eloisa Valdez
SS de Servicos Educativos para el D.F.
Brazil 31 piso 1
Mexico, D.F. 06020 Mexico

University Affiliations and CAMPUS Programs

The Research Program for Foreign Scholars provides 3-6 month grants to scholars from the American Republics area to conduct research at a U.S. educational institution. Minimum master's degree required.

Caribbean and Central American Researcher Programs offer awards for scholars from the Caribbean and Central America to conduct research at U.S. educational institution for 3-6 months. Minimum master's degree required.

Fulbright/IIE Foreign Student Program provides grants to foreign students to earn master's or Ph.D. degrees at U.S. universities in selected fields. Full and partial grants are offered.

CAMPUS Program provides 29-month grants to Central American undergraduates for study at selected U.S. universities and colleges leading to a bachelor's degree in specified fields. Grants provide English language training as necessary.

United States Information Agency
Academic Exchanges Division
American Republics Branch
301 4th Street, S.W., Room 246
Washington, DC 20547; telephone 202/619-5365

U.S. Department of Education

(They signed an agreement with Mexico concerning education.)
Dr. Steward Tinsman
Director of International and Territorial Affairs
Room 3047
United States Department of Education
Washington, DC 20208-5570

U.S.-Mexico Educational Interchange Project

A series of invitational *Educational Leadership Seminars* has been developed to enable key leaders to meet periodically to address specific issues of relevance in North American education exchange. The seminars are designed to share information about the higher education systems in Mexico, the United States, and Canada; increase the mobility of students, professionals, and scholars interested in North American education exchange; and create a stronger sense of a North American identity as policymakers address issues affecting higher education in both countries.

Contact: Margo Schultz, Senior Project Assistance
Western Interstate Commission for Higher Education (WICHE)
P O Drawer P
Boulder, CO 80301-9752
phone: 303/541-0270 or 541-0220
fax: 303/541-0291
E-mail: margoschultz@wiche.edu
(Or)
Sylvia Ortega Salazar, President
Asociación Mexicana para la Educación Internacional (AMPEI)
Liverpool No. 65, Desp. 209
Colonia Juárez
Delegación Cuauhtémoc
México DF 06600 Mexico
phone: (52) 5-533-5570 ext. 150
fax: (52) 5-207-9637
E-mail: ortega@profmexis.sar.net

References

Conference on literacy and adult education. (1991, June/August). *La Paloma,* p. 4.

Diaz de Cossio, R. (1992). Mexico and the Mexican origin population in the United States. Mexico City: Secretaría de Relaciones Exteriores.

Education Section. (1991, January/February). *La Paloma*, p. 9.

Education Section. (1992, October/December). *La Paloma*, p. 7.

Education Section. (1993a, September/December). *La Paloma*, p. 8.

Education Section. (1993b, September/December). *La Paloma*, p. 10.

Flores, A. (1992, July 12). Telephone interview. Director of Scholastic Services, One Stop Immigration.

Mexico Policy News, PROFMEX, Institute for Regional Studies of the Californias, San Diego State University, Fall 1991.

Miller, R. (1991, November). Mexican immigrants can achieve in U.S. schools. *The CATESOL Journal, 4*(1), 91-95.

Mounts, D. (1986). *The binational migrant child. A research report.* Sacramento: California State Department of Education. (ERIC Document Reproduction Service No. ED 277 511)

Orozco, G. (June 16, 1992). Personal interview. Mexico City.

Riding, A. (1989). *Distant neighbors: A portrait of the Mexicans.* New York: Vintage Books.

U.S. Dept. Of Education. (1991, October). *Report on the Border Conference on Education.* Washington, DC: Author.

(This chapter is adapted from an article that originally appeared in *Phi Delta Kappan*, February 1995, pp. 470-474. Reprinted with permission.)

CHAPTER 7

Reauthorized Migrant Education Program: Old Themes and New

AL WRIGHT
LOUISIANA MIGRANT EDUCATION PROGRAM
LOUISIANA DEPARTMENT OF EDUCATION

The Migrant Education Program (MEP) secured a new 5-year lease on life when it was reauthorized in the Improving America's Schools Act (IASA) of 1994, signed into law by President Clinton in October 1994. The new authorization, which went into effect July 1, 1995, required changes in eligibility, priority for services, schoolwide projects, migrant student record transfer, the summer funding formula, and consortium incentives. This chapter describes the new requirements that, taken together, make this the most sweeping one-time change in programming for children of migratory farmworkers and fishermen since it was first enacted as a 1966 amendment to the Elementary and Secondary Education Act of 1965.

Overview

Changes in eligibility removed about 200,000 children from the Migrant Education Program (MEP) but added unknown numbers of older youth. Program priorities were redefined. Included were new requirements for joint planning with other federal and state programs, options for interstate consortia, and modifications in the summer funding formula. Comparable to other IASA programs, in the new authorization there was a call for migrant students to meet challenging academic standards.

Equally dramatic is what was missing from the new legislation: a set-aside for funding a national migrant student database. The Migrant Student Record Transfer System (MSRTS) was discontinued June 30, 1995, but the new legislation nevertheless required Migrant Education grantees to exchange student records.

For all that, however, the MEP retained its essential character and purpose: it remains a state grant program, i.e., state educational agencies will receive and administer the grants; and the stated purpose of the program continues to be "to address the special educational needs of migratory children." The authorizing language carries no mandate to make major modifications in program models and delivery systems previously used to serve migrant children.

But services to migrant children have been affected, to a degree impossible to estimate this early in the process, by changes in the MEP's parent program, the Title I Part A "basic" program. Redefined as a program to help disadvantaged students meet high standards, Title I authorizes the use of funds from a number of sources, including Migrant Education, to serve children in schoolwide projects. The new MEP carries a "special rule" concerning migrant children in such projects.

The MEP is Part C of the new Title I, a designation comparable to that of the basic program, Part A. While Part C is relatively concise compared to Part A, the new MEP authorization is about twice as long as the version that was in effect through June 30, 1995. Additional text includes, for the first time, a statement of purpose specifically addressing the migrant program; program requirements relating the MEP to the Goals 2000 program; definitions formerly carried only in regulations; and mechanisms for coping with the absence of MSRTS, which was used not only to exchange information between schools and MEP sites, but also as the basis for enumerating migrant children and allocating program funds among the states.

Eligibility

About a third of the children previously eligible for the Migrant Education Program (MEP) no longer qualify, owing to the reduction in the eligibility period for children who cease to migrate. The core criteria for initial eligibility were unchanged in the new legislation, i.e., a child (ages 3-21, inclusive) is defined as migratory when he or she moves from one school district to another in order for one or more family members to seek temporary or seasonal work in agriculture or fishing. For the past two decades, eligibility could continue for 6 years after the qualifying move if parents approved their child's designation as formerly migratory after the first year. Beginning July 1, 1995, the eligibility based on a single move was changed to extend for only 3 years.

Children who move more frequently establish a new eligibility each time they make a "qualifying" move. For example, if a family home-based in Texas migrates each year to Ohio and then to Michigan to pick cucumbers, cherries, and apples, the children become eligible on the move to Ohio and then start a new 36-month cycle of eligibility when they relocate to Michigan. But the return to Texas is ordinarily not a qualifying move, because the family is returning home—though for many it is a home they know for only 6 or 7 months a year.

By reducing the term of eligibility, Congress intended to focus more funds on the children who move most frequently. This was consistent with recommendations from many quarters, including the National Commission on Migrant Education and the National Association of Migrant Educators.

The old legislation required that priority in the consideration of services be given to "currently migratory" children, those who have moved within the past 12 months. A steady increase in the number and percentages of children classified as "formerly migratory"—to the point where formerlies outnumbered currentlies about 2:1—led to concern that services for the priority group of children may suffer from the competing demands of the larger group of "settled-out" migrant children.

The new law provides three exceptions for continuing services beyond the 3-year mark: any child whose eligibility expires during a school term may be served until the end of the term; a child whose eligibility ends prior to the start of a term may be served for another year "if comparable services are not available through other programs," and secondary students can continue to be served "through credit accrual programs" until graduation. Because children served under the continuation provisions are not weighted in the funding allocations, services to such children may be limited. However, continuing concern about the still high drop-out rate among migrant students (about 50 percent) may result in use of the continuation option for many secondary students.

The initial effect of the 3-year eligibility period was to produce a redistribution among the states of the MEP appropriation (approximately $305 million for the 1995-96 program year). States previously enrolling larger numbers of migrant children in the 4th, 5th, and 6th years of eligibility lost funds, while states enrolling more children in the first 3 years of eligibility gained.

Another revision in the eligibility definition makes eligible a category of older youth who previously did not qualify. Migrant *workers* and their *spouses* through the age of 21 now qualify. Previously, a worker qualified for the program only if he or she had earlier migrated with a parent or guardian, and spouses did not qualify. It is difficult to estimate the number of migrants in the 16-21 age range who qualify under this provision, but the number could be significant. These are often the prime earning years for farmworkers, who are typically paid by the amount of work performed. The impact on the MEP is uncertain. In some cases, parents and children both may be eligible. Major program adjustments will be necessary if educational and support services are to be provided to a population that is not likely to be enrolled in school.

Priority for Services

There is a major change in the legislative priority for MEP services. In using MEP funds, grantees and subgrantees "shall give priority to migratory children who are failing, or most at risk of failing, to meet the State's challenging . . . standards, and whose education has been interrupted during the regular school year."

Migrant educators generally believe that virtually all migrant children are at risk in relation to challenging performance standards. Even outstanding students are in jeopardy because of state-to-state differences in curriculum and testing requirements. There is greater concern about implications and possible interpretations of the educational interruption priority. This criterion is viewed as a potential disincentive for migrant families to delay departures from their home bases until the end of the school year—a practice that the MEP has promoted for decades with considerable effect. If migrant families believe that allowing their children to complete the school year will result in loss of access to summer programs in receiving states, they may simply withdraw them and migrate earlier.

There is also uncertainty about whether a migrant child's late return to his or her home-base school constitutes an interruption. Many migrant students do not return until October or November each year, and many, especially the older youths who help their parents in the field, have not attended school before their return. Technically, their school year has not been interrupted, because it has not yet begun. Yet, their need to make up class work and catch up with their peers is one of the most critical areas of emphasis in MEP programs in home-base states such as Texas and Florida.

Schoolwide Projects

Title I Part A authorizes the use of Part A funds, "in combination with other Federal, State and local funds," for schoolwide programs. This is generally interpreted as authorizing the commingling of MEP funds with other funds in schoolwide projects that serve migrant children. The provision, however, does not supersede the MEP program requirements for states to assess needs of migrant children and plan appropriate services. In other words, MEP funds can be placed in schoolwide projects if state administrators decide that such projects would meet the needs of migrant children, but there is no mandate to use schoolwide projects as a primary means of meeting their needs.

Additionally, the special rule carried in the MEP authorization requires that any schoolwide projects receiving MEP funds must use those funds to meet needs that result from the migratory lifestyle of migrant children or are not addressed by other programs, or to provide services needed to permit migrant children to participate effectively in school.

Life After MSRTS

The new MEP statute contained an implicit mandate to replace MSRTS by directing the Secretary to seek recommendations on new means of counting migrant children and transferring records, the twin functions of the system defined in the old law. Allocation of funds for the 1995-96 program year was to be based for the last time on data provided by the MSRTS, which was scheduled to begin phasedown of operations after compiling full-time equivalent counts of migrant children in each state in 1994.

The new authorization, like the old, requires state grantees to foster interstate coordination of services, including "the timely transfer of pertinent school records." In the absence of MSRTS, the law called for the Secretary to solicit information and recommendations on the transfer of student records and possible technologies that could be employed, and to make a report to Congress by April 30, 1995. The report included, among other things, information about efforts begun at the state level. Since that time the National Center for Education Statistics has begun work on an electronic records transfer system; two commercial vendors and the Texas Department of Education have also begun multistate systems. Many observers expect that these separate systems will be networked eventually, perhaps via the Internet.

Begun in the early 1970s and originally a showpiece of educational technology at work, MSRTS, a national information system anchored in Little Rock, Arkansas, had come under criticism for its costs—an estimated $25 million at federal, state and local levels—and alleged ineffectiveness. The National Commission on Migrant Education (1991) produced a set of recommendations for improving the system. Before the recommendations could be carried out, however, Congress enacted P.L. 103-59 in 1993, providing for extension of the system only until June 30, 1995. Continuation beyond that point would be at the discretion of the Secretary of Education. When the chairman and ranking minority member of the House Education and Labor Committee subsequently filed a Migrant Education reauthorization bill (HR2679) that specified the discontinuation of MSRTS, the Department of Education took it as its cue to omit MSRTS from its reauthorization package.

Ironically, the new legislation devotes more attention to records transfer than did the previous statutes. Many observers expect the alternate systems for the transfer of records to add substantially to costs. At the time this is being written, the picture remains unclear.

Summer Funding Formula

Summer programs were originally conceived as "safe havens" for migrant children, who might otherwise be with their parents harvesting crops in the field, as well as places for providing a wide range of educational opportunities. Summer schools were inherently more costly than regular-term supplemental programs because they could not piggyback on the existing infrastructure (buildings, maintenance, food service, transportation, etc.). The MEP law was amended to provide an upward adjustment to the allocation to states providing the summer program, producing a formula under which a migrant child generated about four times as much for each day enrolled in summer school as for a day in regular term.

While the adjustment initially achieved its purpose, it became problematic when some MEP grantees began to offer nontraditional, nonschool-based summer programs in which migrant children could be enrolled and served at lower cost. The Department of Education ruled that each state had the right to define an educational program for migrant children according to its own principles and standards. The number of migrant children, especially formerly migrant children, enrolled in low-cost programs dramatically increased because it was possible to generate more funds in supplemental funding than the programs cost to operate. Such programs drew criticism from those who felt the low-cost programs, if conducted primarily to generate additional funds, were contrary to the essential purpose of the programs.

The new law addresses the criticism by directing the Secretary to develop a procedure that more accurately reflects cost factors for the different types of summer programs. The summer provision also introduces the concept of "intersession" programs as equivalent to summer programs. Although not specified in the statute, the intersession provision is intended to apply to the breaks in year-round school schedules.

Consortium Incentives

Although the MEP statute had historically permitted states to join together in applying for their basic grants, no states ever exercised the option. The new law, in an effort to make programs more effective in states receiving smaller grants, provides monetary incentives for doing so. States that join in consortia are eligible to receive additional grants of up to $250,000 from a $1.5 million set-aside. Besides the financial incentive, the statute provides that the Secretary "shall consult" with states receiving MEP grants of under $1 million "to determine whether consortium arrangements with another State or other appropriate entity would result in delivery of services in a more effective and efficient manner."

The consortium provision was enacted in the expectation of reducing administrative costs and making more funds available for direct services. Migrant Education representatives from many of the smaller states had previously told the Office of Migrant Education that actual cost savings were unlikely. Administrative costs are very low in most such states and typically are borne by non-MEP funds.

References

Congress of the United States, House Committee on Education and Labor. (1994). *Improving America's Schools Act of 1994. Report on H.R. 6 together with minority, supplemental, and additional views, Committee on Education and Labor, House of Representatives, 103rd Congress, 2nd session.* Washington, DC: U.S. Government Printing Office. (ERIC Document Reproduction Service No. ED 369 147)

Cox, J. L., Burkheimer, G., Curtin, T. R., Rudes, B., Iachan, R., Strang, W., Carlson, E., Zarkin, G., & Dean, N. (1992). *Descriptive study of the Chapter 1 migrant education program. Final report (Vols. 1-3).* Research Triangle Park, NC: Research Triangle Institute. (ERIC Document Reproduction Service No. ED 355 085)

National Commission on Migrant Education. (1992). *Invisible children: A portrait of migrant education in the United States. Final report.* Washington, DC: Author. (ERIC Document Reproduction Service No. ED 348 206)

National Commission on Migrant Education. (1991). *Keeping up with our nation's migrant students: A report on the migrant student record transfer system (MSRTS).* Bethesda, MD: Author. (ERIC Document Reproduction Service No. ED 350 117)

Pringle, B. A., & Rosenthal, E. D. (1993). *An analysis of the costs of Chapter 1 migrant education program summer services.* Washington, DC: Department of Education (Contract LC 89089001).

Resendez, I., Miller, W., Reyna, T., Rivera, V. A., & Wright, A. (1992). *A comprehensive plan for the education of America's migrant children through elementary and secondary education programs scheduled for reauthorization in 1993.* Sunnyside, WA: National Association of Migrant Educators. (ERIC Clearinghouse Accession Number RC 019972)

This chapter is adapted from an ERIC Digest by the same name, published in March 1995 (EDO-RC-95-1).

CHAPTER 8

Migrant Education Binational Program

DAVID P. DOLSON AND GILDARDO VILLASEÑOR
CALIFORNIA DEPARTMENT OF EDUCATION

In the United States, the Binational Program operates as part of the U.S. Department of Education's Migrant Education Program. It grew from the efforts of a California teacher, who decided to make contact in 1976 with educators in the Michoacán (Mexico) village that was home base for many of her students (see chapter 9 for the full story). Twenty years later, the Binational Program affords 45,000 migrant students the opportunity to continue their education regardless of the country in which they are residing by advocating for appropriate grade-age placement, transference of course credits, school enrollment opportunities, and outreach to increase parents' understanding of the need to enroll students in both countries. This chapter describes the Binational Program from the perspective of the California Migrant Education Program and includes a chronology of its development.

The Binational Program was established by the Migrant Education Program of the California Department of Education (CDE) to coordinate specialized educational projects between the United States and Mexico. The Binational Program focuses generally on migrant students but most specifically on the significant number of binational students, who, as an annual pattern connected to their parents' agricultural labor demands, spend part of the school year in one country and part in the other. Based on information gathered through the Migrant Student Record Transfer System (MSRTS), an average of 45,000 pupils and their families migrate between Mexico and the United States in any given school year. The Binational Program is located in the offices of the Ventura County Superintendent of Schools in Camarillo and consists of a director (Gildardo Villaseñor) and clerical support.

Currently, the Binational Program is involved in the areas of (1) transfer of scholastic records and policy considerations, (2) professional development, (3) teacher exchange, and (4) information and materials clearinghouse. Each of these components is described in this report.

Transfer Document and Policy Consideration

The Binational Commission includes representatives from the state educational agencies (SEAs) of approximately 10 U.S., more than 32 Mexican states (including the *Distrito Federal de México),* and the *Secretaría de Educación Pública.* One of the primary purposes of the commission has been to develop, revise, and promote the use of the Transfer Document for Binational Migrant Students (see sample copy at the end of this chapter). This document contains demographic and educational information on binational pupils that is intended to support continuity of schooling experiences as students migrate between U.S. and Mexican schools on an annual basis. Representatives of the Commission have agreed to use the document within their jurisdictions. The Binational Commission meets twice yearly, once in Mexico and once in the United States, to monitor and evaluate the use of the transfer document. The U.S. subcommittee of the Binational Commission also has two independent meetings annually.

More recently, the Secretaría de Relaciones Exteriores (Dirección General del Programa Para Las Communidades Mexicanas en el Extranjero) has lent its support to the commission. Orientation is provided to Mexican consular officers in the United States, enabling them to advise binational migrant families of the need to obtain a copy of the transfer document for each of their children.

The Binational Program in California plays an important role in assisting schools in both countries to obtain, fill out, process, and transmit the transfer document for individual pupils.

Finally, from time to time, the Binational Commission has served as a forum for discussing important policy issues regarding the education of binational students. For example, based on the recommendations of the commission, the Secretaría de Educación Pública issued an advisory directing school districts in Mexico to normalize enrollment until the beginning of the next school term or even until the next school year.

Professional Development

The Binational Program has been instrumental in arranging summer in-service programs for U.S. teachers serving significant populations of migrant students. With the assistance of the Secretaría de Educación Pública, SEAs from states such as Michoacán and several Migrant Education Service regions have worked together to develop and implement intensive summer in-service programs of several weeks' duration. These sessions have been conducted for the last several years and are now implemented in more than five Migrant Education regions.

These in-service programs provide a setting where Mexican specialist teachers can share information with U.S. teachers regarding (1) bicultural approaches, (2) native language development, (3) special needs students, and (4) the Mexican school system. In many cases, the in-service sessions are coordinated with Migrant Summer School programs so that the Mexican educational specialists can work directly with migrant students and, at the same time, conduct demonstration classes for their U.S. teacher counterparts.

The Binational Program has collaborated with the *Secretaría de Relaciones Exteriores* in conducting short-term in-service programs for individual school districts and Migrant Education Service regions during the regular school year. These sessions are usually coordinated with local Institutions of Higher Education (IHEs). In this way, the Mexican specialists, often renowned educators, are able to make staff development presentations to groups of teachers, university student teachers, Mini-Corps tutors, and college and school district teacher trainers.

The *Secretaría de Relaciones Exteriores*, through four *Centros Culturales* in California, also works with the Binational Program to provide ongoing teacher training courses that address such issues as Spanish language acquisition, bicultural studies, and C-BEST preparation. The purpose of the staff development sessions is to support classroom teachers in obtaining their B/CLAD (Bilingual/Cross Cultural Language and Academic Development) credential from the Commission for Teacher Credentialing.

Teacher Exchange Project

The Binational Program, in cooperation with the SEA in Michoacán, is involved in a pilot teacher exchange program in the Lynwood School District in Los Angeles County and the Salinas Unified School district. At this time, approximately 15 Mexican teachers are assigned in team teaching situations as a way to address the bilingual and bicultural instructional needs of migrant and other pupils. Based on the results of the pilot project, which will be reported in an evaluation study, both the value and nature of the project will be reviewed by the California Department of Education (CDE), the Binational Program, and other migrant education agencies.

Chronology of Binational Program Developments

In the mid-1970s, educators in Pajaro Valley Unified School District (Santa Cruz, California) became aware that a large number of children in their schools all came from Gómez Farías in Michoacán, Mexico. These students spent from 1 to 6 months in Gómez Farías (usually from November through April) but were denied access to the schools because they were in California with their parents who were employed in agriculture when the school year began in September each year.

1976 A Pajaro Valley (CA) district administrator asked teacher Arlene Dorn to find out about the schools in Gómez Farías. Dorn takes up the challenge while in Mexico to study, and begins making contacts. Dorn meets Profesora Irene de la Llata de Anzaldúa, a principal in the American School in Mexico City, who becomes her collaborator. After meeting with a national administrator of elementary education, a regional order is issued to allow migrant children to attend school while in Michoacán.
They travel to Gómez Farías in Michoacán and establish ties with teachers and administrators there and with regional administrators.

1977 Dorn returns to Pajaro Valley school district and begins the Gómez Farías-Pajaro Valley Project, supported by the California Migrant Education Program and her district superintendent. Purposes of project were to begin a collaboration for planning and information exchange collaboration between the two school systems, and thereby develop a model that could be replicated in other California communities.
The first student academic information transfer document is developed and put into use in both communities.

1979 The project loses local district financial support; Dorn seeks private support and secures funding from the David and Lucile Packard Foundation. The fiscal agent became the superintendent of Butte County (CA) Schools, under the auspices of Mini-Corps, a migrant-related program.
The effort is renamed Project MEDIR (Migrant Education Data International Record), and Dorn begins publicizing the needs of binational migrant students and promoting collaboration and use of the transfer document at meetings across California and through federal migrant education meetings.

1980 Dorn conducts a survey of school districts in California and based on the results provides the first research-based estimate of the number of binational migrant children in California: 20,000. Participation in Project MEDIR spreads to other California districts and even more extensively in Mexico.

1984 Project MEDIR again loses its fiscal home and is adopted by La Cooperativa Campesina, a statewide farmworker organization located in Sacramento (CA), with funding from the David and Lucile Packard Foundation. Adriana Salinas Simmons takes over as director.

1986 In January, the first Binational Conference is held in San Diego, California. Eighty-nine educators from Mexico and California attend to promote understanding of the two educational systems, jointly identify solutions to needs of migrant children, and further the development of the Binational Transfer Document.

In July, the second Binational Conference is held in Morelia, Michoacán, and is attended by California and Mexican educators. This meeting results in the further development and use of the new Binational Transfer Document, and the Mexican government issues an official order to enable migrant children to enter Mexican schools regardless of their time of arrival anywhere in Mexico.

Semiannual meetings in Mexico and the United States continue to take place from this time to the present.

1987 The Binational Program was officially moved into the auspices of the California Migrant Education Program through the San Diego (Region 9) County Office of Education. Efforts to expand involvement in the program continue.

1991 By this date, Colorado and Arizona have become collaborating states in the United States, along with the states of Guanajuato, Michoacán, and Baja California in Mexico. Under the directorship of Sheli Cunningham, an informational video is produced in both English and Spanish.

1992 By this date, seven more states have joined the effort: Michigan and Oregon in the United States, and Sonora, Jalisco, Estado de Mexico, Chihuahua, and Zacatecas in Mexico.

1996 Today, 10 U.S. states, all 31 Mexican states, and the federal district of Mexico City have joined participation in the Binational Program. Official Transfer Documents for primary grades (1-6) and secondary grades (7-9) (see copy reproduced in this chapter) have been adopted and disseminated by the Mexican government through its consulates in cities throughout the United States.

An average of 45,000 binational students are expected to migrate between Mexico and the United States during the 1995-96 school year.

(This chronology was based on information provided by Arlene Dorn, Praxedes Martinez, Adriana Salinas Simmons, and Gildardo Villaseñor.)

—*Patricia Cahape Hammer*

Information and Materials Clearinghouse

Through the *Centros Culturales* and the 10 Mexican Consular offices located in California, the *Secretaría de Relaciones Exteriores* has worked with the Binational Program to facilitate the acquisition and use of Mexican educational materials at U.S. schools that enroll large numbers of binational students. For example, one project identifies local schools for receipt of a mini-bibliotecas (small libraries) of grade level-appropriate books in Spanish. Another project provides textbooks and other supplemental books to school libraries and classrooms. The *Centros Culturales* often sponsor cultural presentations (music, plays, puppetry, and films) of interest to schools. The Binational Program, through the various Migrant Education Regional offices, disseminates information regarding these events and other related opportunities. For more information, contact Gildardo Villaseñor, 5189 Verdugo Way, Camarillo, CA 93012: phone (805) 383-1924, (800) 451-9697, FAX (805) 383-6973.

)OCUMENTO DE TRANSFERENCIA

DEL ESTUDIANTE MIGRANTE BINACIONAL

MÉXICO • EUA

PRIMARIA

1° a 6° GRADO

TRANSFER DOCUMENT

FOR BINATIONAL MIGRANT STUDENT

USA • MEXICO

ELEMENTARY

1-6

Sistema Educativo Nacional

Migrant Education

'MENTO DE TRANSFERENCIA ES VÁLIDO EN LOS ESTADOS UNIDOS MEXICANOS Y NO REQUIERE TRÁMITES
ES DE LEGALIZACIÓN
'FER DOCUMENT IS VALID, AND DOES NOT REQUIRE ANY ADDITIONAL LEGALIZATION

ASIGNATURAS COURSES	PROMEDIO DEL PERIODO QUE REPORTA GRADE POINT AVERAGE OR PARTIAL GRADE	OBSER OBSE
ESPAÑOL SPANISH		
INGLES ENGLISH		
MATEMÁTICAS MATHEMATICS		
HISTORIA HISTORY		
GEOGRAFÍA GEOGRAPHY		
EDUCACIÓN CÍVICA CIVICS		
CIENCIAS NATURALES NATURAL SCIENCES		
EDUCACIÓN FÍSICA PHYSICAL EDUCATION		
EDUCACIÓN ARTÍSTICA ARTISTIC EDUCATION		

**ESCALA DE CALIFICACIONES
GRADING SCALE**

NOTACION NOTATION	INTERPRETACION INTERPRETATION		
0-5.9	F	DID NOT PASS	NO PROMOVIDO
6	D	NOT SATISFACTORY	PROMOVIDO
7	C	AVERAGE	
8	B	GOOD	
9	A	VERY GOOD	
10	A+	EXCELLENT	

	SUGERENCIAS SUGGESTIONS

INFORMACIÓN SOBRE EL PROGRAMA BINACIONAL PARA ESTUDIANTES MIGRANTES
INFORMATION ABOUT THE BINATIONAL PROGRAM FOR MIGRANT STUDENT

EN LOS ESTADOS UNIDOS: EN LOS CONSULADOS MEXICANOS
EN EL PROGRAMA BINACIONAL TEL.: 1-800-451-9697

EN MÉXICO: EN EL ÁREA DE CONTROL ESCOLAR DE LA SECRETARÍA DE EDUCACIÓN U ORGANISMO PÚBLICO DESCENTRALIZADO UBICADA EN LA CAPITAL DE CADA ESTADO

EN EL DISTRITO FEDERAL, EN LA DIRECCIÓN GENERAL DE ACREDITACIÓN, INCORPORACIÓN Y REVALIDACIÓN, NETZAHUALCÓYOTL 127, 5º PISO, COL. CENTRO, C.P. 06080 TEL.: 709-96-84 FAX 709-99-57

) AM 27001

ENTO DE TRANSFERENCIA NO ES VÁLIDO SI PRESENTA BORRADURAS O ENMENDADURAS
ENT IS NOT VALID IF IT HAS BEEN ALTERED IN ANY WAY

INFORMACIÓN ACADÉMICA/ACADEMIC INFORMATION

GRADO
GRADE

PERIODO ESCOLAR
SCHOOL YEAR

PERIODO QUE REPORTA REPORTING PERIOD	DEL FROM	DIA DAY	MES MONTH	AÑO YEAR	AL TO	DIA DAY	MES MONTH	AÑO YEAR

NOMBRE DE LA ESCUELA
NAME OF SCHOOL

DOMICILIO
ADDRESS

CIUDAD
CITY

MUNICIPIO
COUNTY

ESTADO
STATE

ZONA ESCOLAR
DISTRICT

CODIGO POSTAL
ZIP CODE

INFORMACIÓN DEL ESTUDIANTE/STUDENT INFORMATION

NOMBRE COMPLETO DEL ESTUDIANTE COMO SE UTILIZA EN MEXICO
STUDENT'S NAME AS USED IN MEXICO

FECHA DE NACIMIENTO (DIA-MES-AÑO)
DATE OF BIRTH (DAY-MONTH-YEAR)

SEXO
SEX

NOMBRE DEL PADRE O TUTOR (APELLIDO-NOMBRE)
FATHER'S NAME / GUARDIAN (LAST-MIDDLE-FIRST)

NOMBRE DE LA MADRE O TUTORA (APELLIDO-NOMBRE)
MOTHER'S NAME / GUARDIAN (LAST-MIDDLE-FIRST)

LEGALIZACIÓN/LEGALIZATION

NOMBRE Y FIRMA DEL PROFESOR O DIRECTOR / TEACHER'S OR PRINCIPAL'S NAME AND SIGNATURE

SE SANCIONARA A QUIEN CON DOLO O FINES LUCRATIVOS REPRODUZCA TOTAL O PARCIALMENTE ESTE FORMAT
ANYONE WHO REPRODUCES PARTIALLY OR TOTALLY THIS DOCUMENT FOR ANY BUSINESS PURPOSE WILL BE PRO

CHAPTER 9

Genesis of the Migrant Binational Program

ARLENE R. DORN
RETIRED TEACHER AND FORMER COORDINATOR OF THE
GÓMEZ FARÍAS PAJARO VALLEY PILOT PROJECT
(NOW KNOWN AS THE BINATIONAL EDUCATION PROGRAM)

This chapter describes, through a personal narrative, the history of the Gómez Farías-Pajaro Valley Project (GFPVP), which was renamed "Project MEDIR" and is now known as the "Binational Program." The Binational Program is administered by the Migrant Education Programs in 10 U.S. states and all 31 Mexican states and the federal district of Mexico City.

This project did not follow the usual pattern of development. Its development was a very personal experience for Arlene Dorn, a classroom teacher from California, who acted as the catalyst. The description of its history and development is based on Dorn's chronological journals, and begins in Mexico in 1976.

The History of the Gómez Farías-Pajaro Valley Project

In 1976 I took a sabbatical leave from Pajaro Valley Unified School District (PVUSD), located in California, where I taught as an elementary teacher, to go to Mexico to study for a master's degree in education. Prior to leaving, an assistant superintendent asked me to find out where the town of Gómez Farías was because many of the Mexican children in the schools came from that village. It was thought that it would be helpful to know something about their education in Mexico.

These migrant children spent from 1 to 6 months (usually November to April) of each school year in Mexico. The majority of the time the children could not enroll in the Mexican schools. This was due to a policy in Mexico that if one did not enroll in September, the beginning of the school year, then one must wait until the following year to enter school. These children were never in Mexico at that time, because their parents were employed in agriculture in California through November. They were denied formal education during the mid-portion of the school year due to that policy in the Mexican public school system. At this time there were approximately 20,000 of these migrant children in California schools.[1] A number of other U.S. states also had a substantial number of migrant students, many in a similar predicament, in their schools. The problems these children faced in gaining their education was tremendous and unique.

First, in California, they were confronted with a foreign language that they had to learn in order to succeed in school. Although there was formalized bilingual education in PVUSD, it was not always available in all schools, and thus there was little language development in the primary language. As a result, many of these children lacked proficiency in both Spanish and English.

Second, school attendance was interrupted by the migratory patterns that their parents followed, so that continuity in the development of academic skills and study habits was never attained. The interruptions in school attendance and undeveloped academic skills caused lack of motivation, low self-esteem, and little appreciation of education by the children. Many dropped out of school at a very early age.

Third, discrimination in both Mexico and the United States followed these children. In the United States, their status was the lowest in society. In their Mexican village, due to comparative material wealth and travel experience to the United States, they held a position perceived to be higher than those who had remained at home. These circumstances brought about unacceptable behavioral responses from children in both societies.

While I was pursuing my studies at the University of the Americas in Mexico City, I went to visit The American School (a school operated by the American School Foundation in Mexico City). One of the principals greeted me and asked me about my interest. I told him about the children from Gómez Farías. He said I must talk to Profesora Irene de la Llata de Anzaldúa. Meeting Profesora Anzaldúa was one of the most significant

[1] A count of these children was not known at this time, 1976. It became known several years later through a count I made, to be explained later in this story.

events in the development of this project. Profesora Anzaldúa was a principal for the elementary grades and liaison to the Mexican Ministry of Education for The American School in Mexico City. She had been educated in both Mexico and the United States. This gave her a unique preparation for involvement in the project.

I explained the circumstances of the international migrants to Profesora Anzaldúa and my idea to locate the village of Gómez Farías. Irene, as she now insisted that I call her, said that we should go to the Secretaría de Educación Pública (SEP) before going to Gómez Farías. Irene told me to write a short description of the problems surrounding the international migrant children and give it to her. Irene said she would translate it into Spanish and then she and I would go to the director of primary education for seven states. His office was in Mexico City. I hurried back to my apartment, wrote the description she had requested, then dashed back to give Irene the letter before school was let out. The following day we went to speak to Professor Juan de Dios Rodriguez Heredia, Director of Primary Education, Secretaría de Educación Pública (SEP), who was in charge of primary education for seven states, among which was Michoacán, where Gómez Farías was located.

Professor Rodriguez was most interested to learn about the international migrant children from his native state. He knew that there were Mexican immigrant students, but he was totally surprised to learn that there were students who migrated *annually* between Mexico and the United States. He was not aware that these children were not admitted to school upon their return to their village. Immediately, he said he would write an order that would allow the children admission to school. Also, he gave me a letter addressed to school authorities in California stating his intentions to permit the children to enter school upon their return to Mexico and his willingness to work cooperatively with California school authorities. He also suggested that Irene and I go to Gómez Farías and meet with the Inspector of Public Education in the area of Gómez Farías for the State of Michoacán. His office made those arrangements, thereby giving our visit official status.

Irene and I went by bus to Tangancicuaro, Michoacán (equivalent to a rural county seat in the United States) to meet with Inspector Ochoa Vega. He was most gracious and interested in assisting in every way possible to aid the children. He suggested that we return for a meeting with the Director and teachers of Benito Juárez School in Gómez Farías at a time he would arrange. Irene and I returned to Mexico City to await the appointment. I returned alone for this meeting toward the end of November 1976 as Irene was back at work.

The meeting at the school went very well. A migrant student, who was about 12 years of age, assisted in interpreting, as I was not fluent in Spanish. The teachers were anxious to try to remedy the problems of the international migrant students. They spoke of the problems they had observed that were similar to those that their counterparts in the California schools had seen. The teachers suggested that I return for a meeting with the parents, which I did. One of the families invited me to be their guest, an invitation I readily accepted.

The following week, a meeting of the village parents was held in the plaza. I spoke in my halting Spanish over the loud speaker that had been set up for the occasion. The parents were most cordial and desirous of being involved in a program for the children. The next day, I went to Zamora, Michoacán, to board the bus for a 6-hour ride back to Mexico City to discuss developments with Irene.

Irene and I also thought it appropriate to contact the PVUSD in Watsonville, California, and ask that the California Master Plan for Migrant Education be sent to us. A friend, Dr. Manfred Shaffer, a professor from the University of California-Santa Cruz, Irene, and Elizabeth Elmer, an American educator, and I spent 5 or 6 hours discussing the possibilities, ideas, and programs that could help the international migrant students. The need to write a proposal and find out to whom it should be addressed was one of our greater concerns.

During Christmas vacation I went to Guatemala. On the first day, in an inn in Guatemala City, during dinner, the six guests were sharing information as to who they were and what they did. The man opposite me said he was Ralph Benner and that he had just retired as Assistant Director of Migrant Education in Sacramento, California. I was so amazed that the

Children at Benito Juárez School, Gómez Farías, Michoacán, Mexico. (Photograph by Arlene Dorn)

food practically fell out of my mouth. The very person I needed to talk to was sitting in front of me, not in Sacramento, but in Guatemala City! A few days later, I received word from home telling me that I had to return immediately due to my mother's poor health.

Upon my return to Santa Cruz, and after seeing that mother was being properly attended to, I went to see the superintendent of PVUSD, Dr. Wallace Raynor. I gave him the letter from Professor Juan de Dios Rodriguez and informed him of all that had taken place in Mexico. Dr. Raynor was very interested in the possibilities of a cooperative effort with the Mexican schools. It was propitious for the development of the project that Dr. Raynor was superintendent. He not only cared about helping these special children, but he had a perspective that allowed him to encompass a project that could not follow a preset notion of development. He said I should go to Sacramento to meet with Fred Wolff, who directed the California Migrant Education Program.

A fellow teacher and friend, Louise Minniear, accompanied me. Together, we presented the needs at the school district level and informed Mr. Wolff of the developments which had taken place in Mexico. I also gave him the letter from Professor Juan de Dios Rodriguez Heredia. Mr. Wolff was enthusiastic about the prospects of a cooperative program with Mexico. He asked me if I would like to have a part in the work. I immediately said yes, not realizing what would transpire over the coming years in the project's continued development.

The Project is Formalized

It was necessary at this time to take several steps to set up a formalized project. A letter from Fred Wolff to Juan de Dios Rodriguez Heredia had to be written, accepting his offer to work with California on behalf of the Mexican migrant children. Fred Wolff did this and gave me the letter to hand-carry back to Mexico upon my return in May, when I received my master's of arts in intercultural education. The next step was to write a proposal placing the pilot project in the PVUSD within the Migrant Education Program. Dr. Raynor had cleared the way for this to take place.

The writing of the proposal turned out to be a considerable task. After an attempt by the project writer at PVUSD, Fred Wolff came from Sacramento to Watsonville and wrote the proposal himself.

Approval of the governing board of PVUSD had to be obtained. The proposal, along with a budget that included my salary as coordinator, had to be approved. (My salary was to remain the same as that of a classroom teacher.) All the money for the project was coming from special funds out of the California Migrant Program. In spite of the fact that the project would not cost the district any money, school officials were hesitant in giving their approval because they were apprehensive of involvement with a foreign government. However, the PVUSD governing board did approve the arrangement at its May 18, 1977, meeting.

In this initial stage other letters were sent to persons that had direct interest in migrant education, as well as to persons whose involvement was more peripheral. One of these letters was from Dr. Wallace A. Raynor to me. He expressed his appreciation for my work and gave me his full support. This letter, dated April 28, was given to me upon my preparation to return to Mexico to finish my degree. My mother's health had been stabilized, clearing the way for me to leave for Mexico.

Upon my return trip I presented Fred Wolff's letter to Professor Juan de Dios Rodriguez Heredia, stating his desire to work with the Mexican educators. At this point, the way was opened for planning strategies between the school in Gómez Farías, Michoacán, Mexico, and schools in the PVUSD. I named the project the Gómez Farías-Pajaro Valley Project. It was a pilot project. Our desire was to develop a program that could be replicated, since, as has been stated previously, there were internationally migrant children in many states in Mexico and in many states in the United States.

A significant letter went to Mr. Vic Rivera, Division of Education for the Disadvantaged, U.S. Office of Education, Washington D.C. The purpose of this letter was to inform Mr. Rivera of the project and also to get his opinion as to the legality of using Migrant Education Program funds for the project.

A fourth letter at this time went to Manual Ceja in the form of a memorandum from Fred Wolff. Mr. Ceja was in an administrative position over the California Migrant Education Program, and he was to become a staunch supporter of the project. In this memorandum Mr. Wolff stated that Licenciado Porfirio Muñoz Ledo, Director of Education for Mexico, had heard of our efforts and also that I had met with Jerry Inman, Cultural Attaché at the American Embassy, Mexico City. Mr. Wolff told of his telephone conversation with Mr. Inman, who assured him of his support. Mr. Wolff asked that a letter from Dr. Wilson Riles, California State Superintendent of Education, be sent to Lic. Muñoz Ledo.

The Gómez Farías-Pajaro Valley Project

Things were now in place for the GFPVP to begin in September of 1977. My year of sabbatical was over and I was again working in PVUSD, but as coordinator of the project. My desk, which I had to purchase out of project funds, was placed in the Migrant Education Office. My immediate supervisor was Francisco Jimenez, Director of Migrant Education. He was supportive of the project, but left the school district early in the Project's history. Mr. Jimenez was under the direction of an assistant superintendent who was in charge of special projects within the district. In my opinion, and many others, the assistant superintendent did not give his support for the GFPVP, although it was in fact he who had initially asked me to find out what I could about the school in Gómez Farías.

Through the early years of the project it was my perception that an attitude of "territorial jealousy" became a hindrance to the project's development in California within the educational community at both the PVUSD level and the California state level. The project was looked upon as being glamorous because of traveling to Mexico and Sacramento and working with people in prestigious positions on both sides of the border.

One incident which stands out in my memory took place in the first year of the project. We were trying to develop a transfer format that would work for both Mexican and California schools to communicate math and reading skills. Dr. Puentes of the California Migrant Education Program had considerable experience in developing record formats of a similar nature, so it was decided that he should go with me to Mexico to meet with the technical department there so that we could work out something together. The technical department was in Mexico City. Our appointment was on a Monday morning. However, we were going out to Michoacán over the weekend to meet with the school director from Gómez Farías, visit the school site, and meet with the inspector whose territory included Gómez Farías.

To prepare for a trip like this it was necessary to have the superintendent of my school district sign various papers. Verbal permission had been granted and tickets purchased. I telephoned Dr. Puentes to arrange our meeting at the San Francisco airport. I went to Superintendent Raynor's office (he had always been supportive of the project) for his signature. Upon arrival he said to me, "You know, Arlene, Dr. Puentes does not want you to go with him." I looked at him in amazement (I had the plane tickets in my purse at that moment) and said "I don't understand. I just talked to Dr. Puentes, 20 minutes ago, making arrangements where we would meet." Dr. Raynor got up from his desk and made a telephone call to Dr. Puentes, who told Dr. Raynor (I learned later) "There is no way I could go out there alone, I don't know how to find these people." Dr. Raynor returned to his desk and signed the papers. My belief is that a person in the school district simply lied. In my opinion the motive was pure jealousy. I ran into many more incidents where this type of hindrance interfered with the development of the project.

Dr. Puentes and I met on that Friday night after a full day's work for each of us, with an hour and half drive to San Francisco. We flew to Los Angeles to board the midnight flight to Guadalajara. The airline now caused us problems; they wouldn't let Dr. Puentes board. I could go, but not he. Naturally, I did not go. We began to find an alternate flight arrangement. By about 3 a.m. we had tickets on a flight to Mexico City, leaving early in the morning! Therefore, we would board a flight to Mexico City, transfer to Guadalajara, retrieve our luggage which had preceded us on the original flight, and arrive for our appointments a day late! We were able to contact the persons in Michoacán a day late and still accomplish our objectives there. But that was not the end. We left Michoacán on Sunday afternoon by bus to return to Guadalajara to get our prearranged flight to Mexico City. Since we had been bumped from the original flight, we were automatically bumped from this flight too. If you are familiar with Mexico on Sunday evening, you know it seems that everyone in Mexico is trying to get home all at once!

How were we going to get to Mexico City for an eight a.m. appointment at the Ministry of Education (SEP)? We taxied to the bus station, but it too was swarming with people. Dr. Puentes enlisted the aide of a local resident, purchasing the last two tickets on a second-class bus, next to the smelly toilet! This was a nonstop bus, arriving at 6 a.m. in Mexico City. We had no chance to get a drink of water since leaving Michoacán and no opportunity now. What to do now? Shut our mouths to keep them moist, think this will end, and be glad not to have to use the toilet. We arrived, got a drink, went to the hotel, changed our clothes, and made our appointment on time! Glamorous? No. Worth it all? Yes.

I believe there was also a legitimate difficulty for the school district in that, through my contacts in Mexico, they were dealing with political entities on a noncorresponding level. This, I feel, put the PVUSD in a somewhat uncomfortable position. Such dilemmas also relate to the California situation and, I believe, had a profound effect on the timely development of the project.

The overall attitude in Mexico was quite different from that in California, though my personal judgment is all I have to rely on in making such claims. From the very beginning, the involved persons in Mexico were excited and willing to put considerable time and energy into establishing the project. Irene Anzaldúa, myself, and others, who later were to join us, were brought before a broad spectrum of officials—many in very powerful positions. Always we were accorded courtesy and sincere attention to the subject of the project and the needs of the children.

One of the main difficulties in Mexico related to timing and to their political system for appointments. It seemed that each time we returned to Mexico new persons were in office. When the president changed, new appointees were everywhere. If there was a new governor, new appointees followed. This didn't just happen immediately, but with a lapse of time that might involve two visits. We would then have to explain the whole project and its history all over again. However, the enthusiasm was always there, and the project was moved further ahead by appropriate persons who could help in getting an institutional home for the project, which was a necessary step for its establishment.

Another difficulty in Mexico was a matter of logistics and the decentralization of Mexican educational institutions. Often it was necessary to go to the locale of the school in Michoacán, or to the state offices in Moralia, Michoacán, to confer with officials. This meant long rides on buses. Even the offices of SEP were located throughout Mexico City. Because of the size of the city and the bureaucracy, one was lucky to accomplish one appointment in a day. Mexican officials we encountered worked long days, but offices were scattered throughout the city.

The fact that the project was in a developmental stage and that this type of international work had never been done before by anyone made it most difficult for a local school board in California to handle the problems.

The Communication Process

The beginning of the actual work on the process of communication of the students' academic record from the California school to the Mexican school, Benito Juárez, took place in California. The California Migrant Education Program appointed Dr. William Kenny as their liaison to PVUSD and me. This was in the early fall of 1977. It was felt that it would be wise for me to have a co-worker travel with me to Mexico, and I agreed. Dr. Kenny asked if I would prefer a man or woman. I felt a man would be best to balance out the team.

Calvin Gunter, a migrant education resource teacher from the Visalia Migrant Education Program, was given this assignment along with his other responsibilities in the Visalia region. Mr. Gunter spoke Spanish fluently. He is a large man, probably six feet two inches tall, and quite blonde. I am five feet tall and very blonde. We made a conspicuous sight in the Mexican village! Our first visit to Gómez Farías was at a time when there was concern in the United States about Mexicans crossing illegally into the states. When we walked down the road in the village, residents thought we were from the INS! People didn't know that we were expected by the school director. Some of the children, back in Mexico from the schools in Watsonville, California, recognized me and the community's fears were put to rest. Along with the demanding work of the project, there were numerous amusing and pleasant times.

However, prior to our trip to Gómez Farías, much had to be done in Watsonville. A format had to be devised for communicating the child's academic record to the Mexican teacher. The question was how much, and in what manner, could information be meaningfully relayed? The two school systems were quite different; they operated on different philosophies. The child was placed in different grade levels in the different systems. Most of the time, the children could not attend the Mexican school because they were not there in September when school commenced and textbooks allocated. Although you will recall that the first Mexican official, Rodriguez, gave a directive that the children could be admitted to school on their return, you probably also realize that things are never as simple in reality as they are on paper. The migrant parents, while still in California, had to be made aware of this directive, as well as all the involved officials in the Mexican state system. While Mexico's educational system was a federal system, the state was also involved.

Several steps had to be taken in California at the beginning of the school year. The Gómez Farías children had to be located out of the whole population of identified migrant students. They were enrolled in a number of different schools throughout the PVUSD. Also, they were in many different classrooms. This group of children numbered about 100. The families were *legal* aliens in California, and many were traveling back and forth in their newly purchased American vehicles.

After locating the children in school and gathering statistical data such as name, age, and so forth from the Migrant Student Record, our duty was to inform the teachers of the project. It would be the teachers who would confer with me as to their ideas on how best to format the information. They would be the ones to fill out the transfer document. This would have to be done, moreover, without prior notification of the students' departure. Generally, when fathers received notification that their work was over (in the late fall) they would pack up and leave the next day. Much of the time the children didn't know they were leaving until they got home from school. In that case, there could be no transfer document sent with the child.

During the same period I met with the teachers, I also had to contact the parents. We wanted them to give the school at least a few days notice of their leaving so the teacher could gather the data to go to the Mexican school. Also, the Gómez Farías parents needed to know that they were able to enroll their children in the Mexican school and that they needed to bring back an academic transfer document from the Mexican teacher the following year. Parents work long hours daily in the fields; consequently, meeting with them meant arranging night meetings at the labor camps where they lived.

There was considerable discussion among all those involved in the project as to the form the transfer document should take. This discussion was necessary as we had to allow for the differences in language and educational systems. Not all students in California were in bilingual classes, and the Mexican teachers in Mexico did not speak English. Then there was the difference in curriculum in the two school systems. Some teachers and school administrators were skeptical as to the feasibility of a transfer document.

Dr. Kenny introduced Dr. Charles Puentes from the California Migrant Education Program into the project. Dr. Puentes had worked extensively throughout the United States in the Migrant Education Program, helping to develop the process for communicating academic and health records for the migrant children who transferred among schools in the United States (the Migrant Student Record Transfer System). Thus, Dr. Puentes came into the project with a wealth of skills. He remained throughout the development of the project as one of its most dedicated supporters and workers, doing a great deal of work on his own time.

Finally, it was decided that the transfer document would be limited to communicating only reading and mathematical skills, attendance, and deportment data. The reading skills could be Spanish or English or both, whatever was appropriate for the child and teacher. The teacher could make any comment he or she felt helpful for the receiving teacher.

Easy? No! For all the reasons stated earlier: Parents leaving without giving the teacher advance notice of their departure; problems in locating the children from Gómez Farías in the classrooms; contacting all of the teachers; and gathering up the transfer documents which would later, in this beginning stage of the project, be taken to Mexico personally by me. In addition, the lack of support from the middle management level in PVUSD made for some very interesting and often frustrating times; but, despite these hindrances, we did it. It wasn't 100 percent, but it was a start.

The first trip to Mexico and the village of Gómez Farías took place in the winter of 1978. We always had to take account of school vacations on both sides of the border and of parents' travel schedules. This, too, was a bit complicated. The families stayed in Mexico for different lengths of time, varying from one to six months. Those who were in Mexico for only one month were not a big concern, as they returned to the California schools without missing too many days. However, all the others *were* a concern, and we wanted to include as many children as possible.

A trip to Mexico, when one is under contract to a school district, doesn't just happen overnight. There are many permission papers to sign and to be signed off on. It takes a bit of explaining. Mr. Gunter was going on this trip and, as we had never met or had an opportunity to plan together, he came to Watsonville from Visalia for a planning session. We had no problem in understanding what we hoped to accomplish and in realizing that plans had to be very flexible to accommodate the degree to which the Mexican authorities might want us to participate. This included activities and meetings with officials at national, state, and local levels. The mode of operation of the U.S. and Mexican bureaucratic process is quite different.

We weren't there to impose something of ours on them, but to work cooperatively for the benefit of the children we both shared. It was not only a political responsibility—but a moral one.

The trip went well at all levels. We met first with Irene Anzaldúa on all our trips. She was our valuable coordinator within Mexico. She knew the educational community well, and she understood our school system. She did all the work with us, gratis! We could not use project money for purposes outside the United States, other than for travel expenses. The project had not yet been institutionalized on either side of the border. We were in a discovering and development mode, and Mexico had not reached the place where they could budget special funds for the project's development.

We met with persons from different administrative levels and persons from the technical department of the Mexican school system (SEP) in Mexico City before going on to Gómez Farías. They were to work with us many times, and they went with us to Gómez Farías.

In Gómez Farías, we met with the director of the school, Professor Roberto Mercado, Inspector Professor Ochoa Vega from Tauganciuaro, and with teachers and parents, and we visited classrooms when in session. Our objective was to introduce the transfer document and to get reaction from the teachers in Gómez Farías as to whether the form was appropriate for the Mexican school. We explained to the school staff the communications from the California teachers. We left Watsonville in the winter before the children returned to California in the spring. During this visit, we were accorded much gracious hospitality by all.

Our next move was to return to Mexico City via the faithful bus trip of about 6 to 8 hours. Then make exit visits to the administrators in the office of Relaciones Internacional of SEP and the Cultural Attaché in the American Embassy. These visits were carried out by Mrs. Anzaldúa and myself. Mr. Gunter needed to return to Visalia for his regularly assigned work. I was always invited to stay in the home of Mrs. Anzaldúa. This, too, was a gracious act on her part, and it made the cost of the trips much less. Always—she gave, expecting nothing in return.

Various Operational Levels

Back in California in April and May, we awaited the return of the children—and hopefully the documents—by mail or by the families themselves. There were a number of things to be accomplished during this time of waiting. In the United States, there were several levels of migrant education conferences to attend. These were on national, state, and regional levels. The purpose was to inform migrant education personnel from other areas what we were hoping to accomplish.

At the national level, other states had a similar population. The children were home-based in many different villages scattered throughout a number of different states in Mexico, but the difficulties experimented by schools on both sides of the border were the same. The hardships the children and families experienced were similar. I had the opportunity, at various conferences, to give slide presentations, showing the Mexican school and depicting life in the village of Gómez Farías. These presentations were well received. We also wanted to keep the persons at the U.S. federal level apprised of our project's progress and activities.

At the California state level, conferences and activities were much the same, probably a little more specific since we were closer to home and the families resided in neighboring areas of Mexico, which made for cultural similarities. At the California state level, there were also migrant parent conferences to attend at different locations as well as one statewide conference. Our presentations in these cases were geared to informing and seeking the help of parents to carry out their role in the communication process. The parents at these conferences showed great interest. Most Mexican parents are anxious for their children to obtain a good education and learn to speak English. They view education and speaking English as the way out of their difficult lifestyle. Often, however, Mexican parents are intimidated by our educational system, so it is difficult for them to participate as we think they should. Also, their work schedule gives them little spare time. So we also wanted to help parents overcome these difficulties and participate in the U.S. educational system.

At the regional level within California, there were presentations made, always to a more specific audience.

At the school district level, presentations involved more contact with classroom teachers, discovering their needs. Often they were ignorant of the unusual problems their international migrant students faced. It was possible that there might be only one such child in the class, and so, for the teacher, it might seem like an isolated case. Some teachers were happy to do the extra work to fill out the transfer documents (which really took little time), but others weren't interested. I found that there were considerable differences from school to school in teachers' responses to the project.

Project Title Change to Project MEDIR

As the pilot project was reaching the close of the 2-year commitment PVUSD had made, it was clear that PVUSD did not wish to continue. Also, in the California State Department of Education, there were changes in leadership, and difficulties at that level had ramifications for the funding of the GFPVP.

At about this time I had discovered the fact that there was a directory of private foundations! I went to the library and began a search for a foundation that would be open to the type of work we were doing. Ignorance is bliss, so it is said, and in my case, this was true. I wrote a letter to ten foundations, among them The David and Lucile Packard Foundation, which responded positively. They supplemented a partial funding from the State of California the next year, and they became the only funding agent of the project for the remaining years of my involvement.

The existence of the project is indebted to the vision and concern of Mr. Colburn Wilbur, executive director of The David and Lucile Packard Foundation, and to the understanding and faith in me and the project by Dolly Sacks, Program Director. The reason I say this is that with the project at this stage of development, one couldn't count any product as concrete evidence except for a few transfer documents that had made the round trip. In fact, the second group of transfer documents that were coming back from Gómez Farías were lost in transit in Mexico. Numerous meetings, a lot of interest shown, and things of this nature were the only concrete evidence to warrant the funding of the project. The fiscal agent for the project at this time was the superintendent of schools for Butte County, California, under the auspices of the Mini-Corps, a program related to the Migrant Education Program, based in Sacramento. Mini-Corps did my secretarial work via the mail; there was no FAX then. I was using my home as my office.

When PVUSD no longer wanted to be involved in the project in 1979, I took a temporary leave from the school district to continue work on the project. The project was renamed Project MEDIR, which stood for Migrant Education Data International Record. It was appropriate to change the name because several other school districts in California had begun to participate. As I recall these were Gonzales, Greenfield, Soledad, Cutler Orosi, Planada, Indio, and some schools served by Region III, headquartered in Merced, California. In Mexico, the development of the project had spread far beyond Gómez Farías, Michoacán, to Guanajuato, Monterrey, Jalisco, Nueva Leon, and other areas where educators were being made aware of the project.

During the first two years of the project, we wanted to explore the possibility of including the Mexican medical record of the child. Adriana Simmons, who was working with the Medi-Corps program, was asked to accompany me and Mr. Gunter to Mexico. The three of us contacted the main health office—similar to a California county health doctor—for the Gómez Farías area in Tangancicuaro. We were informed that it would be necessary to meet with health officials in Mexico City. There isn't the tie-in with health records in Mexico and the schools as there is in California.

We contacted the proper health agency and returned to Mexico City for a meeting. We came away with the sense that to communicate the health record, especially the record of immunizations, would be considerably easier than communicating the academic record simply because there is less ambiguity. Upon our return, Ms. Simmons was not able to bring closure to our efforts. I recall this was about the time PVUSD was withdrawing from the pilot project. Some time later, when I became aware that she could not pursue this work, I contacted the Border Health Organization. Interest was expressed, and I attended one of the meetings in Tijuana, Mexico. I talked with some of the leaders, who suggested that I might present a paper at their next meeting. I felt that at this time I could not take on anything else. So including the child's health record was dropped. I felt there was great potential in this area, because it would be rather simple to show the economic value of this record, and economics speak loudly.

During the first 2 years of the project, Irene Anzaldúa and I thought it would serve the children well if they could bring their Mexican textbook back to California. In all Mexican elementary schools, children are given paperback textbooks that cover all areas of the curriculum. These then belong to the children. However, it was illegal for the books to be taken out of the country. We thought that if the children could bring them to California, it would give them continuity in their studies either by continuing their studies at home or, more probably, in their California classrooms. Having the Mexican texts would also be of help to the California teachers when there were no Spanish-language texts available. This held especially true in science.

We pursued the idea with the Mexican Ministry of Education (SEP), which granted permission. It was quite an involved process. But now, how were we to get that many textbooks to Watsonville from Mexico City? Some young men of a family who were friends of mine retrieved the books from the warehouse, got some makeshift boxes, packed the books, and hauled them to the U.S. Embassy. I then prepared them to go in the official Embassy mail to Texas. Then I paid postage to California from the meager project funds. In Watsonville, I stamped them with the project stamp and began to deliver them to teachers in PVUSD who had international migrant children in their classes.

I followed a regular pattern whenever I was going to Mexico, either alone or accompanied. Before going I contacted Irene and perhaps some Mexican official. Mexico had not assigned any particular person to be coordinator. Irene acted in this capacity purely on a volunteer basis, motivated by concern for these children. Early on in the project's development, she had suggested we contact officials at Relaciones Internacionales[2], a department within SEP. They assisted greatly. Also, I always made an exit visit to the American Cultural Attaché at the American Embassy to

---

[2] Dirección General De Relaciones Internacionales—SubDirección Der Intercambios Culturales, Mexico City.

inform him or her of my activity in Mexico. They, too, were of considerable help.

The personnel of Relacionales Internacionales changed many times. This was also true of other departments. This required me to describe the project again and again. But these repetitions never failed to move the project further ahead, even though it was not institutionalized.

During one of the trips to Mexico when Dr. Puentes participated, we both thought it would be a great advantage for the project's development if we could arrange for the people from Relaciones Internacionales and the people from the technical department to meet jointly with us. We were very pleased when this was accomplished. We also wished to have Irene Anzaldúa appointed as coordinator for Mexico. Our suggestion was that Mexico approach UNESCO to accomplish that goal. This they did, but with very different results.

UNESCO funded a tour of the Migrant programs—starting in Washington, DC, and ending the U.S. phase in California; and then proceeding to Mexico. The Mexican person assigned this tour was Carlos Compos from the technical department of SEP Mexico City, who had been with Irene and me in Michoacán. He was knowledgeable concerning the needs of the project and capable in offering suggestions. He was a very good choice for the task. On the other hand, the man chosen by the Migrant Education Program from Washington, DC, had no experience with the project. I thought a wise choice would have been someone like Dr. Puentes, a consultant with the California Migrant Education Program, who had extensive experience in Mexico and in the furthering of the project. The U.S. and Mexican representatives traveled together in each country observing things in general about migrant education, but as far as I know, this experience did not benefit our project. Unfortunately, Irene Anzaldúa did not get funded as coordinator.

During what might be called the second phase of the project, when it was known as Project MEDIR, I made the first count of international migrant students. The students in this category had never been separated from the count (MSRTS)[3] of all Migrant Students. Their special needs and circumstances were not recognized. No one knew how many students there were who returned to Mexico annually for a 1- to 6-month period and then returned to school in California.

In order to make this count, I sent a letter to all superintendents who had a migrant education program in their district asking for the number, grade

[3]A count made by each state through its migrant program. These records were also stored in a data bank at the MSRTS in Little Rock, Arkansas, as well as for local students at each school district.

level, and location of the students' home base in Mexico. For the most part, local school districts through their migrant program could retrieve this information from their local records. As I recall, I sent out 157 letters and received responses from over 100. From this information (all from relatively small districts) there was a count of about 8,000 children. From this number we estimated, based on general knowledge, that there must be about 20,000[4] students in California who were international migrants, migrating annually back and forth between Mexico and California. This number, taken from things I wrote or said, began to be used by others, with no verification or recognition of its source. I still have in my possession the original letters.

Over the years, I attended various migrant education conferences from national to local levels and at special interest groups, where I made formal and informal presentations. This was in both the United States and Mexico. On one occasion, I invited Profesora Roberta Lajous, from Relaciones Internacionales, to attend a national conference in Virginia Beach. At the conference, I introduced her to Vidal Rivera, national director of the Migrant Education Program. She had had difficulty in arranging appointments with persons with whom she wished to speak in Washington, DC, relative to the children of this project. I suggested she go through the Mexican Embassy, which she did. This opened up some appointments for her, I was told.

As always, the Mexican people and agencies—from local groups of parents and teachers, regional and state officials, to national educational and political persons—acted in favor of our efforts. Wherever we were, treated always with graciousness and hospitality, we worked to further the development of the project.

In 1984 the Butte County Office of the Superintendent was going through some change, and no longer wished to serve as fiscal agent for the project. At this time the La Cooperativa Campecina came into a relationship with the project and served as fiscal agent for only a short period, during which a conference was arranged in Morelia, Michoacán, with school officials from both countries present. One of the representatives, Dr. Jack Shaffer, then director of the California Office of Migrant Education, took the initiative and proposed that Project MEDIR be put under the jurisdiction of the California Migrant Education Program as the Binational Educational Program. It had always been our desire that the project be institutionalized within the Migrant Education Section of the California State Department of Education.

Space does not permit me to write about the involvement of the Ford

[4]This turned out to be a quite valid number.

Foundation, Commission of the Californians; The Research Colloquium on International Migrants held at the University of California, Santa Cruz; and a presentation at a Symposium on Mexican Immigration sponsored by the Center for Ethics & Social Policy in Berkeley. Also, there was work done by Sam Farr, Representative in the California State Assembly (now Congressional Representative), and Representative Leon Panetta, now Chief of Staff at the White House. These people and events all played a role in developing the program.

In August 1995, I was invited to attend the ninth Binational Program Conference in Denver, Colorado, where I was honored as founder of the Binational Program. I appreciated this gracious recognition. I was also glad for the opportunity to give recognition to the work of Profesora Irene de la Llata de Anzaldúa of Mexico as cofounder of the Binational Program. She was killed in an auto accident in Mexico in 1990. As I look back over the history of my part as founder of the program, I believe what I titled my remarks at the opening reception in Denver is true—"God made appointments for me!"

CHAPTER 10

Teachers for Mexican Migrant and Immigrant Students: Meeting an Urgent Need

NORMA VARISCO DE GARCÍA
AND
EUGENE E. GARCIA

The heads of the U.S. Department of Education and the Mexican Secretaría of Educación signed the Memorandum of Understanding on Education Between the Government of the United States of America and the Government of Mexico *in 1991; it has been renewed every 2 years since that time. The U.S. Department of Education's Office of Bilingual Education and Minority Language Affairs (OBEMLA) has provided U.S. leadership in following through on provisions in the* Memorandum *related to teacher education. This chapter describes the rationale for subsequent activities—meant to address bilingual teacher shortages in the United States—and the collaboration taking place among Mexican and U.S. federal, state, and local officials, administrators, and educators.*

Background

Over the past two decades Mexico has remained the country of origin for the majority of immigrants to the United States. An estimated 1,655,843 Mexican citizens have emigrated to the United States since 1981. This figure outnumbers any other nation of origin by over a million for the same time period (Figueroa & Garcia, 1994).

In 1990, the nation's 17.3 million Spanish speakers far outnumbered all other speakers of a foreign language in the United States. According to U.S. Census data, Spanish speakers now account for more than half of all people residing in the United States whose first language is not English. Half of all Spanish speakers live in California and Texas (U.S. Bureau of the Census, 1994).

Unfortunately in light of these facts, there is a scarcity of bilingual teachers to provide instruction to these children. According to a recent study (Fleishman & Hopstock, 1993), there are more than 360,000 teachers providing instruction to these students, but only 10 percent are credentialed bilingual teachers, and only 33 percent have ever taken a college course on culture, language acquisition, or teaching English to limited-English-proficient (LEP) pupils. To further aggravate the problem, the majority of these teachers are not proficient in Spanish (U.S. Department of Education, 1994).

Another study profiling U.S. teachers indicates that only two percent of the teachers in public schools and one percent of those in private schools are Hispanic (Feistritzer, 1986). Furthermore, the National Education Association (NEA) reports that the nation's teachers are still overwhelmingly white and female. A poll of its members shows that 87 percent are white and 72 percent are female. NEA executive Robert Chase said that the failure to attract and keep minority teachers threatens to deny minority students the role models they need (National Education Association, 1992).

It was in light of these facts that the U.S. Department of Education's Office of Bilingual Education and Minority Languages Affairs (OBEMLA) embarked upon a binational effort to increase the number of qualified bilingual teachers and to help other teachers now serving LEP students to learn Spanish and increase their knowledge of the history and culture of students of Mexican origin. Much of this work is being done in collaboration with the Mexican Secretaríat of Education.

The Memorandum of Understanding

On August 17, 1990, the U.S. Department of Education and the Mexican Secretaríat of Public Education entered into a Memorandum of Understanding on Education (Cavazos & Bartlett-Díaz, 1990). This action was taken within the framework of the United States/Mexico Binational Commission, which promotes cooperation between the two nations. The historic document was signed in Nuevo Laredo, Mexico, by former U.S. Secretary of Education Lauro Cavazos and former Mexican Secretary of Education Manuel Bartlett-Díaz. It is the most comprehensive agreement that the U.S. Department of Education has made with any nation. Its purpose is to enhance cooperation between the two countries for improving the quality of education.

The Memorandum of Understanding on Education

Here are some of the main ideas briefly stated from the Memorandum of Understanding:

The Government of the United States of America and the Government of the Republic of Mexico under Article I:

GENERAL EDUCATION

(a) will encourage and develop cooperation and exchanges in the field of education on the basis of equality, mutual benefits, and reciprocity;

(b) such exchanges and cooperation shall be subject to the constitutions and applicable laws and regulations of the respective countries; and

(c) the cooperation provided for in this Memorandum . . . shall attempt to identify new areas for joint activities or where deemed appropriate by all concerned, to strengthen or expand existing programs.

In Article II:

METHODS OF COOPERATION

(a) 1. Encourage and facilitate closer relationships between state education agencies and offices, schools and school systems, postsecondary institutions, other educational entities and organizations, and private sector establishments in the two countries; and

2. Encourage mutually beneficial educational activities involving researchers, scholars, faculty members, teachers, educational administrators, and other specialists to lecture, teach, conduct research, and develop cooperative programs;

(b) 1. Cooperation that facilitates exchanges and dialogue centered on educational management, methods, evaluation, and research; and

2. In support of other bilateral initiatives and programs, the study and teaching of each other's language, culture, and history through the development of exchanges and cooperation.

In Article VI:

TERM OF MEMORANDUM: This Memorandum shall be effective September 1, 1990, and remain effective until December 31, 1991, after which it will be extended for successive 2-year periods...

Additional annexes for subsequent 2-year periods have been signed between both governments (Limon Rojas, M. Letter to U.S. Secretary Richard Riley, July 11, 1995; Riley, R. Letter to Mexican Secretary Limon Rojas, June 2, 1995; Riley & Zedillo, 1993).

The Memorandum of Understanding was timely, because it anticipated the need for increased cooperation that would be brought about by the implementation of the North America Free Trade Agreement (NAFTA). The Memorandum expressed the intention to collaborate for an educational program that would contribute to providing a highly skilled, productive workforce interacting along the border of both countries.

Additional exchange visits by senior officials of both national education agencies occurred in December 1990 and June 1991. These visits resulted in further agreements. Subsequent annexes to the original Memorandum of Understanding were signed that placed further emphasis upon teacher education, teacher exchange, Spanish and English language instruction, technological education, joint university meetings, mathematics and science teaching, and migrant education (Tinsman, 1994).

Border Conference on Education

To enhance cooperative efforts among the 10 border states of the two nations, the Memorandum of Understanding called for a joint Border Conference on Education. The U.S. Department of Education and Secretaría de Educación Pública hosted this conference in Ciudad Juárez and El Paso in October 1991. The conference brought together one of the largest groups of educators (more than 300 chief state school officers, superintendents, university presidents and representatives, business executives, etc.) ever assembled from the two countries to learn about successful existing forms of cooperation and to agree on new and expanded areas of cooperation at both the lower and higher education levels. The conference focused on teacher exchange, the teaching of Spanish and English, teacher training, science and mathematics education, migrant education, literacy, dropout prevention, technical education, faculty and student exchanges, continuing education, and educational technology. Existing border arrangements were strengthened and new relationships were established. Various state education agencies, school systems, and institutions of higher education expanded cooperative efforts to improve education, upgrade the workforce, and stimulate lasting working relationships (U.S. Department of Education & Secretaría de Educación Pública de México, 1991).

Further Agreements

In December 1991, President Salinas appointed Ernesto Zedillo (currently Mexico's President), to replace Secretary of Education Manuel Bartlett-Díaz. Secretary Zedillo immediately hastened the educational reform begun by Secretary Bartlett-Díaz. As a first priority, he turned his efforts to overcoming the internal problems inhibiting reform and federal cooperation. The November 1992 election in the United States and subsequent appointment of a new U.S. Secretary of Education caused some further delay.

Then, in February 1993, Secretary Zedillo called on Secretary Riley, and the two secretaries reaffirmed the joint commitment to cooperate in education, concluding that both nations had much to gain from collaboration. They agreed to sign a new annex to the Memorandum of Understanding that continues the existing forms of educational cooperation and focuses upon those areas of greatest need and, consequently, of highest priority (Riley & Zedillo, 1993).

This Annex Three was signed by Secretary Riley and Secretary Zedillo at the U.S./Mexico Binational Commission meeting held in June 1993, and emphasizes cooperation in the areas of school-to-work transition, teaching of English and Spanish languages, early childhood education, education for the prevention of drug abuse, distance education, and educational research. It also calls for cooperation in the fields of teacher education, adult education, technical education, migrant education, and higher education.

On October 4-5, 1993, a subsequent meeting was held by U.S./Mexico senior education officers in Mexico, D.F., and an agreement of cooperation was concluded in the following three areas: teacher exchange, teacher training, and curriculum exchange. The report on this meeting (Tinsman, 1994) states that this collaborative effort is important due to the interaction of both countries in education, economics, cultural exchanges, and the evermore interlinking demographics.

First Steps in Collaboration

As the first step in advancing the U.S. Department of Education's efforts after the signing of the historic NAFTA agreement, OBEMLA hosted a joint meeting of U.S. and Mexican education representatives at the national meeting of Title VII project directors held in conjunction with the National Association for Bilingual Education conference in Los Angeles, February 18, 1994. For this meeting, OBEMLA director Eugene E. Garcia and his staff prepared a briefing book containing resources on teacher training, teacher exchange, and curriculum examples. The participants agreed that there was an urgent need to share information on existing curriculum, curriculum reform, and materials, with the goal of reenforcing curriculum exchange activities between the two countries.

OBEMLA followed up on the recommendations of participants by organizing a joint invitational symposium, "Curriculum Perspectives: Challenges for the Future [Perspectivas Curriculares: Retos para el Futuro]." This event, meant to accomplish curriculum goals established by the Memorandum of Understanding in education between the two countries, was held in conjunction with the annual conference of the Texas Association of Bilingual Education, November 10-12, 1994, and was sponsored by OBEMLA, the Mexican Secretaríat of Public Education, the Division of Bilingual Education and Special Language Instruction of the Texas Education Agency, the Southwest Educational Development Laboratory, and the Southwestern Bell Foundation. The symposium allowed U.S. and Mexican educators to begin identifying specific materials, resources, methodologies, technologies, and other strategies for elementary and secondary education that can be used by schools in both countries to promote and implement education reform (Richey, 1995).

In order to identify presenters from the United States, input was solicited from state education agency bilingual education directors in Texas, Arizona, New Mexico, and California, the National Clearinghouse for Bilingual Education, and OBEMLA staff. Through collaboration with the Secretaría de Educación Pública, a program for the symposium was developed that included

- curriculum content sessions,
- educational policy,
- educational technology demonstrations,
- educational reform,
- publisher exhibits,
- publisher and educator panel discussions,
- curriculum exhibits,
- workshops, and
- networking.

The symposium drew participants from the 10 U.S. and Mexican border states as well as educators from Florida, Colorado, and Utah. Feedback received from the participants indicates that the symposium was a success, especially in the areas of exchanging materials and methodologies and building partnerships.

The Second U.S./Mexico Symposium took place at the Cibeles Convention Center, Ciudad Juárez, Mexico, September 14-15, 1995. It was cosponsored by OBEMLA and the Mexican Secretaríat of Public Education; the Texas Education Agency; the Southwest Educational Development Laboratory; and the Johns Hopkins University Center for Research on the Education of Students at Risk.

The goal of this symposium was to provide the participants with a unique learning and training experience, bringing them up to date on the latest efforts in the professional development field. An additional goal was to identify additional efforts needed to overcome the shortage of personnel who are well prepared to serve youth in the United States and Mexico.

Approximately 400 educators and members of local and state governments, as well as representatives of state education agencies, OBEMLA, the U.S. Department of Education, and the Secretaríat of Public Education of Mexico, participated in the symposium. The interchange of experiences and ideas identified new possibilities of communication and cooperation, and opened a new era in our bilateral relationship and cooperation in the education field.

Proceedings of the symposium will be published in Spanish and English (Lara & Varisco de García, 1995).

Binational Initiative for Educational Development (El Paso/Ciudad Juárez Region)

In other efforts to alleviate shortages of bilingual teachers, OBEMLA and the University of Texas at El Paso have established the Binational Initiative for Educational Development to enhance education in the El Paso/Ciudad Juárez region. The Initiative has three major activities: (1) a series of meetings and forums to help educators from both sides of the border to become acquainted with each other, to identify topics of mutual interest and concerns, and to explore possibilities for collaborative projects; (2) a series of seminars and workshops of mutual interest to deal firsthand with the problems identified and to implement solutions; and (3) a summer institute involving educators from both sides of the border. These activities are being planned collaboratively with the assistance of the Secretary of Public Education of Mexico. The primary beneficiaries of the activities will be the children and educators of the El Paso/Juárez area. On the United States side, this will include the students and bilingual educators from the neighboring school districts, the El Paso Community College, and the University of Texas at El Paso (especially university students at two Title VII programs). Others who will benefit directly by collaborating with their U.S. counterparts include the children, educators, and researchers in the Ciudad Juárez area (Tinajeros & Lozano, 1994).

Meetings and forums. Educators and researchers from the United States and Mexico have begun a series of meetings to foster the interchange of ideas and expertise, the collaborative identification and the search for solutions, to improve the education provided to children in the border areas.

Seminars and workshops. In order to put the training and interchange of teachers into effect, OBEMLA sponsored three workshops at the NABE International Conference in Phoenix, Arizona, in February 1995 in collaboration with the Secretary of Public Education of Mexico, the border states' state education agencies' directors, and local education agencies' administrators and directors of bilingual education.

- At one workshop, "Teacher Exchange with Mexico: How to Do It," local education agencies from border states that have already conducted teacher exchanges provided materials and information so that other interested local education agencies can learn the nuts and bolts of putting together a teacher exchange.
- The second workshop, "Bilingual Program Personnel Recruitment, Train-

ing, and Certification Activities in Illinois," building on the idea presented by the Secretaría of Educacíon (SEP) of Mexico that normal teachers already living in the United States should be identified and given a course of studies by a university or college, normalize their status, and be provided certification so that they can become part of the U.S. educational system. The administrators of the Board of Education of Chicago, Illinois, and the state education agency director for bilingual education of the state, presented the efforts and the success obtained in their unique program.

- Finally, at the third workshop, "United States Department of Education/ México Secretaría de Educación Education Initiative: Federal, State, and Local," the Director of OBEMLA, a representative from the SEP/ Mexico, and the state director of bilingual education for Texas discussed the philosophy behind and need for the U.S. Department of Education/ OBEMLA-Secretaría de Educación Pública/Mexico Education Initiative, and outlined the next steps planned for its implementation.

The Summer Institute. Dr. Josefina Tinajeros (Sept. 1995) from the University of Texas at El Paso obtained a grant from OBEMLA to conduct summer institutes as a Binational Initiative Educational Development for Enhancement for Education. Local educational agencies (LEAs) attended the Summer Institute from both sides of the border. This Institute was held in Brownsville, September 11-14, 1995. Individual LEAS conducted the summer programs in teacher exchange in Brownsville, Texas.

OBEMLA concentrated its efforts in organizing and conducting the Second Binational Professional Development Symposium, held September 14-15, 1995, in Ciudad Juárez described above.

A committee of educators and researchers from both sides of the border, with support from both OBEMLA and SEP representatives, planned all aspects of the Summer Institute including the program, the length and time of the Institute, and guests and speakers to be invited.

Bridge to Higher Education

OBEMLA has been working with state education agencies in the area of personnel credentialing to ensure that graduates from training programs meet state certification and licensing requirements. This effort has been strengthened by the work to develop national bilingual/ESL competencies, competency standards, and guidelines to assess educator competency in language proficiency and cultural awareness. OBEMLA also has helped plan recruitment efforts outside of the United States. Credentialing of foreign teachers faces formidable obstacles since the expectations and standards differ across the nation (Impine-Hernandez, 1989).

At the higher education level, work remains to be done with universities and colleges in both countries to develop comparable, transferable credits in bilingual education, ESL, Spanish, and culture and civilization. This way, students will be able to work toward a teaching degree accepted in both countries.

Training monies in the continuation programs under Transitional Bilingual Education, Special Alternative Education Programs, and Developmental Education Programs can be utilized to send U.S. teachers to Mexico to improve their Spanish language teaching abilities and skills. These teachers might receive higher education credits in the aforementioned areas of education when they take courses at Mexican colleges or universities.

OBEMLA is also working closely with certain local education agencies in the border states to increase the number of elementary and secondary teachers with bilingual or ESL language certification by modifying its past budget policy to maintain current levels of funding for staff development.

A Border Colloquy: Imagining La Frontera

In addition to the Secretaríal initiatives and activities, collaboration between Mexico and the United States has also taken place in a series of meetings to facilitate collaboration and planning for the education success of children and youth in the U.S./Mexico Border Region. Seven meetings were conducted during 1994: three in Mexico and four in the United States. At these meetings, residents of La Frontera—the region along the boundary between the United States and Mexico—envisioned the future of education for children in an expanded community that spans the boundary. The results sought were to develop common understanding about the educational issues and needs facing La Frontera as it experiences massive cultural and economic change; to foster a binationally shared vision for the education and well-being of the region's children and youth; and to begin the process of developing comprehensive, binational plans to fulfill that vision. The Border Colloquy is sponsored by the Southwest Educational Development Laboratory and funded by the Office of Educational Research and Improvement of the U.S. Department of Education. (See Chapter 11 for more information about this effort.)

Other Recent Developments

The convention between Mexico and the United States for the avoidance of double taxation stipulates that contributions made by a citizen or resident of the United States to a Mexican organization operated for scientific, literary, or educational purposes shall be treated as tax deductible, and vice versa for a Mexican contribution made to a U.S. institution. Through this provision, resources are made available that were once difficult to direct toward education (Luke, 1994).

This is an important step forward, since it allows the involvement of the private sector. A useful further development would be the creation of an umbrella organization to work exclusively on establishing educational exchanges. Schools in both countries currently are conducting educational exchanges; now is an appropriate time to convert those isolated efforts into ongoing arrangements to strengthen and perpetuate the existing linkages.

Conclusions

The teacher exchange summer program and the teacher training summer institute of the Binational Initiative serve as a great challenge for our Hispanic teachers and all other teachers who provide direct services to Hispanic students. OBEMLA, the Secretary of Public Education of Mexico, state education agencies, local education agencies, and institutions of higher education have accepted that challenge to work together to have teachers prepared to help Mexican, Mexican American, and Hispanic students to improve their high school graduation rate.

The Binational Initiative between the U.S. Department of Education and the Secretaríat of Public Education of Mexico, through the Memorandum of Understanding and its annexes, has sparked a number of activities, meetings, and conferences. These activities in turn have produced a strong current of collaboration and understanding, not only at the federal and state levels in both countries, but also in the education community.

Institutions of higher education, administrators, professors, and students are now engaged in programs that study and promote the languages and cultures of the United States and Mexico. Other programs give Mexican and U.S. teachers the opportunity to obtain bachelor's degrees or to update their bilingual teaching skills. Through these efforts, Hispanic students stand a better chance of receiving a more appropriate education, which eventually should help decrease the Hispanic dropout rate and increase the rate of high school completion by Hispanics.

Besides advancing the cause of increasing the supply of bilingual teachers, the Binational Initiative supports the goals of President Clinton's Executive Order on Educational Excellence for Hispanic Americans, which specifically orders an increase in opportunities for Hispanic Americans to participate in and benefit from federal education programs and in their progress toward the achievement of the National Education Goals and other standards of educational accomplishment (Clinton, 1994).

The time has come for specific actions to be taken to improve the education that we provide to our Mexican, Mexican American, and Hispanic students. The NAFTA treaty and the Memorandum of Understanding in Education between the United States and Mexico have provided the appropriate avenues.

References

Cavazos, L., & Bartlett-Díaz, M. (1990). Memorandum of Understanding On Education, Nuevo Laredo, Mexico, August 17, 1990. Washington, DC: U.S. Department of Education.

Clinton, W. J. (1994, February 24). Education excellence for Hispanic Americans, Executive Order 12900. *Presidential documents, 59*(7). Washington, DC: Office of the Federal Register.

Feistritzer, Emily C. (1986) Education vital signs: Teachers. *American School Board Journal, 173* (10), A12-A16.

Figueroa, R. A., & Garcia, E. (1994). Issues in testing students from culturally and linguistically diverse backgrounds. *Multicultural Education, 2* (1), 10-19.

Fleischam, H. L., & Hopstock, P. J. (1993). *Descriptive study of services to limited-English-proficient students.* Study prepared for the Office of the Under Secretary, U.S. Department of Education.

Impine-Hernandez, M. S. (Ed.) (1989). *Colloquium to strengthen educational personnel training programs: Training educational personnel to work with language minority populations.* Washington, DC: Georgetown University Press. (ERIC Document Reproduction Service No. ED 347 124)

Lara, S., & Varisco de García, N. (1995). Report to OBEMLA's director on second U.S./Mexico symposium on professional development, Cibeles Convention Center, Ciudad Juárez, Mexico, September 14-15, 1995. Washington, DC: U.S. Department of Education.

Luke, G. (1994). The educational implications of NAFTA (an edited transcript of a symposium sponsored by the United States Coalition for Education for All, January 14, 1994). Washington, DC: Mexican Cultural Institute.

Richey, R. (1995). *Report to OBEMLA's director on the U.S./ Mexico Symposium on Curriculum Perspectives: Challenges for the Future.* (Austin, Texas, November 9-10, 1994). Washington, DC: U.S. Department of Education, Office of Bilingual Education and Minority Languages Affairs.

Riley, R. & Zedillo, E. (1993). *Annex Three to the Memorandum of Understanding on Education Between the Government of the United States of American and the Government of Mexico.* Activities for 1993-1994. Washington, DC: U.S. Department of Education.

Southwest Educational Development Laboratory. (1994). *Imagining La Frontera: SEDL's Border Colloquy.* Austin, TX: Author.

Tinajeros, J., & Lozano, E. (1994, September 26, draft). *Binational Initiative for Educational Development.* El Paso: The University of Texas at El Paso.

Tinsman, S. (1994). *Report of the U.S.-Mexico Senior Education Officials' Meeting, October 4-5, 1993.* Washington, DC: U.S. Department of Education, Office of Intergovernmental and Interagency Affairs.

U.S. Bureau of the Census. (1994). *We asked . . . you told us. Language spoken at home.* Washington, DC: Author. (ERIC Document Reproduction Service No. ED 382 016)

U.S. Department of Education and Secretaría de Educación Pública de México. (1991). *Border Conference on Education, Ciudad Juárez and El Paso, Texas, 1991.* Washington, DC: U.S. Department of Education.

U.S. General Accounting Office. (1994). *Hispanics' schooling: Risk factors for dropping out and barriers to resuming education (report to Congressional Requesters).* Washington, DC: Author, Program Evaluation and Methodology Div. (ERIC Document Reproduction Service No. ED 374 196)

CHAPTER 11

Exploring Binational Educational Issues: A Report from the Border Colloquy Project

BETTY MACE-MATLUCK AND MARTHA BOETHEL
SOUTHWEST EDUCATIONAL DEVELOPMENT LABORATORY

This article describes the binational concerns that have led the Southwest Educational Development Laboratory (SEDL), one of 10 regional educational laboratories funded by the U.S. Department of Education's Office of Educational Research and Improvement, to establish the Border Colloquy Project. This project focuses on the quality and accessibility of education in the shared border regions of the states of Texas, New Mexico, Coahuila, Nuevo León, Tamaulipas, and Chihuahua. The chapter further describes the Border Colloquy Project's major activities and findings to date, and outlines plans for ongoing cooperative activities among educators in the region known as la frontera.

Background: Issues Facing *La Frontera*

La frontera—the region spanning the boundary between the United States and Mexico—is centered on the most populated international border in the world. More than 16.5 million people live along it. Increasingly, the interactions among these people are leading to overlapping and highly interdependent regional economies, societies, and cultures.

The North American Free Trade Agreement (NAFTA) has redefined the economic significance of a 2,000-mile political line on the map, while migration and cultural influences are helping to smear that line into a regional blur. Tens of thousands of people cross the border each day; many move back and forth between homes in Mexico and jobs, even schools, in the United States. Among those moving North are many who eventually work or settle permanently in communities as far afield as the states of Washington, Illinois, Michigan, and New York.

With immigration a central fact of life along *la frontera,* consideration of border issues carries a huge weight of emotional and political baggage, not only for the region's residents but for U.S. and Mexican citizens throughout the two countries. Many Americans consider *the border* to be a fence, a barrier designed to maintain stability in the country's population, economy, and services (although the gates through this fence tend to open or close depending on U.S. demand for cheap labor). For its part, Mexico considers emigration a drain on the country's resources; the government has enacted measures designed to protect its language and cultures from its larger, sometimes overbearing northern neighbor (Alexander-Kasparik, 1993).

Many border experts believe, however, that NAFTA will serve as a catalyst for the creation of a region that spans current boundaries, a region neither *here* nor *there,* in which neighboring nations remove rather than construct barriers, in which people move freely and the infrastructures that support them—economic, governmental, cultural, and educational systems and services—are compatible and cooperative. The border, then, is conceived not as a line with *us* on one side and *them* on the other but as the central feature in a zone of cooperation, and *la frontera* becomes not a sharp edge between peoples but a community with its own energy, direction, and future.

Although this image of community may seem like idealism or fantasy, the present reality is that territories along the border, such as the "twin cities" of El Paso-Juárez or Laredo-Nuevo Laredo, are already as closely bound as Siamese twins joined at the hip. This interdependency is destined to increase as NAFTA's provisions are phased in over the next 16 years.

With migration and interdependence as givens, the questions that arise are not *shoulds* or *ifs* but *hows.* Some of the biggest *hows* relate to education, which must address a number of complex issues, such as the following:

Poverty and unemployment. These are serious problems on both sides of the border. Thousands of people live in *colonias,* without basic services such as running water. Many families perform migrant labor, moving with the seasons and earning subsistence wages. Health care and other needed social services are largely unavailable. School-based clinics and provision of social services through the schools are slowly gaining favor in the United States, but they are "still talked about more than they are offered" (Alexander-Kasparik, 1994, p. 17). Mexico, on the other hand, provides for health care through its Social Security system; problems there focus less on equity of coverage than on the general inadequacy of resources to address the tremendous need. How can schools on both sides of the border offer poor and transient students the highest quality education? How can schools interact with social service providers to assure all students access to the basic necessities that they must have—food, shelter, health, and safety—in order to focus on learning? How can poor communities provide adequate resources for education?

Differing educational requirements, systems, and structures. Mexico and the United States have different educational requirements, systems, and structures. Contrary to popular perceptions in the United States, Mexico's requirements are sometimes more stringent than those in the United States. To graduate from *secundaría,* for example (*secundaría* encompasses the seventh through the ninth grades), a student must pass Algebra II, which is not required for a high school diploma in Texas (Southwest Educational Development Laboratory, 1994). Students who try to move from one system to the other face major obstacles; Mexican students entering U.S. schools, for example, are sometimes forced to re-take subjects they have already covered in Mexico. How can educational requirements, curricula, and other aspects of schooling be made compatible so that students who move from one system to another are not penalized?

Continuing migration of Mexican students to U.S. schools. U.S. schools will continue to receive students from Mexico; one fifth of all undocumented immigrants are estimated to be children under the age of 15. The challenge, then, is to serve these students—and the rest of the school population—effectively. The schools that have proved most effective in meeting the needs of Mexican immigrant students are schools that are effective in general. They typically "have high expectations for student achievement, cultivate parent involvement in the child's schooling, and display strong and progressive . . . instructional and organizational leadership" (Alexander-Kasparik, 1993, p. 8). In addition to general characteristics of effectiveness, these schools also take specific actions to support immigrant students.

> Such schools also typically value the student's home language and culture; recognize and give immigrant population concerns priority; conduct outreach in parents' home language; train staff to understand and help meet immigrant needs; mainstream immigrant students in

> classes with English-speaking students; and make placement decisions with appropriate assessments and expert consultation (Alexander-Kasparik, 1993, p. 8).

How can we assure that such effective school practices become the norm, rather than the exception?

Teacher training. Training and licensing requirements have been strengthened in both countries in recent years. However, there are still significant differences, and little or no reciprocity or recognition of credentials from one country to the other. Exchange programs are limited and short-term, and those that do exist "currently lean toward the United States for credentialing with no promise of reciprocity" (Alexander-Kasparik, 1993, p. 7). At the same time, too few U.S. teachers are sufficiently trained in bilingual education or English as a second language. How can teacher education and in-service training be made compatible and of consistently high quality, and educators' credentials be honored in both countries?

Language. Many believe that the full potential of this region cannot be realized until all its citizens are bilingual. Bilingual education is still debated in the United States, yet even certified bilingual teachers may not have mastered the levels of Spanish they need to be able to teach in Mexico, or to work most effectively with Mexican students in U.S. schools. Spanish-speaking students in the United States are often precluded from learning other subject matter before they learn English. Developmental bilingual education, often referred to as "two-way bilingual programs" or "dual-language programs," are designed to promote bilingualism among both majority- and minority-language students. In this enrichment bilingual education approach, children learn a second language through subject matter instruction in that language. Most importantly, the students are able to learn a second language and to continue to develop their first language skills. How can schools effectively provide developmental bilingual education for all students in the region, so that they can become fluent in both Spanish and English without any slowdown in content-area learning? And how can teachers receive the language training they may need?

Government sovereignty. Variations in federal, state, and local government structures and policies present barriers to cooperation on both sides of the border. How can governments retain the autonomy they need, yet provide policies, structures, and resources to support multinational initiatives?

Participants in SEDL's Border Colloquy Project are considering these issues and more as they plot a path from current problems to an imagined future. Although participants agree that the challenges to *la frontera* are immense, they also feel strongly that the region is a resource, not a liability, and that with cooperation and good will, these challenges can be met.

The Border Colloquy Project

SEDL's Border Colloquy Project focuses on *la frontera*—the region along the boundary between the United States and The Republic of Mexico—with specific attention to the shared border regions of the states of Texas, New Mexico, Coahuila, Nuevo León, Tamaulipas, and Chihuahua. The Border Colloquy Project is designed to

- develop common understandings about the educational issues and needs facing *la frontera* as it experiences massive cultural and economic change;
- foster an internationally shared vision for the education and well-being of the region's children and youth; and
- encourage the development and use of comprehensive, binational plans to fulfill that vision.

The Border Colloquy Project was initiated in March 1994, after SEDL's Board of Directors targeted the educational needs of *la frontera* as an area of special concern. SEDL has a long history of involvement in border and bilingual, multicultural educational concerns; this work was a logical extension of institutional efforts.

Phase 1 of the project, which extended through November 1994, consisted primarily of a series of seven planning and information-sharing meetings that culminated in the development of an unprecedented binational vision statement for education in *la frontera*. Phase 2 began December 1, 1994, and will extend, at a minimum, through November 30, 1997. This phase of the project focuses on the development and implementation of action plans and on fostering the cooperative relationships that will be essential to effective implementation. SEDL is providing assistance and is facilitating interaction among educational communities on both sides of the border through brokering and networking activities.

Border Colloquy Meetings

The meetings conducted during Phase 1 of the project were designed to culminate in the creation of a vision statement that reflects a shared, binational perspective on the educational future of *la frontera* and its inhabitants. Meeting participants also began to consider elements of the action plans that are being fleshed out and implemented during Phase 2. To complete these tasks, SEDL first sponsored a series of five regional meetings, followed by a meeting in Monterrey, Mexico, with representatives of the departments of education in each of the Mexican states of Chihuahua, Coahuila, Nuevo León, and Tamaulipas. Finally, SEDL sponsored a culminating meeting in Austin, Texas, whose participants were drawn from each of the six preceding meetings.

Regional meetings. The five regional meetings brought together educators and community representatives from specific areas within *la frontera*; they were held as follows:

- McAllen, Texas, April 18-19, 1994, cohosted by the Region I[1] Education Service Center, with 14 participants plus SEDL staff and consultants;
- El Paso, Texas, May 9-10, 1994, cohosted by the Region XIX Education Service Center, with 27 participants;
- Las Cruces, New Mexico, May 10-11, 1994, cohosted by the Las Cruces School District #2, with 27 participants;
- Ciudad Juárez, June 9-10, 1994, cohosted by the Universidad Pedagógica Nacional, Cd. Juárez, with 80 participants; and
- Reynosa, June 15-16, 1994, cohosted by El Centro de Actualización de Magisterio de Nuevo Laredo, with 33 participants.

Participants included students, teachers, principals, bilingual supervisors, and superintendents; staff from state and regional education agencies; legislators and legislative staff members; business, church, and community leaders; university faculty; health and human services providers; and immigration officials.

Participants in the regional meetings were asked to imagine what education should be like by the year 2010, when NAFTA's provisions are to be fully implemented. They first described their image of the ideal community of *la frontera* in general, then focused specifically on schooling, develop-

---

[1]The state of Texas is organized into 20 Education Service Center (ESC) regions. Although working closely with the Texas Education Agency, the centers are independent entities with the responsibility of serving public schools within their defined geographic areas. All ESCs are expected to provide services that support student achievement in the districts within their boundaries, although the ESCs differ in terms of the number and characteristics of member districts.

The ESCs work closely with districts to provide technical assistance in areas of accreditation and curriculum, professional development, and the implementation of PEIMS (Program Evaluation and Improvement Management System), a state-level data system. The ESCs also provide districts with instructional media, data processing services, and assistance in program improvement in areas such as bilingual education, special education, gifted and talented education, and programs for at-risk (of dropping out) students. Some ESCs also provide services in connection with Title I, migrant education, adult education, and similar programs.

ing a vision statement to picture what education should accomplish within that community. Finally, participants outlined the work that must be undertaken—changes in attitudes, values, systems, and services—in order to achieve their vision.

The Monterrey meeting. The Monterrey meeting differed somewhat from the previous five regional meetings. Held on July 21-22, and co-hosted by the Universidad de Monterrey (UDEM), it included representatives from the Secretaries of Education in each of the four Mexican border states of Chihuahua, Coahuila, Nuevo León, and Tamaulipas, along with UDEM faculty and SEDL staff and consultants. The purposes of this meeting were to review learnings from each of the five regional meetings, to identify related activities that are already planned or underway in each of the four states, and to set priorities for cooperative action.

To prepare for the meeting, a group of UDEM faculty members reviewed the summary reports from the five regional colloquies; they presented their analysis of the colloquies as a basis for discussion. After their presentation, participants divided into small groups by state to address two questions: What activities or processes already exist in your state that address the concerns raised in the regional colloquies? And what areas of concern do you believe are most important? Finally, participants divided into mixed-state groups to consider the identified priorities and to add other areas of concern that might have been overlooked.

The Austin meeting. The Austin meeting, held August 1-2 at SEDL headquarters in Austin, Texas, brought together 38 representatives from the previous six meetings. Participants reviewed the vision statements that had been created at the regional meetings and worked to incorporate their ideas into a single, binational vision statement that could serve as a guide to cooperative action within *la frontera*. Participants also began working to develop action plans outlining concrete steps to be taken in order to help actualize their vision.

Findings from the Border Colloquy Meetings

In response to the charge to imagine what conditions in *la frontera* might be like by the year 2010, participants at the five regional meetings projected massive changes, and for the most part equated such change with opportunity, imagining that a changing economic climate will help to produce the resources needed to transform the region. They cautioned, however, that it will be essential to maintain a focus on equality and the well-being of people and the environment. UDEM faculty members summarized their concern this way: "We want to be competitive and productive, but at the same time we look for social equity, respect for human beings, and opportunities for people to be successful."

The border region in the year 2010. In considering what *la frontera* might be like by the year 2010, participants in the regional meetings echoed common themes: economic development that brings with it massive changes in people, cultures, language, resources, and community infrastructures; and the need to assure a continuing focus on human and moral values, with an emphasis on respect for cultural traditions and beliefs. Specific comments included, for example, the following:

> *We will see the attitude that the river is to be used, not just to be crossed.*
>
> *The region will be virtually self-sufficient and consequently able to satisfy the diverse demands of different sectors of its economy.*
>
> *If present tendencies continue, we will have a conflictive and asymmetrical border. However, if tendencies change—and here education plays an important role—the border of the year 2010 could be an integrated, dynamic region with a high standard of living.*
>
> *We believe that we will have a cultural mixture which will affect our language, art, customs, and other facets of both cultures. This "hybrid" culture will be neither a cultural integration nor the submission of one culture under another.*
>
> *There ought to be a way we can cross gently into each other's lives.*

The primary difference among these regional voices was that participants in the two Mexico meetings—in Ciudad Juárez and Reynosa—expressed a more cautious optimism about the anticipated changes. They spoke more in terms of what "should" happen rather than what is likely to happen, and emphasized that current problems will not disappear quickly:

> *There should be a sharing of knowledge, technology, and culture between the United States and Mexico without losing cultural identity.*
>
> *We should get rid of the belief that our intellectual potential depends on whether we come from one or the other side of the border. We must free ourselves from old prejudices and mistaken ideas.*
>
> *We should stop thinking about the communities on both sides of the border as being independent from each other.* 'La frontera' *is a single community.*

Participants at all the meetings described *la frontera* in the next century as an economically and culturally diverse, dynamic, and cosmopolitan region. They expect the divisions between the United States and Mexico to blur somewhat; participants in the U.S. meetings described a greater blurring of national boundaries than did participants from Mexico. All generally described the relatively free movement across the border not only of goods but of people, ideas, resources, and services. Some anticipate the creation of a regional government or oversight agency that spans national boundaries. Participants see tremendous population growth, leading to the need for improved infrastructures and human services—improved, high-tech transportation and communication; basic facilities such as water, electricity, and sewage; and services such as health and education. All groups perceive technology as increasingly important both to the economy and to education. Participants also were united in a focus on the environment; while some see increased opportunities for "clean" industry, others expressed concern that current environmental problems will increase.

Participants described an open, multicultural society in which bilingualism is an essential skill. However, every group expressed, in some form, the conviction—and the concern—that, no matter how global the economy or cosmopolitan the population, the inhabitants of *la frontera* will not lose their individual cultural heritage and values; the region will be characterized by "integration without erasing cultural differences, but rather supporting them." There will be a continuing concern for equality and individual well-being.

Education in *la frontera*. Participants in the regional meetings were generally in agreement about the kind of education that will be needed in *la frontera*. They described an educational system that is an integral part of community life. Two different groups used the phrase "full-service schools" to describe the concept of schools working with other community agencies to provide a full spectrum of services for students and their families—child care, parent education, health services, adult training, and the like. Specific comments included the following:

The quality of the school systems on both sides of the border would be equal.

Open the school from its isolated condition and engage it with the life of the community on both sides of the border.

We conceive education as an effective means for equalization, mobilization, and transformation.

We totally will reject failure in our schools.

We need an international set of standards. That would mean raising our standards, especially at the elementary level, to those of the Mexican system. Standards and mastery become the key, not grade levels.

Our schools [will be] the central focus of the community, providing child-centered, comprehensive educational, health, and human services.

Education will need to prepare students for both work and citizenship; schooling will include a strong vocational focus, but also will impart values, teaching about students' own cultural traditions and encouraging respect for others. All students will need to become bilingual; technology will be integrated into instruction at all levels. Progress through school will be based on concept mastery rather than on grade levels; students will be able to move freely from school to school as their needs dictate.

To support this kind of education in *la frontera*, rules, policies, and resources will need to change. All participants anticipate greater cooperation and exchange between the educational systems in the United States and Mexico; some expect the creation of a binational, regional governing board. Educational standards will need to be uniformly high. Accreditation, teacher certification, and student entry and exit requirements will need to be coordinated. At the same time, almost every group noted the need to maintain local flexibility, so that local school districts can tailor their offerings to meet specific community needs.

Faculty from the Universidad de Monterrey, after analyzing the reports of each of the five regional meetings, identified elements of curricular change that would support economic growth and bicultural understandings while helping to maintain each country's identity and cultural and moral values. In their presentation at the Monterrey meeting, they identified six major elements:

- "human development," which includes a focus on respect for oneself, family, and society as well as on an integrated, humanist education;
- "the development of teaching-learning models for a bicultural environment," which involves "a personalized education that would use different educational models according to each student's learning pace";
- instruction in both Spanish and English, so that all students on both sides of the border will become fluent in both languages; the presenters noted, "Two neighbors that want to work together have to understand each other";
- the development of multimedia instructional materials, using technology to promote cultural exchanges and interactions;
- teacher training, in language particularly but also in other curricular areas; better training, the presenters noted, should help teachers become better valued and respected in their communities; and

- administrator training, with a focus on new approaches to managing the educational system; new concepts that focus on "bottom-up" decision-making hold promise for building new understandings.

Concerns and Priorities

Participants in the regional meetings described the kinds of changes they feel must occur in order to assure a productive future for *la frontera* and all of its inhabitants. They characterized their concerns in terms of changes in perceptions and attitudes, knowledge, resources, and binational cooperation.

Changing perceptions and attitudes. Participants in all five regional meetings focused intensively on misperceptions about the border region and on racial and ethnic stereotypes, describing these as major barriers to be overcome. Participants described public perceptions in the United States regarding Mexico and the border region as highly negative and seriously inaccurate; Mexico and its people are too often considered only as a drain on the United States, which overlooks the richness of its languages and culture, the resources it has to offer, and the quality of many of its educational policies.

Participants focused strongly on perceptions about language and language differences. One misperception among many Americans, they noted, is "about the superiority of English to Spanish." "We must accept differences in languages," one U.S. group stated; similarly, a participant in one of the Mexico meetings said, "It is time for some organizations and people from the United States to stop being intolerant and accept the use of our language in their communities."

Participants also pointed out that the United States and Mexico are economically interdependent, but there is a general perception, as a participant in a U.S. meeting stated, "that Mexico needs us and we don't need them." Related to this is the misperception of the border area as "economically deprived" rather than "economically viable."

Finally, participants in three of the five groups noted that people must alter their attitudes about change itself: "We have to get beyond seeing change as a problem all the time; we need to move people to where they embrace change."

Filling gaps in knowledge. Participants feel that residents in both Mexico and the United States need to learn more about each other's history, cultures, and educational and social systems:

> *We must get to know the border and become familiar with the cultural patterns of both countries.*

We need knowledge regarding the ways in which both sides of the border maintain social, cultural, and economic relationships.

They generally feel that such learning can best occur through working together. Some groups also called for comparative studies focused on public schools and curriculum; one group spoke of the need for greater knowledge about "how to work with diversity."

Filling resource gaps. Participants see a substantial need for increased resources. The greatest problem, one group noted, lies with "seemingly insurmountable gaps related to federal funding" and the differences in the two countries' relative economic power. Alleviation of poverty is a major priority for most; so is funding to make good education accessible to all. One group detailed the need for increased teacher salaries, opportunities for teachers' professional advancement, funds for teacher preparation, and provisions for better educational facilities, technology, and materials.

Extending binational cooperation. Participants feel that strong leadership is needed at federal, regional, and state levels to accomplish change in *la frontera*. The governments of both Mexico and the United States need to develop cooperative arrangements that provide for common resources and regulations, while at the same time allowing for greater local autonomy and flexibility for the border region. Most critically, governments need to facilitate the sharing and equalization of financial resources; one group suggested moving toward common financial and currency systems, following the model of the European community.

One group focused in some detail on the need for cooperative efforts to address the environmental problems that have been raised by the development of heavy industry along the border. The border region needs to be able to attract "clean" industry; participants noted, "We need a notion of economic development which could include the promotion of *frontera* art, culture, music, and agriculture—not just heavy industry."

Discussions of binational cooperation focused primarily on education. Cooperation in education should focus on development of systems for international accreditation; exchanges of teachers, students, and materials; a focus on bilingual, multicultural education, including teacher training in these areas; and shared research. Some participants suggested the creation of "a similar educational infrastructure on both sides of the border through a common fund" and/or a regional board of education.

A Common Vision for Education

A major goal of the Border Colloquy Project's Phase 1 activities was the creation of a common vision regarding the future of education in the border region, a vision that can guide planners, policymakers, and practitioners from both countries as they consider the purposes and practice of schooling in *la frontera*. To accomplish this task, SEDL first asked participants in the five regional colloquies to draft vision statements based on their discussions about the future of the border region. These five statements then provided a base from which participants in the regionwide Austin meeting—who included representatives from each of the regional colloquies and the Monterrey meeting—worked to develop a final, binational vision statement reflecting the group's shared goals.

Though they were phrased differently, and though some were composed in Spanish and some in English, the vision statements developed in the five regional meetings all reflect remarkably similar goals and concerns. All focus on the "holistic well-being" of students, on assuring that all children have the opportunity to grow up as productive, fulfilled members of society. That society, according to all five vision statements, will be "bicultural" or "multicultural," changing and dynamic. Most of the vision statements picture a close relationship between school and community; according to one statement, "the educational process will integrate school and community"; another states that "schools are the central focus of the community."

The vision statements also focus on character, dignity, and moral and democratic values. The goal of education, it is clear, is to prepare students not only vocationally and intellectually but morally and culturally as well. Education will offer "academic excellence, moral values, bicultural understanding and respect, and preparation for participation in work and society," enabling students to be "dynamic members of a multicultural society." Two of the vision statements address the concept of lifelong learning; one refers to "comprehensive educational, health, and human services."

Participants in the Austin meeting carried each of these concepts into the development of a unified vision statement. This vision statement—drafted, revised, and approved by educational and community leaders representing six of the border states in the United States and Mexico—is, to SEDL's knowledge, the first of its kind, a symbol of the movement toward cooperation and mutuality among the inhabitants of *la frontera*.

Binational Vision Statement
Developed by Participants in the SEDL Border Colloquy
Austin, Texas, August 1-2, 1994

We in the Mexico-United States border region, looking toward education in the year 2010, consider our children to be our most precious resource. Therefore, every individual has the right to equal educational opportunities through which she/he will develop self-

esteem, dignity, cultural pride, understanding of others, and the capacity to become a positive, contributing member of society.

To respond to the needs of this international, multilingual, multicultural community, we will have a binational educational system that is open, flexible, integrated, of high quality, and adapted to the region's common needs in an atmosphere of community. Recognizing the family as critical in the child's development, this system will offer health and human services and family education. It will include staff development and programs teaching environmental improvement, international understanding, cultural and moral traditions and values, and the skills to compete in a global economic society. It will use technology resources and multicultural, multilingual strategies.

Making the Vision Real: Initiating Cooperative Work

The SEDL Border Colloquy Project is designed to move from ideals to action. After the establishment of a common vision for *la frontera*, the next tasks are to consider initiatives that may be already underway and to develop plans and networks of support for those plans.

Existing initiatives. Participants in both the Monterrey and Austin meetings outlined some of the efforts already underway that support elements of the binational vision for education in *la frontera*. Their reports are summarized below.

The Monterrey meeting. In Monterrey, representatives of the Secretaries of Education from the four border states of Chihuahua, Coahuila, Nuevo León, and Tamaulipas reported on current activities in their states. Participants from Chihuahua noted that interactive, multimedia approaches to education are essential tools for helping children to learn and to develop pride and respect, and a focus on this area is a strong priority for the state. The need for instructional materials "is fundamental in teaching"; for that reason, the state is developing a plan by which every teacher in the state can learn to work with computers to access the teaching materials they need. There is also a concern to expand student instruction using computerized programs; courses in mathematics, Spanish, and Mexican history already have been developed.

Representatives from Coahuila focused on two general areas of concern: education for the development of individual and social capabilities, and the application of science and technology to improve production. Specific initiatives that address these broad areas include a focus on educational quality. To support quality in education, the Foundation for Educational Excellence is designed to "reward the effective classroom performance of teachers on every educational level." Another effort is the consolidation of a research group at the Universidad Autónoma de Coahuila, whose research includes binational projects. One study examined the acquisition of Spanish and mathematics skills by children in the border area (Núñez López, 1994). Participants spoke in detail about the importance of educational research, noting that "educational attention has to be based on research, which is the starting point for decision making."

Representatives from Nuevo León identified bilingualism as "the number one problem," noting that the state has implemented a program for fourth, fifth, and sixth graders that reaches almost 8,000 children. A second concern is with the quality of the educational system; here, the state receives support from specialists in New Mexico and Texas, who participate in teacher training conferences. A third priority is teacher training in Spanish, mathematics, and science; in this area, the state has initiated Saturday programs focused on these subjects. Quality language instruction is also a concern; initiatives are being tried in which students work on their English skills using a computer center and special software. Technology is a final concern; some schools already are equipped with parabolic antennas, allowing for distance education and teacher access to new resources.

Representatives from Tamaulipas noted that the government in that state is supporting a number of initiatives, including a movement "towards the rescue of cultural values." One program that is being upgraded is "school for parents," which provides education regarding child care, health and hygiene, and drug and crime prevention. In terms of teaching-learning models, there is some exploration of "dynamic school" and "specialized teaching" principles. Language instruction is a somewhat weak area, because English is considered a "foreign language" rather than an essential second language; however, one promising pilot program is in place. There are also teacher and administrator training initiatives, including a border pilot program allowing for teacher exchanges. Participants noted that the various administrator training initiatives need to be better integrated.

The Austin meeting. In Austin, Dr. Roberto Zamora, Executive Assistant to the Texas Commissioner of Education, noted that the Texas Education Agency and the Mexican Secretaríat of Education have worked cooperatively for many years. He described a range of activities that have occurred over the past three years, including international conferences and seminars focused on the U.S. and Mexican educational systems, bilingual education, English as a second language, and instructional strategies and approaches; exchange agreements that include training programs for educators; and research activities.

Dr. Alberto Zamora, Associate Superintendent of the Learning Services Division of the New Mexico State Department of Education, noted that the

New Mexico legislature has allocated funds specifically for improving communication between Mexico and the United States. New Mexico has also helped to sponsor and participate in international conferences and has developed agreements with the states of Nuevo León and Guanajuato focused on educational exchange and improvements.

Prof. Isidro Martínez Duarte, Director General of the Secretaría de Educación y Cultura for the State of Chihuahua, described a cooperative effort between his state and El Paso Community College to teach English to elementary school students in Ciudad Juárez. The use of technology in education is also a priority in Chihuahua, with several initiatives underway in that area.

Lic. Temístocles Núñez López, Director de Enlace y Vinculación con Instituciones de Educación Superior de la Secretaría de Educación de Coahuila, described cooperative research projects conducted with Laredo State University focused on values and learning acquisition in children from both sides of the border. He also described the project focused on educational quality that was mentioned at the Monterrey meeting and noted the importance of the border governors' conferences to the furtherance of educational improvements.

From Tamaulipas, Ing. Oscar E. Guerra Corza, Director de Educación Media, Superior y Extraescolar, Secretaría de Educación, Cultura y Deportes, highlighted the formation of an education commission as part of the meetings of the border governors. The commission's purpose is specifically to identify and address border issues.

New initiatives emerging from the Border Colloquy. At the Austin meeting in August 1994, participants divided into regional work groups and began outlining action plans for cooperative work. Since then, these groups have been moving on a number of projects, with facilitation and, in some cases, resources provided by SEDL staff.

The *El Paso-Cd. Juárez-Las Cruces* work group has begun a series of cross-border seminars through which educators in the two countries can share their knowledge, experience, and concerns. The seminars are structured so that, in the first meeting, educators from Cd. Juárez speak to U.S. educators about Mexico's educational system; a few weeks later, the roles are reversed. Work group members are also arranging for cross-border visits to schools and educational agencies. The work group has been invited by the Secretary of Education in Chihuahua to learn in detail about the state's education agency and how it works. As a result of this exploration, the work group has scheduled a meeting to explore the possibility of a joint summer institute for school administrators. Finally, the work group is planning a technology fair in which representatives from Cd. Juárez, El Paso, and Las Cruces will share examples of technology uses in education.

The *Las Cruces-Deming* work group is pursuing the idea of a cross-national school for the communities of Columbus, New Mexico, and Palomas, Chihuahua. Work group members and SEDL staff have met with representatives from the Columbus, Palomas, and Deming schools to investigate the feasibility of such a plan and also have talked with state education agency staffs about the idea. In February 1995, the Chihuahua Secretary of Education, New Mexico Commissioner of Education, SEDL staff, work group members, and representatives from the Los Alamos National Laboratory met in Santa Fe to explore plans and discuss policy issues.

The Tamaulipas/Texas area work group, with support from SEDL staff, conducted a joint meeting in October 1994 with representatives from the Reynosa, Monterrey, and McAllen meetings attending. Participants in this meeting decided that their first step would be to involve a broader set of voices in the determination of activities needed in the area. They have arranged for and conducted a series of local forums in four sites to obtain local input for regional action plans.

In addition to assisting with regional work group activities, SEDL staff have formed a *Policy/Planning Advisory Group* for the project, with representation from each of the state-level educational agencies involved in the project and from each of the six regional information sharing meetings that were conducted during Phase 1 of the project. The group's purposes are to consider policy issues as they arise in the course of project activities, to facilitate local group interaction, and to serve in an advisory capacity to SEDL staff. The advisory group's first meeting was held in Austin in late February 1995, with cosponsorship by SEDL and the Texas Education Agency.

Plans for the Future

It is SEDL's goal, provided federal funding priorities and other circumstances allow, to continue the Border Colloquy Project at least through November 30, 1997. Based on input from meeting participants and educational issues outlined in the literature, it is clear that comprehensive change will take time, and that there is much to be done. Projects that SEDL staff hope to facilitate through the Border Colloquy Project include

- development of a model for successful teacher-administrator exchange;
- support for the use of educational technology to develop the concept of bilingualism;
- the pursuit and development of models for binational schools;
- efforts to align certification and accreditation; and
- joint research, including a comparative study of the two countries' educational systems.

Conclusions

With the sustained involvement and commitment of participants from the Border Colloquy meetings, SEDL hopes to establish a foundation from which educational systems, policies, and services can be adapted to the future needs of *la frontera*. However, the barriers are not insubstantial. Public resources are scarce in both countries. Adapting laws and policies to accommodate binational cooperation is virtually unprecedented. And attitudes among the public, in both countries, tend at times to be negative and suspicious. As one regional meeting participant noted, "This reality, this beautiful reality that we talked about creating this morning, we're going to have to drag some people along kicking and screaming all the way."

The gap between planning and implementation is also a challenge. As participants pointed out again and again, the kinds of discussion fostered by the Border Colloquy are essential, but similar meetings have been held in the past, without significant change. Follow-up action among all involved is essential. Only if everyone involved is committed to action will the promise of *la frontera*'s imagined future be realized:

The year 2010 is not far away; we must start working today.

Note: This article draws substantially from a report on the Border Colloquy Project, *Imagining La Frontera: SEDL's Border Colloquy* (Austin: Southwest Educational Development Laboratory, 1994). Information in the section titled "Background: Issues Facing *La Frontera*" was drawn primarily from two articles by Rosalind Alexander-Kasparik (Ed.): "Border Issues in Education (Part 1)," *SEDLETTER*, September-December 1993, pp. 2-18; and "Border Issues in Education (Part 2)," *SEDLETTER*, January-April 1994, pp. 2-22. Reprints of both documents are available from SEDL, 211 East 7th Street, Austin, Texas, 78701. Telephone: 512/476-6861.

References

Alexander-Kasparik, R. (Ed.). (1993, September-December). Special report: Border issues in education (Part 1). *SEDLETTER*, 2-18. Austin, TX: Southwest Educational Development Laboratory.

Alexander-Kasparik, R. (Ed.). (1994, January-April). Special report: Border issues in education (Part 2). *SEDLETTER*, 2-22. Austin, TX: Southwest Educational Development Laboratory.

Núñez López, T. (1994, August). Presentation at the SEDL Border Colloquy Project Meeting, Austin, TX.

Southwest Educational Development Laboratory. (1994). *Imagining la frontera: SEDL's Border Colloquy*. Austin, TX: Author.

CHAPTER 12

Binational Health Care for Migrants: The Health Data Exchange Pilot Project and The Binational Health Data Transfer System

CONTRIBUTORS ON BEHALF OF THE TASK FORCE:[1]
HÉCTOR EDUARDO VELASCO MONDRAGÓN, M.D.,
JOHNSON MARTIN, PH.D, AND HENRY STEVENSON-PEREZ, M.D.

As the economic integration of Mexico and the United States intensifies, so does the cross-migration of labor forces. Subsequently, when migrant workers or their family members become ill, health care is often disjointed and suboptimal. Binational health data exchange among providers of health care becomes essential. This demonstration project represents a vital step toward assessing health risk, epidemiologic surveillance, and assuring quality health care for mobile populations. The system is de-

---

[1]Written on behalf of the Binational Health Data Transfer Task Force, which includes Drs. Carlos Santos-Burgoa, Fernando Chacon-Sosa, Héctor Eduardo Velasco Mondragón and Jorge Oviedo of the Instituto Nacional de Salud Pública, Escuela de Salud Pública de México, Karen Mountain of the Migrant Clinicians Network, Drs. Joe Davis and Eric Svenkerud of Centers for Disease Control and Prevention, Drs. Marta Esquivel Arrona, Armando Pérez-Cabrera, Mario Bronfman, Fidencio Pedraza Magaña and Leticia Zamora Ramos of the Secretaría de Salud del Estado de Guanajuato, Edward Powers and Johnson Martin, Ph.D. of the Pennsylvania Department of Health, Olivia Carter-Pokras, Ph.D. of the Office of Minority Health, Henry Stevenson-Perez, M.D. of the National Institutes for Health, David Wall, Ph.D. and Lea Pellet, Ph.D. of Christopher Newport University, and David Much, Ph.D. of Muhlenberg College.

signed to test the technical, financial, legal, and political aspects of data sharing between the two countries. Demographic and clinical data on Mexican migrant patients are collected and made available to front-line health care providers in Mexico and in the United States. Data transfer concentrates on four tracer conditions of binational concern: sexually transmitted diseases, tuberculosis, leprosy, and hepatitis. This chapter contains details on the development of the data transfer system, including system objectives, system design, software and data entry procedures, data analysis, procedures to protect client confidentiality, and preliminary evaluation.

Introduction

Providers who offer health services to Mexican migrant workers in Guanajuato State, Mexico, and the Commonwealth of Pennsylvania, United States, often confront medical information gaps that preclude the prevention, diagnosis, and follow-up of disease exposure. Therefore, a binational task force comprising representatives from the United States and Mexico met throughout 1993 to discuss strategies to increase the coordination of care. The task force is composed of representatives from the Instituto Nacional de Salud Pública, Escuela de Salud Pública de México, Migrant Clinicians Network, Secretaría de Salud del Estado de Guanajuato, Pennsylvania Department of Health, Centers for Disease Control and Prevention, Office of Minority Health, National Institutes of Health, and Muhlenberg College. Their collective efforts are evidenced in the relationship that has been forged between Guanajuato and Pennsylvania over the last 2 years. More important, they have implemented a direct method by which Guanajuatan and Pennsylvanian providers can share demographic and clinical data on mutual clients. This demonstration system of data transfer is commonly referred to as the GUAPA (incorporating the first three letters of Guanajuato and the state abbreviation for Pennsylvania) Project. "Guapa" means handsome woman in Spanish and has made for a memorable project name. The background, design, impact, challenges, and vision of this pilot project are described in the following pages.

Background and Rationale for GUAPA

Over the last five centuries, two major global changes have occurred: the transition from isolation to communication and, subsequently, from communication to interdependence of countries. The joining of several countries into the European Community and the signing of the North

American Free Trade Agreement (NAFTA) are the latest evidences of globalization.

The expanded economic integration of Mexico and the United States will boost the already intensive exchange of travelers, workers, and goods. This exchange, in turn, will augment the import-export of infectious diseases; health risks will increase, creating the need for increased binational coordination of health services. Thus, health information exchange and joint database development between Mexico and the United States are strategic necessities of the post-NAFTA reality. Communication and coordination are vital steps toward health risk assessment, epidemiologic surveillance, and health care quality assurance for mobile populations.

Recent estimates have placed the special U.S. population of temporary agricultural residents at approximately 4.5 million persons per year (Oliveira & Cox, 1988). The geographic patterns of migration (commonly called "streams") have become well understood over the last 10 years by public health officials on both sides of the border. Moreover, it is known that the majority of these migrant workers do not participate in any established health care plan, either while in the United States or in Mexico (Knochenhaur, 1991). Perhaps more important, the health care problems faced by the population of largely male Mexican migrant workers in the United States reflect directly on the quality of life of their families who remain in Mexico. For example, migrating workers that acquire infectious diseases in the United States have a substantial likelihood of transmitting these diseases to their families upon their return to Mexico.

The migrant worker's health status, and thus, endurance of physical labor, has a profound socioeconomic impact on family members. It is estimated that approximately five individuals in Mexico are dependent on the resources sent by each Mexican farmworker in the United States (Velasco Mondragón, 1993). In the most extreme example, those workers who bring their families with them also expose their youngsters to the problems associated with the migratory lifestyle. For children, these include suboptimal vaccination, reduced monitoring of developmental milestones, increased injuries, and decreased access to care (Dever, 1991).

To date we have no uniform methodology for sharing information on a specific patient who migrates between states. There is a very real concern that, in the absence of a single-payer national health care plan, these "information islands" may actually worsen. The importance of and urgency for a coordinated system is underscored by considering some of the ramifications of inadequate and inaccessible health care: development of multidrug-resistant strains of Mycobacterium tuberculosis and the documented spread of tropical diseases such as malaria in both California and New Jersey (Brook, Genese, Bloland, Zucker, & Spitalny, 1994). Thus, health data transfer that is accurate and "real time" (available immediately for patient treatment) is no longer just a technological nicety but rather a medical necessity in the health care management of the U.S. migrant farmworker population. A twenty-first century version of today's GUAPA project has the potential to facilitate comprehensive health care for migrant workers and their children on both sides of the U.S.-Mexico border.

In the planning phase of GUAPA, all reviewers of the proposal universally endorsed the need for exchanging "real time" health data. U.S. health professionals expressed a desire to receive from their Mexican counterparts a "sentinel warning" or notice prior to the arrival of individuals who could be expected in specific migrant worker locations. Additionally, U.S. health providers need an effective way of knowing which pre-existing health problems and disease entities Mexican farmworkers bring with them. The client's verbal report is often not adequate, and many do not bring medical documentation with them. Nonetheless, an accurate medical history is critical in the care of individuals who have chronic diseases, such as the ubiquitous diabetes or hypertension. Equally important from a public health perspective are the detailed medication histories of those with contagious diseases, such as tuberculosis. If a drug regimen is begun in one country, it often must be maintained in the other country in order to achieve a cure.

Similarly, from a Mexican health professional's perspective, it would be very cost effective to receive early warning of those infectious diseases diagnosed in Mexican workers while they are in the United States. In this way, exposure of family members could be determined, and appropriate therapy could be offered immediately. For those family members not yet exposed to the infected worker, such information would be extremely valuable to prevent familial transmission upon the person's return to Mexico.

For example, Guanajuato's health care providers estimate that up to 8 percent (128) of leprosy cases already under treatment are lost to the U.S. migrant streams (Yañez Velasco, 1995). A higher percentage of uncontrolled leprotic individuals might travel undetected to the United States. Also, AIDS fatalities may be occurring at higher rates among migrant farmworkers and their families than among their nonmigrating counterparts, according to the latest findings from a migrant census underway in Moroleón and Yuriría (Peréz-Cabrera, 1994). To address these complex issues, two key ingredients are indispensable: (1) binational collaboration between governmental, management, and clinical counterparts; and (2) binational, bilingual, bicultural systems of communication and epidemiologic surveillance. In developing and implementing the data transfer system, task force members are striving to put these ideals into practice.

Feasibility and Planning of GUAPA

Unfortunately, the Mexican migrant community working within and between the United States and Mexico presents numerous challenges to data sharing, surveillance of infectious diseases, and, often, to quality health care itself. The extreme mobility of migrant workers is both the reason for, and one of the larger barriers to, the binational exchange of health data.

Binational task force members examined current efforts to identify and follow up mobile populations along the Mexico-U.S. border and in other parts of the world, and found that this migrant health information pilot project is the first to test client data transfer and binational epidemiologic surveillance.

Over the course of 12 months, U.S. and Mexican health care providers, health officials, and researchers met on six occasions to discuss the nature of the problem and potential solutions and plans of action. These meetings resulted in the decision to implement this particular project, a demonstration of health data sharing between providers in Guanajuato, Mexico, and Pennsylvania, United States. To maximize outcomes, it was decided that the pilot project would focus on those infectious diseases for which early intervention and treatment are effective and warranted. Four tracer conditions of binational concern were selected: tuberculosis, leprosy, sexually transmitted diseases (STD) (gonorrhea, chlamydia, syphilis, and HIV), and hepatitis.

There are approximately 3,000 Mexican farmworkers who travel annually to southeast Pennsylvania. Use of this limited population will give an initial barometer reading as to the usefulness and feasibility of future expanded endeavors of a similar nature. This step-by-step approach incorporates the fact that successful systems are often, if not always, the result of motivated individuals. Clinical and public health counterparts in Pennsylvania and Guanajuato who care for a mutual population have a built-in incentive to work together. However, a desire on the part of health care providers to work together was not a sufficient condition to guarantee success. The project would be successful only if target population surveys were conducted both in Guanajuato and Pennsylvania. These surveys were intended to determine the level of interest as well as the nature of any concerns expressed by the target population.

The task force analyzed the potential for establishing such an up-to-the-minute health data transfer system. A variety of challenges were identified:

- acceptance of such a system by the migrant workers;
- acceptance by the families of such workers;
- endorsement by both Mexican and U.S. health care professionals who treat these workers;

- maintenance of patient confidentiality (including information relating to immigration status);
- ascertainment of optimal technical "hardware and software" systems;
- decisions regarding specific content of health data transmissions;
- establishment of compatible definitions for clinical pictures, diagnoses, treatment protocols, and medicine regimens for the index diseases;
- need for bilingual data transfer;
- establishment of a binationally recognized minimum standard for implementing a culturally competent action plan for a specific patient or family; and
- determination that GUAPA's binational health data transfer objectives are supported by common constitutional principals shared by both the United States and the Republic of Mexico.

Following a series of written exchanges, telephone conference calls, and two face-to-face binational meetings, consensus decisions were reached on each of these topic areas. Many of these concerns are reviewed under the section entitled *Challenges*.

Project evaluation is currently addressing the extent to which each of these challenges was met. Evaluation encompasses the project's technical, financial, legal, political, ethical, cultural, and operational aspects, and will identify areas and methods of improvement. Findings will form the basis of a Binational Migrant Health Information System Protocol. This protocol will facilitate the expansion of the system to other diseases and states, and will establish the preferred design, implementation, monitoring, and evaluation of a Mexico-United States health data transfer system.

GUAPA Project Goals

As with any demonstration project, a primary goal of GUAPA is to test the feasibility of a permanent migrant health information system between Mexico and the United States. The project clearly aims to maintain and expand communications between individuals who would utilize the mistakes and successes of GUAPA in planning additional international health care collaborations.

The more specific goals of the data transfer system are threefold: (1) to provide the kind of exchange of patient information that would allow a health clinic in either Pennsylvania or Guanajuato to monitor the treatment of a particular migrant patient who has been diagnosed with one of the tracer conditions; (2) to contact persons who may have been exposed to one of the tracer conditions; and (3) to provide the opportunity for binational epidemiological surveillance, clinical comparative analysis, and health systems research with regard to the four tracer conditions.

Key supportive actions are needed to reach the above goals. First, all documents concerning the pilot project and all information transferred through the system are in both English and Spanish. Second, the following "call to action" objectives were committed to by both the state of Guanajuato and Pennsylvania: (1) through the personnel exchange and long-term training, health professionals on both sides of the border will endeavor to understand more about their patients' experiences on the other side; (2) both states will endeavor to ensure continuity of appropriate, culturally sensitive, and comprehensive care; and (3) many services are rendered free of charge, and every effort is made to minimize fees for services not covered by mandatory program funds.

The timetable for the GUAPA project is as follows:

- June 1994 through February 1995
  Pilot Phase Implementation

- March 1995 through June 1995
  Analysis and Evaluation of Pilot Phase

- June 1995
  Second Binational Health Data Transfer Conference

GUAPA System Design

The design of the data transfer system is best illustrated by describing the component structures that support it. They are located at the following sites:

- General Hospital, Uriangato, Guanajuato, Mexico
- State Department of Health, Harrisburg, Pennsylvania, USA
- School of Public Health, National Institute of Public Health, Cuernavaca, Morelos, Mexico

The plan focuses on the Mexican migrant sender state of Guanajuato and capitalizes on the decentralization of the Mexican health system that is currently underway.

The General Hospital in Uriangato is strategically placed between the two municipalities (Moroleón and Yuriría) with the highest rates of migration to Pennsylvania. Use of the system and recruitment of new cases is currently being promoted by the Guanajuato Secretary of Health, a task force member. Individuals newly diagnosed with one of the four tracer diseases will follow the usual health care channels within the Guanajuato Health Jurisdiction. However, in addition, that data pertaining to migrants to the United States will now be transmitted to the U.S. GUAPA module.

The U.S. module is located at the Department of Health in Harrisburg, Pennsylvania, which routinely collects all epidemiological data for Pennsylvania. Together with the Migrant Clinicians Network, Pennsylvania Department of Health officials are in charge of promoting the new system. The following networking avenues have been used: the computer communications software "WONDER System" of the Centers for Disease Control (CDC), migrant health bulletins and newsletters, and direct communication with migrant health care providers along the three U.S. migrant streams.

The Pennsylvania Department of Health oversees and facilitates prevention and treatment activities of health care providers (including its own county health departments). The prototype Migrant Health Data Registry was developed by members of the task force. This registry exists in two forms: (1) Migrant Health *Paper* Register, and (2) Migrant Health *Computer* Register. The information that is collected and shared includes discrete demographic data items, ad hoc data files on request, and standard CDC information on notifiable diseases (regarding exposure, diagnosis, treatment, and follow-up). In the clinical setting the health care provider solicits from the patient the necessary background information and adds to that the relevant medical information regarding the clinic visit (diagnosis, treatment, etc.). This information is then transferred from the patient's clinical chart to a paper format developed for the project. This constitutes the Paper Registry. The information is then input into the Computer Registry. Information in the Computer Registry is transferred from the Guanajuato GUAPA Registry to the Pennsylvania GUAPA Registry and vice versa, via the CDC WONDER communications system.

Files in the Migrant Health Computer Registry are kept, updated, and shared, until the outcome of the clinical event is documented. At that time, a final report is generated and shared between the appropriate counterparts. In this way, the two Registries serve as hotlines of information and binational referral for providers of migrant farmworkers. As well, a copy of the completed Migrant Health Paper Register is given to individual clients before they migrate. They are urged to share this copy with subsequent health care providers in either country.

A monitoring module is located at the School of Public Health in Mexico (ESPM), National Institute of Public Health, Cuernavaca, Morelos. This component supports the following activities: (1) linking GUAPA participants in Guanajuato and Pennsylvania for the implementation, development, and evaluation of the project; (2) collecting project results for analysis by the research team; (3) coordinating clinical, epidemiological, and health systems research; and (4) producing the final Binational Health Information System Protocol to be used in expanding the program.

Software

The database computer program being used was specifically designed for this demonstration project. This new software program is called MUST (Mexico United States Transfer) and is written in CLIPPER. MUST is a menu-driven, screen-based data entry program. The MUST program creates a series of files that are then exchanged between Pennsylvania and Guanajuato via the CDC's WONDER program. WONDER is the CDC's electronic communication program that is accessible by modem through an 800 number. It is used to transfer information, including E-mail, and has the ability to search the Public Health Data Base at CDC. Currently WONDER has over 18,000 users and was the logical choice for the GUAPA health information highway. By tapping this resource, the MUST system allows GUAPA participants to enter, exchange, and analyze their data. A compatible Spanish version of MUST has been produced by the Secretaría de Salud de Guanajuato and ESPM.

Data Entry

Data sources for the system are clinical records of migrant subjects with tuberculosis, leprosy, STD, or hepatitis who are seen at any migrant health care facility, private practitioner's office, hospital, state health service, or migrant health clinic in Guanajuato State or the United States.

As written responses from the Paper Registry are entered into MUST, they are automatically subjected to a range and validity check. For example, MUST will not allow the entry of a diagnosis that does not fall within one of the four tracer disease categories. Likewise, MUST checks for valid entries for variables such as gender and marital status. Pull-down menus of valid options are another way in which MUST promotes both ease and accuracy of data entry.

Collected information includes form number, case number, date, file status, name, gender, age (DOB), RFC (Mexican federal taxpayer number), occupation, marital status, number of family members, hometown address in Guanajuato, home base address in United States, relative in United States, relative in Mexico, and states visited in the previous 12 months. Since the clinical picture of the four tracer diseases differ, there are four variations to the health portion of the form. Each includes "routine" data (clinical and laboratory), as well as free text for descriptions and inquiries appropriate for that disease entity.

Data Exchange

MUST's send and receive functions have encryption built into them (via numeric codification of text), thus preserving patient confidentiality. MUST is also designed to return follow-up information to the initiating agency from the investigating agency. Space is provided for reporting what happened as a result of investigation, test results, diagnosis, treatment provided, or for requesting additional information, if needed. Hard copy reports, as well, are sent to providers.

Due to complicated software difficulties, language translation capabilities have not been built into the MUST system. Translation is often done by the coordinator in each country, but remains a weakness in design.

Since Guanajuatan laborers migrate to states other than Pennsylvania, health care providers anywhere in the United States may participate by sending paper files by mail, facsimile, or modem to the Pennsylvania GUAPA module. There they are manually entered into the computer and then sent to the module at the Ministry of Health, Guanajuato State. Study cases from Guanajuato State are also manually captured and sent to the Pennsylvania module. Pennsylvania distributes the information to the requesting or concerned health care office within a 48-hour period.

Once information is received by the counterpart module, it follows the usual flow of information throughout the health delivery system, including epidemiology departments. Guanajuato cases are reported to Dirección General de Epidemiología, social work offices, laboratories, hospitals, and community centers. Front-line health care users of information are asked to acknowledge and return information on outcomes through the documented resolution of the case.

Data Analysis

For project analysis and evaluation, MUST allows built-in summarizing of reports and the inclusion of ad hoc reports. The MUST system creates a series of databases in dBase format. Because this is such a widespread and well organized database format, the information from the MUST system can be imported into a wide variety of software programs for further analysis. These include spreadsheet and graphics programs (Lotus 1-2-3, QuattroPro, etc.), statistical analysis programs (SAS, SPSS), and geographic information systems (GIS, GISPlus). Several of these software programs are currently being used by GUAPA participants to analyze pilot project data.

Each GUAPA component is now establishing direct and simultaneous communication with each of the other components. All information transfer is acknowledged and registered by sender and receiver modules, thus keeping a logbook of uploading and downloading operations. Databases are updated and purged every quarter by the administrator of each module. The research team is currently developing a directory of system users, listing them in chronological order as they have used the GUAPA system. Additionally, every two quarters the research team determines and disseminates to participants any needed changes in system policies, technology, and practices.

Confidentiality

Patient confidentiality and the ethics of professional-patient interactions are well established traditions in Mexico and the United States. As such, these standards of practice have become firmly entrenched in medical and legal guidelines for implementing new systems of care. The task force reached consensus that medical ethics standards and patient confidentiality would not be compromised by the establishment of a new binational health data transfer system. However, assuring patient confidentiality in the immediate patient population under study (Mexican migrant farmworkers) does pose some special challenges.

Protection of all information pertinent to the immigration status of the client is central in gaining his or her confidence in the new system. This goal is being accomplished by rigorous assurance that immigration questions are not asked of any individuals participating in the system. Additionally, legal measures were taken to assure that all records pertaining to migrant worker clients are not subject to outside scrutiny.

Whenever data are shared with those who are neither treating project clients nor managing the project, data are stripped of all identifiers. Patients are informed that all identifiable data, shared by the design and purpose of the system, are released only after obtaining their written, informed consent. The consent form indicates that (1) no immigration information will be sought by this system, nor will any information about participating clients be shared with non-health-care professionals participating in the system; (2) all mechanisms possible will be utilized to ensure the security and confidentiality of information transmitted across the border; and (3) only those farmworkers and their families who have jointly signed an informed consent document (indicating that they both wish free exchange of health data information between the migratory worker and family) will be entered into the system.

Patients have the authority to withdraw their permission to disclose their records, without explanation and at any time during the project. Once information is released to health care providers in either country, it is subject to the respective laws, regulations, and procedures regarding confidentiality. Only qualified health care providers or offices, who are subject by law to ensure confidentiality of clinical information, will be eligible to share and use the system's data. These assurances of confidentiality are the responsibility of the Pennsylvania and Guanajuato health authorities. Any confidentiality gaps or threats (none to date) would be registered and reviewed by both the research team and the binational task force.

Data Security

The security of data is assured through a number of strategies. On-line access to files is granted only after verification of user's identity, by using the CDC's WONDER system password. After use of the system, access is recorded. In the event of nonauthorized access, a record would also be made and the respective authority would be notified.

Updated records are labeled with the date and the label "updated." No alteration of registers is permitted. If modifications are needed, the original record is kept and the modified record is labeled "amended." The transmission of information is limited to the three modules described, and to the clients' health care providers.

Files are encrypted for transmittal with the client's RFC (Mexico's federal taxpayer number), known only by the database administrator of the module. After completion (resolution) of the event that prompted the record transmittal, that file is locked out of the database and will be used only for future consultation or evaluation purposes. That is, it is not possible to consult completed cases on-line routinely.

Activities to Date/Preliminary Evaluation

On July 27, 1994, the first successful exchange of sentinel disease information took place between Pennsylvania and Guanajuato. This transfer of information enabled the Guanajuato Department of Health to locate and bring to medical care the sexual contact of a migrant diagnosed and treated for syphilis in Pennsylvania. This information sharing represents the first successful electronic interface of public health systems in different countries for the purpose of intervening in the spread of a communicable disease by way of contact tracing.

Other first-year GUAPA activities centered on fulfilling the task force's objective of increasing the capacity for cross-cultural health outreach and education. The stated goal is to increase prevention and early case detection of the four tracer infections. To this end, the Pennsylvania Department of Health, in cooperation with Muhlenberg College, the Chester County Department of Health, and Comunidad Hispana, began an outreach education and screening program for Mexican migrant workers in southeastern Pennsylvania. To facilitate this effort, the Guanajuato Secretary of Health assigned a physician, Jose Ramírez Valenzuela, to work in Pennsylvania. Furthermore, the State of Guanajuato developed, and made available, relevant and culturally sensitive educational materials published for patient education in Mexico.

Dr. Ramírez Valenzuela conducted educational programs for over 800 farmworkers during the course of his 4-month stay in Pennsylvania. He facilitated several screening projects, conducted by the Pennsylvania Department of Health, during which over 200 workers were screened for syphilis and HIV. Additionally, he worked with the Chester County Health

Department in their tuberculosis screening of 40 Mexican farmworkers. Those screening efforts, while limited by personnel, time, and funds, identified 2 cases of untreated syphilis, 1 HIV-positive worker, and 11 individuals with positive tuberculin tests. With informed consent, the names and addresses of these individuals' contacts were transmitted to Guanajuato in order to medically examine, educate, and treat them, if needed.

Simultaneously with the Pennsylvania outreach project, the State of Guanajuato initiated a major STD screening project in public family planning clinics in the two cities that are major migrant sender communities, Moroleón and Yuriría. These screenings included testing for syphilis, gonorrhea, and chlamydia, as well as locating individuals with Hansen's disease. The two screening efforts in Guanajuato and Pennsylvania have identified several previously undiagnosed cases of tuberculosis, syphilis, chancroid, chlamydia, and HIV.

Now the basic technological requirements for GUAPA have been accomplished. Technologically speaking, after initial compatibility issues were corrected, the system has worked perfectly. Both the Mexican Instituto Nacional de Salud Pública and the Health Department of Guanajuato have decided to make minor system modifications and include a disease registry. Software for such a registry is currently available from the CDC Division of STD/HIV Control and Prevention.

In the analysis of the feasibility of system implementation, health professionals on both sides of the border discovered a wide range of concerns ranging from very technical issues (such as standard identifiers and hardware/software choices) to very serious infrastructure problems (such as the lack of information on migrant demographic, socioeconomic, and health needs). A major infrastructure weakness is the present inability of both countries to rapidly share information among their own states. This lack of internal communication severely limits binational collaborations in exchanging data and resources.

A detailed cost effectiveness analysis relating to the implementation of a more geographically comprehensive binational health data transfer system is beyond the scope and capabilities of the task force. Perhaps a formal governmental entity, such as the Agency for Health Care Policy and Research (AHCPR) of the U.S. Public Health Service or El Instituto Nacional de Salud Pública of Mexico, might find such a topic suitable for in-depth research. However, it would seem that the implementation of a fully binational system would not require significantly more people in either country. Given the virtual explosion in new technologies of the "information superhighways," the actual cost for pertinent hardware and software and the operations of this equipment appear minimal, especially when considering the public health savings of early intervention and prevention of disease.

What would be needed, however, is the education of providers about cross-cultural skills and different types of care effective with various mobile populations. An educational process on both sides of the border is needed to enhance bilingual skills, bicultural sensitivity, and understanding of the clients' lifestyles.

GUAPA Challenges

The principal barriers to utilization of the data transfer system appear to be financial and political. Other major barriers include a lack of culturally sensitive health care in Pennsylvania, use of different drugs and differing standards of diagnosis and care between Guanajuato and Pennsylvania, a lack of participation by U.S. receiver states other than Pennsylvania, and ambiguities regarding provider responsibility upon receipt of shared data.

Accessibility to health care for migrant farmworkers must be considered a major difficulty and barrier to communicable disease intervention and prevention. For example, testing for tuberculosis is often severely limited by both provider and patient financial constraints. Moreover, U.S. providers appear to have many misconceptions regarding the availability and quality of health care in Mexico and have expressed reluctance to gather and send information to Mexico for purposes of contact tracing. Mexican providers, on the other hand, have expressed reluctance to share locating information on individuals working in the United States with questionable legal status.

Outreach to the migrant community is frequently conducted by persons unfamiliar with both the process of disease intervention and the cultural milieu of the migrant farmworker. This results in an inability to adequately disseminate and gather the information necessary to engage the provider in disease intervention and prevention offered by the GUAPA Project. Binational and bicultural dialogue would allow a more comprehensive approach to the health needs of migrant populations. Perhaps one of the most sobering aspects of the development of a binational health data transfer system was discovering the significant divergence in medical standards of prevention, diagnosis, treatment, and follow-up for infectious clients. Not only do the United States and Mexico have significant differences in these areas, but the various states within the two countries also vary greatly from each other. For example, certain U.S. clinics require laboratory confirmation of a chlamydia infection in order to secure diagnosis and institute therapy, whereas others do not. Many clinical operations in Mexico do not utilize this laboratory technology as yet. Similarly, the specific steps required to pronounce a patient "cured" of an infectious illness (such as syphilis) vary substantially not only between the United States and Mexico, but also among the different states within each country.

No easy solution to this apparent medical "Tower of Babel" is apparent. The problems inherent in the adoption of standardized definitions of diagnosis and outcomes do not appear to be rooted in differences of scientific theory or opinion. Moreover, the difficulties in such basic transfer of health data information do not appear to be related to any provincial desire to withhold information from one region (or country) to the other. Instead, wide differences of opinion exist with regard to the convenience of utilizing specific laboratory diagnostics in confirming clinical impressions. There certainly exist significant differences with regard to the resources available for use of technologies in the different regions on both sides of the border.

It is likely that in time, a "lowest common denominator" standard for diagnosing and treating outcomes will be adopted by the World Health Organization (WHO). In the meantime, there is a clear benefit to the immediate implementation of a binational system that would at least allow counterpart health professionals to be aware of each other's diagnostic and treatment criteria.

The system for drug approval and drug regulation in Mexico differs significantly from the system that has been adopted in the United States. Thus, it is likely that a patient who is diagnosed with tuberculosis in the United States may start the first 3 months of therapy with a specific drug regimen and 3 months later (upon return to Mexico) be unable to secure those drugs. Moreover, it is possible that health professionals on either side of the border may be unable to dispense drugs obtained in the other country, even if an appropriate amount of drug to complete therapy is provided to the patient. Similarly, the current treatment protocols for handling toxicity of treatment and other complications may also differ between the two countries. An immediate task at hand for the task force is to identify those drugs on both sides of the border that have sufficient compatibility to be utilized interchangeably.

Yet another realization of GUAPA regards the need for increased consortia building among migrant receiver states in the United States. Data entry into the pilot project has not been forthcoming from areas other than southeastern Pennsylvania. It may be that a lack of understanding of the health care delivery system in Mexico and a concern for the preservation of patient confidentiality are barriers to participation. To address these concerns, the Pennsylvania and Guanajuato Departments of Health have prepared an educational video describing the structure of the health care delivery system in Mexico, services provided, and policies and procedures regarding the preservation of patient confidentiality.

A specific medical, social dilemma, with distinct ethical ramifications, emerged even in the planning phase and continues to limit the success of the project. Specifically, what are the ethical and legal obligations of health professionals on either end of the data transfer system to respond to the health information that they receive? To add to this concern, the United States suffers from a severe lack of bilingually and biculturally sensitive health care professionals.

In lieu of systemic infrastructure changes, realistic and cost-effective solutions have been improvised for the above concerns in order to support GUAPA activities. Moreover, the participants have reached consensus on far greater and overriding issues: the implementation of such a system is the expressed desire of potential system clientele and will be cost effective.

It is clear that the implementation of a binational system of health data exchange is critical to any major economic integration between the two countries. Yet, there is a long history of political distrust and cultural misunderstanding between the United States and Mexico. With this project, we have before us an expression of intent to overcome these historical barriers to communication for the purpose of improving health care on both sides of the border.

Not surprisingly, the National Institute of Health of Mexico reports that other states in Mexico are lining up to participate in a broader binational exchange. In fact, Illinois and Morelos are beginning collaborative conversations with each other and with GUAPA designers in hopes of replicating the pilot project.

GUAPA demonstrates that the exchange of information is technologically possible with relative ease and minor expense. The bigger challenge is now clear—to surmount the political, cultural, and economic barriers that impede the provision of health care on both sides of the border.

In the context of NAFTA, a spotlight has been directed on the provision of health care in both countries. A minimum standard of health care for migrant farmworkers is an essential component of any binational collaboration on disease control. The GUAPA project certainly promotes the reality of a minimum and quality standard of care.

The development of a master plan for further binational collaboration on data transfer should consider the perspectives of the task force and system users. The specific steps for incrementally augmenting the amount of health data exchanged between the United States and Mexico, and the timetables for doing so, will necessarily require more feasibility information. This process will include the analysis of the GUAPA demonstration.

Task force members agree that the formal adoption of a true binational agreement must await the clearance of the respective state departments. Official, high level endorsement will ensure that such an agreement is rooted in mutual and constitutional legality, the authorization of which is beyond the scope and abilities of the task force members.

Task force deliberations began before the approval of the North American Free Trade Agreement. The obvious need for this supportive medical infrastructure has only increased following NAFTA's ratification. One must remember that as we enter the twenty-first century, a possibility for increased migration between our two countries (not only from Mexico to the United States, but also vice versa) should be anticipated. The capacity to increase the level of binational economic interchange will depend on the ability of a wide range of professionals on both sides of the border to implement appropriate sociological infrastructures, including health data transfer.

References

Brook, J. H., Genese, C. A., Bloland, P. B., Zucker, J. R., & Spitalny, K. C. (1994, July 7). Brief report: Malaria probably locally acquired in New Jersey. *The New England Journal of Medicine.*

Dever, G. (1991). Profile of a population with complex health problems. *Migrant Clinicians Network, 1*(16).

Knochenhaur, M. (1991). Mexican public health official in charge of newly created health insurance program for Mexican migrant workers in the United States, interviewed at Western Stream Migrant Forum, San Diego, CA.

Oliveira, V. J., & Cox, E. J. (1988). *The agricultural work force of 1985: A statistical profile.* Washington, DC: U.S. Department of Agriculture.

Peréz-Cabrera, A. (1994). Personal communication.

Velasco Mondragón, H. E. (1993). Study conducted on the health care needs of Mexican migrant farmworkers in Southeastern Pennsylvania.

Yañez Velasco, L. B. (1995). Anecdotal report.

Part III

Working in Districts, Schools, and Classrooms

CHAPTER 13

Bilingual, Bicultural, and Binational Cooperative Learning Communities for Students and Teachers

MARGARITA CALDERÓN, PH.D.
CRESPAR/JOHNS HOPKINS UNIVERSITY

As NAFTA opens the border between the United States and Mexico, the need for binational cooperation in education becomes ever more imperative. This chapter provides a rationale for binational education and describes a variety of cooperative bicultural programs for students and teachers. These programs include two-way bilingual classrooms in which English-speaking and Spanish-speaking students are grouped in heterogeneous cooperative learning teams, teachers' learning communities that provide collegial support for implementing a complex cooperative learning model, and binational staff development activities involving U.S. and Mexican teachers from neighboring cities along the border. Particular emphasis is placed on an effective binational staff development process that helps teachers transfer appropriate knowledge and behaviors into the bilingual cooperative classroom, and provides ongoing support for personal development, interpersonal relationships, and program implementation.

This chapter will focus on providing a rationale for binational education followed by examples and recommendations for joint educational endeavors. The examples of cooperative activities are based on contextualized longitudinal studies (Calderón, 1984-1995; Durán, in press; Hertz-Lazarowitz & Calderón, 1994; Hertz-Lazarowitz, Ivory, & Calderón, 1993; Slavin & Madden, 1995; Stevens, Madden, Slavin, & Farnish, 1987). Collectively, the studies have given us a framework consisting of best instructional approaches: ways of training teachers, administrators, and communities; providing follow-up support to all staff development activities; and dealing with innovation implementation in whole-school efforts. The basic elements of each of these components will be described, and will be interrelated in the final section.

Why Binational Education? What Are the Benefits for the Majority Population?

The benefits for the majority culture in the United States are many. For instance, it is projected that by the year 2000, the effects of NAFTA will boost the dollar value of already vigorous Texas trade with Mexico by about 13 percent to $29.2 billion, adding approximately 113,000 new jobs (Texas Education Agency, 1995). Other border states and states where Mexico's twin-plants are situated such as Michigan, Ohio, Georgia, and Florida, will surely benefit. However, without a shift in educational goals, Cummins' conclusions might prevail:

> Dwindling resources in an era of dwindling commitment to second language acquisition add up to an increasingly high number of tongue-tied Americans. The consequences of generalized language incompetence include an international trade gap that threatens both short- and long-term economic stability, inadequate intelligence [information], and insufficient expertise in international communication that threatens national security and exacerbates cultural isolation (1993).

Although a planned strategy is not yet in place, recently there has been increased interest in second-language study for economic purposes.

> It was automatically assumed that anyone studying a second language as a major field was going to be either a teacher, an interpreter, or a translator and had no other career options. There is still a need for people in those professions. There is also a growing need for individuals who possess advanced skills in second languages and are trained in various technical areas. This is a result of increased activity in international business, the inflow of large amounts of foreign capital to the United States, increased internationalization, and an expanded awareness of the need to conduct not only business but also diplomatic relations in the language of the host country (Weatherford, 1986).

Interpreters and translators in the United States have more work than ever. Large companies are now seeking employees who possess a combination of bilingual and business/managerial skills. Such people have an edge over others without language capability. The supply and demand deficit in bilingual education is especially felt in the education profession. Every state in the nation has a dramatic shortage of bilingual teachers. California has an annual shortage of approximately 20,000 (California State Department of Education, 1994). Texas needs an average of 14,000 a year (Texas Education Agency, 1995). Due to such shortages, bilingual teachers can pick their school and generally receive an additional stipend for being bilingual.

What are the benefits of a binational education for the language-minority population?

The population of language-minority students is quickly growing. In 1985-86, there were 1,472,000 limited-English-proficient students enrolled in U.S. schools. In 1992-93, 7 years later, the enrollment was up to 2,736,000.

It is a well-known fact that U.S. schools with large language-minority student populations are typically Chapter 1 schools. Chapter 1 schools are generally the most underfunded, understaffed, and ineffective in our nation (Slavin, Dolan, Wasik, Ross, & Smith, 1994). With respect to change and innovations, these schools have been dormant for many years, supporting a level of mediocrity and status quo that is hard to change. Unfortunately, many of these schools also lie near the U.S.-Mexican border.

In Texas, many of the schools labeled as "low performing" schools by the Texas Education Agency (1993) are also those with bilingual programs and a 90-97 percent Hispanic enrollment. They also have the highest percentage of teachers on temporary teaching permits. These schools espouse the mind-set that bilingual programs are remedial programs and a vehicle for students to learn English quickly and forget their mother tongue. Many of the best teachers learn to move out of these depressing situations, leaving novices or less capable teachers to deal with language-minority students. These types of compensatory bilingual programs perpetuate the stereotypes and stigmas that lead students to academic and personal failure.

Why are schools the way they are today? Some reasons we all are very familiar with are as follows:

- Schools fail to incorporate minority students' language and culture into the total school program.
- They exclude minority communities from participation in school decisions.
- They assume a transmission approach to pedagogy that relegates students to a passive role, instead of a constructivist approach in which students become active learners.
- They use a Band-Aid approach to staff development.
- Students who have attended school in their native countries are often

ahead of U.S.-born students in mathematics and science. However, they are typically placed in unchallenging courses.
- Secondary-school-age immigrants are either expected to read sophisticated textbooks to learn complex subject matter or are placed in watered-down remedial courses.
- The clash of differences between the native culture and the U.S. culture leads to intergenerational conflict in many immigrant families.

In addition, researchers also find that

- Most high-school-age immigrant students need to work; many have little access to quality health care, information, or means of support; many live in crowded, poorly maintained apartments (McDonnell & Hill, 1993).
- Schools and state educational agencies approach assessment in a way that places the blame for failure on the student rather than on the educational context (Cummins, 1981).
- Only about half of the high school students who take the first year of a second language go on to a second year, and fewer than 4 percent of all high school students go on to a third. In many other countries, secondary school students must take at least 4 years of a second language (Draper, 1989).
- Between 1966 and 1979, the number of U.S. colleges requiring second-language study for admission fell from 34 percent to 8 percent (Draper, 1989)
- By 1988, second-language teaching at the elementary school level had virtually disappeared, reaching less than 1 percent of all students (Draper, 1989).

These are but a few well-known examples out of many which impact negatively on language minorities, and particularly low-schooled immigrant students. As joint educational endeavors begin to target quality education, language-minority students stand to gain considerably. A set of recommendations are listed below that targets changes in school structures to ensure language-minority-student success.

Binational Exchanges Have Existed for Many Years

While economic links between the United States and Mexico continue to grow, legislative and popular commitment to language programs ebbs and flows. "Binational education" is starting to catch on, but it will be some time before funding allocations are appropriated specifically for such efforts. Therefore, local initiatives have sprouted that display a spirit of cooperation but not much money. Chapter 2 in this book describes such an intervention and how it was triggered by research.

It is these types of contextualized efforts that are going to bring about short- and long-range success for students. However, contextualized interventions and research must be accompanied by systematic approaches to professional development and learning communities where all participants expand their knowledge and skills in order to develop appropriate and effective schooling practices.

Up-Scaling Binational Exchanges

The border cities of El Paso and Cuidad Juárez have a long tradition of small-scale border exchanges that come and go with the persons who initiate them. As interest intensified on both sides of the border with the ratification of NAFTA, the Leadership Enhancement Academy for Binational Education (LEA) evolved.

The LEA is sponsored by a grant from the Texas Education Agency that focuses on recruitment, retention, and support systems for minority teachers and teachers of critical shortage areas—mainly bilingual education. The purpose of the LEA is to establish a comprehensive systematic mechanism for educators from both sides of the border who seek to improve schooling practices for Latino students.

The Leadership Enhancement Academy for Binational Education

Principals, assistant principals, and coordinators from both border cities are collaborating to develop and mold the Leadership Enhancement Academy. Administrators, teachers, Chamber of Commerce representatives, and parents meet monthly at various school districts on both sides of the border to study the multiple issues of bilingual and binational education.

The 1-day sessions consist of several speakers who are experts on topics such as NAFTA, binational teacher exchanges, and effective bilingual instructional practices. State and federal education agency officials also come to present cutting-edge information. For instance, the Director of the Texas Teacher Recruitment, Retention, and Assistance (TTRRA) Program talked about relevant plans by the agency, and expressed the need to take back to the Texas Education Agency the ideas generated by the group to integrate into Texas state plans. At that same session, the vice presidents of the Juárez and El Paso Chambers of Commerce presented information on the impact NAFTA has already had on the border. They also touched on implications for educators and suggested ways both sectors could begin to collaborate. Educators, in turn, suggested ways the business sector could collaborate with and contribute to education.

After listening to speakers, participants discussed the implications and ideas derived from each speaker and converted those into immediate plans and activities. The participants clustered in teams by levels: pre-K, elementary, and secondary. University and private sector representatives joined a team of their choice. Each team began with a round-robin strategy in which participants took turns sharing their purpose for involvement in the project. Next, individuals listed what they or their school could contribute to other schools and what they needed or would like to receive in return. For the final activity, schools from El Paso partnered with schools from Juárez and scheduled visits. The agendas for months to come will continue to intensify these relationships. A future meeting was set aside for teachers and administrators from both sides of the border to do 15-minute roundtable presentations on "best practices" in teaching, curriculum, educational policies, and school reform. Other binational programs such as "Hands Across the Border," a program for elementary and secondary student exchanges, will be integrated into future meetings.

Purpose, Goals, and Objectives

The purpose of the Leadership Enhancement Academy for Binational Education in El Paso, Texas, is to help educators implement, research, and improve bilingual/binational education; promote bilingualism for all students; and develop a global perspective about the future. The vehicles to accomplish this are joint comprehensive staff development programs and school projects. For this purpose, the LEA team has been studying ways of coordinating binational efforts on a short-term experimental basis while keeping in mind long-term comprehensive elements and goals.

The Texas Centers for Border Economic Development, which are currently working with the LEA, have identified the following key features of a comprehensive binational education program:

- curriculum development for K-12 schools;
- a mentoring program, with substantive interaction between industry and education (K-12);
- continuing education;
- exchange programs;
- intern programs;
- certificate programs;
- conferences and seminars;
- a speakers bureau; and
- applied research (Acosta, 1995).

The LEA has adopted these recommendations and expanded upon them as a target of activities. Five goals have been developed by the LEA as follows:

Goal 1. Cultivate relationships.

- Set up the structures that support the development of relationships across the border.
- Organize learning communities for continuous growth.
- Create a center for coordination and cooperation.

Goal 2. Orchestrate professional development opportunities on both sides of the border for

- teams of administrators, teachers, parents, and community members on effective bilingual programs, cultural understanding, research-based innovative practices, etc.;
- English and Spanish mini-courses;
- equivalency credentials;
- internships in schools; and
- administrator academies on bilingual or binational school restructuring, organizational development, leadership training, supervision, coaching, and other related themes.

Goal 3. Provide access to information.

- Establish mechanisms for continued learning and sharing in communities.
- Organize conferences, seminars, teacher exhibits, and calendars of events.
- Link up with the TTRRA/UNITE bulletin board and set up an assortment of data files, news bits, and communication links.
- Work with the business sector to secure the technology and multimedia necessary for long-distance learning and staff development.
- Create a newsletter, occasional papers, program/project summaries, reports.

Goal 4. Develop an integrated systemic approach to address the multiple aspects of binational education.

- Set up a bilingual/binational pilot project in 10 schools in El Paso and Juárez.
- Coordinate collaborative efforts.
- Support school-site endeavors.
- Identify resources for sharing, and write proposals for on-going funding.

Goal 5. Conduct research and evaluation.

- Conduct workshops on research and evaluation processes.
- Conduct research on target projects.
- Set up an evaluation process for all activities to determine impact and continue development of interventions.
- Scale up effective practices.

It is subsumed in these goals that the vehicle for implementation of innovations is systematic staff development and follow-up support systems. Fortunately, there are ample literature- and researched-based examples to help us understand the process of change and how to incorporate it into new programs.

Why a Systematic Approach to Binational Professional Development?

Staff development has been one of the most talked about and least misunderstood concepts of our century. Michael Fullan (1990), Judith

Warren Little (1982), and other well-known researchers have written books about the ineffectiveness of staff development and faulty implementation of educational change. Now, in the context of NAFTA, staff development and educational change become particularly complex when we examine them from a bilingual perspective. As we get ready for the next century, we need to look at staff development in new ways that put it in sync with the educational needs of our global society.

Some guiding questions are

- What will the staff development practices of the future be like?
- How can we bridge not only knowledge gaps but human relations gaps through effective personal and professional development practices?
- How do we bridge the gap between mind-sets about binationalism, cultural pluralism, and multilingualism?
- How do we create the types of schools that will develop the talents and intellect of diverse student populations?

The binational programs are taking new risks with staff development. They are experimenting with new ways of collaborative learning across the border. It's not easy. The language of the presentations is always an issue when participants are limited in one or the other language. The logistics of holding meetings and sessions on both sides of the border are somewhat cumbersome. Communiqués are disseminated through personal delivery because the mail takes a long time to cross the border. In spite of hurdles such as these, the willingness to connect is strong enough to find solutions.

Nothing is as valuable and effective as face-to-face interaction. As administrators, teachers, and students begin meeting frequently to study the art of schooling, they are acquiring much more than knowledge about schooling. They develop sensitivity to "the other culture," a deeper understanding of others and themselves, a new view of education and their immediate surroundings, and, above all, a renewed enthusiasm for creating better opportunities for both student learning and their own professional growth.

What Should Schools for a Binational Society Look Like?

Through collaboration and combined intellectual and financial resources, schools can reconfigure existing structures to meet the demands of a global society. Schools can capitalize on the languages and talents of immigrant students and expand the pathways to their success. Schools can begin by espousing a philosophy and practices that reaffirm these standards:

- Immigrant and language-minority students are part of a whole-school integrated system.
- There are opportunities for all students in the school to become bilingual or multilingual.

- Special instructional interventions for limited-English-proficient students are of high quality and integrated into the whole-school system.
- There is equity and excellence in all aspects of schooling for immigrant students.
- The first language is used in two-way bilingual programs and has equal status with English.
- The instructional approach facilitates language acquisition and content-area mastery through multiple active-learning contexts (cooperative learning, discovery field trips, learning centers, internships, and mentors).
- There is a climate that values all cultures.
- There is a climate of collaboration and team spirit.
- There are high expectations for all students coupled with supportive systems.
- There is a high level of family engagement in schooling.
- The business community makes this school their business.
- Comprehensive staff development is ongoing and all teachers participate.
- Communities of learners are established for students, teachers, staff, administrators, and parents.
- "Bridge" programs with community colleges and local universities insure successful career paths for immigrant and all students.
- Health services and counseling are available.

A Typical Program of the Future

El Paso has a population of 750,000 and is the largest city on the Texas-Mexico border. The El Paso Independent School District, the largest in the city, has a student enrollment of 64,859 with a Hispanic student population of 72 percent and 14,742 limited-English-proficient (LEP) students. Juárez has a population of 1 million and continues growing through constant migration from the interior of Mexico and Central America.

In a border town such as El Paso, especially considering the effects of NAFTA, it is not enough to set up programs so that the district's LEP students acquire English. In fact, it is a myopic and single-sided vision of education to focus on one language in a bilingual city that faces environmental, social, political, and economic issues resulting from mutual concerns with Mexico. In contrast to the low-skilled assembly lines of the past, or maquiladoras of today (twin plants), tomorrow's work sites will require employees to frame problems, design their own tasks, evaluate outcomes, and cooperate in finding novel solutions to problems (Drucker, 1989). If students live in multicultural, bicultural, or binational communities, they must also understand and evaluate multidimensional issues that impact their society.

The Accelerated Two-Way Bilingual Program was designed to address these needs (Calderón & Carreón, 1994). The program was initiated 3 years ago at two elementary schools in El Paso Independent School District. Academic achievement, language acquisition, and biculturalism are natural partners in the program. The two-way bilingual design builds on the intellectual power of bilingualism (Cummins, 1981; Krashen & Terrell, 1983; Diaz, 1985). The program's mission is to prepare children for a multilingual multicultural world of advanced technology—a world in which they can become leaders who think critically and work collaboratively to solve the complex problems that they will face on the border.

Each class in the two-way bilingual program is staffed by two teachers, a bilingual teacher and monolingual teacher, who collaborate in the teaching process. The teacher teams have found that working together offers new opportunities for personal and professional growth. The teachers benefit from their mutual strengths. They have increased their repertoire of teaching strategies, enhanced their professional background, learned to work effectively as a team, taken turns becoming mentor and peer coach, and become more reflective and self-motivated. In addition, the teachers have a better understanding of the interaction of cultures and the value of bilingualism. To their amazement, the English-speaking teachers are acquiring Spanish along with their students!

Benefits of Two-Way Bilingual Programs for Students

What we have learned thus far from two-way bilingual education is that it provides schools an excellent tool to address the academic, language, social, and economic challenges of a bicultural and binational community. The students in the program reflect the ethnic and language makeup of the community. This program brings English speakers together with monolingual Spanish speakers to learn together in two languages. The classes at each grade level (K-5) include approximately 15 Spanish-speaking and 15 English-speaking students. As the students participate in cooperative learning activities conducted in Spanish for half of the day and in English for the other half, they acquire each other's language and gain new insights into each other's culture. They learn to work together in a mutually supportive and highly interactive environment and learn to solve problems by building on strengths in language as well as on academic knowledge.

Cooperative Learning for Students

The instructional approach used in the two-way bilingual program centers on the Cooperative Integrated Reading and Composition (CIRC) model of instruction (Calderón, 1991, 1994a-i; Hertz-Lazarowitz & Calderón, 1994; Stevens, Madden, Slavin, & Farnish, 1987). There is a strong research base on the implementation of this model in both monolingual and bilingual settings (Slavin & Madden, 1995; Slavin et al., 1994;

Stevens et al., 1987). Students in CIRC classrooms repeatedly outperform their peers in more traditional classrooms in academic, social, and linguistic development. The Bilingual CIRC provides a context for accelerated language development in two languages because the students continuously discuss, solve problems, read with partners, write extensively, and edit each other's work. They learn to collaborate in decision making, testing of organizational strategies, and accomplishing tasks efficiently and effectively.

The development of biliteracy skills through the bilingual CIRC model affects the success students experience in math, science, technology, and social studies. Content areas are learned through techniques borrowed from CIRC and also through Bilingual Group Investigation (Hertz-Lazarowitz & Calderón, 1994) projects. Cooperative learning is integrated throughout the day, and includes even simple cooperative strategies such as the round-robin.

Benefits of the Bilingual Cooperative Learning Program for Students

From other field studies in bilingual contexts, we have found that the Bilingual Cooperative Integrated Reading and Composition (BCIRC) model creates a context for quality interaction for bilingual or language-minority students. As second-language learners, students in BCIRC classrooms experience ample opportunities for expressing ideas, exchanging information, and building comprehension for literacy development. Literacy skills are practiced and developed through literature and content-area textbooks.

The BCIRC model consists of a sequence of cooperative, independent, teacher-directed learning strategies that can take 2-6 weeks to implement. Because it is based on a constructivist approach to second-language acquisition, teachers find the model adaptable to different grade levels and program options (Calderón, 1991, 1994i). For instance:

- BCIRC is being used in middle schools and high schools for teaching ESL. It is just as effective in 50-minute periods as it is in newcomer classes that are 2 or more hours long.
- BCIRC is being used in middle schools and high schools for teaching sheltered social studies, science, and math courses. It is particularly effective in schools that have class periods of 1 hour and 45 minutes, although 50-minute sessions spread out over 2 or more weeks are also effective.
- BCIRC is being used in elementary schools for transitional bilingual language arts programs, because it creates a natural transition between first- and second-language reading and writing skills.
- BCIRC is being used in elementary schools as a "reading across the

curriculum" model for content-area reading for students who need additional practice.

- BCIRC is being used for literature-based approaches, because the reading activities and writing process render an appreciation and a thorough exploration of a variety of literature for and by children.
- BCIRC is being used with basal readers, because the "Treasure Hunt" questions that teachers and students develop provide more critical thinking than the basal questions. The story-related mapping and writing suggestions also yield higher quality of student products in comparison to basal suggested activities.
- BCIRC is being used for thematic interdisciplinary units, because the 20 or so activities of 6-week units make profound learning fun. It creates a context for integrated experimentation and discovery.
- BCIRC is being used for bilingual instruction in two-way bilingual programs because students are learning through interdisciplinary interactive discussion, reading and writing in two languages with a more capable peer.

Cooperative Learning Provides a Better Context for Bilingualism

The research on these BCIRC applications during the past 5 years has found many benefits for students. The benefits found systematically across the different grade level programs that focused on the *learning of English* were that:

- BCIRC increases the variety of and frequency of second-language practice because it provides varied concrete experiences, as recommended by Krashen and Terrell (1983).
- The input from peers while working in pairs and teams of four is much more comprehensible.
- Team work on treasure hunts offers students the opportunity to hear more complex language than from the teacher in whole-class discussion.
- The variety of team activities creates natural redundancy in communication as students exchange information and requests, as recommended by Long, Brock, Crookes, Deicke, Potter, and Zhang, 1984.
- Oral communication is integrated with literacy development and is the basis for making meaning of reading texts.
- Instead of language drills or choppy pieces of language, students use continuous, ongoing discourse that relates to particular tasks, problem solving, or creative endeavors; thus, language learning becomes subconscious as students focus on cognitive endeavors.
- The carefully structured sequence becomes an information processing model that develops internal mental structures and schemata for processing information in the first language for the first few months—then the processing in the second language becomes obvious as students master subject matter.

Cooperative Learning for Biliteracy and Biculturalism

In addition to deriving the seven benefits listed above (Calderón & Carreón, 1994), students participating in two-way bilingual programs also enjoy these advantages:

- There are more possibilities for natural correction from peers and for students to develop their own self-correction devices through the frequent debriefing strategies.
- There are higher levels of linguistic accuracy and information processing accuracy, because students are always interacting with native speakers of each language.
- The questions formulated by students are genuine or what Long et al. (1984) calls referential—those where the questioner really needs the information. This is in contrast to the display questions "Is this a pencil?" that are typical in ESL programs. Students in two-way bilingual programs have to negotiate for meaning within a variety of tasks all day long!
- The students' first language acquires high status, and their self-esteem flourishes as they become experts for other students.
- When students become experts for other students in team and partner activities, the bilingual program becomes an enrichment program for all students rather than a compensatory intervention for limited-English-proficient students.
- Students understand the global aspects of literacy as well as those aspects that belong to each language and culture.
- Because students use the whole range of their first-language capabilities (through the cycle of academic and social activities), these learning and thinking processes are then naturally transferred into the follow-up cycle in the second language. Going through a cycle in each language enables faster learning of a second language while developing a high level of the first.
- The bilingual/bicultural cycle enables inclusion of a greater variety of curricular materials, real-life experiences, and authentic literature from diverse cultures.
- A safe context is created for newly arrived immigrants. Newcomers find that their language expertise and cultural capital are valued and nurtured.
- In a supportive, nonthreatening cooperative context, students learn important life skills for working in binational or multiethnic contexts.
- BCIRC consists of a sequence of team formation, team building; class building; role assignment; social and cooperative norms development; vocabulary building; formulating and testing predictions; developing oral, silent, and peer reading strategies; debriefing strategies for content, process of learning and thinking, and social behavior; reading comprehension; answering and formulating questions; writing meaningful sentences; pronunciation practice; spelling practice; mapping stories and

characters; doing different types of writing in teams and individually; editing; publishing; storytelling; presenting; and peer- and self-evaluation through portfolio rubrics, checklists, and reflection activities. As students complete this cycle in 2-to-6-week units, the myriad of skills, content, and language learned is too great to describe in this synthesis of research (Calderón, 1994b).

Documented Student Academic Achievement

BCIRC developed into a dual-language management system that enables teachers to keep track of student biliteracy progress. Students are continuously engaged in meaningful and challenging activities at all times, and time on reading and writing increases as much as 500 percent, compared to other reading methods used in bilingual classrooms. Many positive student gains in linguistic, academic, and social achievement have been documented through the 5-year study in Ysleta Independent School District in El Paso.

In the Ysleta ISD study (1988-1994), students in BCIRC experimental classrooms outperformed students in control classrooms. In this 5-year project, hundreds of experimental and control students were initially matched by levels of English and Spanish at each grade level and were tested at the end of each year with standardized tests, a criterion-referenced test for reading comprehension, writing tests in two languages, a self-esteem and cooperative attitudes inventory, and portfolio contents.

Some Students' Gains from the Ysleta Project:

- BCIRC students made greater academic gains than the control classrooms on two standardized tests: the Texas Assessment for Academic Skills and the Norm-Referenced Assessment Program for Texas.
- More students transitioned into regular classrooms sooner and had sustained academic success.
- Many students transitioned into gifted classes.
- The more continuous years that students were in BCIRC (when all grade levels implemented the model), the greater the academic, linguistic, and social gains.
- BCIRC students did better than control groups on criterion-referenced tests that measured reading and writing proficiencies in both languages.
- BCIRC students typically won first place in school and district writing contests, science fairs, and other academic contests.
- BCIRC student writing samples were rated higher on quantity and quality in comparison to their equivalent groups. They had longer narratives and higher "quality" scores for writing in two languages. (See Hertz-Lazarowitz & Calderón, 1994; and Calderón, 1994c for additional descriptions of the results.)

Better Anglo/Hispanic Relations and Liking of "Spanish"

Student attitudes toward working in cooperative groups and toward the language of instruction were assessed with the Cooperative Attitude Reaching Education (CARE) scales. On a scale of 1-3 (1=very much, 2=some, 3=not at all), the great majority of students in the two-way bilingual program rated items dealing with their feelings toward others as a 1. The cumulative percentage of students selecting the ranking of 1 or 2 ranged from 87 to 97 percent. The majority of students also felt that their classmates liked them, and 64 percent gave the item a ranking of 1. Students also gave high rankings to items related to their attitude towards school and specifically their class. When asked if they liked to read and write in English and Spanish, a cumulative percentage of 92 percent indicated that they liked to do so in English, 86 percent indicated the same for Spanish, and 88 percent of the students liked to read and write in either language in groups. These are the most positive results gathered in the past 3 years of utilizing this instrument with students from various school districts and in comparison with different types of bilingual programs.

Benefits for Teachers: A Positive Context for Teachers To Construct Their Own Knowledge

Many studies in El Paso and Juárez have focused on identifying the best promising staff development and teacher support practices for implementing a complex cooperative learning model such as BCIRC (Calderón, 1994c, 1994d). The results of these studies give us insights on the following components:

- elements of a positive school context for teacher development;
- the content and process of the most effective development activities;
- how and which cooperative learning strategies can be used as effective staff development tools;
- stages that teachers go through when implementing cooperative learning models;
- how teachers construct their Teachers' Learning Communities (TLCs) for continuous improvement and types of collaborative activities conducted in weekly TLCs; and
- how teachers become researchers and trainers of other teachers and curriculum developers (see Calderón, 1994a, 1994b, 1994c; Calderón & Durán, in press; Hertz-Lazarowitz & Calderón, 1994).

Professional Development for the Year 2000 Begins Now for Teachers

The preparation for the two-way bilingual program was far from fast flimsy fixes. The teachers, principals, resource teachers, and project director attended a 3-hour workshop every Wednesday for the first year.

They also worked on curriculum development and attended more in-service training during the summer. The comprehensive staff development components of process and content were presented in *both* Spanish and English.

The process consisted of presentation of theory, modeling of teaching strategies, peer practice at the workshops, peer coaching in the schools, and lesson development. The content consisted of theories of first- and second-language acquisition; culture, history, and values of the students; and an extensive repertoire of teaching strategies and alternative assessment techniques.

The teaching strategies and models consisted of the inquiry model (Joyce, Weil, & Showers, 1992), bilingual group investigation (Hertz-Lazarowitz & Calderón, 1994; Sharan, 1992), the Bilingual Cooperative Integrated Reading and Composition (Stevens et al., 1987; Calderón, 1994i), concept attainment, and discovery models (Joyce et al., 1992). Teachers and administrators also studied research on staff development, implementation of change, systems thinking, building communities of learners, Accelerated Schools' philosophy, and collegial models.

In addition to the Wednesday staff development sessions, teachers conducted their Teachers' Learning Community (TLC) sessions once a month, where they shared their student products, successes, and failures; read journal articles to each other; and used a variety of activities to construct their own learning experiences and fine-tune their implementation.

What Do Teachers Accomplish in Learning Communities?

Teachers need a place where they can solve complex problems of implementation. They need a place to reflect on their practice, share exciting successes, gauge their performance, and solve problems with the help of others who are "in the same boat" (Little, 1982; Fullan, 1990). These self-directed collaborative study groups are places in schools or universities where colleagues can

- identify areas of interest, problems, and solutions;
- plan, organize, and evaluate their professional development activities;
- share knowledge, teaching skills, and student products;
- schedule peer observations and coaching; and
- plan binational activities.

Observations of Teachers' Learning Community (TLC) activities in bilingual settings provide ample variety of activities that teachers have constructed to create meaning of their learning (Calderón, 1994a). Any place in the school can be designated as a TLC. One example of a TLC is a group of sixth-grade teachers from Harris Middle School in San Antonio

Independent School District. They selected their science lab as their TLC. On *Mondays* they talk about curriculum, *Tuesdays* are for meeting with the principal to take care of "school business," *Wednesdays* are for studying articles and furthering their knowledge base, *Thursdays* are for solving problems about individual students, *Fridays* are for catch-up or "unfinished business." They bring "goodies" to eat and celebrate the accomplishments of the week.

Cooperative Learning As a Tool for Staff Development

Staff development interventions for teachers must provide ongoing, interactive, cumulative learning on the multiple aspects of education of language-minority students in order to develop new conceptions, skills, and behaviors. The basis of learning is interaction. Teachers learn by interacting with consultants and university faculty, but mainly with peers (Tharp & Gallimore, 1988; Fullan, 1990; Calderón, 1992). Interactions take place during training activities, observation, and discussion of teaching demonstrations; practice of the teaching behaviors; peer feedback and coaching cycles; and, at intense levels, during problem solving in TLCs.

Teacher development designs can capitalize on the essentially social nature of teaching and learning and use cooperative learning for both purposes. Cooperative learning structures help teachers learn how to use cooperative structures in their classroom but also help teachers develop in several other ways. For instance, cooperative learning (CL) can be included in the process for in-service training with four purposes in mind:

1. to teach the content of the training focus;
2. to teach, apply, and internalize principles of adult learning, coaching, feedback, and support techniques;
3. to conduct reflection, decision making, and problem solving activities; and
4. to learn how to use CL strategies in the classroom. (For a full description of how to conduct this type of in-service training, see Calderón, 1994e, 1994f, 1994g.)

Binational Staff Development Activities

Last summer, the staff development component took on a new twist. Teachers attended a 1-week summer institute in Juárez on Bilingual Cooperative Integrated Reading and Composition (BCIRC) and on group investigation, conducted in Spanish by teachers from Juárez who are also implementing those models. Juárez teachers attended a 1-week institute on BCIRC in El Paso, conducted in English. They not only learned BCIRC teaching strategies but also fine-tuned their English. Teachers from El Paso went to a 1-week institute in Juárez and learned BCIRC strategies and fine-tuned their Spanish.

During the school year, teachers from Juárez presented workshops in Spanish to teachers in El Paso. Relationships flourished, and the contact and exchanges have continued. There are plans to continue the summer institutes in both cities.

The Dangers of Quick Fixes and Superficial Exchanges

The successes that have been documented across multiple settings prove the effectiveness of a comprehensive model for change that includes curriculum, teaching methods, theory, staff development designs, and teachers' learning communities. It is important to highlight, however, that the successes were commensurate with a strong philosophy of implementation and teacher support. In several other settings, the erosion and misapplication of BCIRC were observed when commitment to its philosophy and teacher support were missing.

First, BCIRC is a mind-set for the project implementers that involves a strong philosophy of equity, quality, and high expectations for all learners. The learners include administrators, teachers, parents, and students. The social development of intelligence is the mechanism that ultimately produces observed benefits. Therefore, cooperative learning is an integral part of literacy, social, and cognitive development. Teachers and administrators believe that cooperative learning is the best way for students to learn and they themselves practice collegial learning, coaching, collaborative decision making, planning, and ongoing assessment and improvement.

The mind-set of cooperation becomes the source for creating positive change and innovation (Senge, 1990). Although change does not come quickly, change becomes a desirable goal when colleagues have an opportunity to take control of organizing their learning. Addressing the needs of language-minority students must become a cooperative and comprehensive program.

Placing students in groups and encouraging them to work together through cooperative structures is not sufficient to produce significant learning gains. In classrooms of teachers who attended only a few days of inservice on cooperative learning, the following pattern has been observed (Hertz-Lazarowitz & Calderón, 1994):

- students working with low-level content in teams,
- students working with unchallenging tasks,
- one or two students doing the work for the team,
- students working with a low level of cooperation, and
- unchanged student achievement and test scores.

When interviewed, the teachers of these students identified the following barriers to effective implementation of cooperative learning:

- inflexible schedules (little time for group activities);

- the need to "cover certain material" or else they would be in trouble;
- curriculum designed for the traditional classroom;
- no time to teach social norms or the discourse of cooperation;
- no time for lesson development;
- problem students would not cooperate;
- not enough knowledge to make situational decisions about team formation, team building, teaching strategies to use, etc.;
- grading difficulties;
- pressure to teach to the district's or state's test;
- administrators wanted dramatic results immediately; and
- supervisors did not know how to evaluate cooperative learning lessons.

These barriers exist when schools do not provide comprehensive staff development and follow-up support systems for teachers.

Effective Staff Development Process

The staff development portion of our Cooperative Learning in Bilingual Settings study (Calderón, 1994c, 1994d) focused on (1) the content that teachers needed in order to promote a cooperative learning philosophy, appropriate teaching skills, and fidelity to the mode; (2) the process of teacher development; and (3) ways of organizing support systems for teachers trying to shift into a new instructional philosophy and delivery system.

In essence, the findings confirmed that although comprehensive coverage of content at the teacher in-service sessions is vitally important, the process for renewal and follow-up support systems for collegial learning are critical. Without certain processes for preparing teachers, the content never transfers into their active teaching repertoire. Therefore, the teaching philosophies and methods we would like teachers to espouse never transfer into the classroom—no matter how many hours or days or monies are spent on in-service workshops!

The professional development processes that help teachers transfer desired knowledge, behaviors, and appropriate decisions into the classroom can be summarized as follows:

- presentation of theory, philosophy, and research on cooperative learning, literacy development, alternative assessment, and teacher professional development; followed by extensive observation of CIRC and BCIRC teaching models conducted in both languages;
- analysis and discussion of student adaptation and modification to meet diverse needs;
- management of heterogeneous grouping in two languages for instruction;
- activities for teachers and students for developing cooperative skills and positive collegial relationships;

- communication skills and protocols for peer coaching, e.g., offering help, accepting help, and making suggestions to the teacher for improvement;
- guided practice with feedback from peer coaching, mentoring, and interactive peer journals;
- video analysis and reflection activities of own teaching performance and decisions;
- time blocks for adapting school curriculum and lesson planning;
- study and analysis of student performance, alternative assessment processes, and portfolio assessment; and
- ways to sustain self-directed collaborative study groups or Teachers' Learning Communities at schools where colleagues continue to refine their practices, celebrate their successes, and deal with problems.

Genuine Change at the Teacher Level Is Multidimensional.

When attempting to implement cooperative learning, there are at least four dimensions of personal change for *mainstream classroom teachers*:

- the integration of new teaching approaches into the teacher's repertoire,
- the use of new revised materials to go with those approaches,
- the possible alteration of beliefs or pedagogical assumptions, and
- the incorporation of new classroom norms into the teaching process.

For *bilingual teachers* there are at least two more:

- the development of proficiency in two languages and fluency for delivering the new teaching approaches, and debriefing of higher-order thinking and processing of complex information; and
- the techniques to address students' mixed levels of linguistic and conceptual complexity.

This comprehensive staff development program has major implications for school restructuring efforts. The critical elements of effective teacher development should be incorporated into the school's organizational development plan. In essence, teachers of language-minority students need to know how to create the kind of classroom environment that will facilitate bilingual literacy, content learning, and pride in being bilingual and bicultural. Without appropriate support, teachers will have an insurmountable task.

Why Cooperative Learning for All?

Since no one has the answers to the complex problems facing our border schools today, educators from both sides must work together to solve them. The more adults work together, the more opportunities they create for unlocking complex challenges and for solving problems with trust and mutual respect (Liebermann, 1986). For years, Johnson and Johnson

(1987), proponents of cooperative learning, have been proposing collegial support groups as a tool for educational reform. They found that competitive and individualistic environments are less effective in achieving positive outcomes for adults. They concluded that cooperation among adults promotes achievement, positive interpersonal relationships, social support, and self-esteem.

Cooperative learning provides the structures that

- enable and support difficult work;
- facilitate joint reflection on new knowledge; and
- teach group skills, conflict management, consensus building, decision making, and critical inquiry, while maintaining the dignity of individual team members.

In Juárez and El Paso, cooperative learning has provided a common theme, a common strategy, a point of departure where everyone is a learner. There are no experts and novices. The teachers in Juárez are highly skilled in using CL for middle schools, while the teachers in El Paso have tremendous expertise at the elementary level. Each takes turns being expert and novice. Both will become novices as staff development incorporates technology as another tool for cooperative learning.

Pulling It All Together

This chapter has described research-based projects involving student achievement, immigrant students, second-language acquisition, biliteracy, instructional methods, bilingual teacher development, staff development design, cooperation among adults, learning communities, and program implementation. All of these come together to form the theoretical and practical underpinnings of the Binational Model. Graph 1 (page 224) illustrates how these projects are triangulated to relate to one another, all the while creating an impact on the students.

The Binational Model operates simultaneously on five levels: (1) cultivating relationships, (2) providing comprehensive staff development, (3) providing continuous information and networks, (4) implementing innovations in schools, and (5) conducting research and evaluation.

The comprehensive model addresses various layers simultaneously. (See Graph 2, page 225.)

Most attempts at binational exchanges tend to stay at the information stage. Or, they are one-sided in nature. For instance, Mexican teachers are recruited to teach in U.S. schools but not vice versa. Teachers from the United States go to Mexico for brief courses, but rarely is the same opportunity offered to Mexican teachers. Exchanges must be two-way exchanges. With this in mind, the Binational Model seeks to promote equivalent structures where there are ample opportunities for everyone who wants to participate.

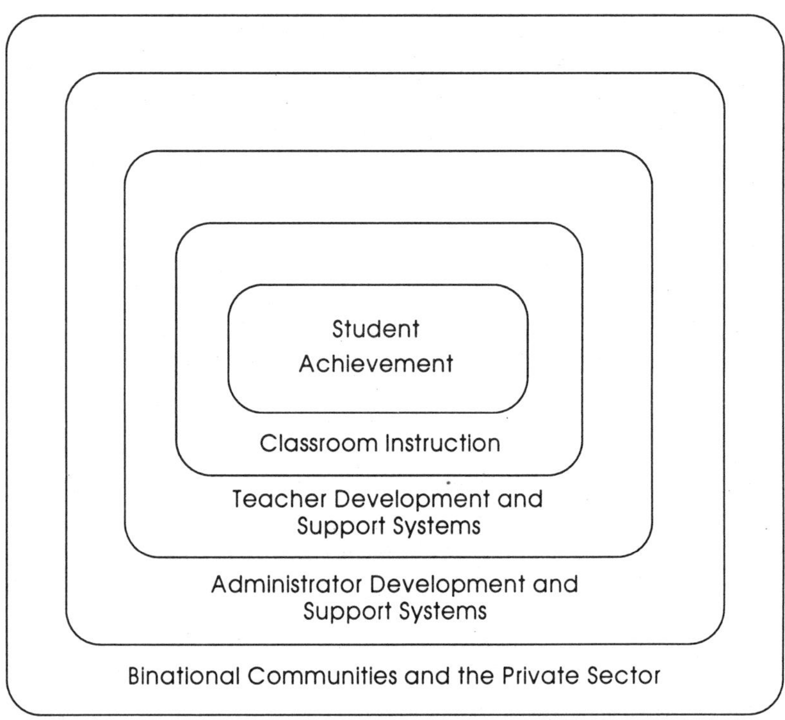

Graph 1

The model of staff development is currently organized to provide opportunities to participants for

- acquisition of knowledge and information processing;
- skill development (teaching, writing, researching, using technology);
- acquisition of a second language;
- rewriting of curricula and materials;
- gathering and disseminating local culture (folk stories, art, history, etc.); and
- gathering and disseminating children's literature in Spanish and English.

The mechanism for knowledge and skill development is orchestrated through

- joint workshops;
- conferences and seminars;
- university courses;
- certificate programs;
- intern programs;
- peer coaching across the border;
- mentoring programs;

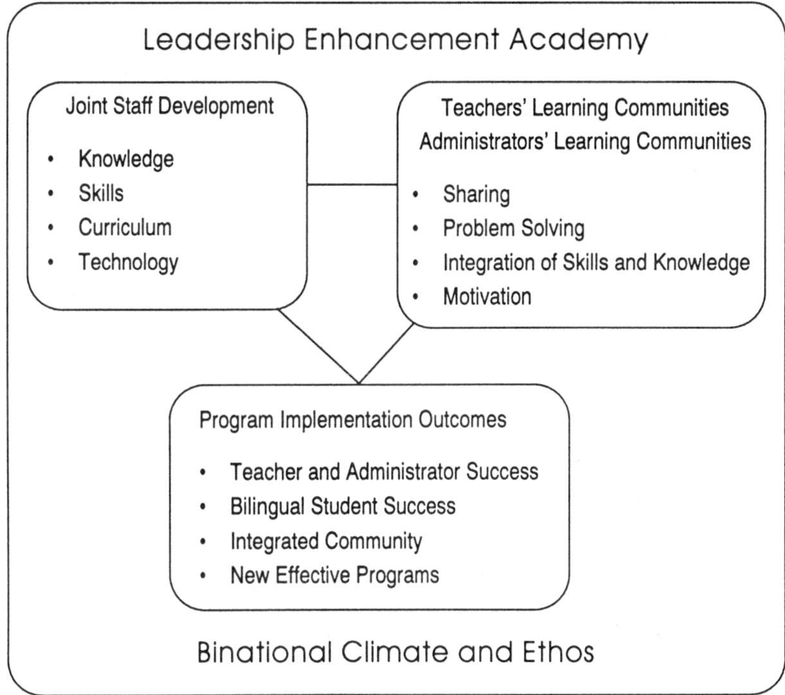

Graph 2

- principals shadowing principals;
- student, teacher, and administrator exchanges;
- school visitations and classroom observations;
- joint curriculum development;
- joint research; and
- teachers training teachers.

Implications from this program, which will be studied for the next 5 years, have already singled out some premises about the future of staff development:

1. Bilingualism and biculturalism are developed to a higher degree of comfort and quality in a context where the two cultures interact.
2. The best context for complex learning is through interaction in cooperative heterogeneous teams.
3. Learning is enhanced when participants are assisted by more capable peers (Vygotsky, 1978), and each cohort of teachers takes turns being the more capable peers.
4. Language and cultural differences dissipate when educators are learning that which is meaningful and relevant to their students' needs.
5. Staff development approaches, themes, and strategies; instructional repertoires for teachers; and leadership models cut across cultures. We

all have the same problems, dreams, aspirations, fears, and need for companionship.

6. Resources can stretch a long way when shared with others. The more you give, the more you receive.

Webster's Dictionary defines the word "collaboration" as working with the enemy or the invader. Binational staff development helps all of us learn to work with the real enemy—our own fears and biases that invade us constantly. By working with others, we learn to work out those fears.

References

Acosta, M. (1995). Unpublished presentation at local school district.

Calderón, M. (1984). *Second language acquisition and organizational change through an effective training model. Bilingual Education Selected Paper Series. Los Angeles*: California State University: Evaluation, Dissemination, and Assessment Center.

Calderón, M. (1984). *Training bilingual trainers: An ethnographic study of coaching and its impact on the transfer of training.* Unpublished doctoral dissertation, San Diego State University, CA.

Calderón, M. (1989). Applying research on effective bilingual instruction in a multidistrict in-service teacher training program. *National Association for Bilingual Education Journal, 12*(2), 133-152.

Calderón, M. (1989, September). Cooperative learning for limited-English-proficient students. *IDRA Newsletter*. San Antonio, TX: Intercultural Development Research Association, 16(9), 1-7.

Calderón, M. (1990). *Cooperative learning for limited-English-proficient students.* Baltimore: Johns Hopkins University.

Calderón, M. (1990-91). Cooperative learning builds communities of teachers. *Teacher Education and Practice, 6*(2), 75-79.

Calderón, M. (1991). Benefits of cooperative learning for Hispanic students. *Texas Research Journal, 2,* 39-57.

Calderón, M. (1992). Dynamic assessment of teachers and language-minority students through cooperative learning. *Cooperative Learning. 13*(1), 27-29.

Calderón, M. (1994a). *The important role of BCIRC for effective bilingual programs: Annual report.* Baltimore: Johns Hopkins University Center for Research on Effective Schooling for Disadvantaged Students.

Calderón, M. (1994b). *Transforming learning and curriculum of language-minority students through cooperative learning.* Symposium at the American Educational Research Association, New Orleans, LA.

Calderón, M. (1994c). *Bilingual teacher development within school learning communities: A synthesis of the staff development model: Annual report.* Baltimore: Johns Hopkins University Center for Research on Effective Schooling for Disadvantaged Students.

Calderón, M. (1994d). *Professional development for teachers implementing cooperative learning.* Paper presented at the American Educational Research Association, New Orleans, LA.

Calderón, M. (1994e). *The Bilingual Cooperative Integrated Reading and Composition Model: Resource book for staff development specialists and teachers.* El Paso, TX: MTTI Inc.

Calderón, M. (1994f). *El aprendizaje cooperativo en las universidades.* El Paso, TX: MTTI, Inc.

Calderón, M. (1994g). *El aprendizaje cooperativo en primarias y secundarias. Manual para maestros.* El Paso, TX: MTTI, Inc.

Calderón, M. (1994h). Mentoring, peer-coaching, and support systems for first-year minority/bilingual teachers. In R. A. DeVillar, C. J. Faltis, & J. P. Cummins (Eds.), *Cultural diversity in schools: From rhetoric to practice.* Albany, NY: SUNY Press.

Calderón, M. (1994i). Cooperative learning for bilingual settings. In R. Rodriguez, N. J. Ramos, & J. A. Ruiz Escalante (Eds.), *Compendium of readings in bilingual education: Issues and practices.* San Antonio, TX: Texas Association for Bilingual Education.

Calderón, M. (1995). *Dual language programs and bilingual teachers' professional development.* Symposium at the American Educational Research Association, San Francisco, CA.

Calderón, M., & Carreón, A. (1994). Educators and students use cooperative learning to become biliterate and bicultural. *Cooperative Learning Magazine, 4,* 6-9.

Calderón, M., & Durán, R. (in press). *Restructuring schools for language-minority student success.* New York: Scholastic, Inc.

California State Department of Education. (1994). Telephone conversation with Assistant Superintendent of Instruction.

Cummins, J. (1981). The role of primary language development in promoting educational success for language-minority students. In California State Department of Education (ed.), *Schooling and language-minority students: A theoretical framework* (pp. 3-50). Los Angeles: California State University; Evaluation, Dissemination, and Assessment Center.

Cummins, J. (1993). Empowerment through biliteracy. In J. Tinajero & A. F. Ada (Eds.), *The power of two languages.* New York: Macmillan/McGraw-Hill, 9-25.

Diaz, R. M. (1985, January). Intellectual power of bilingualism. *Quarterly Newsletter of the Laboratory of Comparative Human Cognition, 7*(1).

Draper, J. B. (1989). *The state of the states: State initiatives in foreign languages and international studies, 1979-1989.* Washington, DC: Joint National Committee for Languages. (ERIC Document Reproduction Service No. ED 320 390)

Drucker, P. (1989). How schools must change. *Psychology Today, 5,* 18-20.

Durán, R. (in press). Cooperative learning for language-minority students. In R. A. DeVillar, C. J. Faltis, & J. P. Cummins (Eds.), *Successful cultural diversity: Classroom practices for the 21st century.* New York: SUNY Press.

Fullan, M. G. (1990). Staff development, innovation and institutional development. In B. Joyce (Ed.), *Changing school culture through staff development* (pp. 3-25). Washington, DC: Association for Supervision and Curriculum Development.

Hertz-Lazarowitz, R., & Calderón, M. (1994). Implementing cooperative learning in the elementary schools: The facultative voice for collaborative power. In Sharan, S. (Ed.), *Handbook of cooperative learning methods.* Westport, CT: Greenwood Press.

Hertz-Lazarowitz, R., Ivory, G., & Calderón, M. (1993). *The Bilingual Cooperative Integrated Reading and Composition (BCIRC) project in the Ysleta Independent School District: Standardized test outcomes.* Baltimore: Johns Hopkins University Center for Research on Effective Schooling for Disadvantaged Students.

Johnson, R. T., & Johnson, D. W. (1987). How can we put cooperative learning into practice? *Science Teacher, 54*(6), 46-48, 50.

Joyce, B. R., Weil, M., & Showers, B. (1992). *Models of teaching*. Boston: Allyn & Bacon.

Krashen, S. D., & Terrell, T. D. (1983). *The natural approach: Language acquisition in the classroom.* San Francisco: Alemany Press.

Liebermann, A. (1986). Collaborative work. *Educational Leadership, 45*(5), 4-8.

Little, J. W. (1982). Norms of collegiality and experimentation: Workplace conditions of school success. *American Educational Research Journal, 19*(3), 325-340.

Long, M. H., Brock, C. A., Crookes, G., Deicke, C., Potter, L., & Zhang, S. (1984). The effect of teachers' questioning patterns and wait-time on pupil participation in public high school classes in Hawaii for students of limited-English proficiency (Technical Report No. 1). Honolulu: University of Hawaii at Manoa, CSLCR.

McDonnell, L. M., & Hill, P. T. (1993). *Newcomers in American schools: Meeting the educational needs of immigrant youths*. Santa Monica, CA: Rand.

Reich, R. B. (1992). *The work of nations: Preparing ourselves for 21st century capitalism.* New York: Vintage Books.

Senge, P. M. (1990). *The fifth discipline: The art and practice of the learning organization.* New York: Doubleday.

Sharan, Y. (1992). Group investigation. *Cooperative Learning Magazine*, 13.

Slavin, R. E., & Madden, N. A. (1995). *Effects of Success For All on the achievement of language learners.* Paper presented at the American Educational Research Association, San Francisco, CA.

Slavin, R. E., Madden, N. A., Dolan, L. J., Wasik, B. A., Ross, S., & Smith, L. (1994). Whenever and wherever we choose...The replication of Success for All. *Phi Delta Kappan, 75*(8), 639-647.

Stevens, R. J., Madden, N. A., Slavin, R. E., & Farnish, A. M. (1987). *Cooperative integrated reading and composition: Two field experiments.* Baltimore, MD: Center for Research on Elementary and Middle Schools, Johns Hopkins University. (ERIC Document Reproduction Service No. ED 291 075)

Texas Education Agency. (1995, May). Texas teacher retention, mobility and attrition (Report Number 6). Austin, TX: Author.

Texas Education Agency. (1993, September). *Final report on district and campus accountability rating.* Austin, TX: Author.

Tharp, R. G., & Gallimore, R. (1988). *Rousing minds to life: Teaching, learning, and schooling in social context.* New York: Cambridge University Press.

Vasquez-Ramos, A. (1993). Educational policy recommendations under the North American Free Trade Agreement. *Latino Educators' Committee on Free Trade and Education.* Los Angeles: USC Embassy Residential College, June 21, 1993.

Vygotsky, L. S., (1978). *Mind in society: The development of higher psychological processes.* (Cole, M., John-Steiner, V., Scribner, S., & Souberman, E., Eds. and Trans.) Cambridge, MA: Harvard University Press.

Weatherford, H. J. (October, 1986). *Personal benefits of foreign language study* (ERIC Digest). Washington, DC: Clearinghouse on Languages and Linguistics. (ERIC Document Reproduction Service No. ED 276 305)

CHAPTER 14

Programming For Success Among Hispanic Migrant Students

MARY V. MONTAVON AND JERI KINSER
COBDEN UNIT DISTRICT #17
COBDEN, ILLINOIS

The farms surrounding Cobden, Illinois, have employed seasonal migrant labor for decades but, before 1990, few migrant students attended local schools and services for them were minimal. As the number of migrant students has grown, Cobden School District has developed a quality bilingual education program incorporating native-language instruction for students who speak Spanish, content courses in Spanish, and English-as-a-Second-Language (ESL) classes. Begun in 1994, a summer Migrant Education Program provides increased Spanish instructional time and opportunities for students to experience Mexican culture. This chapter provides details on the development of the program; placement and assessment tools; program content at the elementary school, junior high school, and high school levels; instructional materials and strategies; parental involvement; participation of Mexican exchange teachers in the summer program; and program problems and successes.

Establishing Migratory Patterns

Cobden, Illinois, is situated about 330 miles south of Chicago in the fruit-growing hills of southern Illinois. These foothills of the Ozarks are filled with apple, peach, and plum orchards; vineyards; fields of strawberries, blueberries, blackberries, and raspberries; and a variety of vegetables that include tomatoes, peppers, cucumbers, and squash. In order to harvest such an array of produce, much seasonal labor is needed. Few local people are willing to do the work. So, the majority of this agricultural labor is provided by workers who follow the central migrant stream, a pattern of migration beginning in Mexico, Texas, or Florida; passing through southern Illinois; and continuing north to Michigan before returning south each year.

Over the years, the ethnic background of the migrant population coming to Illinois has changed. Many years ago, there were many African American and Anglo American laborers. Since the early 1950s or so, the farm labor migrant population in southern Illinois has consisted primarily of Mexican Americans and Mexicans (Avery, 1995), the latter coming mainly from the state of Michoacán in southeastern Mexico. Many are of Tarascan heritage; some still speaking the language. Others are from the state of Guanajuato in central Mexico. In recent years, they have been joined by workers from the Central American countries of Guatemala and El Salvador (Certificates of Eligibility, 1993-1995).

In our school system, the history of one family with eight children illustrates the pattern of movement to the Cobden region. This family came to Cobden from Cherán, Michoacán, Mexico. As in many other families, the father came first to the United States with his brother. They found work in Texas in 1987 and then continued north to Alabama, North Carolina, and finally southern Illinois. The work they found along the way included cattle ranching, wood cutting, and fruit picking. The orchards near Cobden offered them the opportunity to earn more money than other types of work they had found. In 1990, the mother joined her husband and brought along the youngest daughter. The following year, three sons arrived. And finally in 1992, the entire family of 20 was reunited in southern Illinois. Despite substandard living conditions in a two-bedroom home with no running water, the father's joy was effusive as he spoke about being together again.

During the time this family has been in the Cobden School District, the children have been successful in school, and one graduated from high school in the spring of 1995. Family members have found nonseasonal local employment and become contributing members of the community. They have been able to secure loans from the local bank to purchase cars and a home and have established good credit in the area.

This family and others come to the southern Illinois region for economic opportunities that do not exist for them in Mexico. Most families would prefer to remain in Mexico, but they are unable to find work there. The orchard growers here like the Mexican workers because they work hard and are dependable. Growers in Cobden and other areas need these farmworkers as much as the workers need the growers.

For the winter, Cobden's migrant workers usually return to Arcadia, Florida; McCallen, Texas; or their Mexican hometowns of Cherán, Michoacán, or Salvatierra, Guanajuato. They return to southern Illinois in early spring. The migrant labor camp, where most currently migratory families live, opens the first of April and closes in November.

Previously, the majority of migrant workers were adult males who came to southern Illinois without their families. The Amnesty Act in 1986 (IRCA) allowed many of them to legally bring their families to the United States. This has impacted the schools. An increasing number of families have "settled out," remaining in the Cobden area throughout the entire year. In February 1995, there were 69 migrant students in the district, compared to only 22 students 5 years ago. Many families have bought property in the area or have found living quarters in public housing projects.

Commencement of Program of Instruction

In the fall of 1990, the services provided to migrant students in the Cobden Unit School District were minimal. Students took up space in the classroom but rarely were engaged in learning activities. Some teachers viewed the students as transient and, therefore, not worth spending time with. At this time, there were 55 migrant students in the district in the fall—22 of whom remained during the winter. One classroom was set aside to work with migrant students, but there was no instructional program per se. One teacher and two bilingual noncertified teacher aides were available to help students who came to this classroom. Individual classroom teachers determined whether or not their students needed to be served, but followed no established criteria for sending students to this program. Once students gained minimal conversational skills, they were no longer seen as needing additional instruction.

Some students spent large amounts of time in the migrant room as their regular teachers would send textbooks and assignments for the entire day. Other students would come without assignments or books. Because they were seen as temporary, many students were not even given textbooks for their mainstream classes.

Program Development

In 1990, there was an urgent need to develop an educational program to meet the needs of migrant students, to assess students' language ability upon entry into the program, to provide native-language instruction for those with little or no English proficiency, to offer ESL instruction, and to provide a support system for migrant students in mainstream classrooms.

The State of Illinois mandates a transitional bilingual education program in all school districts that have more than 19 students of the same language background. In addition to ESL instruction, this approach involves the teaching of content areas wholly or partially in the student's home language until skills in English are strong enough that the students can function in the mainstream English-speaking classroom. The current program in the Cobden School District was developed both to meet the mandates of the State of Illinois and to provide a quality educational program for the migrant bilingual student. A crucial part of the program was provision of native-language instruction. The work of researchers such as Cummins (1989), Krashen (1985), Krashen and Biber (1988), and Ovando and Collier (1985) was used to support this approach.

To provide more instruction in native-language skills as well as English, a second teacher and a certified bilingual aide were hired in the fall of 1991. The aide was a former migrant student from the district who had graduated and was studying in the University. Of the two bilingual ESL teachers in the district, one was primarily responsible for kindergarten through sixth grade and the other for junior high and high school. In 1992, an ESL teacher was added to focus on the second-language acquisition needs of students at the grade-school level. An essential part of the bilingual curriculum, this allowed the bilingual instructors to spend more time on native-language instruction.

In 1994, a summer Migrant Education Program was started with the use of Chapter 1 Migrant Education funds. This program extended the students' time in the district to at least 8-9 months. It also increased Spanish instruction time, which was limited during the regular school session. The summer program focused on providing language development and mathematics in the Spanish language to strengthen native-language skills. All teachers, except one, were bilingual.

In addition to the academic program, the summer school gave students the opportunity to explore more fully all aspects of Mexican culture. They were able to experience the music, dance, and art of Mexico and to share their accomplishments with friends and family. It was during this session that a traditional folklóric dance troupe was formed, and local artists provided workshops on mask making and papier-mâché to the students. Recorder lessons were given to all students in grades 4-8. This was a very popular class. It was the first time many students had their own musical instrument and learned to play music. Students also learned to sing typical Mexican songs. For many, it was the first time they had learned words to a song.

Bilingual Assessment Instrument

In addition to a curriculum that met the needs of the students, a plan of assessment and evaluation was developed in the district to make the program accountable. After reviewing various instruments for language proficiency, the Woodcock Language Proficiency Battery (Woodcock, 1991) was chosen as the language assessment tool. Every student, whose home language is one other than English, is given this test upon entry to the program and again in the fall of each successive year. Students who fall below the 50th percentile are placed in the bilingual program. Since the district began using this tool in the fall of 1992, only one student has tested above the 50th percentile either initially or at follow-up. This level of performance is an indication of the extreme need of our students, a need that was not being met within the mainstream program of instruction.

In order to track the progress of all students, the district administers the Iowa Test of Basic Skills (1986) in the fall of each year and the Riverside Achievement Test (La Prueba de Realizacion, 1991) in Spanish in the spring. These tests are not used for placement but, rather, to set a baseline to determine whether progress is being made academically.

Alternative assessment measures are used during the summer Migrant Education Program. Journals track students' writing development and gives staff additional insight into students' reaction to their school day and to the various activities. Writing prompts for functional writing are given to students in grades 3-8 at the beginning and end of the summer, and students' essays are scored based on Illinois' Write On program. A math achievement test is given at the end of the summer.

Program Content

In grades K-6, children whose home language is Spanish are taught to read and write in Spanish. Students receive a language arts grade in Spanish in grades K-4 and are taught social studies in Spanish in grades 5-6. Students also attend ESL classes to acquire the English skills necessary to function in mainstream classrooms. Due to staff limitations, the emphasis in ESL is on those students with very limited English proficiency. Students are pulled out of their regular classroom for 30 minutes per day. Individual needs are taken into account in an afternoon tutorial program. Dependent on need, some students are pulled out of their regular classes less than others for tutoring.

The migrant program also works with the Chapter 1 program to identify students who may benefit from reading and mathematics assistance.

At the junior high school, the bilingual students receive instruction in social studies in Spanish, help with regular classroom work during study hall, and an ESL class. Students with limited English ability struggle through the regular program curriculum. Again, with limited staff, students are not provided first-language instruction in all subject areas. There is still much to be done with the junior high students in terms of additional programming.

High school students are able to take individualized courses in Spanish, mathematics, social studies, science, and health. These PASS (Portable Assisted Study Sequence) courses, which originated in California in 1978, allow students to earn credit towards high school graduation. Each course consists of 10 units. For each unit the student must read the materials, complete the activities, and take a test on the material. After the 10 units are completed, the student receives a full year's credit.

Cobden High School teachers have examined these materials and approved credit for these courses in their subject areas. Spanish language courses are used with students who have little or no English. Students can continue these courses in the summer during the evenings. In addition to these courses in Spanish, ESL is offered at two levels in the high school. With this program and regular courses such as physical education, Spanish language, and art, limited-English-proficient students are able to receive 2 years of high school credit before they plunge completely into an all-English program. Much hard work and assistance is needed for these students to make it through the final 2 years of high school; however, it is being done. In the spring of 1995, two students graduated from this program. Both students began their studies in the district with little English but were able to complete their courses in the regular classroom.

Materials and Strategies for Instruction

In the primary grades, whenever possible, the skills being taught in the Spanish language correspond to those being taught in the mainstream curriculum. It is a goal of the program to work closely with the classroom teacher to coordinate curriculum between the bilingual and the mainstream programs. This has not always been an easy task and there is still much work to be done. The language arts program used in the bilingual curriculum is literature based, taught with a whole language approach. Students read in order to find information and for the sheer enjoyment of reading. This is a program that integrates a variety of language arts skills using many different books, tapes, and posters.

At the kindergarten level, students express their ideas through drawings and the teacher records the commentary given by the child; these drawings and commentaries are saved and put together to form a book. The student may then "read" her/his picture book. They take a great deal of pride in these books, which also can be used as an assessment tool to show their progress throughout the semester.

A variety of activities accompany readings. When reading the story "The Three Little Pigs," for example, students may construct houses using straw, sticks, and blocks; they also may act out the roles of the pigs and the wolf. With a unit about the circus, the classroom floor may be taped to represent the circus ring and the tight rope, and students can act out the roles of people and animals in the circus. At the same time, vocabulary enhancement and language development are being achieved.

Students at the elementary level also like to express themselves through drawings. Students may work on a mural together. They decide what they want in the mural and then work together over a period of time to complete the task. After the mural is finished, writing assignments may include vocabulary generated by the portrayals on the mural.

Students at this level enjoy learning through music, and it is important to provide plenty of opportunities to sing and listen to songs. After students learn a few songs or finish a mural, the teacher may use a video camera to film their work. Students really enjoy seeing themselves perform.

Students may also role-play by acting out the story of "The Three Bears." Props are used for porridge, chairs, and beds, and each student takes a turn playing the part of Goldilocks or one of the three bears.

Alternative methods of assessment may be necessary with these students. Students with reading difficulties may require oral testing on subject matter content (i.e., social studies}. Students with writing difficulties may compose an essay with the help of a tape recorder and later transcribe their work onto paper.

Awareness of the contributions of minority cultures can be brought into the classroom in many ways. Students may be assigned projects and activities that allow them to demonstrate culture-specific knowledge and skills; special holidays may be honored through discussions, projects, or demonstrations. For example, students may compare Mexico's Day of the Dead to the U.S. Halloween and celebrate the appropriate customs, have a fiesta to celebrate Mexican Independence Day on September 16, make murals about the work in the fields, develop related discussion and writing projects, or write a history of their parents' migration to the United Stated.

In the junior high U.S. history class, opportunities to discuss issues relevant to immigrants to this country, treatment of Native Americans, Spanish influence, or Mexican history can make history come alive for these students. The junior high/high school ESL class at the beginning level emphasizes the vocabulary of everyday situations and school subject areas. In the second course, greater emphasis is placed on reading and writing in the English language. Students are exposed to literature and work on using the English language to express themselves.

Parental Involvement

Over the years, parental involvement has grown. The single greatest indicator of parental concern is the fact that many families have chosen to "settle out" and have bought property in the district or found residence in the public housing projects. They realize the great detriment to their children of moving from school to school. Some families make a tremendous sacrifice to stay in the area, because there are often no jobs available from November to March. They have chosen to stay in the Cobden area, because they are concerned about their children's education. They encourage their children in school and hope that their children's lives will be easier than their own.

For those families who do move away for the winter, getting their children enrolled in school as soon as they return in the spring is their first priority. Students coming from Texas have already been promoted to the next grade in their Texas school, but the parents make sure they are back in school in Illinois, if only for a few weeks.

The school open-house theme in 1993 was "Mexican Heritage." The Mexican mothers prepared and served more than 500 meals to the school community. There were dissatisfied customers when the food ran out. These mothers took great pride in seeing the Cobden natives enjoy their Mexican home cooking.

Parents feel free to come to the classroom with questions or concerns and have become much more vocal and responsive in parent meetings. Parents have supported the program staff and have made their voices known at school board meetings.

Parents are more likely to show up for a parent meeting if there is a planned activity for their children at the same time. Parents do not have child care readily available. During December, a parent meeting was scheduled in conjunction with a Christmas cookie bake and party planned by the high school Spanish Club for the younger children. The turnout was tremendous. The children had a good time, and the parents felt at ease without their children in tow and assured that they were well provided for. The Cobden Spanish Club students loved hosting this event for the children.

Exchange Programs

Two Mexican teachers took part in the summer Migrant Education Program. They were part of a group of teachers who were sponsored by the Secretaría de Relaciones Exteriores in Mexico to work with Mexican communities in the United States. Both were graduates of the Escuela Superior de Educación Física. One was from Mexico City and the other from Tijuana. Their contribution was a tremendous benefit to the program. These teachers were extremely adept at working with the students and teaching them about Mexican history and culture. They used role play, storytelling, and games to engage the students in learning activities. They were understanding and keen by being aware to the particular needs of migrant students.

It is hoped that such a program can be continued in the future and that teachers from other Spanish-speaking countries can participate. Teachers in Guatemala have expressed an interest in exploring possibilities for participation, but nothing concrete has developed yet.

Additional Factors to Consider

Needless to say, there are many difficulties in a program such as this. One of the greatest concerns for staff members is the ratio of students to staff. One teacher spends short periods of time with many students. One half hour of native-language instruction and one half hour of ESL instruction are not enough for students who begin school with little or no knowledge of English and with many basic skill deficiencies. Sad to say, money is a factor in hiring additional staff, and administrators' priorities are not always in sync with educational needs of the students.

Along with the these problems, there is the controversial nature of bilingual education in the United States and in the Cobden School District. Some educators, parents, and legislators believe students should be moved into all English classes as quickly as possible. They believe that the more English the students are exposed to, the more quickly and better the students will learn English. Despite research to the contrary, they are firm in this view. Most agree to the need for ESL classes but not to the need for native-language instruction. Many staff members do not understand what the purpose of native-language instruction is or why it is necessary. They do not realize all that is involved in learning another language. Some do not understand the particular needs of migrant students. Much more in-service training for mainstream teachers is needed.

Some migrant parents do not want their children to participate in the program because they want them to "learn English" or they do not want them stigmatized by being separated from the native English-speaking students. More parent education is also needed.

Another difficulty in teaching is the varying educational and literacy levels of the students. Dialects vary depending on whether the student was born and raised in the United States, in a "rancho," or in a "pueblo" in Mexico. Vocabulary and usage depend upon the area from which the child comes. Our experience has shown that children who arrived from Mexico with a good foundation in Spanish are more successful in learning English than U.S.-born Mexican American children. The task is to enhance their Spanish vocabulary and expose them to literature and other language usage that will develop their abilities in the language.

Despite the difficulties, there have been program successes. Most parents are happy and proud that their children can read and write in Spanish. Receiving instruction in Spanish has given children pride in their language and culture that was lacking in the past. The individualized programs at the high school level in subjects such as health and science in Spanish are very positive. Courses in Mexican history and literature have given students a sense of pride in their heritage and history and have made them more aware of who they are.

The folklóric dance troupe formed during the summer session has subsequently been invited to perform for the Mexican Independence Day celebration in the town square and for the Arts in Celebration Festival. The students were also invited to perform for the International Student Festival at Southern Illinois University and to participate in a dance recital with a local dance instructor. Both students and their parents felt good about this.

Though it will take several years to show the academic success of the program, the socio-psychological benefits seem apparent. Students are enthusiastic about their studies; absenteeism is down; parents participate more in school activities. Students want to be a part of school activities, ask questions about why they are treated in prejudicial ways, and have begun to dream about what they want to do when they grow up. One of our students, a junior in high school, just revealed that he wants to be a bilingual teacher!

References

Avery, V. (1995). Personal Communication. State of Illinois, Department of Employment Security.

Certificates of Eligibility. (1993-1995). Cobden, IL: Cobden Migrant Education Program.

Cummins, J. (1989). Empowering minority students. Sacramento: California Association for Bilingual Education.

Iowa Test of Basic Skills. (1986). Chicago, IL: Riverside Publishing Company.

Krashen, S., & Biber, D. (1988). On course: Bilingual education success in California. Sacramento, CA: California Association for Bilingual Education.

Krashen, S. (1985). *Inquiries and insights.* Hayward, CA: Alemany Press.

La Prueba de Realizacion. (1991). Chicago, IL: Riverside Publishing Company.

Ovando, C. J., & Collier, V. P. (1985). *Bilingual and ESL classrooms.* New York: McGraw-Hill.

Woodcock, R. (1991). Woodcock Language Proficiency Battery - Revised. Allen, TX: DLM Teaching Resources.

CHAPTER 15

Latino Voices in Children's Literature: Instructional Approaches for Developing Cultural Understanding in the Classroom

JOHN M. KIBLER
ILLINOIS RESOURCE CENTER

As the Mexican American community continues its growth as the largest language minority population within the U.S. educational system, an investigation of literature that accurately and authentically reflects Mexican American students' cultural experience is necessary for any teacher. This chapter outlines strategies integrating children's literature, specifically Mexican American children's literature, into the structure of a classroom environment through both curricular and social methods. Multicultural literature and its uses in building literacy, academic competencies, and comprehension within ESL, bilingual, and monolingual classroom curricula are also examined. Viewing the Latino community in the United States realistically and understanding the concept of authenticity in cultural teaching must serve as a foundation for this integration. A framework for evaluating and selecting multicultural resources is also emphasized.

And one thing I would really like to tell them about is cultural relativity. I didn't learn until I was in college about other cultures, and I should have learned that in the first grade. A first grader should understand that his or her culture isn't a rational invention and that

> there are thousands of other cultures and they all work pretty well; that all cultures function on faith rather than truth; that there are lots of alternatives to our own society. Cultural relativity is defensible and attractive. It's also a source of hope. It means we don't have to continue this way if we don't like it.
>
> —*Kurt Vonnegut, Jr. (1974)*

Introduction

What is culture? What are its components? How does it affect the creation of an individual? How does it affect the organizations and systems in which individuals participate? A discussion of these four questions provides a strong theoretical foundation for the integration of cultural resources into curricular content areas.

Culture is more than mere custom that can be shed or changed like a suit of clothes. It is dynamic, learned, and creative. It is both conscious and unconscious. It is symbolic, influential, and organized. It is also highly individual. It is not merely the five F's of food, fashion, festivals, famous people, and folklore. Nor is it the artifacts and materials used by people or a laundry list of their behaviors, values, and actions. It defies stereotypic depiction of groups of people in television, movies, newspapers, and other media.

Culture in its clearest reality is a means of survival. As educators begin to build multicultural learning environments in which students positively and substantively interact across cultural lines, multicultural programming concerning curricular integration and student awareness appears very attractive and seems a strong solution. There are, however, several key components to this process that merit the utmost attention. The intent, the preparation, and the training of all individuals involved are paramount, and in many instances, overlooked.

In schools all over the United States, groups of students with different cultural and social histories are brought together, and unprepared educators with the best of intentions simply hope for positive results. No program will be effective if implemented as a solution to the "problems" associated with a culturally different group of persons. The most typical scenario of this process is exemplified by the unstructured and superficial integration of culture into the educational environment through such efforts as ethnic food festivals and international cultural fairs. However, even then, if this integration of diversity doesn't work, the students are blamed or chronic problems concerning bigotry are cited as the core reason why such action was unsuccessful.

What is missing from these scenarios is a real understanding of what culture is, its impact on the creation of an individual, as well as the context that cultural awareness provides for communication and relationships in the intercultural environment.

A useful framework for conceptualizing the impact which culture has on an individual's personality development can be gleaned from Lewin's (1935) and Bronfenbrenner's (1979) formulas for identifying the underlying components of human behavior and human psychological development. Lewin contends that behavior is a joint function of an individual person interacting with his environment. Bronfenbrenner extends this formula to describe the dynamic process of human personality/psychological development as a joint function of person and the environment. A person is defined as an interrelated collection of complex characteristics that are the results of that person interacting with the environment over time. The environment is also defined as a dynamic interrelated collection of complex characteristics that are evolving over time and influenced by the persons and organizations existing within it.

Bolger, Caspi, Downey, and Moorehouse (1988) provide a clear understanding of that ever-changing environment through their description of it as a complex system of physical, cultural, and historical factors that interact with each other and with the developing individuals. It is Bolger's contention that individuals share experiences and influences that can be linked to their membership in higher-level systems, such as families, organizations, communities, societies, and historical periods. Thus these developmental contexts are couched within hierarchical structures that range from macro-level settings such as social class or culture to micro-level contexts such as family, school, work, or a leisure setting. This theoretical framework serves as a foundation for understanding the complex process of psychological development and cultural development of all students. This framework also underscores the fallacy of seeking to understand any system or organization in which individuals participate without a clear and in-depth understanding of culture and its effect on human development.

This important knowledge must be a part of the planning and implementation of any educational program. Context is everything. Success or failure depends on how well the environment has been prepared and whether practitioners have been trained to handle the inherent challenges with confidence, awareness, empathy, and respect.

It is important to be realistic about the great skill required for an educator to be capable of creating a classroom where no great rift exists between racial, ethnic, social, and linguistic groups, and where students are open to welcoming new and different members into their classroom culture. It is unrealistic to expect teachers to know everything about all groups of people. It is, however, realistic to expect both teachers and students to be open to learning about other people and their experiences, and to use one another's knowledge as resources to become multiculturally competent (Nguyen & Kibler, 1993). This practice is the key to the integration of linguistically or culturally different students into the intercultural classroom environment.

As the pool of educators whose cultural membership is within so-called "minority groups" continues to diminish, the integration of authentic cultural information into classroom instruction must become the responsibility of all educators (Zeichner, 1990). It is not the role of ethnic communities to educate the world about their histories and current dimensions, unless they choose to do so. Cultural information should be utilized by all teachers for educating all students because it is relevant and important, and provides an effective pedagogical tool for the teaching of higher-order thinking skills and multiple-perspective problem solving. It is time to move from teaching students *what* to think to sharing with students a framework for *how* to think about academic content areas and human relationships. A number of beliefs provide the framework for this philosophy.

The world is increasingly interdependent, complex, and changing. Isolationism is not a viable solution. Culture is the filter through which each individual makes sense of the local environment. An awareness of the impact that culture has on any student's intellectual and personal development is a vital part of teacher education and necessary for creating successful student learning environments.

Interconnections exist among cultural concepts, and students should understand these connections. Understanding who we are and how we got to be that way is an integral part of understanding the world. In its clearest essence, this means becoming aware of culture and its impact on each of our lives.

In the multicultural United States, we must think locally, regionally, and nationally, in addition to thinking internationally. The sequence from local to international is paramount. It is important that students see themselves and their culture reflected in their environment. They must grow comfortable with the idea that perceptual differences exist between various cultural and social experiences. Too often teachers think in terms of "strange lands and friendly peoples"; it is assumed that the world is culturally diverse, but our own neighborhoods are not (Hoffman, 1992). It is only by knowing our neighbors better, however, that we can better know the world. It is important that educators recognize that the present, the past, the commonplace, the familiar, and the local are resources for knowing our global community. Diversity exists all around us; we need only to look at our neighborhoods to see it. It is not necessarily something that is outside of ourselves or our everyday lives.

The term *intercultural* will be used in this chapter, instead of *multicul-*

tural, *global*, or *international*. This usage emphasizes the interconnected "feel" or psychological state that exists within the concepts of community and environment. How do diverse persons come together in an environment and create a way of living together productively? We can have multicultural classrooms that consist of children from many different cultures, but they may not be interacting and learning to understand one another (Hoffman, 1992). The term "intercultural" addresses this issue most effectively.

Any piece of quality literature can serve a multitude of purposes, one of which is providing cultural information, exposure, and understanding.

Viewing the Latino Community and Language Minority Education Realistically

"Just tell them who we are and that we are not all alike," was Margarita Avila's response to Earl Shorris' question about what to tell the world about Latinos in his 1992 book. To the people of Spanish-speaking countries, there is no generic Latino/Hispanic experience, and the various groups that make up what we simplistically refer to as "Hispanic" or "Latino" are not interchangeable.

The Mexican American population is no less diverse than when it began (Gómez-Quiñones, 1990). It is a heterogeneous population with distinct subgroups that manifest different experiences and adaptation processes to life in the United States. Some Mexican Americans are more integrated into U.S. society than others. Consequently, there are differences in class, cultural orientation, ethnic identification, and consciousness, as well as differences between immigrants and nonimmigrants (Shorris, 1992).

It is important to remember that individuals who come from the cultures of Central and South America are not typically called "Hispanic" or "Latino" until they arrive in the United States. U.S. diversity seems to demand generic terms for large and diverse groups of people. The usefulness of these terms, however, is quite limited. These general categorizations are applied to individuals as if each person shared a common background. In reality, the categorical label of "Hispanic" or "Latino" simply narrows the origin of a person down to about one fifth of the world.

Shorris (1992) shares some important information about categories and terms of reference that help to clarify issues of ethnic labeling. He explains that geographically, "Hispanic" is preferred by Spanish-speaking peoples in the Southeast and much of Texas, while New Yorkers from Central and South America use both "Hispanic" and "Latino." In Chicago, where Mexican Americans are a majority, the preferred term is "Latino" or "Chicano." In California, the word "Hispanic" has been barred from the Los Angeles Times, in keeping with the strong feelings of people in that community. Some people in New Mexico prefer "Hispano." Shorris feels that politically "Hispanic" is often linked to policy issues that can be considered conservative or moderate, while "Latino" can be linked to policy issues that are moderate or more liberal. Acuña (1988) contends that the term "Hispanic" belongs to the middle class, which seems most pleased by the term. The explanation is that Anglos and people who oppose bilingual education and bilingualism, such as those who belong to English-only groups, seem to prefer "Hispanic," which makes sense, since "Hispanic" is an English word meaning "pertaining to Spain." Following Shorris's usage, the term "Latino" will be used in this chapter for linguistic reasons: "Latino" has gender, which is grammatically linked to Spanish, as opposed to "Hispanic," which follows English rules. In addition, the term "Anglo" will be used to describe any person who is not Latino, Asian, Native American, or Black. The term is not meant to be derogatory but descriptive (Shorris).

In Shorris (1992), Margarita Avila also provides advice for understanding the Latino community, which she says is a combination of culture and the nuances of language and history. This community is most readily accessible in good Latino literature, whether it be fiction or nonfiction. The first-person reflections of characters' personal lives in an authentic piece of literature accurately captures the "we-are-not-alike" phenomenon that Avila articulates. This is certainly true of children's literature, as well. Authentic books for children and young adults demonstrate the vast diversity and complexity within the Latino community. Books that speak for individuals and families rather than communities accomplish this modeling of diversity most effectively. Their personal voices create an opportunity for individuals of all backgrounds to see themselves in the events and characterizations. The key to a realistic understanding of an ethnic community is to encourage readers to view an ethnic community as they do their own—as a rich and diverse setting.

An important contribution of the growing Latino population is that it forces the people of the United States to reflect upon political and social beliefs concerning language and identity (Tucker, 1984). The sociolinguistic aspect of Latino life is explored in authentic literature through the narration of characterization and plot, as well as through the utilization and interaction of Spanish and English. The tenuous and multidimensional relationship that these two languages create in the lives of many literary characters is a recurring theme.

Cortes (1990) considers the debate concerning how the United States will handle its growing diversity as one of the four greatest decisions of U.S. history. Latino literature reflects upon this question of linguistic diversity and ponders the role that language plays in our national identity. Another issue that these literary sources confront is the status of certain languages within U.S. culture. G. Richard Tucker (1984) suggests that language is the unrecognized thread that runs through many issues fundamental to U.S. national development. Tucker believes that although linguistic and cultural pluralism characterize many societies around the world, this rarely motivates groups of people to evaluate the ways in which various linguistic and cultural groups coexist. Since this doesn't happen in political and social institutions of society, Tucker feels it is inevitable that educational institutions become the focal point of this debate. Latino voices in young adult and children's literature are a powerful aid in helping students understand that the world's peoples speak a variety of languages, and that each of these distinct and complex languages provides a system for the universal challenge of communicating with one another. Considering the growing linguistic diversity of our nation, it is important that students grow more comfortable with such things as translation, multilingual communication environments, and the complexities that linguistic diversity creates for the planning and implementation of intercultural environments. The reality for today's children is that these new skills will become important for life, as well as employment. Fortunately, in the publishing world, the most readily available (though few in number) bilingual resources come in Spanish and English, which bodes well for the largest language-minority population within our schools.

The implementation of high quality native-language instructional programs continues to be the best and most efficient way to teach English as a second language. The retention of first language and first culture enhances academic success (Ramírez, 1992). It is time to stop pretending that we don't have the research information needed to educate language-minority students. A careful overview of recent research indicates that native-language instruction, when done correctly, is the most effective component of a program for language-minority students (Collier, 1995).

Bilingual education, like mainstream education and every other profession, has practitioners whose expertise runs the gamut from paltry to brilliant. The hysteria surrounding bilingual education is counterproductive. Due to the diversity of languages that students bring to the classroom, bilingual education is a luxury in many places. Native-language instruction, however, remains the most effective and successful pedagogical strategy for integrating language-minority students into U.S. schools (Ramírez, 1992). In addition, the attitudes of bilingual programs toward retention of first language and first culture can serve as guides to creating effective programmatic structures to help language-minority students become academically successful, regardless of an instructional program's focus on native-language instruction or ESL.

Understanding the reasons for the success or failure of language-minority students is not difficult. Language-minority students often enter our schools intellectually gifted by virtue of their bilingualism and biculturalism, and yet many of them fail academically or drop out because they feel alienated (Cummins, 1986). Approximately one third of U.S. children are academically at risk and the majority of these children are not native speakers of English (Scarcella, 1990). Before implementing educational changes designed to prevent language-minority students from failing in school, it is important to understand some of the reasons for their failure: feelings of alienation, teacher prejudice, home/school discontinuities, learning style discontinuities, language attitudes and linguistic prejudices, socioeconomic status, inadequate pedagogy, unfair assessment procedures, stress, minority students' perception of their own status in the United States, and institutional racism (Cummins, 1986, Trueba, 1988). Others in this volume have shared important information about various aspects of a student's academic, family, and cultural life, and this information can serve as a guide in choosing cultural literary resources that reflect the realistic and authentic experiences of Latino language-minority students (whether immigrant, refugee, migrant, sojourner, or born and raised in the United States). These intercultural resources also provide a way for monolingual students to gain a better understanding of the psychological, social, and personal issues that language-minority students confront on a daily basis.

The schizophrenic and unsuccessful context of current U.S. second-language teaching policy is another issue for consideration. Educational policies encourage English monolinguals to study foreign languages at great cost and with great inefficiency, and at the same time destroy the linguistic gifts of students from non-English backgrounds (Baker, 1993). This strange and unexplainable dichotomy tends to value foreign language but not the foreign speaker. An educator must always balance the teaching of native language and the acquisition of English skills for any language-minority student, but in the end, the choice of language usage in social situations outside the classroom should be the choice of the language-minority student, as it is for any student.

Developing and implementing a second-language learning program without adequate preparation and training may be considered a desperate move to contend with students as problems to be solved. This kind of policy decision ensures the failure of the program. The students are not to blame, nor is the concept of native-language instruction. Educators must begin to recognize that with the research and information we have concerning human learning and second-language acquisition, it is foolish to believe that quick fixes can work. When short-term results are examined, the result is an inaccurate picture of true student achievement (Collier, 1988). Lack of educators' knowledge, preparation, training, and expertise are the reasons for failure—not lack of student effort, willingness, or cognitive abilities.

Authenticity in Cultural Teaching

Teachers who wish to utilize cultural resources authentically in their teaching practices should seek simply to help students make sense of the world in which they live (Hoffman, 1992). Without this ability, the world can be a bewildering and intimidating place for any student. Hoffman goes on to contend that our educational system today is filled with students who do not want to interact with others different from themselves; they often seek to escape or withdraw, adopting behaviors incompatible with democratic values and with values necessary to a healthy, happy, and productive life.

Students need knowledge and interpretive skills to make sense of the complex world in which they live. Each student, however, also needs the courage to complete this process of understanding by grappling with complex human issues. This assertion relates directly to the difference that exists between teaching students *what* to think and teaching them *how* to think. Adults who are important in students' lives can serve as models for this truth-seeking process, and it is clearly true that teachers are often among the most significant of these adults (Hoffman, 1992).

One of the simplest and yet most difficult ideas to internalize is the concept of perceptual difference: the idea that everyone perceives the world differently, and that members of one culture group may share basic sets of perceptions that differ from those of other culture groups (Hoopes, 1979). The key to achieving authenticity in cultural teaching is to aid students and other educators in becoming functionally aware of the degree to which our behavior is culturally determined. Functionally aware has been defined as an ability to understand and integrate cultural awareness into relationships and academic study (Hoopes). It also means simply learning how to think in ways that move out of one's insulated world into the often complex negotiation of building communities.

Students are often aware of the many interconnections among people at a very early age but lack a thorough understanding of both the genesis and implications of these interconnections. Hoffman (1992) believes that children typically come to formal education curious about and connected to all others, but in the educational process lose this concept of interdependence among peoples. This reality may be largely inadvertent, but the resulting damage is intense. The curriculum is divided into disconnected subject areas, utilizing a one-nation, one-gender approach to understanding and interpreting history. It becomes a question of "us" studying about "them" (Hoffman). Us-them studies of culture and the overutilization of teacher-centered transmission of information are part of the reason for students' isolation from world reality. This approach to education reflects the philosophy that it is more important to teach students *what* to think rather than *how* to think.

A major problem is that the education system perpetuates two myths related to cultural differences and interpersonal conflicts. Confronting these myths would mean dealing with some painful truths about how we educate children and the realities of the world.

The first myth concerns the balance between similarities and differences in individuals. It is, of course, a reassuring concept to view ourselves as part of a world family. The image of holding hands around the world in harmony and love is beautiful but fails to convey that membership in this world family, like all families, can be quite frustrating and disconcerting at times. Familiar platitudes such as "We may be different on the outside, but on the inside we're all alike" may make us feel good, but what are the implications of such a statement?

Students need to view universal human qualities as the basis for building bridges among people of different backgrounds (Cortes, 1990). At the same time, however, students must learn about the real and meaningful group variations in cultural, racial, ethnic, and social experience. Platitudes about how we are all basically alike or proclamations of color blindness will never eradicate the necessity of this important awareness.

The second myth concerns three false ideas about interacting with others: (a) getting along with others is easy, (b) conflict is bad and should be avoided at all costs, and (c) we have to like or love others to interact respectfully with them.

It's time we stopped talking about love. Respect should be our focus. A lack of love or liking has been used as an excuse for abuse and violence and separation for far too long. Conflict doesn't always mean someone is at fault. It isn't always easy or possible to be friends with everyone. Relationships may be uncomfortable, painful, strange, weird, wonderful, functional, or dysfunctional.

What is the result of propagating these two myths? I believe it has left children with very few choices when they encounter individuals who are different from themselves. If we really are all the same, regardless of culture, interacting with other people should be fairly easy. This uninformed way of thinking leads students to believe that if conflict occurs, or discomfort pervades, or miscommunication happens, something must be wrong with that other person or with themselves. There must be a reason for this "negative" occurrence. Such experiences and thought processes reinforce the idea that someone is at fault; someone should be blamed.

Marker (1992) believes that if we give children "a continued diet of feel-good, New Age pseudocultural pap," we really are not accomplishing much toward the development of interculturally competent individuals. The result will be "a generation of ethnocentric ignoramuses ill-prepared to deal with the complexities of a bewildering modern world." Educators who believe that eating tacos and learning an ethnic dance are the only ingredients necessary for an in-depth, cross-cultural study will scratch their heads in confusion at the prospect that after all this talk about multicultural education, our first-grade students still run around war-whooping and scalping each other.

The more aware we are of our own contextual ideals, the better able we are to resolve, maintain, understand, and mediate cross-cultural relationships and ideals. This is not a philosophical construct but an economic necessity because as our world diversifies, such skills are needed for participation in an ever-changing workforce. This contextual understanding also provides a productive format for viewing, understanding, and dealing with racism, sexism, homophobia, linguistic and religious intolerance, and the bigotries faced daily by the physically and mentally challenged. The real problem is our expectation that interpersonal relationships will be easy. They are not.

Without some sense of cultural awareness, cultural experiences hide from even their own members much more than they reveal (Hall, 1976). A majority of individuals with whom I interact seem to believe that developing cultural awareness is a process of looking outward when, in reality, cultural awareness is a process of looking inward. It is a process of viewing ourselves juxtaposed against other, different individuals as a way of better understanding and *illuminating* ourselves. Cross-cultural experiences can offer this important and transformational vantage point.

Schools provide such opportunities daily by forcing this juxtaposition upon educators and students. The homogeneity of our living communities rarely provides this opportunity. It is important to balance the safety and comfort of home with the diverse experiences and challenges that are necessary for the psychological development of each individual.

Conflict is normal. It is natural. It should be expected. In all relationships, frustration is balanced with learning; hurt is balanced with insight; anger is balanced with concern; affection is balanced with respect. For educators to expect otherwise and to share that unrealistic expectation with children is a disservice to them. To see conflict as presenting an opportunity for growth requires a significant shift in attitude and world view (Kreidler, 1990).

Seekers of intercultural knowledge may attend workshops, listen to speakers, or read fact sheets dealing with world cultures, but if they do not perceive themselves to be cultural beings, they can never facilitate that understanding in others. Understanding as much as possible about one's own cultural context must precede aiding others in the understanding of theirs.

Some pedagogical structures achieve the goal of integrating intercultural resources into content areas more effectively than others. Figure 15-1 provides examples of classroom practices that integrate cultural learning and academic instruction. Intercultural literature can serve as a strong foundation for engaging students in authentic cultural learning.

Holding hands with each other is far from enough. It is time for us to

Figure 15-1. Guidelines for Utilizing Cultural Experiences in the Classroom

A teacher integrates cultural learning with academic instruction when he or she:

- makes the most of cultural resources and experiences of individuals in the class;
- uses content-based instruction that is grounded in diverse, real-life purposes and contexts;
- raises students awareness of the complexity and interconnectedness of human knowledge;
- treats cross-cultural conflict as a natural part of communication that can be positively resolved;
- teaches directly or indirectly cross-cultural communication and problem-solving skills;
- uses and legitimizes alternative ways of expressing knowledge and solving problems;
- engages students in cross-cultural decision-making and communication situations;
- aids students in understanding how culture operates in their own and others' lives;
- illuminates and corrects stereotypic depiction of groups of people;
- demonstrates the need to understand and view universally human qualities as the basis for building bridges among people of different backgrounds;
- aids students in growing more comfortable with learning about the real and meaningful group variations in culture, race, and ethnic experience;
- creates situations where students develop and practice effective human relations skills;
- facilitates understanding of how prejudice, bigotry, and oppression operate;
- creates experiences that challenge a student's own cultural assumptions; and
- compares and contrasts subject matter of similar themes, genres, or historical significance.

Source: Ngoc-Diep thi Nguyen and John Kibler (1993)

look at diversity in our culture as a chance to enrich our own lives—to expand ourselves, to respect what we don't understand, and even to accept what might make us a little uncomfortable.

Insider and Outsider Perspectives in Multicultural Children's Literature

On July 4, 1744, the Iroquois chief, Canassatego, replied with clarity and insight to an offer of the Virginia Legislature to the Six Nations, inviting them to send six youths to be educated at the Williamsburg College of William and Mary.

> We know you highly esteem the kind of Learning taught in these Colleges, and the maintenance of our young Men, while with you, would be very expensive to you. We are convinced, therefore, that you mean to us Good by your Proposal; and we thank you heartily. But you who are so wise must know that different Nations have different Conceptions of things; and you will not therefore take amiss, if our Ideas of this kind of Education happens not to be the same with yours. We have had some experience of it. Several of our young People were formerly brought up in the Colleges of the Northern Provinces; they were instructed in all your Sciences; but, when they came back to us, they were bad Runners, ignorant of every means of living in the Woods, unable to bear either Cold or Hunger, knew neither how to build a Cabin, take a deer, or kill an enemy, spoke our language imperfectly, were therefore neither fit for Hunters, Warriors, nor Counselors; they were totally good for nothing. We are however not the less obliged for your kind Offer, tho' we decline accepting it; and to show our grateful Sense of it, if the Gentlemen of Virginia shall send us a Dozen of their Sons, we will take great care of their Education, instruct them in all we know, and make Men of them (Fenelon, 1993, p. 1).

Canassatego has a great deal to teach U.S. educational institutions about culture and teaching. His words reflect the vital insights that membership in a culture provides for understanding a particular cultural experience. As well, his words speak eloquently of what can result when one, through education, is robbed of one's first language and first culture. Practices that seek to force an outside cultural view onto a particular cultural experience as a way of assessing or judging that experience are oppressive in nature. Any outsider view must originate from a position of respect, equality, and familiarity. Accuracy matters greatly. Writers and illustrators make dangerous and stereotypical errors by not knowing a culture intimately.

Writers who attempt to portray an unfamiliar culture often produce works that are sterile or nonspecific; those who use non-English words without proper understanding may portray their contextual foundations incorrectly (Barrera, 1992). Outsider views alone will never accurately reflect a cultural experience unless balanced by insider perspectives.

Membership in a culture alone, however, doesn't make a writer a quality presenter of that culture's experiences. Gifted writers of all kinds write about their cultures and beyond. Fiction and nonfiction writers of all nationalities utilize stereotypical depictions of characters whenever they fail to see characters as individuals. Authenticity matters greatly, but there is no specific outline for how one acquires it (Rochman, 1993).

Nancy Cloud (1993) believes that the work of educators who interact with linguistically and culturally diverse children extends far beyond the role of language teacher. She contends that educators serve many functions in the second-language classroom in addition to language instruction, and that all linguistically and culturally diverse students experience psychological, social, and cultural effects during acculturation in the classroom. These students are learning a new language and various sets of new cultural rules for school and society. The rigidity of these cultural patterns and the reactions of others to their adaptation can be overwhelming at best and stigmatizing at worst. In addition, because of their life experiences, many ESL students face more serious emotional issues caused by disruption and violence, traumatic resettlement, dramatic changes in family composition, losses, and separation.

Cloud argues that children's books normalize the experiences of children by validating their lives and providing a safe environment for the exploration of feelings and painful experiences. She believes that by empathizing with a story's characters, linguistically and culturally diverse children can acknowledge and share their own feelings associated with similar circumstances without feeling threatened, vulnerable, or exposed. Students whose cultural experiences are not directly reflected in a piece of literature are enriched by putting themselves in another's circumstances, which contributes to the acquisition of problem-solving and higher-order thinking skills, as well as the development of intercultural understanding. Story reading allows students to participate when they are ready, and in whatever way they prefer. Just listening to a story can provide the same benefits to both sets of students with similar results (Cloud, 1993).

In his work with Foxfire, Eliot Wigginton (1991) proposes that the utilization of cultural resources in pedagogy should result in the creation of a tangible product. He contends that the personal investigation of culture resonates deeply with students and has the potential to lift the classroom out of the routine into another dimension. Wigginton goes on to explain that empty assertions that students should be proud of their culture have negligible impact on students' intellectual and personal development. Equally as negligible are guest speakers at an assembly, ethnic food festivals, and "once-a-week" multicultural enlightenment sessions. Cultural information and resources are only effective in pedagogy through sustained exposure in an environment characterized by independent student research and inquiry, where aspects of culture are discovered, brought to a level of consciousness, and used (Wigginton, 1991). Intercultural literature is an integral part of classroom culture that seeks to open students to investigating and making sense of the world around them, regardless of their participation inside or outside of a cultural experience. The way each student interacts with a piece of literature is individualistic; insiders see themselves reflected in it, while outsiders gain insights into experiences that differ from their own.

Selecting and Evaluating Multicultural Children's Literature

Rudine Sims Bishop (1992) defines multicultural children's literature as "literature by and about people who are members of groups considered to be outside the socio-political mainstream of the United States." Hazel Rochman (1993) offers a counter-interpretation, asserting that these books should focus on breaking down borders.

The combination of these viewpoints provides a sense of balance in understanding what a book can accomplish in the intercultural classroom. Intercultural children's literature should illuminate cultural experiences that have, for too long, been considered outside of the U.S. mainstream. This powerful literature should also be used by educators and parents to break down borders.

The process of creating a realistic view of any cultural experience can seem a daunting task. Nieto (1992) posits that the search for an authentic literature is not the search for an always-positive, romanticized, or idealized perspective. Authentic literature is neither unrealistically heroic nor destructively negative, but, rather, attempts to reflect the range of issues and possibilities within community experiences.

The key to the selection process is understanding why one chooses a book and how it will be used. A book is not good just because it reflects other cultures. Further evaluation can be based on criteria adapted from the work of educators in the field of intercultural children's literature.

Teachers should first look at the existing curricula and the concepts to be shared with students over the course of the school year. An existing curriculum serves as a framework for identifying academic goals. It is a starting point for considering where intercultural diversification and enhancement are most appropriate. In addition, the teacher needs to consider (1) expected outcomes, (2) the background of students, (3) the students' prior knowledge and exposure, (4) language proficiency level(s), and (5) the languages used in the literary resource. The teacher should also consider the mode of transmission of the resource, the format for integration into the curriculum, academic concepts outlined, and cultural learning concepts explored. Figure 15-2 identifies some literary and cultural criteria for evaluating cultural resources and creates a scale for assessing each literary item on a variety of issues. This guide can serve as a framework for the integration of any cultural resource in the classroom.

The excited exclamation of "that's about me" from a second-grader after his teacher reads a story is an everyday experience for children within the majority culture. Children from other cultures, however, do not often have the opportunity to see themselves in books (Nieto, 1992). Teachers and schools have the responsibility to make it possible for all children to see themselves and their experiences reflected in the books that they read, and to balance that with literature that reflects experiences of others different from themselves. It is important to remember that a single book cannot accomplish everything and, therefore, each book need not provide information on each and every aspect of culture. Balance, achieved through multiple resources, is the key to selecting and integrating cultural resources successfully.

Mexican, Mexican American, and Latino Voices in Children's Literature

Hazel Rochman (1993) believes that a good book can help to break down barriers, making a difference in the lives of readers by dispelling prejudice and building community. A story should lead the reader to imagine the lives of others in all their complexity by reaching beyond stereotype to depict unique individual characters. Rochman contends that once a reader views a character as a flawed, complex, striving individual, stereotypes are dispelled.

The term "Hispanic American" or "Latino" is a new one for many within the library and publishing business, denoting dual membership in the cultural heritages of Latin America and the United States. In the past, finding books about ethnic heritages of Latin America and the Caribbean was difficult because of misinformation or neglect on the part of mainstream U.S. publishers. Barrera's (1992) analysis supports the assertion that those who did publish such works typically projected a stereotypically romanticized view of how Mexicans (and by implication, other Spanish-speaking persons) were supposed to act, speak, and be. Her examination of the two or three Caldecott and Newberry award-winning books that reflect

Latino themes since 1940 reveals stereotypical characterizations, atypical representations, and negative themes. Barrera's insights demonstrate two outstanding themes that characterize this type of literature: the Anglo benefactor who saves characters from themselves and the emphasis on English as the only route to salvation for Spanish-speaking youth (Council on Interracial Books for Children, 1975; Duran, 1979). Even though the overall scope of Latino literature today is vastly improved, books for children and young adults that reflect Mexican American life and culture are still severely underrepresented, considering the proportion of the U.S. population that is of Mexican American background (Barrera, 1992). Today, Mexican Americans comprise over five percent of the U.S. population and are the largest and fastest-growing ethnolinguistic group in the United States, totaling almost 14 million persons (U.S. Bureau of the Census, 1991).

In the late 1960s, the stage began to be set for the emergence of children's literature written by Mexican Americans. Barrera (1992) indicates the many factors that contributed to this emergence, mainly the literary expression of participants in the Chicano movement of the 1960s and 1970s creating a new ethnic consciousness for Mexican Americans. Even though little of this writing was for young people, nonetheless it created a backdrop whereby literature for children could find psychological and artistic support. The Bilingual Education Act of 1968 was also an instrumental force in the emergence of children's literature about Mexican American culture and life written by Mexican Americans (Barrera). Some of the earliest works that emerged from this movement included those of Ernest Galarza; the reading series for grades 1-6 titled *Serie Tierra de Encanto*, created under the direction of Dolores Gonzáles, 1972-1977; and the children's books of Nathaniel Archuleta. In the 1960s and 70s, the few works of Latinos that were published by major U.S. publishing houses conformed to the prevailing mainstream views that speaking Spanish was a flaw to be overcome, and that assimilating as soon as possible into mainstream U.S. culture was the most attractive and intelligent choice for any Latino immigrant. Some authentic resources for children were published by small presses, which developed as a result of the need to produce curriculum materials for bilingual children. While much of this publishing was in Spanish, many noteworthy titles appeared in English or in a bilingual format. The Children's Book Press was especially successful even before the concept of publishing multicultural books for children came into vogue. The Raintree Hispanic Stories series is a well written and strong resource for bringing important Latino historical figures to life for young readers (these historical figures having been omitted from most state-approved textbooks).

The immigrant and refugee experience continues to be an important

Figure 15-2. Cultural and Literary Guidelines for Selecting Literature

Cultural Information: Accurate and Authentic
i.e., does it offer an "insider's" or informed "outsider" perspective?

Very Successful | Unsuccessful
[1] [2] [3] [4] [5] [6] [7] [8] [9] [10]

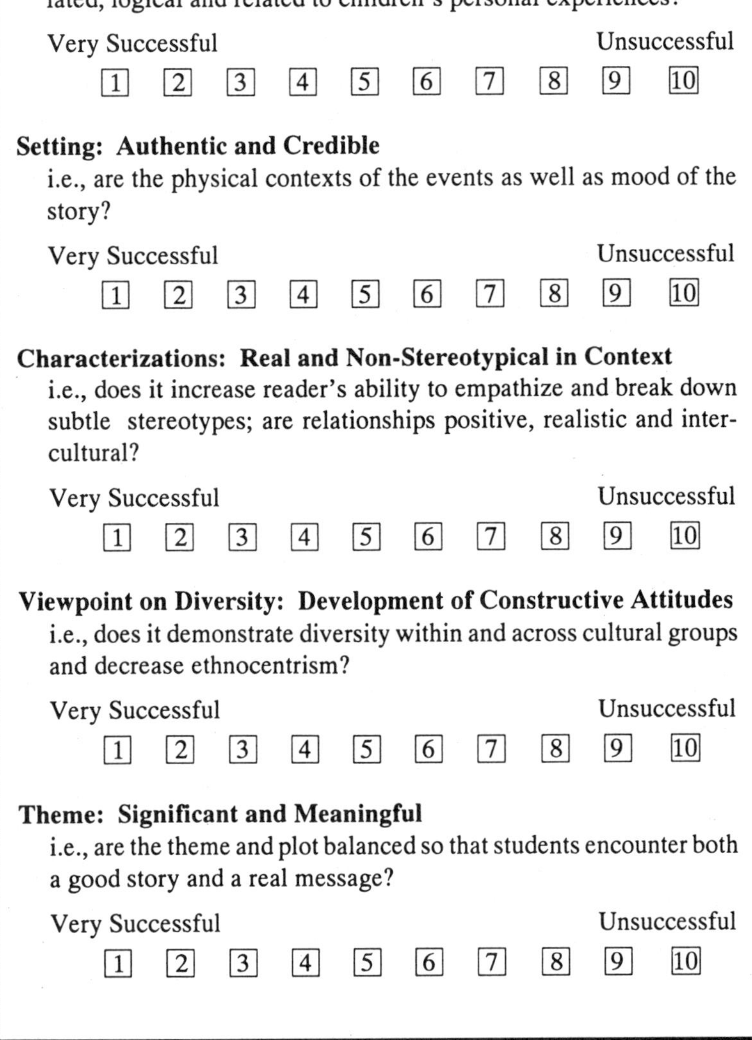

Plot: Well constructed and substantial
i.e., is it well organized with actions and events that are interrelated, logical and related to children's personal experiences?

Very Successful | Unsuccessful
[1] [2] [3] [4] [5] [6] [7] [8] [9] [10]

Setting: Authentic and Credible
i.e., are the physical contexts of the events as well as mood of the story?

Very Successful | Unsuccessful
[1] [2] [3] [4] [5] [6] [7] [8] [9] [10]

Characterizations: Real and Non-Stereotypical in Context
i.e., does it increase reader's ability to empathize and break down subtle stereotypes; are relationships positive, realistic and intercultural?

Very Successful | Unsuccessful
[1] [2] [3] [4] [5] [6] [7] [8] [9] [10]

Viewpoint on Diversity: Development of Constructive Attitudes
i.e., does it demonstrate diversity within and across cultural groups and decrease ethnocentrism?

Very Successful | Unsuccessful
[1] [2] [3] [4] [5] [6] [7] [8] [9] [10]

Theme: Significant and Meaningful
i.e., are the theme and plot balanced so that students encounter both a good story and a real message?

Very Successful | Unsuccessful
[1] [2] [3] [4] [5] [6] [7] [8] [9] [10]

Perspectives: Multiple, Balanced, and Inclusive
i.e., does it offer positive yet realistic situations or correct distortions or omissions of significant cultural or historical information?

Very Successful Unsuccessful

1 2 3 4 5 6 7 8 9 10

Self-Esteem: Reinforcement of Positive Impact on Reader
i.e., does it provide for a discussion of self-esteem of students from both inside and outside the cultural group(s) involved?

Very Successful Unsuccessful

1 2 3 4 5 6 7 8 9 10

Global Perspective: Seeing the World as an Interdependent System
i.e., does it develop constructive attitudes toward conflict, ambiguity and change?

Very Successful Unsuccessful

1 2 3 4 5 6 7 8 9 10

Multicultural Awareness: Understanding Prejudice and Bigotry
i.e., does it acknowledge the devastating effect of inequality and offer solutions and understanding?

Very Successful Unsuccessful

1 2 3 4 5 6 7 8 9 10

Adapted by Ngoc-Diep thi Nguyen and John M. Kibler from *Multicultural Literature for Children: Making Informed Choices* by R. S. Bishop (1992); *Toward Cooperation and Integration*, page 65, Foreign Language and International Studies, New York State Department of Education, and *Skill Development in Elementary Social Studies* by Barbara J. Winston and Charlotte C. Anderson (1977).

theme for Latino writers of both fiction and nonfiction for all ages, with the migrant worker and his life experiences being a new and welcome addition, mostly in nonfiction.

The border is fact and metaphor for many Latino writers, serving as an image of the borders of place, language, family, and memory and of the individual between two worlds (Rochman, 1993).

The young adult market, however, continues to be deficient in most Latino themes. Until recently, little was published in English. I have attempted to include in an annotated bibliography some good nonfiction, especially in photo-essay form, about new immigrants in urban and rural places and the scope of migrant workers, focusing as much as possible on the experiences of Mexicans and Mexican Americans. With the notable exception of Gary Soto and a few others, young adult fiction is limited to the adaptation and usage of adult novels.

An excellent chapter entitled "Ideas a Literature Can Grow on: Key Insights for Enriching and Expanding Children's Literature About the Mexican American Experience" (Barrera, Liguori, & Salas, 1992) is perhaps the best resource to be found on the topic. The chapter asserts that the Mexican American experience shares both universally human, as well as uniquely personal and distinctive qualities, and provides an outline of the basic understandings that an educator needs to utilize resources of this genre effectively.

The annotated bibliography that follows this chapter identifies resources for three groupings of grade levels, as well as further resources in poetry; entries within each section are organized alphabetically by author. Recommendations and opinions expressed within the bibliography are solely my own. Published recommendations of Rudine Sims Bishop and the Multicultural Booklist Committee (1994); Rosalinda B. Barrera, Olga Liguori and Loretta Salas (1992); Hazel Rochman (1993); Masha Kabakow Rudman (1993), Ngoc-Diep thi Nguyen (1993), and Oralia Garza de Cortes (1992), as well as recommendations made in the bibliography *Our Families, Our Friends, Our World* (Miller-Lachman, Ed.) were used extensively as a guide in the search for resources to analyze. In addition, the guidance, encouragement, and advice of Judy Kwiat, director of the InterAmerica Midwest Multifunctional Resource Center, proved invaluable.

Depending on its use, a particular book may be appropriate across various grade levels. Many books that younger readers could never read on their own may be read to them and utilized for areas of language learning and retention.

As an Anglo educator deeply concerned about the educational and social issues facing Mexican American students and teachers in America's school, I turn in conclusion to Barrera, Liguori, and Salas (1992) as a way to balance my outsider's perspective with an insider's clarification:

> If literature is to do all the extraordinary things literature professionals are presently saying it can do, namely to empower and transform human minds, then the present corpus of children's literature must first be transformed into a literature that represents all the cultural diversity in this country. If not, then literature will be empowering only in a selective way, more for children from some cultural groups than others. Given that a 'new world' and 'new America' are unfolding before our eyes, it makes sense that a new literature for children, one grounded in human diversity and human understanding, be promoted (p. 236).

Annotated Bibliography of Resources for Students and Teachers

PreSchool-Grade 3

Ada, Alma Flor. (1991). *The Gold Coin [Moneda de oro].* New York: Atheneum.
Illustrated by Neil Waldman. Translated from the Spanish by Bernice Randall. The tenacity of a kind old woman transforms a thief into a responsible man.

Brown, Tricia. (1986). *Hello Amigos.* New York: Holt.
Photographs by Fran Ortiz. A young Mexican American boy in San Francisco introduces the reader to his family, his community, and his culture on the occasion of his birthday.

Bunting, Eve. (1990). *The Wall.* New York: Clarion Books.
Illustrated by Ronald Himler. A 1991 ALA Notable Book and a 1990 Notable Children's Trade Book in the Field of Social Studies, this poignant picture book shares the story of a young Latino boy and his father as they visit the Vietnam Veteran's Memorial in Washington, DC.

Cisneros, Sandra. (1994). *Hairs = Pelitos.* New York: Knopf.
Illustrated by Terry Ybáñez. A vignette from the author's best-selling adult novel, *The House on Mango Street*, this bilingual story looks at the diversity of hair in a loving family.

Delacre, Lulu. (1989). *Arroz Con Leche.* Bergenfield, NJ: Scholastic.
A bilingual collection of Latin American songs and chants on various themes.

Dorros, Arthur. (1991). *Abuela.* New York: Dutton Children's Books.
Also available in Spanish. Illustrated by Elisa Kleven.
A 1992 ALA Notable Children's Book and 1991 Notable Children's Book in the Field of Social Studies, this marvelous story, which features collage artwork, depicts the imagined flight of a young girl and her grandmother over New York City.

García, María. (1987). *The Adventures of Connie and Diego = Las aventuras de Connie y Diego*. Rev. ed. San Francisco, CA: Children's Book Press.
Translated into Spanish by Alma Flor Ada. Illustrated by Malaquias Montoya. Illustrated by a noted California muralist, this modern bilingual fairy tale explores the important role that self-acceptance plays for two children dealing with prejudice and bigotry.

Havill, Juanita. (1992). *Treasure Nap.* Boston, MA: Houghton Mifflin.
Illustrated by Elivia Savadier. A nap story turns into an exploration of family folklore for a young Mexican American girl as she explores the treasures of her great-great-grandmother's trunk.

Lomas Garza, Carmen, as told to Harriet Rohmer. (1990). *Family Pictures = Cuadros de familia.* San Francisco, CA: Children's Book Press.
Translated into Spanish by Rosalma Zubizarreta. A marvelous introduction to one of America's finest Mexican American artists, this bilingual book reflects the childhood memories of the artist in a rural South Texas setting.

Mora, Pat. (1992). *A Birthday Basket for Tía.* New York: Macmillan.
Illustrated by Cecily Lang. A beautifully illustrated story of how a young Mexican American girl and her cat surprise her 90-year-old great-aunt on her birthday. Also of note by this author is *Tomás and the Library Lady* (Knopf) and *Pablo's Tree* (Macmillan).

Most, Bernard. (1990). *The Cow That Went Oink.* San Diego: Harcourt Brace Jovanovich.
One of my favorites, this story looks at two animals who struggle with the process of becoming bilingual.

Roe, Eileen. (1991). *Con Mi Hermano = With My Brother.* New York: Bradbury Press.
Illustrated by Robert Casilla. Spanish translation by Jo Mintzer. A bilingual story of the warm and caring relationship between two Latino brothers.

Schoberle, Cecile. (1990). *Esmeralda and the Pet Parade.* New York: Simon and Schuster Books for Young Readers.
A good and unusually illustrated story of a group of Mexican American children and their goat, Essie, and the adventures they have at the Sante Fe Pet Parade.

Stanek, Muriel. (1989). *I Speak English for My Mom.* Niles, IL: Albert Whitman.
Illustrated by Judith Friedman. A strong and evocative tale of the role and responsibilities of a young Mexican American girl who serves as translator for her widowed mother.

Stevens, Jan Romero. (1993). *Carlos and the Squash Plant = Carlos y la planta de calabaza.* Flagstaff, AZ: Northland Publishing.
Illustrated by Jeanne Arnold. A wonderful story of a young Mexican

American boy who lives on a farm with his loving family and discovers what can happen when you refuse to wash behind your ears.

Weiss, Nicki. (1992). *On a Hot, Hot Day.* New York: Putnam's. Simple illustrations and repeated rhymes depict what a young boy and his mom do in order to stay cool on a hot day.

Grades 4 - 7

Ashabranner, Brent K. (1987). *The Vanishing Border: A Photographic Journey Along Our Frontier with Mexico.* New York: Dodd, Mead. Photographs by Paul Conklin. Narrative, interviews, and photographs portray the cities, towns, and citizens of the Texas-Mexico border.

Beatty, Patricia. (1981). *Lupita Mañana.* New York: Morrow. The harrowing story of two undocumented Mexican children who, in an attempt to supplement their single mother's income, experience the dangers, temptations, and painful realities of life in the United States.

Bethancourt, T. Ernesto. (1985). *The Me Inside of Me.* Minneapolis: Lerner Publications.
A positive and affirming story of a 17-year-old Latino adolescent who explores social pressures, class, and self-identity as he must adjust quickly to sudden wealth and what it can do to one's life.

Carlstrom, Nancy White. (1990). *Light: Stories of a Small Kindness.* Boston: Little Brown.
Illustrated by Lisa Desimini. A collection of stories set in different cultures (including Mexican culture) explores universal themes through small kindnesses and mystical events.

Codye, Corinn. (1990). *Vilma Martínez.* Raintree Hispanic Stories. Milwaukee: Raintree Publishers.
Translated into Spanish by Alma Flor Ada. Illustrated by Susi Kilgore. This inspirational bilingual story looks at the life of a female Mexican American lawyer and serves as a testament to similar stories in Mexican American history.

Hewett, Joan. (1989). *Getting Elected: The Diary of a Campaign.* New York: Lodestar Books.
Photographs by Richard Hewett. This marvelous photo essay looks at the campaign of Gloria Molina, the first Chicana elected to the California Assembly.

Hewett, Joan. (1990). *Hector Lives in the United States Now: The Story of a Mexican American Child.* New York: Lippincott.
Photographs by Richard Hewett. Another strong photo essay by the Hewetts looks at the daily life of a 10-year-old Mexican American and his family in a residential area of Los Angeles.

Hughes, Shirley. (1991). *Wheels: A Tale of Trotter Street.* London: Walker.

A family story focused on a Latino boy's hope for a new bike and a brother's generosity.

Krull, Kathleen. (1994). *Maria Molina and the Days of the Dead.* New York: Macmillan.
Illustrated by Enrique O. Sánchez. A strong and easily understood explanation and experience of a family's participation in the Days of the Dead celebration.

Mazzio, Joann. (1992). *The One Who Came Back.* Boston: Houghton Mifflin.
A 1993 Recommended Book for Reluctant Young Adult Readers, this realistic coming-of-age novel explores interracial friendship, familial relationships, and bigotry directed toward Mexican Americans.

Roberts, Naurice. (1986). *Cesar Chávez and La Causa.* Picture-Story Biographies. Chicago: Children's Press.
A simplified but moving biography of an important Mexican American who dedicated his life to helping farmworkers gain rights and respect through the United Farm Workers of America. Other biographies of note in this series are those on Everett Alvarez, Jr., Evelyn Cisneros, and Henry Cisneros.

Soto, Gary. (1987). *The Cat's Meow.* San Francisco, CA: Strawberry Hill Press.
Illustrated by Carolyn Soto. The noted Chicano poet and novelist's first book for younger children explores the nature of communication through the device of a girl's cat who possesses the unique ability to speak a foreign language—*Spanish.*

Tafolla, Carmen. *Patchwork Colcha: A Children's Collection.*
A collection of poems, stories, and songs in Spanish and English by this Chicana poet and bilingual children's television writer. A further collection of her work that includes some of the stories from above, but also poetry, is the children's chapter in *Sonnets to Human Beings and Other Selected Works by Carmen Tafolla: A Critical Edition.* (Santa Monica Press).

Taylor, Theodore. (1986). *The Maldonado Miracle.* New York: Avon Books.
The engrossing and harrowing story of a motherless 12-year-old Mexican youth who ventures north to the United States in search of his migrant worker father.

Ulibarrí, Sabine. (1982). *Pupurupu: Cuentos de Niños/Children's Stories.* Berkeley, CA: Quinto Sol.
Eleven varied short stories in both Spanish and English for older elementary readers.

Grades 8 - Adult

Anaya, Rudolfo A., & Márquez, Antonio. (Eds.). (1984). *Cuentos Chicanos: A Short Story Anthology*. Rev. ed. Albuquerque: New America, University of New Mexico Press.
A strong and balanced anthology of contemporary short fiction by such prominent authors as Rudolfo Anaya, Ron Arias, Denise Chávez, and Alberto Rios.

Anaya, Rudolfo. (1972). *Bless Me Ultima*. New York: Warner Books.
Anaya is the recipient of the Premio Quinto Sol (national literary award for best written work by a Mexican American), and in this novel for older readers he explores a young boy's experiences and feelings as he watches a community accuse the local curandera (faith healer), who lives with his family, of witchcraft. Also recommended is his more recent *The Farolitos of Christmas: A New Mexico Christmas*.

Arias, Ron. (1987). *The Road to Tamazunchale*. (3rd ed.). Tempe, AZ: Bilingual Press.
Illustrated by Jose Antonio Burciaga. Nominated for the National Book Award, this novel mixes fantasy and reality as the dreams and imagination of the central character provide commentary on various issues in contemporary society.

Barrio, Raymond. (1985). *The Plum Plum Pickers*. Binghamton, NY: Bilingual Press.
A beautiful novel about a Mexican American family of migrant workers in the fields of California.

Bode, Janet. (1989). *New Kids on the Block: Oral Histories of Immigrant Teens*. New York: Franklin Watts.
The anxieties of entering the United States illegally and the fears of deportation are depicted by the Mexican entry in this collection of testimonies of 11 recent immigrant teenagers.

Carlson, Lori M., & Ventura, Cynthia L. (Eds.). (1990). *Where Angels Glide at Dawn: New Stories From Latin America*. New York: J. B. Lippincott.
Illustrated by Jose Ortega. Introduction by Isabel Allende. Translated by the editors, this excellent anthology features Mexican writer Jorge Ibarquengoitia and nine others exploring varying themes across many cultures in North, Central, and South America.

Cisneros, Sandra. (1991). *The House on Mango Street.* New York: Vintage Books. (Also in Spanish: *La casa en Mango Street.*)
This short story collection chronicles the collective cultural experience of the author's childhood in the urban barrios of Chicago.

Corpi, Lucha. (1989). *Delia's Song*. Houston. TX: Arte Público Press.
An important voice in Mexican American fiction, this novel explores the Chicana perspective through the female protagonist's journey to self-discovery.

Fernández, Roberta. (1990). *Intaglio: A Novel in Six Stories*. Houston, TX: Arte Público Press.

This sensitive novel is formed around the stories of six diverse and multidimensional Mexican American women growing up and living along the Río Grande.

Galarza, Ernesto. (1971). *Barrio Boy.* Notre Dame, IN: University of Notre Dame Press.

This classic study explores an immigrant family's voyage from their mountain village in Mexico to their home in a northern California barrio.

Hernández, Irene Beltrán. (1989). *Across the Great River*. Houston, TX: Arte Público Press.

A harrowing, realistic, and often violent story from a young girl's perspective of the experiences endured by a Mexican immigrant family in their journey across the Río Grande.

Paredes, Américo. (1990). *George Washington Gómez: A Mexicotexan Novel.* Houston, TX: Arte Público Press.

Originally written in the 1930s and nominated for the American Book Award in 1990, this novel chronicles the history of a family living along the Texas-Mexico border.

Rebolledo, Diane, Gonzales-Berry, Erlinda, & Marquez, Teresa. (Eds.). (1988). *Las Mujeres.* Albuquerque, NM: El Norte Publications.

An excellent collection of the best writing by Mexican American women authors, delineated by various topics.

Rivera, Tomás. (1987). *Y no se lo tragó la tierra = And the Earth Did Not Devour Him*. Houston, TX: Art Público Press.

Bilingual ed. English translation by Evangelinal Vigil-Piñon. This classic of Chicano literature portrays the harsh, violent, and nightmarish lives of Mexican migrant farmworkers.

Ríos, Alberto Alvaro. (1984). *The Iguana Killer: Twelve Stories of the Heart.* Lewiston, ID: Blue Moon and Confluence Press.

A short story collection that reveals through personal and intimate perceptions the experiences of the Mexican American immigrant.

Rodriguez, Richard. (1982). *Hunger of Memory: The Education of Richard Rodriguez.* Boston: D. R. Godine.

This controversial autobiography chronicles the life of the author growing up in the barrios of Sacramento.

Soto, Gary. (1990). *Baseball in April and Other Stories.* San Diego: Harcourt Brace Jovanovich.

A wonderful collection of short stories about the lives of young Latinos in California by one of our finest writers of young adult fiction.

Soto, Gary. *Living Up the Street: Narrative Recollections.* (1985). San Francisco, CA: Strawberry Hill Press.

Winner of the 1985 American Book Award, this fine collection of short stories poetically relates the experiences common to adolescents growing up in a Mexican American barrio.

Soto, Gary. (1992). *Pacific Crossing.* San Diego: Harcourt Brace Jovanovich.
Two Mexican American boys experience a six-week student exchange program in Japan and discover new things about their hosts and themselves.

Soto, Gary. (1991). *Taking Sides.* San Diego: Harcourt Brace Jovanovich.
A realistic and moving novel concerning a Mexican American eighth-grader who must confront family and social issues alike when he and his mother move from an urban barrio to a White suburb.

Thomas, Joyce Carol, (Ed.). (1990). *A Gathering of Flowers: Stories About Being Young in America.* New York: Harper & Row.
Gary Soto is featured in this high-quality short story collection about the childhood and adolescent experiences of various authors in particular ethnic communities in the United States.

Ulibarrí, Sabine R. (1989). *El Cóndor, and Other Stories.* Houston, TX: Arte Público Press.
A bilingual collection of this master storyteller's folklóric tales.

Viramontes, Helena Maria. (1995). *The Moths and Other Stories.* 2nd ed. Houston, TX: Arte Público Press.
This collection of short stories explores the feminist perspective in Mexican American culture and the struggles of various female characters who challenge the cultural expectations of traditional roles.

Poetry

Catacalos, Rosemary. (1984). *Again for the First Time.* Sante Fe, NM: Tooth of Time Books.
The first collection by this excellent Mexican American poet offers surprisingly personal and provocative views of Mexican American culture.

Cervantes, Lorna Dee. (1981). *Emplumada.* Pitt Poetry Series. Pittsburgh: University of Pittsburgh Press.
This marvelously accessible collection focuses on personal and community change in the barrio over the last 25 years from a woman's perspective.

Mora, Pat. (1991). *Communion.* Houston, TX: Arte Público Press.
An adult poetry collection by the noted children's author. Other poetry collections by this poet are *Borders* (1985) and *Chants* (1984), both published by Arte Público Press.

Ríos, Alberto. (1985). *Five Indiscretions: A Book of Poems.* Riverdale-on-Hudson, NY: The Sheep Meadow Press.
This rich collection of poetry explores Mexican American life and culture close to the United States-Mexico border.

Salinas, Luís Omar. (1987). *The Sadness of Days: Selected and New Poems*. Houston, TX: Arte Público Press.
This wonderful collection explores selections from throughout the poet's literary career.

Soto, Gary. (1990). *A Fire in My Hands: A Book of Poems*. New York: Scholastic.
A notable 1991 Children's Trade Book in the Field of Social Studies, this book of 21 poems reflects the author's youth in the San Joaquin Valley of California.

Soto, Gary. (1992). *Neighborhood Odes*. San Diego: Harcourt Brace Jovanovich.
Illustrated by David Diaz. A Notable 1992 Children's Trade Book in the Field of Social Studies, this book of poems brings a Mexican American neighborhood to life for all readers.

References

Acuña, R. (1988). *Occupied America: A history of Chicanos* (3rd ed.). New York: Harper & Row.

Baker, C. (1993). Foundations of bilingual education and bilingualism. Philadelphia, PA: Multilingual Matters, Ltd.

Barrera, R. B. (1992). The Mexican American experience in children's literature: Past, present and future. *Oregon English Journal*.

Barrera, R. B., & Liguori, O., & Salas, L. (1992). Ideas a literature can grow on: Key insights for enriching and expanding children's literature about the Mexican American experience. In V. Harris (Ed.), *Teaching multicultural literature in grades K-8*. Norwood, MA: Christopher-Gordon.

Bishop, R. S. (1992). Multicultural literature for children: Making informed choices. In V. Harris (Ed.), *Teaching multicultural literature in grades K-8*. Norwood, MA: Christopher-Gordon.

Bishop, R. S. (Ed.). (1994). *Kaleidoscope: A multicultural booklist for grades K-8*. Urbana, IL: National Council of Teachers of English Publication.

Bolger, N., Caspi, A., Downey, G., & Moorehouse, M. (1988). Development in context: Research perspectives. In N. Bolger, A. Caspi, G. Downey, & M. Moorehouse (Eds.), *Persons in context: Developmental processes* (pp. 1-24). New York: Cambridge University Press.

Bronfenbrenner, U. (1979). Interacting systems in human development. Research paradigms: Present and future. In N. Bolger, A. Caspi, G. Downey, & M. Moorehouse (Eds.)., *Persons in context: Development processes* (pp. 25-49). New York: Cambridge University Press.

Cloud, N. (1993). *Literacy and second language acquisition*. Keynote address conducted at the 16th annual Illinois conference for teachers of linguistically and culturally diverse students.

Collier, V. (1988). *The effect of age on the acquisition of a second language for school.* Silver Spring, MD: National Clearinghouse for Bilingual Education (NCBE).

Collier, V. (1995). Acquiring a second language for school. *Directions in language and education, 1*(4). Silver Spring, MD: National Clearinghouse for Bilingual Education (NCBE).

Cortes, C. (1990, March/April). A curricular basic for our multiethnic future. *Doubts and Certainties Newsletter, 6,* 1-5.

Cortes, O. G. de. (1992). United States: Hispanic Americans. In L. Miller-Lachman (Ed.), *Our family, our friends, our world: An annotated guide to significant multicultural books for children and teenagers* (pp. 121-154). New Providence, NJ: R. R. Bowker.

Council on Interracial Books for Children. (1975). Chicano culture in children's literature: Stereotypes, distortions, and omissions. *Interracial Books for Children's Bulletin, 5,* 7-14.

Cummins, J. (1986). Empowering minority students: A framework for intervention. *Harvard Educational Review, 56(1),* 18-36.

Duran, D. F. (1979). The Latino literary renaissance: Its roots, status, and future. In D. F. Duran, *Latino materials: A multimedia guide for children and young adults* (pp. 3-12). New York: Neal Schuman Publishers.

Fenelon, J. (1993, September 3). *Multiple intelligences, cultural curriculum and the four directions model.* Workshop conducted for Todd County High School, Mission, SD.

Gómez-Quiñones, J. (1990). *Chicano politics: Reality and promise, 1940-1990.* Albuquerque: University of New Mexico Press.

Hall, E. T. (1976). *Beyond culture.* Garden City, NY: Anchor Press.

Hoffman, D. (1992). A case for creating the intercultural classroom. In W. Enloe (Ed.), *Linking through diversity.*

Hoopes, D. (1979). Intercultural communication concepts and the psychology of intercultural experience. In M. Pusch (Ed.), *Multicultural education: Across cultural training approach.* New York: Intercultural Press.

Kreidler, W. J. (1990). *Elementary perspectives: Teaching concepts of peace and conflict.* Cambridge, MA: Educators for Social Responsibility.

Lewin, K. (1935). *A dynamic theory of personality: Selected papers.* New York: McGraw-Hill.

Marker, M. (1992, November). The education of little tree: What it really reveals about the public schools. *Phi Delta Kappan, 74,* 226-227.

Nguyen, N. D. T. (1993). The refugee experience: Its impact on student adjustment and schooling. *Linguathon, 9*(3), 12-14. Des Plaines, IL: The Illinois Resource Center.

Nguyen, N., & Kibler, J. (1993). *Transformation through transition and trauma: The immigrant and refugee experience.* Workshop conducted at the 16th Annual Illinois Conference for Teachers of Linguistically and Culturally Diverse Students.

Nieto, S. (1992). We have stories to tell: A case study of Puerto Ricans in Children's Books. In V. Harris (Ed.), *Teaching multicultural literature in grades K-8.* Norwood, MA: Christopher-Gordon.

Ramírez, J. D. (Winter/Spring 1992). Executive summary of the final report: Longitudinal study of structure of English immersion strategy, early-exit and late-exit transitional bilingual education programs for language-minority children. *Bilingual Research Journal, 16.*

Rochman, H. (1993). *Against borders: Promoting books for a multicultural world.* Chicago: American Library Association.

Rudman, M. K. (Ed.). (1993). *Children's literature: Resource for the classroom* (2nd ed.). Norwood, MA: Christopher Gordon Publishers.

Scarcella, R. C. (1990). *Teaching language minority students in the multicultural classroom.* Englewood Cliffs, NJ: Prentice Hall Regents.

Shorris, E. (1992). *Latinos: A biography of the people.* New York: W. W. Norton.

Trueba, H. T. (1988). *Raising silent voices: Educating the linguistic minorities for the 21st century.* Cambridge, MA: Newbury House.

Tucker, G. R. (1984). Toward the development of a language-competent American society. *International Journal of Social Language, (45)*, 153-160.

U.S. Bureau of the Census. (1991). *1990 census of population: General population characteristics in the United States.* Washington, DC: Author.

Wigginton, E. (1991, December). Culture begins at home. *Educational Leadership, 49(4)*, 60-64.

Vonnegut, K., Jr. (1974). *Wampeters foma and granfalloon (opinions)*, p. 267. New York: Delacourt Press/Seymour Lawrence.

Zeichner, K. (1990). Preparing teachers for democratic schools. *Action in Teacher Education, 11*(1), 5-10.

CHAPTER 16

Incorporating Mexican American History and Culture into the Social Studies Classroom

KATHY ESCAMILLA
UNIVERSITY OF COLORADO, DENVER

Despite dramatic changes in nation's population in the past 25 years, the social studies curriculum in most U.S. schools has remained oddly static. Because social studies, in particular, constitutes the curriculum for dealing with such changes, curricular changes are needed to restore some of its original purposes. This chapter explains why Mexican American history and culture should be better represented in the social studies curriculum, analyzes issues related to curriculum development and the selection of instructional materials, and advocates school cultures that affirm diversity.

Introduction

Latinos are now the fastest growing and one of the least educated ethnic groups in the United States (Estrada, 1988; Broun, 1992). Mexican Americans make up 63 percent of the entire population of the group collectively referred to as "Hispanic" (Estrada, 1988). Over the past 25 years, educators have initiated many programs and policies with the hope of improving educational attainment among Mexican Americans and other Hispanics.

To understand the historical need for initiatives to improve the educational attainment of Mexican Americans, consider the following statement from Andersson and Boyer (1970):

> The failure of our schools to educate Spanish speaking students is reflected in the comparative dropout rates in five Southwest States. Anglos, 14 years and older, have completed an average of 12 years of school compared to 8.1 for Spanish surnamed students. According to the 1960 Census, the state of Texas ranks at the bottom with a median of only 4.7 years of school completed for Spanish surnamed persons (p. 6).

Unfortunately, not much has changed over the past 25 years. The following information was reported in the April 1992 issue of the *NABE News* ("Excerpts," 1992):

- The Hispanic high school drop-out rate is 50 percent and higher in most urban areas;
- Three out of four Hispanic students can't pass a math test involving fractions;
- Only 51 percent of Hispanics over 25 are high school graduates;
- Only 10 percent are college graduates; and
- 56 percent are functionally illiterate.

While much has been written about this tragic situation, not much has changed with regard to school practices as they pertain to Hispanics, in general, and Mexican Americans in particular.

Many writers assert that one of the causes for the alarming statistics (low school achievement and completion rates of Mexican American students) is the narrow school curriculum. The typical public school curriculum continues, in 1996, oddly as it was in 1968—homogeneous, monolithic, and ethnocentric in its content. It has traditionally ignored and omitted the histories of many ethnic communities, particularly Mexican American communities (Anaya, 1992; Banks & Banks, 1989; Sleeter & Grant, 1994).

Anaya (1992) refers to this situation as a "censorship of neglect" and argues that in spite of the fact that Mexican Americans (Chicanos)[1] consti-

---

[1]The terms Mexican American and Chicano are used interchangeably throughout this article. Mexican Americans, as well as Chicanos, are persons of Mexican heritage who now reside in the United States. The term Chicano has a meaning that is deeply rooted in the history of Mexico. It was adopted by young people in the 1960s as a symbol of pride and as a means of acknowledging and accepting the Mexican Indian side of their heritage as well as the more socially acceptable Spanish, European part. Chicanos, in general, felt that schools should place more value on the teaching and learning of Spanish and on the study of the history of their people. The term *Chicano* is thought to be more political than the term *Mexican American*, and writers in the field use both terms based on their own self-identification and personal preference (Tatum, 1990, p. 12).

tute the fastest growing ethnic group in the United States, their history and literature are still virtually unknown and seldom taught in American classrooms. Anaya describes the situation eloquently:

> The Chicano community stretches from California to Texas and into the Northwest and Midwest. But not one iota of our social reality, much less our aesthetic reality, is represented in the literature read or history studied in the schools. So damaging has been this neglect that its result has been that the teachers of this country literally cannot see the children of twenty million people (p. 19).

One effort to improve educational attainment among Mexican Americans is to replace the outdated school curriculum that is universalist and monolithic in its view of the history of the United States with a curriculum that incorporates, in positive ways, all the voices of our country. This chapter will discuss the importance of this effort with regard to the education of Mexican Americans in the United States and will focus its discussion of curriculum reform on the social studies curriculum in particular.

The chapter considers the incorporation of Mexican American history and culture into the social studies classroom around three topics. These include (1) reasons for teaching Mexican American history and culture, (2) selecting texts and topics for curriculum integration that accurately represent the Mexican American experience in the United States, and (3) creating a total school climate that values and affirms diversity.

Reasons for Teaching Mexican American History and Culture

Several questions are often asked by teachers and school administrators about *why* it is important to teach Mexican American history and culture in social studies classrooms. They include:

1. Who needs to know this information?
2. I don't have any Mexican American students in my school. Why should I include Mexican American studies in my curriculum?
3. Mexican American students already know about their culture. Wouldn't our time be better spent teaching them the mainstream U.S. culture?

With regard to the first question, I argue that the answer is *everyone*! Knowledge of the contributions, struggles, history, and contemporary life of Mexican American students is important for *all* students in U.S. schools; however, it is especially important for students who are themselves Mexican Americans or Chicanos, a point I will return to later in this section.

Banks (1989) argues that it is crucial that schools provide opportunities for all students to learn about their unique ethnic heritage. However, it is not enough for Mexican American students or any students to learn only about their *own* cultural heritage and history. They must learn to appreciate and respect other cultural groups as well. Banks maintains that all students need to develop "ethnic literacy." Ethnic literacy is not a set of discrete facts about a particular cultural group. Rather, it is a knowledge of the role and function that ethnicity plays in our daily lives; in our society; and in our transactions locally, regionally, and transnationally. Ethnic literacy allows all students to understand their uniqueness, to understand the complexities of ethnicity and culture, and to take pride in who they are as people as well as learn to respect other cultural groups.

It has been argued that, in the United States, ethnic literacy is more important for dominant culture (White) students than it is for ("minority") students of color (Banks & Banks, 1989; Sleeter & Grant, 1994; Gollnick & Chinn, 1994).

The importance of ethnic literacy for White persons is that, in spite of the changing demographic situation in the United States, many people, particularly White people, live in neighborhoods that are segregated ethnically and linguistically, and they go to schools where the majority of students are also White. Further, 95 percent of the teaching force (for *all* students) is White (Chavez-Chavez, in press). In short, opportunities for dominant culture students to interact formally and informally with people who are linguistically and culturally different are limited. The study of the history and culture of various ethnic groups in schools is important if these students are to develop the multiple perspectives and ethnic literacy needed to participate in the 21st century (Córtes, 1990).

In view of the above, when people question the relevance of incorporating Mexican American history and culture into social studies classrooms in schools where there are few Mexican Americans, I reply that these are the very schools where this type of study is most needed!

Conversely, there is much evidence that the assumption that Mexican American students already know their culture, and therefore don't need to study it in school, is an erroneous one. For example, in 1987 I helped to conduct a major study of 10th-grade students in a large urban school district in Southern Arizona (Escamilla, 1987). It is important to realize that this school district is about 40 percent Mexican American and is located in a city where fully one third of the residents identify themselves as Hispanic. Further, it is only 65 miles from the Mexican border. One might assume that, in such a location, both Mexican American and White teenagers would have a thorough knowledge of Mexican American culture and history. Through the study I hoped to discover what high school sophomores knew about contributions to life in the United States that had been made by Mexican Americans and other cultural groups. Our study was informal, but quite informative. We simply asked all sophomores in the 10 high schools in the school district to answer two questions. There were over 3,000 students involved in the study. These were the questions asked:

1. Name two contributions that the United States has given to the world.
2. Name two contributions that Mexican Americans have given to the United States or to the world.

The results of these two open-ended questions were revealing. First, 80 percent of the students, no matter what their ethnicity, were able to readily identify two contributions that they felt the United States had given to the world. Their answers ranged from television to the atomic bomb to democracy. Not surprisingly, the three most common answers were popular culture answers—rock and roll, blue jeans, and Coca-Cola.

Sadly, however, only 20 percent of the students in the study could identify two contributions that Hispanics had given the United States or the world. The students were evenly divided by ethnicity; that is, no ethnic group knew any more about Hispanic contributions than any other ethnic group. This study, again, took place in a city whose predominate architecture reflects Hispanic contributions, where popular rock singer Linda Ronstadt was born and raised, and where street names, school names, and the very name of the state are in Spanish. In spite of being surrounded by Hispanic historical and cultural influences, high school students in this area had great difficulty identifying (and identifying *with*) cultural contributions of Hispanics. Even more telling, I feel, is that not one student in the survey identified a Hispanic contribution as being an *American* contribution to the world (question #1).

I concluded from this very informal study that neither Mexican Americans nor other cultural groups had a good understanding of the culture, history, or contributions of Mexican Americans to life in the United States. Further, we needed to explore new ways of incorporating the history and culture of Mexican Americans into our school curricula (social studies as well as other subjects).

Many others have written about the need for Mexican Americans in the United States to study their own cultural heritage and history. Gollnick and Chinn (1994) argue that opportunities to see oneself in the school promote a positive ethnic affiliation among Mexican Americans (and other groups). This, in turn, greatly influences individual development in many ways, including life choices, values, opinions, attitudes, and approaches to learning. Others argue that positive ethnic identification improves self-esteem and that there is a positive relationship between self-esteem and academic achievement (Nieto, 1992; Córtes, 1990; Banks, 1989; Sleeter & Grant, 1994).

Conversely, other writers assert that the tradition of omitting Mexican

American history and cultural studies from the curriculum has had the effect of alienating Mexican Americans from schools and from U.S. society in general. My 1987 study seemed, in fact, to suggest that just such a situation prevailed among high school sophomores. Contrary to knowing their own culture, Mexican American students often become alienated from both the dominant U.S. culture and from their own culture as well. The Chicana poet Gloria Anzaldua (1993c) eloquently evokes this alienation in several of her poems. Excerpts from two of them are included below to give the reader a sense of the frustration of cultural alienation:

> To live in the Borderlands means you . . . are neither hispana india negra española ni gabacha[2] eres mestiza, mulata half-breed caught in the crossfire between camps while carrying all five races on your back not knowing which side to turn to, run from; To live in the Borderlands means knowing that the india in you, betrayed you for 500 years, is no longer speaking to you, that mexicanas call you rajetas[3], that denying the Anglo inside you is as bad as having denied the Indian or Black (p. 96).

For Mexican Americans, the cultural alienation also includes linguistic alienation as described once again by Anzaldua (1993b) in her poem "Linguistic Terrorism." She says:

> Deslenguadas. Somos los del español deficiente.[4] We are your linguistic nightmare, your linguistic aberration, your linguistic mestisaje[5], the subject of your burla[6]. Because we speak with tongues of fire we are culturally crucified. Racially, culturally and linguistically, somos huérfanos[7]—we speak an orphan tongue (p. 293).

The above words are poignant reminders that one of the major reasons for incorporating Mexican American history and culture into the social studies classroom is to avoid the cultural alienation that has typified the experience of generations of Mexican Americans in the United States. Before these students are asked to learn to respect other cultural and ethnic groups they must first have the opportunity to learn to respect themselves, and this must begin with positive self-identity. As Anzaldua (1993b) says, "Awareness of our situation must come before inner changes, which in turn

---

[2]A Chicano term for a white woman.

[3]Literally split, that is having betrayed your word.

[4]"Tongueless. We are those with deficient Spanish."

[5]A reference to the language of the Chicano being similar to the cultural heritage which is mixed racially and often referred to as Mestizo-mixed.

[6]Joke

[7]We are orphans.

comes before changes in society. Nothing happens in the "real" world unless it first happens in the images in our heads" (p. 87).

Thus, the most compelling reason for the incorporation of Mexican American studies into U.S. schools may be to erase the negative image that many Mexican Americans and others have of their culture and heritage.

In fact, goals for these educational experiences should include making students proud of their various cultural heritages. To illustrate what I have in mind for all Mexican American students via study of their own history and heritage, consider the example of positive self-identity related by Raúl Yzaguirre (1988). Raúl is the current president of the National Council of La Raza. Raúl says it was not until he became an adult that he realized the great cultural advantages he had because of his Chicano heritage. In fact, he felt proud of not one background, but of his three distinct backgrounds. When he moved to Washington, DC, and people did not know the difference between being Mexican and Chicano, and would often say disparaging things about Mexico, Raúl would proudly say, *"Soy Mexicano"* (I am Mexican). When he would go to Mexico and people would notice he looked "Americanized," and would criticize Mexican Americans as being "pochos," he would proudly say, *"Soy Chicano"* (I am Chicano). When he went to Europe and heard the critics put down the United States, he would proudly say, *"Soy Americano"* (I am American). He had come to know that he was enriched by all his cultural identities, and was no longer alienated from any of them.

In short, it would seem that classrooms and schools should strive to create environments that minimize the cultural alienation felt by so many Mexican American students and the cultural myopia characteristic of so many White students. Suggestions for ways to do this are included in the next sections.

Selecting Texts and Topics for Curriculum Integration That Accurately Represent the Mexican American Experience in the United States

Perhaps the most important element in the selection of materials about the Mexican American experience in the United States is diversity. The Mexican American experience in the United States is diverse, complex, and dynamic. No single definition or story characterizes the Mexican American experience, just as no single story captures any other ethnolinguistic group.

Given this diversity, it is important to define the Mexican American experience first and foremost as a human experience. Many identify its beginnings around 1848 with the Treaty of Guadalupe Hidalgo, when

Mexico ceded a third of its land to the United States. This area today is California, Nevada, Utah, Arizona, New Mexico, Texas, and part of Colorado (Barrera, 1992). Others say, however, that the history of the Mexican American began in Pre-Columbian times (Tatum, 1990).

After the Treaty of Guadalupe Hidalgo, the Mexicans who chose to remain on the ceded land became the Mexican Americans. Domination and subordination characterized the subsequent experiences of the various Mexican groups. For persons teaching Mexican American history, it is important that they know that many Mexican Americans have been here for generations, while others will be arriving today. Social studies classes incorporating Mexican American history must be aware of each of these realities.

It is important also to note that there are many materials currently available to teach about Mexican American culture and history. However, as Banks and Banks (1989) have noted, many of these materials limit their presentation of the Mexican American experience to the discussion of isolated holidays and events such as the *16 de septiembre* (Mexican Independence Day) and *5 de mayo* (an important holiday in Mexico commemorating the beginning of the victory of Mexico over the French who were occupying Mexico in 1862).

Further, these same materials tend to present historical figures in two extremes. One extreme is the "hero" presentation which describes a few exceptional historical figures as superhumans who overcame insurmountable odds to achieve greatness. More often though, social studies curricula depict the Mexican American people as helpless victims of poverty and discrimination.

The dichotomy of heroes and victims produces a distorted account of the Mexican American experience. Perpetuating the stereotypes of Mexican Americans as victims is harmful to all students in a classroom, but poses special dangers to students of Mexican American heritage. The view that only the exceptional succeed while the majority fall victim—combined with the sporadic and inaccurate treatment of the contributions of Mexican Americans in the curriculum—may lead students to conclude that if they are not truly exceptional (and most of us are not!), then there is no hope for them, unless they reject their heritage and learn to "act White." Further, students may be misled to conclude that their heritage has contributed very little to the development of the Western Hemisphere.

The heroes and victims syndrome of the presentation of the Mexican American experience has the potential of leaving students with few realistic role models. Most students are not likely to achieve the greatness of a Caesar Chávez, nor will they likely live in a state of abject poverty. Many students will find it difficult to identify with Mexican American culture as presented in most social studies curriculum. The result is a conceptual vacuum that defeats one of the main purposes of integrating Mexican American studies into the curriculum—to develop a sense of ethnic pride.

So how do we select materials and choose topics to incorporate Mexican American history and culture into the social studies curriculum in a way that does not focus solely on discrete historical events, token contributions, famous people, or hopelessness?

I offer the following guidelines for incorporating materials about Mexican American history and culture into the social studies curriculum. First, these collections should include the range of Mexican American history and not be limited to contemporary history or the history of "Westward Expansion." (At present, the latter two conditions, and not the former, prevail.) Second, Mexican American history is American history, and it should be presented together with traditional topics in U. S. history. Third, school classrooms and libraries should have collections of books and materials (trade books as well as textbooks) that represent the Mexican American diaspora (i.e., immigrant and emigrant populations) and range of experiences and viewpoints.

Significant eras in Mexican American history are presented below; these eras need to be represented in social studies textbooks dealing with general American history. The discussion also provides a list of texts and materials that can be used by teachers to inform themselves about Mexican American history so that they can then create integrated lessons. These eras need to be taught at both elementary and secondary levels. This list of resources is by no means exhaustive but is offered as a way of encouraging teachers to learn more about Mexican American history and to begin to consider ways to integrate Mexican American history without making it a separate subject in an already crowded curriculum.

Major Eras In Mexican American History

- Pre-Columbian History (prior to 1492)
- Spanish and Mexican Periods (1528-1848)
- Mexican American Period (1848-1960)
- Contemporary Period - The Civil Rights Era (1960-present)

Textbooks and other materials useful to teachers attempting to incorporate this history into the social studies curriculum include the following:

Elementary/Middle History Texts

Hispanics in America to 1776. (1993). Paramus, NJ: Globe Book Co.

Hispanics in the U.S. (1989). Englewood Cliffs, NJ: Globe Book Co.

Hispanics in U.S. history. (1983). Tucson, AZ: University of Arizona Press.

Pinchot, J. (1973). *The Mexican Americans in America.* Minneapolis, MN: The Learner Co.

The Latin experience in U.S. history. (1994). Paramus, NJ: Globe Fearon.

High School History Texts

Acuña, R. (1988). *Occupied America: A history of Chicanos* (3rd ed). New York: Harper & Row.

Chávez, J. (1984). *The lost land: The Chicano image of the Southwest.* Albuquerque: University of New Mexico Press.

Moore, J. (1976). *Mexican Americans.* Englewood Cliffs, NJ: Prentice Hall.

Nova, J. (1973). *The Mexican American in American history.* New York: American Book Co.

500 years of Chicano history in pictures. (1992). Albuquerque, NM: Southwest Organizing Project.

Literature

With regard to materials selection that includes literature to represent the Mexican American diaspora and multiple experiences, I suggest that social studies texts be supplemented with literature for children and adolescents. The history of a people cannot be separated from their literature, stories, and poetry. In fact, the inclusion of these stories in the curriculum is crucial to accurate portrayal of Mexican American people and their history. Literature helps make history "come alive." Fortunately, during the past few years, several excellent resource books have been produced for teachers to use in finding literature that represents the broad range of experiences in the Mexican American culture. These resources include but are not limited to the following:

Harris, V. (Ed.). (1992). *Multicultural literature in grades K-8.* Norwood, MA: Christopher Gordon Pub.

Latino poetry. (1994). Paramus, NJ: Globe Fearon.

Mexican American literature. (1993). Englewood Cliffs, NJ: Globe Book Co.

Ramírez, G., & Ramírez, J. (1994). *Multiethnic children's literature.* Albany, NY: Delmar.

Tatum, C. (Ed.) (1990). *Mexican American literature.* Orlando, FL: Harcourt, Brace & Jovanovich.

Using the above resources and others, it is now possible for both elementary and secondary teachers to integrate Mexican American heritage into the social studies curriculum through literature as well as through textbook topics. With such resources, teachers can expand their presentation of the treatment of Mexican Americans beyond heroes and victims (heroes and victims are also important, too, but as a part of this literature and not in isolation). Types of literature needed to supplement the historical topics listed above are described below, with several examples.

Historical fiction. Historical fiction can be used to supplement all the historical topics listed, from the stories of fifth-generation Mexican Americans to the stories of first-generation Mexican Americans. For example, the book *Kids Explore America's Hispanic Heritage* (1992) presents stories about people like Casimiro Barela, who was born before the Mexican American war in 1848 and who helped to write the Colorado Constitution; and Rodolfo "Corky" Gonzalez, a contemporary writer and civil rights activist who can trace his heritage in the United States back four generations. Other books, such as *Lupita Mañana* (Beatty, 1981), present stories about the contemporary struggles of recent arrivals who are undocumented workers.

Folk tales and legends. As with historical fiction, folktales and legends can help to provide a human side to the study of historical topics. Further, folktales and legends provide an interesting and stimulating tool for comparing and contrasting cultural viewpoints. Stories such as *La Llorona* (Hayes, 1987), *The Farolitos of Christmas* (Anaya, 1987), *The Moon God of the Maya/El Dios Maya de la Luna* (1983), and *The Sweethearts/Los Novios* (1983) provide interesting ways to illustrate within-group diversity and enrich social studies lessons. These last two items are not commercially available materials, incidentally.[8] They were developed, in all probability, as a local effort. Developing folktales and legends in this way can help forge links between schools and communities.

Contemporary culture, including the changing status of women. If students are to understand culture truly, they must learn that cultures are continually changing. Contemporary stories help to illustrate the changing nature of the Mexican American culture. Their use can help social studies teachers reduce the "folksy" treatment that many cultural groups receive in social studies textbooks. Books such as Soto's *Taking Sides* (1990) or Cisneros' *House on Mango Street* (1983) present stories that relate to "real people" living in the contemporary United States and the cultural struggles that contemporary Mexican Americans face. Other books, such as Atkinson's *Mar a Teresa* (1979), are also important in their presentation of the changing circumstances of Mexican American women in the United States. For

[8]*El Dios Maya de la Luna* and *Los Novios* are available on request from Kathy Escamilla, School of Education, University of Colorado at Denver, Campus Box 106, P. O. Box 173364, Denver, CO 80217-3364. Please include a self-addressed, stamped envelope (two first-class stamps).

example, in *Mar a Teresa*, the mother is a graduate student who moves from New Mexico to Ohio to pursue a degree.

Real people. In any social studies class, particularly those with historical foci, the "real people" stories are important ways of illustrating how average people live in particular points of time. But equally important is their use to show the diversity of "average experience" between and within different cultural groups. Stories such as Lomas-Garza's *Family Pictures* (1990), Soto's *Baseball in April* (1990), and Bruin's *Rosita's Christmas Wish* (1985) present "people stories" that students from many cultural groups can understand and appreciate.

Heroes and heroines. As stated previously, the inclusion of heroes in the study of Mexican American heritage is problematic if the study of heroes represents the entire treatment of Mexican American culture. However, the study of heroes and heroines is a feature of a balanced curriculum. Mexican Americans have made significant contributions to U.S. history and deserve recognition for their work. Stories about heroes and heroines should be chosen to fit the appropriate period of history being studied so that topics are presented in an integrated way. Fortunately there are many such books. Examples include Clinton's *Everett Alvarez Jr.: A Hero for Our Times* (1990), which is a story of the first American pilot shot down over North Vietnam who also became the first POW in 1964. Similarly, Munson's book, *Our Tejano Heroes: Outstanding Mexican Americans in Texas* (1989), provides short biographies of historical and contemporary figures who have contributed in significant ways to the history of Texas.

Victims and discrimination. As with heroes and heroines, reading about discrimination visited upon Mexican Americans is important to a complete understanding of the history of this group. And a complete understanding of the Mexican American experience is important if students are to become active agents in the continuing quest for social justice in the United States. However, as with heroes and heroines, topics of discrimination and victimization should be presented as a *part* of the Mexican American experience (and one American experience), but not its entirety. Books such as de Ruiz's *La Causa: The Farmworkers' Story* (1993), Anzaldua's *Friends From the Other Side* (1993a), and Tafolla's *Sonnets to Human Beings* (1992) are wonderful classroom collections, not only because they present stories of victimization, but also because they simultaneously illustrate the heroism so often involved in resisting or coping with discrimination.

Used with an integrated presentation of Mexican American history, literature powerfully and positively incorporates Mexican American issues into social studies classrooms. The use of literature also honors the fact that literature and history depend on one another.

One cannot hope, however, to create positive ethnic pride and instill respect and appreciation for the Mexican American culture by simply changing the social studies curriculum. Classrooms are microcosms of larger school environments (just as schools are microcosms of communities). True integration cannot really succeed unless the entire school environment affirms and honors the Mexican American culture and the students and families who represent that culture. Students need visible symbols of Mexican American culture and heritage, schoolwide, every day.

Creating a School Climate that Appreciates Diversity

Student attitudes about school and their sense of self are shaped by what happens both in the classroom and throughout the school. The benefits of effectively incorporating Mexican American history and culture into classroom instruction will be diluted unless the school as a whole appreciates not only the Mexican American culture but also the living, breathing, speaking students who represent that culture *because they are that culture* (Banks & Banks, 1989).

Changing a curriculum does not necessarily change a school. To illustrate this point, let us consider the following example. Teachers in the high school where I did my 1987 study (Escamilla, 1987) were often heard making comments such as, "I love living in the Southwest—the architecture is great, the lifestyle is wonderful." This same school also had cultural activities, a ballet folklórico dance group, a Spanish club, and a MESA club for Hispanic students who were interested in careers in engineering. Further, they also had a social studies curriculum that reflected Mexican American contributions. Yet in this school, when teachers described the Mexican American students, they often made statements such as they are "at-risk," "not competitive," "not future oriented," "have families that don't value education," and are, in general, "problems." Researchers in this area describe such attitudes as valuing *"lo mexicano"* (Mexican things), but not *"los mexicanos"* (Mexican people) (Paz, 1987). Students can expect to make few gains in a school environment that purports to value their culture (in the abstract) while at the same time disdains them as human beings.

For these reasons, any attempt at creating an environment that affirms diversity must consider the larger environment as well as the curriculum. Banks (1989) has identified eight characteristics of a multicultural school. These include three issues that could be viewed as issues to be addressed inside a classroom and five that could be viewed as larger school issues.

The characteristics are as follows:

1. The teachers and school administrators have positive attitudes toward all students, and they respond to them in positive and caring ways.
2. The formalized curriculum reflects the experiences, cultures, and perspectives of a range of cultural and ethnic groups as well as both genders.
3. The teaching styles used by the teachers match the learning, cultural, and motivational styles of the students.
4. The school environment shows respect for the students' first languages and dialects.
5. The instructional materials used in the school show events, situations, and concepts from the perspectives of a range of cultural, ethnic, and racial groups.
6. The assessment and testing procedures used in the school are culturally sensitive, and students of color participate in gifted and honors classes at a proportional rate.
7. The school culture and the informal curriculum reflect cultural and ethnic diversity.
8. The school counselors have high expectations for students from different racial, ethnic, and language groups and help these students to set and realize positive career goals.

Banks' list has been further supported by researchers specifically studying Mexican Americans (Tikunoff, 1984; Lucas, Henze, & Donato, 1990). The above list of characteristics and others like it demonstrate that real improvement results from changing schools and their attitudes as well as changing curriculum.

Integrating Mexican American history and culture into the social studies classroom is a worthy and important goal for all schools—especially those with large populations of Mexican American students. Effective integration requires that teachers have accurate materials that represent the diversity of the Mexican American experience and the broad range of contributions that Mexican Americans have made to life in the Western Hemisphere. Further, this study should motivate children and youth not only for learning but for positive social change on behalf of the common good.

However, quality materials and enlightened curricula will have little impact in schools where the environment is still alien or hostile to the very students such schools purport to help. Therefore, creating a school environment that values Mexican American students is essential. To truly incorporate Mexican American history and culture into the curriculum requires that the entire school and all its teachers and staff take individual responsibility in learning to teach in new ways and with new perspectives. As educators, we are professionally responsible for entering different existential worlds in order to enrich ourselves and our teaching and to serve as models for others. This enrichment lies at the heart of pluralism and excellence, and it illumines the search for equity and social justice. Nothing less will create meaningful change.

References

Acuña, R. (1988). *Occupied America: A history of Chicanos* (3rd ed.). New York: Harper & Row.

Anaya, R. (1992). The censorship of neglect. *English Journal, 81*(5), 18-20.

Anaya, R. (1987). *The farolitos of Christmas.* New York: Hyperion Books for Children.

Andersson, T., & Boyer, *M. (Eds.). (1970). Bilingual schooling in the United States.* Austin, TX: Southwest Educational Development Laboratory. (ERIC Document Reproduction Service No. ED 039 *527)*

Anzaldua, G. (1993a). *Friends from the other side.* San Francisco, CA: Children's Book Press.

Anzaldua, G. (1993b). Linguistic terrorism (poem). In T. D. Rebolledo & E. S. Rivero (Eds.), *Infinite divisions: An anthology of Chicana literature.* Tucson, AZ: University of Arizona Press.

Anzaldua, G. (1993c). *To live in the borderlands means you* ...(poem). In T. D. Rebolledo & E. S. Rivero (Eds.), *Infinite divisions: An anthology of Chicana literature.* Tucson, AZ: University of Arizona Press.

Atkinson, M. (1979). *Mar a Teresa.* Carrboro, NC: Lollipop Power.

Banks, J., & Banks, C. A. (1989). *Multicultural education: Issues and perspectives.* Boston: Allyn & Bacon.

Banks, J. (1989). *Multiethnic education: Theory and practice* (2nd ed.). Boston: Allyn & Bacon.

Barrera, R. (1992). Ideas a literature can grow on: Key insights for enriching and expanding children's literature about the Mexican American experience. In V. Harris (Ed.), *Teaching multicultural literature in grades K-8,* (pp. 203-242). Norwood, MA: Christopher-Gordon Pub.

Beatty, P. (1981). *Lupita mañana.* New York: William Morrow & Co.

Broun, A. (1992). Building community support through local educational funds. *Journal of the National Association for Bilingual Education: NABE News, 15*(4&5), 11, 26-27.

Bruin, M. A. (1985). *Rosita's Christmas wish.* San Antonio, TX: Tex Art Services, Inc.

Chávez-Chávez, R. (in press). *Multicultural education in the everyday: A renaissance for the recommitted.* Washington, DC: AACTE.

Chávez, J. (1984). *The lost land: The Chicano image of the Southwest.* Albuquerque: University of New Mexico Press.

Cisneros, S. (1983). *House on Mango Street.* New York: Vintage.

Clinton, S. (1990). *Everett Alvarez Jr.: A hero for our times.* Chicago: Children's Press.

Córtes, C. (1990). Multicultural education: A curricular basic for our multiethnic future. *NEA/NY Advocate, 17*(1), 8-9.

de Ruiz, D. (1993). *La causa: The farmworkers' story.* Chicago: Children's Press.

Escamilla, K. (1987, February). *Do they really know their culture?* Paper presented at the annual conference of the Arizona Association for Bilingual Education, Flagstaff.

Estrada, L. F. (1988). Anticipating the demographic future: Dynamic changes are on the way. *The Magazine of Higher Education, 20*(3), 14-19.

Excerpts from the condition of education for Hispanics in America. (1992, July). *NABE News* (15)7, p. 6.

500 years of Chicano history in pictures. (1992). Albuquerque, NM: Southwest Organizing Project.

Gollnick, D., & Chinn, P. (1994). *Multicultural education in a pluralistic society* (4th ed.). New York: Macmillan.

Harris, V. (Ed.). (1992). *Teaching multicultural literature in grades K-8.* Norwood, MA: Christopher-Gordon.

Hayes, J. (1987). *La llorona: The weeping woman.* El Paso, TX: Cinco Puntos Press.

Hispanics in America to 1776. (1993). Paramus, NJ: Globe Book Co.

Hispanics in the U.S. (1989). Englewood Cliffs, NJ: Globe Book Co.

Hispanics in U.S. history. (1983). Tucson, AZ: University of Arizona Press.

Kids explore America's Hispanic heritage. (1992). Santa Fe, NM: John Muir Pub.

The Latin experience in U.S. history. (1994). Paramus, NJ: Globe Fearon.

Latino poetry. (1994). Paramus, NJ: Globe Fearon.

Lomas-Garza, C. (1990). *Family pictures (Cuadros de familia).* San Francisco: Children's Book Press.

Lucas, T., Henze, R., & Donato, R. (1990). Promoting success of Latino language minority students: An exploratory study of six high schools. *Harvard Educational Review 60*(3), 315-140.

Mexican American literature. (1993). Englewood Cliffs, NJ: Globe Book Co.

The Moon God of the Mayans (El dios maya de la luna). (1983). Story disseminated at the annual conference of the California Association for Bilingual Education (CABE), Anaheim, CA.

Moore, J. (1976). *Mexican Americans.* Englewood Cliffs, NJ: Prentice Hall.

Munson, S. (1989). *Our Tejano heroes: Outstanding Mexican Americans in Texas.* Austin, TX: Eakin Press.

Nieto, S. (1992). *Affirming diversity.* New York: Longman.

Nova, J. (1973). *The Mexican American in American history.* New York: American Book Co.

Paz, E. (1987, February). *Appreciating people and artifacts.* Address given to the Arizona Association for Bilingual Education Annual Conference, Flagstaff.

Pinchot, J. (1973). *The Mexican Americans in America.* Minneapolis, MN: The Learner Co.

Ramírez, G., & Ramírez, J. (1994). *Multiethnic children's literature.* Albany, NY: Delmar.

Sleeter, C., & Grant, C. (1994). *Making choices for multicultural education: Five approaches to race, class, and gender.* New York: Merrill.

Soto, G. (1990). *Baseball in April.* San Diego, CA: Harcourt, Brace & Jovanovich.

Soto, G. (1990). *Taking sides.* New York: Harcourt, Brace & Jovanovich.

Tatum, C. (Ed.). (1990). *Mexican American literature.* Orlando: Harcourt, Brace & Jovanovich.

Tafolla, C. (1992). *Sonnets to human beings.* Santa Monica, CA: Lalo Press.

The Sweethearts (Los Novios). (1983). Story disseminated at the annual conference of the California Association for Bilingual Education (CABE), Anaheim.

Tikunoff, W. (1984). *Applying significant bilingual instructional features in the classroom.* Rosslyn, VA: InterAmerica Research Associates.

Yzaguirre, R. (1988). *The importance of positive ethnic identity to build pride in Hispanic youth.* Keynote address given at the annual conference of the Arizona Association for Bilingual Education (AABE), Phoenix.

Chapter 17

Teaching Mathematics For Understanding To Bilingual Students[1]

Walter G. Secada
University of Wisconsin-Madison

Yolanda De La Cruz
School of Education and Social Policy
Northwestern University

[1]The development of this chapter was supported in part by the National Center for Research in Mathematical Sciences Education (NCRMSE), which is funded by the Office of Educational Research and Improvement (OERI), U.S. Department of Education (grant number R117G10002), and which is administered through the Wisconsin Center for Education Research (WCER), School of Education, University of Wisconsin-Madison. Additional support was provided by the Spencer Foundation and the National Science Foundation (NSF) under Grant No. RED 935373 to Northwestern University, Evanston, IL. The findings and opinions expressed in this chapter belong to the authors and do not necessarily reflect the views of NCRMSE, NSF, OERI, the Spencer Foundation, or WCER. Karen Fuson, who directs the Children's Math Worlds project, and her staff at Northwestern University have been working with teachers at Esperanza Elementary School in developing the ideas from which we have drawn the Mercado examples. Many of our ideas on teaching for understanding have been tried out and developed in workshops with teachers of bilingual students in New York City, Brownsville, Dallas, El Paso, Laredo, San Antonio, and other parts of Texas. Their feedback proved very helpful in our efforts to present these ideas accessibly. Finally, Judith LeBlanc Flores, Elizabeth Fennema, and two anonymous reviewers provided valuable feedback on an early, (very) rough draft of this chapter. Our thanks to all of them.

A variety of issues arise when schools and teachers plan for the mathematics education of binational students. Educators might be interested to know about their students' general educational experiences and, more specifically, the mathematics they are learning in both countries; about students' cognitive and linguistic strengths in either or both languages; and about learning styles (Cocking & Mestre, 1988; De Avila & Duncan, 1985; Irvine & York, 1995; Simmons, 1985). This chapter is organized around the core theme of teaching for understanding, because teaching for understanding is a hallmark of the mathematics education reform (Cohen, McLaughlin, & Talbert, 1993; Lampert, 1986, 1989, 1990; National Council of Teachers of Mathematics, 1989, 1991, 1995; National Research Council, 1989; Schoenfeld, 1992). Through this chapter, the authors strive to make information about teaching for understanding accessible to people engaged in the education of binational and bilingual students.[2]

Why Understanding?

Educators have been relatively successful in teaching basic computational skills to high degrees of proficiency, as evidenced by the steady rise in achievement scores beginning in the 1980s (reviewed in Secada, 1992). Unfortunately, educators have been much less successful in teaching children when to apply those skills in real-world settings, advanced mathematics, or the sciences (Dossey, Mullis, Lindquist, & Chambers, 1988; Dossey, Mullis, & Jones, 1993; Mullis, Dossey, Foertsch, Jones, & Gentile, 1991; Mullis, Dossey, Owen, & Phillips, 1993). Teaching for understanding is thought to be a solution to this problem, not just for so-called mainstream or majority students, but also for students of diverse social backgrounds (Carey, Fennema, Carpenter, & Franke, 1995; Knapp and Associates, 1995; Knapp & Shields, 1991; Peterson, Fennema, & Carpenter, 1991; Silver, Smith, & Nelson, 1995; Villaseñor & Kepner, 1993).

Children enter school understanding and being able to do a lot of mathematics (Carpenter, 1985; Fuson, 1988). For instance, Secada (1991b) found that Hispanic bilingual first graders could solve arithmetic word problems in both English and Spanish that, according to conventional

[2]Additional work on teaching mathematics and science for understanding to bilingual students can be found in Rosebery, Warren, & Conant (1992), Secada (1991a), Warren & Rosebery (1992, 1995), Warren, Rosebery & Conant (1989, 1994).

wisdom, they should not have been able to solve[3]. Not only did their invented solutions[4] tend to result in correct answers, but also, their explanations of those solutions were sensible and demonstrated that they understood many of the problems. In contrast, the computational facts on which bilingual children are all too often drilled seldom make much sense to them; hence, at least initially, young children tend to ignore computational facts and instead to rely on their own strategies (that is, their own mathematics) when solving word problems.

Beyond the fact that children will ignore or misapply what they do not understand—as do all people—the disconnection between how primary-graders reason about mathematics versus how students are taught poses two additional problems. First, this disconnection lays the foundation for failure in school mathematics. When children cannot do computations in the book's way or they cannot do paper-and-pencil algorithms quickly and efficiently—because neither makes much sense to them—they are often corrected, have their papers marked wrong, and drilled further. In other words, children begin to fail in mathematics. For bilingual children, the consequences of this initial "failure" become even more severe since they add to the stereotypical belief that students acquiring English cannot engage in mathematics that involve substantive use of language, such as word problems.

---

[3]These children had been identified as limited English proficient (LEP), a term that has a 20-year history of local, state, and federal usage. During the past few years, the term LEP has been severely criticized for its pejorative overtones in focusing on students' purported deficiencies as opposed to their knowledge and skills (Casanova & Arias, 1993). At a time when the United States' educational systems are being challenged to produce an informed citizenry who can participate in an increasingly multilingual and multicultural society and who can help that society in a technological and multinational economy, a new term is needed to communicate the potential resources that are represented by students who, in addition to knowing languages other than English, are learning English as a second or third language. These terms include "students acquiring English," "English learners," and "learners of English as a second language." Recognizing that there has been some confusion and in some cases outright resistance to terminology that departs from the conventional use of the term LEP, we nonetheless will use the term "bilingual" to refer to the population of students who have some competence in two or more languages and the term "students acquiring English" to refer to students whose command of the English language is deemed less than optimal. Hence, our use of the term "bilingual" includes "students acquiring English"; it is all a matter of degree.

[4]There is a large body of research on children's informal, invented solution strategies for arithmetic word problems (see, for instance, Carpenter, 1985; Carpenter & Moser, 1983, 1984; Carpenter, Moser, & Romberg, 1982; Riley, Greeno & Heller, 1983). These strategies are invented because they are not taught in school. In addition, schooled and unschooled children as well as bilingual and monolingual children use many of the same strategies when confronting word problems (Adetula, 1989; Ghaleb, 1992; Secada, 1991b).

The second consequence of failing to encourage children to understand the mathematics they encounter and to solve problems in ways that make sense to them is that they begin to believe mathematics should *not* make sense. Mathematics then becomes the rapid production of nonsensical stuff (see Carpenter, 1985, for a fuller elaboration of this argument). In contrast, students who are taught mathematics so that they understand it will be socialized into expecting that its teaching should make sense to them.

In developing this chapter, we adopted the position that student understanding of worthwhile mathematical content is the *sine qua non* of mathematics education, and everything else—curriculum, instruction, and assessment—is a means to that end. Our position means that the chapter's two additional themes—student bilingualism and the use of children's home and cultural backgrounds in mathematics—are important considerations for teachers and other school personnel insofar as they help teachers to promote student understanding of mathematics[5]. Our examples[6] illustrate how teaching for understanding might look in a classroom that includes bilingual or binational students; they also weave student bilingualism and the use of home and cultural backgrounds into the fabric of teaching for understanding.

---

[5]The astute reader will see other themes reflected in the examples that we use. For instance, students' sharing their reasoning and problem-solving strategies with one another in small-group settings reflects the use of cooperative groups. That some students use counters for solving arithmetic problems, while others use their fingers, is consistent with a focus on teaching through multiple modalities. And as we have already noted, students who are schooled in Mexico are likely to be learning different algorithms than are taught in U.S. schools. We are aware of these issues and we agree that they are important. Our central point remains: cooperative groups, manipulatives, learning styles, and the like are important insofar as attending to them helps teachers to promote student understanding. Rather than try to cover everything that is relevant to the teaching of binational students, we decided to focus on fewer ideas (student understanding, bilingualism, and home cultures) and to develop those ideas in depth.

[6]The following vignettes are *composites* of the many classrooms that we have observed where there is teaching of mathematics for understanding. The core of many vignettes are from Yolanda De La Cruz's observations of Mrs. Sara Avelar, a teacher who has asked that her real name be used. At the time that Yolanda was observing Mrs. Avelar's classroom, Sara was one of eight primary-grade teachers and over 200 children at Esperanza School who were participating in the *Children's Math Worlds* curriculum development project. Esperanza is the fictitious name of an urban elementary school in a largely Hispanic neighborhood. Almost all the children were, to some degree, bilingual. Roughly half were dominant English speakers and were enrolled in four English-language classrooms, one for each of grades K through 3. Of these children, most were first generation U.S. born. The other half were students acquiring English and were enrolled in one of four Spanish-English bilingual classrooms. Over 80 percent of Esperanza's bilingual children were of Mexican descent; many had been born in Mexico. Sara Avelar taught 28 second graders in her bilingual class. All came from Mexican homes where little or no English was spoken.

Mathematics Teaching

Let us enter a second-grade bilingual classroom in which 28 children are using both English and Spanish to talk among themselves as they work with fraction strips and a pair of dice. The strips of paper come in six different sizes: the longest is a whole, and the children refer to it as the *one* (*el uno*). The next size is half the size of the one, that is, it is the half (*un medio*); followed by 1/3 (*una tercera parte*), 1/4 (*una cuarta parte o un cuarto*), 1/8 (*una octava parte o un octavo*), and 1/16 (*el decimosexto*, which children refer to as *the smallest* or *el más pequeño*). Children play in pairs; each child rolls a die whose faces are marked 1/2, 1/4, 1/8, 2/8, 1/3, and 1/16. Each child takes the fractional strip that corresponds to the number that is rolled and places the fractional strip on top of the 1-strip. The first child to cover, exactly, the 1-strip with the correct, corresponding fractional strips, wins. On a separate sheet of paper, children record the fractions that they roll.

As we go from pair to pair, we overhear different conversations. Children check one another to be sure that the strip matches the fraction that was rolled. One child asks his partner, who has played the 1/4-strip though the die shows 2/8, to explain why she did so. "Porque los dos son iguales (Because both are equal)," she answers. Unsure what is meant, the first child asks for more of an explanation, "¿Cuáles son iguales? (Which ones are equal?)." Taking two of the 1/8-strips and one 1/4-strip, the second child covers the 1/4-strip with the two 1/8s. She explains, "Estos dos son lo mismo que la cuarta parte. Mira (these two [she holds the 1/8-strips in one hand] are the same as 1/4 [she holds the 1/4 in the other hand]. See [she covers the 1/4-strip with the two 1/8-strips])."

Two children do not place the 1/3-strips on the 1-strip, even when they roll 1/3. "Why don't you use these?" an adult asks. Seeing the puzzled look on their friend's face, a third child explains, "Quieren saber porqué no usas estos (They [the visitors] want to know why you don't use these [points to the 1/3 strips])." "Tenemos que llegar a uno, y es mas difícil con éstas." Translating, the teacher explains, "They say they have to reach the one and it's more difficult with the 1/3-strips."

Another pair notices that they can exchange two 1/8-strips for one 1/4-strip. As they discuss the trade, two more children join in and suggest that they work together to see what other trades can be made. The teacher suggests that the four record the results of their exploration in order to share them with the rest of the class. "Be sure you can explain how you figured things out so that everyone understands you," she reminds them.

Circulating among the children, watching how they're doing, the teacher poses questions to clarify children's thinking and to help them think of ideas for winning the game. Jesús[7] seems unable to find fractions that total 1 and he is becoming increasingly frustrated from losing the game. Since it is almost time for recess and children are finishing their activity, she makes a mental note to call Jesús' mother. Instead of Jesús repeating the same fraction game at home, his mother and teacher decide that he should help with cooking so that he can see fractions in use.

Later, as Jesús is measuring the ingredients for making pancakes, he notices "¡Oh, ésto es lo que estamos haciendo en la clase! (Oh! This is what we're doing in class!)" Jesús then explains to his mother how each smaller measuring cup is part of the big one. She, in turn, explains that had Jesús used the wrong cups, the pancake mix would not have turned out right.

The next math class begins with children discussing the results of their game. Children go to the board to write all the different ways that they got to 1. Their teacher tells the students that if someone else has written down what they did, to just put a checkmark by that way. To begin the class discussion, Jesús explains how he and his mother measured the ingredients for pancake batter and how he used half cups (which were easier to handle) for the flour, an eighth of a cup for the oil, and so forth.

Teacher: ¿Cuánta harina usaste? (How much flour did you use?)

Jesús: Una tasa y media. (One and a half cups.)

Teacher: ¿Cómo supiste que tenías una tasa si estabas usando media tasa? Enséñale a la clase con estos papelitos. (How did you know when you had a full cup since you were using only a half cup? Show the rest of the class with these paper strips.)

Jesús: Llené la tasa con dos. Así. (I filled the cup with two. Like this.) [At the overhead projector, Jesús places two of the 1/2-strips right next to the 1-strip, and shows how they cover it.]

Teacher: ¿Cuántas de las medias tasas usaste? (How many of the half cups did you use?)

Jesús: Tres. Porque dos son una tasa; y una más para tasa y media. (Three. Because two are one cup; and one more for one and a half cups.)

As Jesús sits down, the teacher points out where the class has written that two 1/2s make a whole. "Vamos a ver cómo se pueda sumar a uno. . . Let's see how we can add to one." she translates. As the children review the different ways that they got to the 1-strip, they see that not everyone wrote their expressions the same way: some had used plus (+) signs; others, commas; and still others had just listed the fractions in no order. After a short discussion, the children agree that they need to find a single way of writing things because otherwise, things could get confusing.

[7]All names are fictitious.

The consensus is to use the plus sign because these are numbers that "add to 1."

As they recopy the list of fractions, some children argue that 1/3+1/4+1/2 cannot equal one; others argue that it does.

Teacher: ¿Quiénes piensan que éstos suman a uno? (Who thinks that these add up to one?) [A group of children raise their hands] ¿Y quiénes dicen que *no*? (And who says *no*?) [Some other children raise their hands.] ¿Y quién no sabe? (And who doesn't know?) Bueno, discútenlo entre ustedes mismos. (Well, discuss it among yourselves.)

In a spirited conversation, some children bring out strips to show others how 1/3+1/4+1/2 is too big to equal 1. Other children write on paper. Listening to each group's reasoning, the teacher sends groups that achieve consensus to the other groups to help them resolve the problem. After a while, there is quiet.

Teacher: ¿Qué decidieron? (What did you decide?)

María: Es más que uno. (It is more than 1.)

Teacher: ¿Cómo lo sabes? (How do you know that?)

María: [Comes to the overhead and talks while she places the fraction strips next to one another and compares them to the unit strip] Porque, maestra, si pones juntos los papelitos, es más grande que uno. (Because, teacher, if you put the fraction strips together, it's larger than 1.)

Teacher: ¿Están de acuerdo? ¿Todo el mundo le entendió a María? ¿Explícalo otra vez para estar segura que te entendieron? (Does everyone agree? Did everyone understand María? [Some No's] Please explain it another time to be sure that everyone understands you.)

María re-explains. As there are no questions from her classmates, she goes to sit down.

Teacher: ¿Quién lo hizo de otra manera? ¿Liliana? (Who did it a different way? Liliana?)

Coming to board, Liliana writes:

1/4	+ 1/4 + 1/2 = 1
1/3	+ 1/4 + 1/2

Liliana: Dos cuartas partes más la media parte son uno. Pero la tercera parte, aquí, es más que un cuarto. Así es que, la suma tiene que ser más que uno. (Two 1/4s plus 1/2 equals 1. But 1/3, here, is more than 1/4. Hence, the sum has to be more than 1.)

Liliana circles the 1/4 and the 1/3 as she says that 1/3 is more than 1/4.

Teacher: ¿Y por qué creen que alguien escribió eso? (Why do you, the class, think that someone wrote that [pointing to the 1/3 + 1/4 + 1/2]?)

The children call out various reasons. Maybe someone wrote down the wrong numbers. Maybe the person didn't match the fraction to its proper piece of paper. Maybe the person forgot that the idea was to get exactly to 1.

At this point, the teacher calls on the four children who explored the various trades that could be made among fractions to explain what they have discovered. Their results include relatively simple equivalences such as 1/2 equals two of the 1/4s or 1/4 equals two of the 1/8s; but also, their results include more complex equivalences such as 1/2 equals four 1/8s. They take turns showing how they traded fraction strips using the overhead; some of the other children ask them to slow down so that they can try the trades for themselves. One child notices that 1/3s were never traded; another child notices that—except for the equation 1 = 1/3 + 1/3 + 1/3—the 1/3-strips were never used: "No se mezclan (They don't mix)." The teacher ends the class:

Teacher: Para discutir mañana, tengo dos preguntas. ¿Es verdad que no pueden mezclar una tercera parte con otras fracciones para hacer uno? También, deben de notar que nuncan sumaron a ocho a los octavos, ni a 16 a los pequeñitos. ¿Por qué pasó eso? Miguel, dime de lo que vas a pensar para mañana. . . . ¿Teresa? (To discuss tomorrow, I have two questions. Is it true that we can't mix 1/3 with the other fractions to add up to 1? Also, notice how no one added eight of the 1/8s nor 16 of the tiny ones. Why did that happen? Miguel, tell me what you will think about for tomorrow. [listens to his response] . . . Theresa? [listens to her response]).

While admittedly a hybrid of many examples of teaching for understanding, the above vignette illustrates how the teacher is not afraid to withdraw into the background to allow the discussion among children to develop. She intervenes, however, to keep the discussion moving productively, to insure that everyone has a chance to contribute something substantive, and to ask children to elaborate on their initial answers so that others can understand them. Moreover, students realize that they are expected to give reasons for their answers; after a while, it becomes part of the classroom's culture that when anyone gives an answer, he or she follows up with an explanation, "because . . . ." Teachers will vary among themselves in how they do these things, based on their personal teaching styles and on the specific goals of their mathematics lessons and units. Yet four principles guide their decision making and practices: (1) be constantly assessing what your students understand; (2) choose mathematical content that is interesting, open ended, and accessible to students of varying skills and abilities; (3) focus on developing children's understanding by building on their prior knowledge of mathematics; and (4) develop mathematical language in context.

Assessing Student Understanding

Teachers who teach for understanding are constantly assessing how well their students—both individually and as a class—are understanding the mathematical ideas in the lesson and discussion so that they can decide what to do next. If the students are not "getting it," the teacher can help the student think things through, give an easier but related problem, or ask someone to re-explain what he or she did. These teachers use many cues to help them assess student understanding. For instance, the teacher above noticed the *confused looks* of one of her students when she was asked something in English. Also, teachers can recognize the *"Aha, now I've got it!"* expression that students get when something clicks and they begin working furiously on solving a heretofore obscure problem. Jesús' teacher saw that he was seldom *right* when adding up fractions to equal 1 and she could see his increasing *frustration* in not "getting how" to play the dice game. She *asked students if they understood* one another's explanations.

While student cues provide a direct way of assessing understanding, teachers can also rely on other, more subtle ways by which people in their everyday lives can tell if someone understood something. Teachers often listen to see if students are *restating what has been said in their own words*. For instance, María used her own words to explain how the strips 1/3, 1/4, and 1/2 were bigger than the 1-strip, and hence why 1/3 + 1/4 + 1/2 was bigger than 1. At the end of the class, the teacher asked two of her students to, tell her in their own words, what they would be talking about the next day. This allowed her to check whether they understood the mathematical ideas behind the questions with which she was ending that class.

People show that they understand something when they *relate an idea or what has been said to a different event.* For instance, Jesús explained how his measuring the ingredients for the pancake mix was related to making and to adding fractions. With his teacher's help, he discussed how two halves make a whole (cup). Hence, he was able to relate fractions, the in-class use of fraction strips, and measurement (done out of class) to one another.

Teachers often ask students to *explain and/or elaborate their reasoning*. Throughout the two lessons, children explained their reasoning when they said how they had figured something out or why something was right or wrong. This was a deeply embedded part of the class culture on how things were done. Without any prompting, for instance, Jesús explained why the 3 half-cups of flour that he used totaled 1 and 1/2 cups. Also, when asked why she had used the 1/4-strip in place of two 1/8-strips when the die said 2/8, a student (during the first lesson) at first said that they were equal. Realizing that her partner did not understand what she meant, she explained by showing how two of the 1/8-strips could be made to fit exactly on the 1/4-strip.

People show that they understand an idea when they *put a new twist on that idea.* For instance, from their observation that the 1/4-strip could be used in place of two of the 1/8-strips came the four students' investigation on fraction equivalence. That is, they were trying to see how far this idea of trading fraction strips for one another could be generalized.

People understand a problem when they *relate and/or apply new ideas to the problem.* For instance, Liliana related two facts—that 1/4 + 1/4 + 1/2 = 1 and that 1/3 > 1/4—to explain why 1/3 + 1/4 + 1/2 > 1.

When people *point out something that is wrong (or, at least, is a problem) with an idea,* they show that they understand that idea. For example, after the long class discussion about 1/3, 1/4, and 1/2, the students diagnosed possible reasons for why this error had occurred in the first place. It wasn't enough to explain why they were right in saying that 1/3 + 1/4 + 1/2 could not equal 1; the class also explained what was wrong with someone's original reasoning.

Teachers who teach for understanding often ask if anyone has *solved a problem in a different way or can give a new way of justifying an idea.* For example, consider another bilingual first-grade classroom where a teacher poses the word problem: "Clara tiene 13 carritos de juguete. Seis de sus carritos son rojos y el resto son azules. ¿Cuántos de los carritos son azules? (Clara has 13 toy cars. Six of her cars are red and the rest are blue. How many of her cars are blue?)" A child might solve this problem using colored blocks. He would model the problem by first putting six blue blocks out on a surface. Then he would keep adding red blocks until he got to a total of 13. To get the answer, he would count the seven red blocks. Another child might solve this problem by reasoning about number facts. She would know that 6 + 6 = 12; so the answer has to be 7, since 7 + 6 = 13.[8] In this case, their teacher might infer that both children understood the problem, but that the second child could draw on her more sophisticated knowledge of number facts to solve the problem.

Over the long term, children can show that they understood an idea by *remembering that idea or by applying it in new settings.* In the example just above, the child who remembers that 6 + 6 = 12 and can apply it in order to infer that 7 + 6 = 13 has shown an understanding of how numbers are related to each other.

Teachers who teach for understanding attend to these and many other cues as to how well their children understand the mathematical content that is the subject of the lesson. They base their instructional decisions not just

---

[8]This kind of reasoning about numbers, which relies on children using those number facts that they have memorized (usually doubles) to derive other number facts, is much more common among primary grade children than people give them credit for (Carpenter & Moser, 1983, 1984).

on whether answers are right or wrong, nor on the need to cover a certain amount of material. Although these may be considerations, the primary concern is to ensure that all students actually understand something of what is being taught and discussed.

Content

The mathematics that students engage in should be *worth understanding* (see National Council of Teachers of Mathematics, 1989). At the very least, it should be substantive and focused on *contexts that promote problem solving, applications, and higher order thinking;* the upshot is that students make connections within and across different areas of mathematics. Notice how, in the vignette above, what could have been a rather superficial activity involving fractions and paper folding becomes much more. The inclusion of 1/3 and 2/8 in the dice-rolling activity means that students will confront messy situations in which questions about different ways of adding fractions that sum exactly to 1 and about the equivalence of fractions are likely to come up. What is more, by discussing the small fractions (1/8 and 1/16) and an "unmixable" fraction (1/3) which, in the words of one student, "no se mezclan (did not mix with the other fractions)," students will connect the ideas about chance with their list of ways of adding to 1.

The tasks and activities that make up lessons should be related to one another so that there is the *development of depth over breadth.* The above vignette illustrates a flow from the first to the second day's activities. What is more, one can envision how the teacher and students will use subsequent days to build on what happened during the first two days. They will refer to the two lists (the list of equivalent fractions and the listing of different ways by which they had summed to 1) to develop their ideas about fractions. One can see students coming to class ready to report on other uses of fractions that they have encountered in the real world. Throughout these days, students will be developing deeper and more interconnected understandings about fractions.

The activities, tasks, and problems that students encounter should be *accessible to students with a wide range of knowledge and skill.* That is, students with diverse backgrounds should be able to understand what is required, make meaningful attempts to do the activity, and understand some of the simpler strategies that other students may use. Both the fraction activities and the word problem, discussed above, are examples of exercises in which bilingual children with a broad range of language and mathematics backgrounds can be engaged. They include manipulatives or paper and pencil, which students can use to support their reasoning and problem-solving efforts. Moreover, word problems such as the one described above can be made more accessible to children who do not understand them or a bit more difficult for children who find them too easy. The mathematical content of word problems can be modified by using smaller or larger numbers. The content can also be modified by using numbers that can be more or less easily related to one another, such as doubles (3,6; 4,8; 5,10; 6,12, etc.), numbers separated by 10 (3, 13), or numbers that are not obviously related to one another. Primary grade teachers will often vary a word problem's difficulty in order to give a child a problem that will stretch the child's thinking a bit while remaining accessible.

Also, mathematics problems, activities, and tasks should be *open-ended enough to allow students and teachers to take the activity in a variety of directions.* Not only did the fractions activity—with its inclusion of 2/8 and 1/3 on the dice—allow students to explore new but related topics, it almost seemed to encourage such an exploration.

Problems and activities should be *interesting* to students. The term *interesting* (not *fun*) is used purposefully to convey the intellectual quality of a problem that is engaging and can require hard intellectual work. While fun activities might also be interesting, the overlap is far from perfect: too many fun activities are mindless and contain little mathematical substance. Moreover, the fun comes from doing interesting and engaging mathematics.

Student interest can be engaged in various ways, for instance, by using children's own names in word problems or allowing them to write their own problems. It has been our experience that children will often write and solve problems that are more complex than those that adults would think of posing. Problems that grow out of children's everyday lives or are applicable to their lives can be more interesting than problems and activities that are not connected to their lives. Jesús, in the vignette above, became more engaged in fractions when he could see and apply them in his mother's kitchen. After a field trip to the zoo, a first-grade teacher posed a series of word problems based on the animals eating different kinds of food. Also, student interest can be engaged by students exploring topics that they have never experienced directly, by using fantasy.

Prior Student Experiences

Since understanding develops out of what people already know, teachers who teach for understanding constantly try to connect new problems (and other mathematics activities) to their children's prior mathematical knowledge and backgrounds (see Smith & Silver, 1995). For instance, the dice-rolling activity from the fractions unit created a common core of background information that students would mine over the next few days to discuss equivalence and the addition of fractions. For some students, this activity tapped into other knowledge that they had about fractions—for instance, the knowledge that 1/3 > 1/4 or that 2/8 = 1/4. Binational students may come to school having learned different algorithms for the number operations than are commonly taught in the United States (Secada, 1983); teachers need to be alert to how these students think about computations. Also, the metric system is used in most real-world settings and is taught in schools outside of the United States. Hence, many binational students are likely to have a better understanding of metric measure than their American counterparts. At the very least, teachers should ***not*** assume—as we have seen in at least one basal mathematics series—that students acquiring English should be drilled on the meanings of the common prefixes (kilo, centi, milli) that are used in metric measure.

Just as Tikunoff (1985) found that effective bilingual teachers use their children's home cultures to support classroom management and student learning, so, too, should teachers try to tap into binational children's home cultures to support their mathematics learning. For instance, the teacher discussed possible at-home activities with Jesús' mother in an effort to support his learning about fractions.

Teachers might use a context or theme with which their students are familiar to serve as an umbrella out of which they generate mathematical activities and problems. For instance, teachers at Esperanza Elementary School are participating in the development of the *Children's Math Worlds* curriculum (De La Cruz, under review; Fuson & Perry, 1993; Fuson, Zecker, Lo Cicero, & Ron, 1995). The curriculum has three strands: word problem/graphing, place value/multidigit arithmetic, and geometry/measurement. *Children's Math Worlds* is designed to create an ongoing interaction between Latino/Latina children's mathematics learning in class and their experiences outside by bringing children's mathematical knowledge (from both inside and outside of the classroom) into the classroom and by providing families with activities that they can do at home with their children. One group of activities is based on the Mercado, the marketplace that is common in Mexico, where many of these bilingual, binational children and their parents go to visit extended family members. What is more, the school's neighborhood features its own Mercado, which is very similar to what can be found in Mexico. For instance, ambulatory vendors use pushcarts to sell bocaditos (snacks) and other small items.

The Mercado provided a context where children enact, through role playing, a variety of mercantile transactions. In this way, children have learned about money; how to identify and know the value of coins (penny, nickel, dime, quarter) and bills (dollar, five dollar, ten dollar); how to make change for less than $10.00; adding and subtracting up to two 4-digit numbers with decimals; how to solve two-step story problems involving the addition and subtraction of up to two 4-digit numbers; the meaning of multiplication; how to solve story problems involving multiplication; and how to write and solve word problems using the Mercado as a context. For example, bilingual second graders would work with partners where one would be el vendedor (the vendor), the other, el cliente (the buyer). El cliente would select an item from a grocery and use plastic money to make the purchase; el vendedor would ensure that enough had been paid and in some cases would make change. After several purchases, students would switch roles.

In follow-up activities, students would create shopping lists from teacher-made grocery lists. Students would list the names of the items they were going to buy with their prices; then they would find the total cost of their lists. If they had enough money to make the purchases, they would do so. As students became more proficient with these transactions, they would use real grocery ads to create their shopping lists—involving the use of larger numbers—and make their purchases.

A typical word problem for students to solve would be this:

> Tú quieres un dulce. El dulce cuesta 19 centavos. Le das al vendedor 25 centavos. ¿Cuánto vas a recibir de cambio? (You want to buy some candy. Each candy costs 19¢. You give the seller 25¢. How much change will you receive?)

When asked to write a problem based on spending $400 or less, Armando wrote:

> Voy a comprar un stereo para mi familia. Tengo $381.10. Pienso que me va a quedar si compro uno en menos de $300. Quiero un stereo que tiene todo: uno para tocar discos, para casetera, y que tenga reloj. Con lo que me sobra, le voy a comprar algo para mi mamá. (I want to buy a stereo for my family. I have $381.10. I think I will have [money] left over if I buy one for under $300. I want a stereo that has everything: one that plays disks [records], plays cassettes, and has a clock. I am going to buy something for my mother with the money I have left over.)

Armando drew a picture of his stereo with a price tag. He worked out the subtraction problem to show that he would have money left over to buy a gift for his mother.

The Mercado provides a rich context that is familiar to the children, that supports children's doing mathematics since the problems they encounter will have meaning and be interesting, and that can be used as a basis for children to write their own problems about things that are important to them. Armando's writing sample shows how the problems that children generate contain both substantive mathematics and referents to their home cultures and values (as in buying something for one's family and a gift for mom).

Mathematical Language

While students develop understanding working alone or using objects to help them model problems, they also develop understanding by discussing mathematics. Asking children to share ideas about mathematical topics and asking how they figured out a problem or why, such as in the above example of the second grader who used a 1/4-strip instead of two 1/8-strips, are among the ways in which students can develop their understandings. For such discussions to be productive, classrooms need shared norms for listening and the expectation that everyone will explain her or his reasoning. For instance, Jesús, in the fractions vignette above, spontaneously explained why three half-cups of flour were the same as one and a half cups.

Beyond sharing norms for explaining their reasoning, students need to be able to discuss their ideas without much ambiguity. The use of mathematical language[9] is intended to help people talk about mathematics clearly and with little ambiguity. The teacher's use of language, in the fractions vignette above, illustrates some uses of mathematical language during instruction. For example, she modeled the proper, conventional usage of mathematical terminology in her own conversations with children.

But also, her focus remained communication. Though she used the proper names for almost all of the fraction strips, she used the students' term of "the little one (el pequeño)" when referring to 1/16. In that particular context, there would be no confusion since everyone understood that the little one referred to the smallest paper strip and seemed comfortable with that term. What is more, the use of *one sixteenth* would likely have, itself, been too confusing for second graders.

When a student used the term "mezclar" (mix) in describing how 1/3 did not appear on the list of fractions that were successfully added to one another in order to get to 1, the teacher used the student's own terminology since, once again, the student's term seemed to capture what was meant in

---

[9]Mathematical language consists of the specialized symbols, technical terms and phrases, and ways of speaking that (a) help people to communicate with one another when they are talking about mathematics and (b) mark people as knowing how to do mathematics (see, for instance, Cuevas, 1984; Dale & Cuevas, 1987; Lampert, 1986, 1990; Pimm, 1987; Spanos, Rhodes, Dale, & Crandall, 1988).

a way that other students could understand without too much ambiguity. Also, she allowed students to refer to the strips without using their fractional names, as would happen when children would indicate a particular sized strip with "mira" (look). At some time in the future, students would be expected to use more precise terminology, but for the purposes of that class in that context, the precise use of mathematical language was leavened with the use of children's own language.

On the other hand, the teacher recognized that confusion would likely arise if students tried to use three different ways of listing the fractions that added to 1. Rather than allow that to happen, she pointed the problem out to the class, and together (with her prodding), they decided to use number sentences, such as 1/2 + 1/4 + 1/8 + 1/8 = 1, to list the fraction combinations that had added to 1.

The point is that mathematical language, like language in general, develops in context to support communication. The way to increase students' use of precise language is to use contexts that require such precision.

One unfortunate use of mathematical language occurs when students look for certain key words or phrases in a word problem as a short cut for solving the problem.[10] For instance, *in all*, *altogether*, and *total* are said to be cues for students to add; *left* or *remaining*, to subtract. The only reason that these words can be such cues, however, is because of the restricted content of the elementary school curriculum, and not for any mathematically relevant reason. Consider the following word problems, which can be solved by primary graders who do not rely on key words:

Addition:	Tanya has 8 chocolate chip cookies and 7 raisin oatmeal cookies. How many cookies does she have *in all*?
Subtraction:	Tanya has 15 cookies *in all*. Seven (7) of them are chocolate chip, and the rest are raisin oatmeal. How many of Tanya's cookies are raisin oatmeal?
Multiplication:	Tanya has 4 friends coming over to play today. She wants to give each of her friends 3 cookies for snack time. How many cookies does she need to have *in all*?
Division:	*In all*, Tanya has 15 cookies to share with her 4 friends for snack time. If she and each of her friends get the same number of cookies, how many cookies will each person get?

A student who relied on key words to solve these problems would get just one of them right. The use of key words to go directly (and thought-

[10]Many teachers, especially teachers of students acquiring English, encourage this practice.

lessly) from a word problem to a solution should be discouraged. Students need to think about what words mean in the context in which those words are used.

Additional Language Concerns

An ideal solution to the issue of teaching mathematics with understanding to binational children, particularly in classrooms along the U.S.-Mexico border, would be to hire teachers who are bilingual and to support their learning to teach mathematics with understanding in either language. For instance, bilingual curriculum materials are being developed to support teaching-for-understanding approaches in English and Spanish, and there are many professional development opportunities for teachers who are interested in these approaches.[11] By modifying some of their instructional approaches, monolingual teachers can also teach for understanding to binational students who are acquiring English. While maintaining a focus on student understanding, these teachers will need to compensate for the fact that they and their students are stronger in different languages.

One of the most difficult things for a monolingual teacher to decide is if errors by a student who is acquiring English reflect a lack of mathematical

---

[11]Primary grade teachers may be interested in the project known as *Cognitively Guided Instruction* (CGI) (see Carey et al., 1995). For professional development opportunities on *CGI*, please contact *Cognitively Guided Instruction*, Wisconsin Center for Education Research, University of Wisconsin-Madison, 1025 West Johnson Street, Madison, WI 53706.

Mathematics in Context (National Center for Research in Mathematical Sciences Education, in press) is being developed as a dual language curriculum for middle school students. For information about the project and professional development opportunities, please contact *Mathematics in Context*, National Center for Research in Mathematical Sciences Education, Wisconsin Center for Education Research, University of Wisconsin-Madison, 1025 West Johnson Street, Madison, WI 53706.

An elementary through middle school curriculum project is *Visual Mathematics* (Forman & Bennett, 1995). For information about the project and professional development opportunities, please contact Mathematics Learning Center, P. O. Box 3226, Salem, OR 97302.

High school teachers might be interested in the *Interactive Mathematics Program* (Resek & Fendel, in press). For information about the program and professional development opportunities, please contact IMP, 6400 Hollis, Suite 5, Emeryville, CA 94608.

SummerMath (Schifter & Fosnot, 1993) provides professional development opportunities for teachers at all grade levels. For information please contact SummerMath for Teachers, Mount Holyoke College, South Hadley, MA 01075.

EQUALS, which has developed bilingual versions of *Family Math* (Stenmark, Thompson, & Cossey, 1986) and other equity-based materials, provides professional development on a wide range of topics for teachers of all grade levels. Please contact EQUALS, Lawrence Hall of Science, University of California, Berkeley, CA 94720.

understanding or some problems with English. For instance, consider the case of a ninth-grade mathematics class that was being taught completely in Spanish by a mathematics teacher who is bilingual. At the start of this class, students were putting up the solutions to homework problems from an English language text. One problem was this: *There are two complementary angles. One is twice the other. What are the angles?* A girl had written two equations: $x+y=90$, $x=2y$. She had solved for x and y by substituting 2y for x in the first equation: $3y=90$, $y=30$, $x=60$. Her explanation to the class was in Spanish. She noted that since the angles were complementary, their sum was 90 ; and since one was twice the other, $x=2y$. She explained why she had substituted for x in the first equation, and how she simplified the equations to get her solution.

Also observing this class was a school administrator who interrupted the class to ask the girl to repeat her explanation in English. Due to her grammatical difficulties, some of this girl's statements were mathematically incorrect. Had one of us not heard her simple and concise explanation in Spanish, we would have been convinced that she simply had not understood the problem and would have wondered if she—or someone else—had done her homework.

Given the importance of ongoing assessment in order for the teacher to figure out what understandings are developing among students, the problem becomes particularly acute when the teacher and student have difficulty in understanding each other. In cases like these, it still is important for the student to be able to discuss his problem-solving strategies with other students. The teacher might encourage a student acquiring English to explain the solution to someone else in the class who has a stronger command of both languages. Assuming that the teacher has been teaching mathematics for understanding all along, then she should monitor whether the Spanish-language explanation made sense to the class's bilingual students. Students should be encouraged to discuss errors or points of misunderstanding among themselves as a means of self-correction. From time to time, the classroom teacher might ask a more strongly bilingual student to translate what has been said from Spanish into English so that the rest of the class can have an opportunity to participate in the conversation.

Secondly, teachers might have some of their curricular materials translated into Spanish or rewritten in simplified English so that they are more accessible to children in their classes (see examples from Secada & Carey, 1990, for how this can be done). In their studies with bilingual children, Secada (1991b) translated arithmetic word problems into Spanish, one sentence at a time. Problems were translated back into English by someone who did not know what the original problems had been. Then, the back-translations were checked to see how well they matched the original versions of the problems. If there was a match, then it seemed reasonable to assume that the original translations maintained fidelity to the problem's original intent. Prior to asking children to solve those problems, Secada asked each bilingual teacher who worked with the children to read the translations and to suggest locutions and alternative vocabulary that would make their problems more understandable to the children. For instance, one bilingual teacher noted that *lapiz de color*, while technically a correct translation for *crayon*, was not a commonly used term; her suggestion, *Crayolas,* was used instead.

English word problems can be simplified by ensuring that sentences are short, maintain active voice, and use present tense. Sentences that contain complex grammatical constructions—such as phrases or subordinate clauses within clauses—should be broken up and simplified. The names of familiar objects should replace unfamiliar objects; for instance, a word problem about blocks, toy cars, or candies is likely to be more accessible to children than one about things that they seldom encounter. The use of children's own names will often make a problem more accessible.

Translated problems, as well as simplified-English versions, can be used to begin a series of lessons. They should be saved, updated, and shared with other teachers who are encountering similar difficulties.

Many students acquiring English receive little encouragement to speak about their ideas, in part due to the belief that they will find it too difficult to express themselves. Many Hispanic girls are socialized to defer to boys. Hence, if teachers tend to call on students who answer first, students acquiring English and girls will be left out of the conversation. Teachers need to reach out to these children—either through increased wait time, or by warning them that they will be called on—in order to be sure that they are included in the classroom's processes.

Teachers of students acquiring English may find that their students are struggling with new vocabulary in mathematics or that they may speak very little English in general. The teacher should always keep in mind that the real issue is to ensure that students actually understand each other. Hence, a teacher should use the strategies that she would use in any other subject. In addition to simplifying oral language, teachers should expand on student responses and build on those when posing their next question. Some students pass through what is known as a silent period when they are just beginning to learn a second language; during this time, they are listening and trying to make sense of the rules for conversation in the classroom as well as in the larger world. Teachers will need to give students time and look for nonverbal cues as to whether they understand the gist of the lesson. Also, other bilingual students should be asked to speak with that student.

Generally, classroom conversations about mathematics are slow in starting; but when students are socialized into the norms of those conversations, the conversations can be quick and full of implicit referents. Teachers will need to monitor exchanges carefully to ensure that students acquiring English actually participate.

Concluding Comments

There are many other suggestions for mathematics teachers to use when they encounter students acquiring English (see, for example, Secada & Carey, 1990). As is the case with general techniques for teaching mathematics, these techniques are intended to ensure that students can communicate their understandings with their teachers and with one another. It is important to remember that the goal, in all cases, is for the student to understand the mathematics that he or she is encountering. The teacher needs to assess whether or not this is happening and to decide what to do next (give an easier problem, provide help that is pitched so that the student still has to do some reasoning, add context to a problem, translate, or simplify the language) based on judgments of how well the students are understanding and based on the goals for the lesson. The curriculum needs to support the teacher by providing mathematics content that is worth understanding, by having problems and activities that create opportunities for students to make sense of what they are doing, and by being sequenced so that students can make connections between what they know and what is being presented. Finally, the students need to continue to do the work we know they do when they enter school; that is, they need to make sense of the mathematics they encounter, talk about how they figured things out so that they can check with one another (regardless of the language they speak), and listen respectfully when another student is making a point. In other words, the entire mathematics classroom needs to change in its norms for behavior.

The exciting thing is that we are beginning to get evidence that mathematics *can* be taught in this way. What is more, when mathematics is taught for understanding, teachers feel increasingly effective in their teaching and students actually learn more mathematics.

References

Adetula, L. O. (1989). Solutions of simple word problems by Nigerian children: Language and schooling factors. *Journal for Research in Mathematics Education, 20*, 489-497.

Carey, D. A., Fennema, E., Carpenter, T. P., & Franke, M. L. (1995). Equity and mathematics education. In W. G. Secada, E. Fennema, & L. B. Adajian (Eds.), *New directions for equity in mathematics education* (pp. 93-125). New York: Cambridge University Press.

Carpenter, T. P. (1985). Learning to add and subtract: An exercise in problem solving. In E. A. Silver (Ed.), *Teaching and learning mathematical problem solving: Multiple research perspectives* (pp. 17-40). Hillsdale, NJ: Erlbaum Associates.

Carpenter, T. P., & Moser, J. M. (1983). Addition and subtraction concepts. In R. Lesh & M. Landau (Eds.), *Acquisition of mathematics concepts and processes* (pp. 7-24). New York: Academic Press.

Carpenter, T. P., & Moser, J. M. (1984). The acquisition of addition and subtraction concepts in grades one through three. *Journal for Research in Mathematics Education, 15(3)*, 179-202.

Carpenter, T. P., Moser, J. M., & Romberg, T. A. (Eds). (1982). *Addition and subtraction: A cognitive perspective.* Hillsdale, NJ: Erlbaum Associates.

Casanova, U., & Arias, M. B. (1993). Contextualizing bilingual education. In M. B. Arias & U. Casanova (Eds.), *Bilingual education: Politics, practice, and research. Ninety-second Yearbook of the National Society for the Study of Education* (Part II, pp. 1-35). Chicago, IL: National Society for the Study of Education.

Cocking, R. R., & Mestre, J. P. (Eds.). (1988). *Linguistic and cultural influences on learning mathematics.* Hillsdale, NJ: Erlbaum Associates.

Cohen, D. K., McLaughlin, M. W., & Talbert, J. E. (Eds.). (1993). *Teaching for understanding: Challenges for policy and practice.* San Francisco: Jossey Bass.

Cuevas, G. J. (1984). Mathematics learning in English as a second language. *Journal for Research in Mathematics Education, 15(2)*, 134-144.

Dale, T. C., & Cuevas, G. J. (1987). Integrating language and mathematics learning. In J. A. Crandall (Ed.), *ESL through content-area instruction: Mathematics, science, social studies.* (pp. 9-54). Englewood Cliffs, NJ: Prentice Hall.

De Avila, E. A., & Duncan, S. (1985). The language minority child: A psychological, linguistic, and social analysis. In J. W. Segal, S. F. Chipman, & R. Glaser (Eds.), *Thinking and learning skills. Volume 2: Research and open questions* (pp. 245-274). Hillsdale, NJ: L. Erlbaum.

De La Cruz, Y. (under review). *A case study of supporting teachings with mathematics reform in language minority classrooms.* [Available from the author at Northwestern University]

Dossey, J. A., Mullis, I. V. S., Lindquist, M. M., & Chambers, D. L. (1988). *The mathematics report card: Are we measuring up?* Trends and achievement based on the 1986 National Assessment. (NAEP-17-M-01). Princeton, NJ: National Assessment of Educational Progress, Educational Testing Service. (ERIC Document Reproduction Service No. ED 300 206)

Dossey, J. A., Mullis, I. V. S., & Jones, C. O. (1993). *Can students do mathematical problem solving? Results from constructed-response questions in NAEP's 1992 mathematics assessment* (ETS-R-23-FR01). Washington, DC: National Center for Education Statistics. (ERIC Document Reproduction Service No. ED 362 539)

Forman, L., & Bennett, A. (1995). *Visual mathematics.* Salem, OR: Mathematics Learning Center.

Fuson, K. C. (1988). *Children's counting and concepts of number.* New York: Springer-Verlag.

Fuson, K. C., & Perry, T. (1993). *Hispanic children's addition methods: Cultural diversity in children's informal solution procedures.* Paper delivered at the biennial meeting of the Society for Research in Child Development, New Orleans, LA.

Fuson, K., Zecker, L., Lo Cicero, A., & Ron, P. (1995). *El Mercado in latino primary classrooms: A fruitful narrative theme for the development of children's conceptual mathematics.* Paper delivered at the annual meeting of the American Educational Research Association, San Francisco, CA.

Ghaleb, M. S. (1992). *Performance and solution strategies of Arabic-speaking second graders in simple addition and subtraction word problems and relations of performance to their degree of bilingualism*. Unpublished doctoral dissertation, University of Wisconsin-Madison.

Irvine, J. J., & York, D. E. (1995). Learning styles and culturally diverse students: A literature review. In J. A. Banks & C. A. McGee Banks (Eds.), *Handbook of research on multicultural education* (pp. 484-497). New York: Macmillan.

Knapp, M. S. & Associates (1995). *Teaching for meaning in high-poverty classrooms.* New York: Teachers College Press.

Knapp, M. S., & Shields, P. M. (Eds.). (1991). *Better schooling for children of poverty: Alternatives to conventional wisdom.* Berkeley, CA: McCutchan.

Lampert, M. (1986). Knowing, doing, and teaching multiplication. *Cognition and Instruction, 3,* 305-342.

Lampert, M. (1989, March). Arithmetic as problem solving. *Arithmetic Teacher,* 34-36.

Lampert, M. (1990). When the problem is not the question and the solution is not the answer: Mathematical knowing and teaching. *American Educational Research Journal, 27*(1), 29-63.

Mullis, I. V. S., Dossey, J. A., Foertsch, M. A., Jones, L. R., & Gentile, C. A. (1991). *Trends in academic progress: Achievement of U.S. Students in science, 1969-70 to 1990; mathematics, 1973 to 1990; reading, 1971 to 1990; and writing, 1984 to 1990* (Report No. ETS-21-T-01). Washington, DC: National Center for Education Statistics. (ERIC Document Reproduction Service No. ED 338 720)

Mullis, I. V. S., Dossey, J. A., Owen, E. H., & Phillips, G. W. (1993). *NAEP 1992 mathematics report card for the nation and the states: Data from the national and trial state assessments* (Report No. RN-23-ST02). Washington, DC: National Center for Education Statistics. (ERIC Document Reproduction Service No. ED 360 190)

National Center for Research in Mathematical Sciences Education and Freudenthal Institute. (Eds.). (in press). *Mathematics in context: A connected curriculum for grades 5-8.* Chicago: Encyclopedia Britannica Educational Corporation.

National Council of Teachers of Mathematics. (1989). *Curriculum and evaluation standards for school mathematics.* Reston, VA: Author.

National Council of Teachers of Mathematics. (1991). *Professional standards for teaching mathematics.* Reston, VA: Author.

National Council of Teachers of Mathematics. (1995). *Assessment standards for school mathematics.* Reston, VA: Author.

National Research Council. (1989). *Everybody counts: A report to the nation on the future of mathematics education.* Washington, DC: National Academy Press. (ERIC Document Reproduction Service No. ED 309 938)

Peterson, P. L., Fennema, E., & Carpenter, T. P. (1991). Using children's mathematical knowledge. In B. Means, C. Chelemer, & M. S. Knapp (Eds.), *Teaching advanced skills to at-risk students* (pp. 68-101). San Francisco, CA: Jossey-Bass.

Pimm, D. (1987). *Speaking mathematically: Communication in mathematics classrooms.* New York: Routledge and Kegan Paul.

Resek, D., & Fendel, D. (with the help of L. Alper & S. Fraser), (in press). *Interactive mathematics program.* Berkeley, CA: Key Curriculum Press.

Riley, M. G., Greeno, J. G, & Heller, J. I. (1983). Development of children's problem solving ability in arithmetic. In H. P. Ginsburg (Ed.), *The development of mathematical thinking* (pp. 153-200). New York: Academic Press.

Rosebery, A. S., Warren, B., & Conant F. R. (1992). Appropriating scientific discourse: Findings from language minority classrooms. *Journal of Learning Sciences, 2*(1), 61-94.

Schifter, D., & Fosnot, C. T. (1993). *Reconstructing mathematics education: Stories of teachers meeting the challenge of reform.* New York: Teachers College Press.

Schoenfeld, A. (1992). Learning to think mathematically: Problem solving, metacognition, and sense making in mathematics. In D. A. Grouws (Ed.), *Handbook of research on mathematics teaching and learning* (pp. 334-370). New York: Macmillan.

Secada, W. G. (1983). *The educational background of limited-English-proficient students: Implications for the arithmetic classroom.* Arlington Heights, IL: Bilingual Education Service Center. (ERIC Document Reproduction Service No. ED 237 318)

Secada W. G. (1991a). Evaluating the mathematics education of limited-English-proficient students in a time of educational change. In U.S. Department of Education, Office of Bilingual Education and Minority Languages Affairs: *Focus on evaluation and measurement: Proceedings of the second national research symposium on limited-English-proficient student issues* (Vol. 2, pp. 209-256). Washington, DC: Author. (ERIC Document Reproduction Service No. ED 349 828)

Secada, W. G. (1991b). Degree of bilingualism and arithmetic problem solving in Hispanic first graders. *Elementary School Journal, 92*(2), 213-231.

Secada, W. G. (1992). Race, ethnicity, social class, language, and achievement in mathematics. In D. A. Grouws (Ed.), *Handbook of research on mathematics teaching and learning* (pp. 623-660). New York: Macmillan.

Secada, W. G., & Carey, D. A. (1990). *Teaching mathematics with understanding to limited-English-proficient students* (Urban diversity series no. 101). New York: ERIC Clearinghouse on Urban Education, Institute on Urban and Minority Education, Teachers College. (ERIC Document Reproduction Service No. ED 322 284)

Silver, E. A., Smith, M. S., & Nelson, B. S. (1995). The QUASAR Project: Equity concerns meet mathematics education reform in the middle school. In W. G. Secada, E. Fennema, & L. B. Adajian (Eds.), *New directions for equity in mathematics education.* New York: Cambridge University Press.

Simmons, W. (1985). Social class and ethnic differences in cognition: A cultural practice perspective. In J. W. Segal, S. F. Chipman, & R. Glaser (Eds.), *Thinking and learning skills. Volume 2: Research and open questions* (pp. 519-536). Hillsdale, NJ: Erlbaum.

Smith, M. S., & Silver, E. A. (1995, September-October). Meeting the challenges of diversity and relevance. *Mathematics Teaching in the Middle School, 1*(6), 442-448.

Spanos, G., Rhodes, N. C., Dale, T. C., & Crandall, J. (1988). Linguistic features of mathematical problem solving: Insights and applications. In R. R. Cocking & J. P. Mestre (Eds.), *Linguistic and cultural influences on learning mathematics* (pp. 221-240). Hillsdale, NJ: Erlbaum.

Stenmark, J. K., Thompson, V., & Cossey, R. (1986). *Family math.* Berkeley, CA: University of California, EQUALS.

Tikunoff, W. (1985). *Applying significant bilingual instructional features in the classroom. Part C Bilingual Education Research Series.* Rosslyn, VA: National Clearinghouse for Bilingual Education. (ERIC Document Reproduction Service No. ED 338 106)

Villaseñor, A., & Kepner, H. S. (1993). Arithmetic from a problem-solving perspective: An urban implementation. *Journal for Research in Mathematics Education, 24*(1), 62-69.

Warren, B., & Rosebery, A. S. (1992). Science education as a sense-making practice: Implications for assessment. *Focus on evaluation and measurement: Proceedings of the second national research symposium on limited-English-proficient student issues.* (Vol. 2, pp. 273-304). Washington, DC: U.S. Department of Education, Office of Bilingual Education and Minority Languages Affairs. (ERIC Document Reproduction Service No. ED 349 829)

Warren, B., & Rosebery, A. S. (1995). Equity in the future tense: Redefining relationships among teachers, students, and science in linguistic minority classrooms. In W. G. Secada, E. Fennema, & L. B. Adajian (Eds.), *New directions for equity in mathematics education* (pp. 298-328). New York: Cambridge University Press.

Warren, B., Rosebery, A. S., & Conant, F. B. (1989). *Cheche Konnen: Science and literacy in language minority classrooms.* Cambridge, MA: Bolt, Beranek, & Newman. (ERIC Document Reproduction Service No. ED 326 060)

Warren, B., Rosebery A. S., & Conant F. B. (1994). Discourse and social practice: Learning in bilingual classrooms. In D. Spencer (Ed.), *Adult literacy in the United States.* Washington, DC: Center for Applied Linguistics.

Part IV
Working with Families

CHAPTER 18

Voices of Latina Migrant Mothers in Rural Pennsylvania[1]

STEPHANIE L. BRESSLER
KING'S COLLEGE

Latina migrant mothers who traveled with their families to pick tomatoes in rural northeastern Pennsylvania were interviewed about the goals and expectations of their childhood as defined by family and culture, the reality of their adult lives as migrant mothers, and their expectations for their children's future. The telling of their stories encouraged the mothers to explore the impact of the values and norms of Latina and migrant cultures, as well as family commitment to education, on their own limited life choices. Their stories are shared here to provide a resource for teachers and administrators in the United States who are responsible for educating migrant children from Latina cultures.

Introduction

Most of the farmworkers who arrive in northeastern Pennsylvania each summer to pick tomatoes work their way from the South (Florida or Texas) to the North and back again. Poor economic conditions at home and the need to travel to remain employed characterize

[1]The presentation of her oral history findings has been supported in part by the Pennsylvania Humanities Council, a statewide organization funded partially by the National Endowment for the Humanities. It does not necessarily express the views of the Council or the Endowment.

the lifestyle of these migrant workers. They travel through the East Coast states, taking on whatever work they can find. Many of these workers are citizens or legal residents of the United States or have documented permission to seek employment in this country. However, many Mexicans and Central Americans continue to cross the border without the U.S. government's permission in order to search for economic opportunities. Some of these undocumented workers also find their way to Pennsylvania to pick crops.

Among the farmworker groups representing varying points of origins, lifestyles, and legal statuses are families with school-age and preschool-age children. These families arrive in northeastern Pennsylvania in late July or early August and stay until late September to hand-harvest a multimillion-dollar fresh market tomato crop. The children of these families attend a special summer school program provided by Pennsylvania Migrant Education and are integrated into local district schools when the regular school year begins. The mothers of these children interact often with staff from Pennsylvania Migrant Education and other farmworker support agencies to plan their children's school attendance and to secure other needed services (e.g., health care, transportation, supplemental food). During these interactions, Latina mothers often have expressed concerns that their children are losing their cultural heritage by living in the United States. In an attempt to help these mothers preserve their heritage for their children, Dr. Stephanie Bressler, an assistant professor of political science at King's College, Wilkes-Barre, Pennsylvania, and Barbara Hludzik, Northeast (Pennsylvania) Migrant Education Program, conducted an oral history project during the summer of 1994. As the project progressed, the researchers chose to focus on the mothers themselves, encouraging them to tell their stories in their own language (i.e., Spanish) of growing up in and now raising their children in the migrant lifestyle. The telling of their stories encouraged mothers to explore the impact of cultural values and family commitment toward education on their own life choices and hopes for their children. Their stories are shared here to provide important insights for teachers and administrators in the United States who are responsible for educating migrant children from Latina cultures.

Methodology

Four Latina migrant mothers ranging in age from 22 to 37 years were interviewed for the oral history project. Two of the mothers, Rosa and Elia, consider the United States their permanent home. One mother, Rigoberta (not her real name), grew up in Guatemala but moved to Mexico with her family to flee war at home; she plans to go back to Guatemala soon but hopes to return to the United States with her family. The fourth mother,

Griselda (not her real name), whose husband recently secured a job in the meat packing industry, moved her family from a farm labor camp into private housing. She is unsure how long her family will stay in northeastern Pennsylvania and talks about returning to Mexico. At the time of the interviews, Rosa, Elia, and Rigoberta resided with their families in grower-provided farm labor camps. These camps are located in isolated areas and consist of cinder-block barracks that are almost always overcrowded. While the mothers' level of formal education ranged from "very little" to 9 years, all four were articulate and comfortable with the interview process, which fit in well with the familiar oral tradition of their Latina culture.

Although the concept of oral history implies a focus on interviewees' recollections of their past, the mothers were also asked to reflect on their present lives and on the future of their children. Each mother participated in a series of interviews. Interview questions were planned and organized to solicit each mother's thoughts on the interrelationships among her own childhood as defined by family and culture, the reality of her adult life as a mother, and her expectations for herself and her children in the future. (See appendix at the end of this chapter for outline from which interviewer generated questions in Spanish.)

While carefully planned oral history is accepted as a scholarly approach to collecting information about individuals' lives, the researchers acknowledge the subjective nature of this information and the limitations of its use as evidence to generalize about a group of people. However, the observations made by the women interviewed for this project suggest values, norms, and ways of understanding life that are likely shared by many other Latina migrant women. Their reflections, supported by the researchers' observations of migrant families collected during the past 10 years, are offered here not as conclusive evidence of the lifestyle of all Latina migrant mothers but as a primary source of information about how some of these mothers view their own and their children's lives.

Findings and Discussion

Latina migrant mothers represent a unique population. These women grew up in a rural Latina culture with traditional differentiation and stratification of male and female roles. The women were socialized, as were their mothers, to be primarily responsible for domestic and child-rearing tasks and to respect the authority of men. Reflecting on her father's advice that terminated her schooling after only 3 years, Rigoberta shared this:

> *Cuando yo entré en la escuela, a mí me gustaba mucho la escuela....* When I started school, I liked school a lot. But my father said, "It isn't going to do you any good to be studying or earning good grades

> because you are *niñas* (little girls), my daughter. You are going to grow up. You are going to look for husbands and what I am going to give you isn't going to be good for anything." *Mi hermano* (my brother), the one who is younger than me, they gave him schooling. But what happened is that he didn't want to study. And therefore, I liked school, but my father only gave me permission to go for 3 years.

Latina migrant mothers continue to uphold many of the traditional roles and values of this rural culture, as Elia observed in the following:

> *Yo enseño a mi niña cosas de trabajo de limpiar....* I teach my girl housework and harvest and how things are done for when she's married so that she can help her husband. My oldest son, Joe, goes with my husband to move trucks when there's no school and to help him with what he needs help in.

While Latina migrant families mostly follow traditional gender roles, the economic uncertainty with which these families constantly live dictates that mothers work in the fields or in related jobs. Migrant women do nearly every kind of farm labor, including harvesting crops and sorting and packing produce (Farmworker Women Speak Out, 1994, p. 2). In addition, Latina migrant women handle all domestic responsibilities. Their husbands rarely help with household chores and child care. The double burden experienced by these women is reflected in their comments.

> *Está más dura la vida de la mujer....* The life of a woman is harder because she has to go to the field to work and has to cook and do everything. Later the man goes out with other men.

> *Para una mujer, ese trabajo es pesado....* The work is heavy for a woman. But when one wants to work, well, one has to put up with it.

> *Entonces tú trabajas todo el día en la labor....* Then you work (as a woman) all day in the fields, and then in the afternoon, at night, you have to take care of the children, take them to the clinic, to the hospital when they get sick. This is always one's job (as a woman).

At the same time, these women are surrounded by and work and live in mainstream American culture, in which the changes in gender roles are more visible. They see women working in jobs that they consider men's work (i.e., doctors), and they see men assuming primary responsibility for caring for children (i.e., day care workers). Their children participate in mainstream culture in school where men's and women's roles are less differentiated, but both migrant mothers and children are expected to remain part of a more traditional culture at home. The children experience many contradictions, which sometimes makes it difficult for them to learn appropriate behaviors.

As services for migrants and their families are further developed, mothers are encouraged by agency workers to participate in public activities such as parental involvement groups. Interaction with educational staff is almost always the responsibility of mothers. Fathers almost never play a role in their children's education. According to Rosa:

> *Una madre siendo migrante tiene que cuidar sus hijos....* A mother who is a migrant must take care of her children because no one is going to take care of them for her, and she must see that they can go to school, grow up, and do something better than their mother and father could do.

But at home—in the farm labor camps—these women live in a male-dominated culture where their husbands' jealousy and suspicions often means that they must ask permission to take part in these and almost all other activities. Rigoberta recalled that as a young woman recently arrived in the United States, she was obligated to seek her father's permission before speaking to or being seen with the man who was later to become her husband. Another mother worried that her husband would be annoyed that she was wearing shorts when being photographed as part of the oral history project. Yet this same mother had convinced her husband to allow her to accept a temporary job at the summer school where she hoped she would be in a better position to encourage her children to work hard in school. As a result of living in two cultures, migrant mothers and their children often experience role and value conflicts. The changes these women see in their lifetimes as exemplified by the roles and statuses of women are significant. They are changes that more often evolve over several generations in other parts of society.

While the oral histories provide much evidence of the impact of Latina culture on the mothers' lives, the women's stories reveal that the migrant lifestyle has a more direct influence on how these families live their lives. A culture of migrancy has previously been identified by ethnographers who report common behavioral patterns among migrants of different ethnic/cultural backgrounds (Prewitt-Diaz, Trotter, & Rivera, 1990). Low earnings and the need to travel to remain employed heavily influence this lifestyle. Elia reflected:

> *Desde que yo fui nacida....* Ever since I was born my father and mother always have traveled to the jobs. Now I come to different places. I'm still a migrant.

As is true for most migrants, the mothers began working when very young and continue to work now. Griselda recalled:

> *Tenía como catorce años y trabajaba yo en los tomates....* I was 14 when I worked in tomatoes, getting up very early at four in the morning to make the lunch to carry to the fields. Afterwards, we would pick there all day.

While their parents sometimes verbalized support for education, these women's schooling was regularly disrupted and eventually abbreviated by the need to travel. School was viewed as competing for the time of young girls whose work in the fields could supplement meager family incomes or whose help was sorely needed by their own mothers, who cared for large families of 13 or 14 children. Migrant families' ambivalence toward education has been well documented by earlier studies (Reul, 1974; Friedland & Nelkin, 1971; Coles, 1970). The migrant mothers interviewed for the oral history assumed adult roles at a young age as worker and surrogate mother to younger brothers and sisters. The mothers remembered:

> *Todos trabajábamos a la hora de ir por la escuela....* All of us worked until it was time to go to school. They came to find us at work and took us to school, and Papa was angry that they put us there.

> *Yo les ayudé mucho a mis padres también....* I helped my parents a lot also. I was growing up, went to school. Lots of times I couldn't go to school, because I had to stay and help my mother with my brothers and sisters that were much younger.

Distracted by their families' demands and frustrated by the frequent disruptions in their education, all of the mothers interviewed left school at an early age. All expressed dissatisfaction and, at times, embarrassment with their lack of education. They viewed their failure to finish education as a major factor in their continuing inability to leave the migrant lifestyle and improve their lives.

> *No van a ser iguales como yo que no entiendo....* They (my children) are not going to be like me—like one who does not understand.

Out of respect for their own parents, however, these women blame themselves for their failure to continue their education. When asked whether it was her decision to leave school, Elia recalled:

> *Se me hace que yo, fue mi problema....* I think it was me, it was my problem. I wanted to quit really. I didn't pay attention to my mother and father telling me to go. I just didn't want to go and they didn't force me to go either, so I didn't. For my mother, I think it was better

> because I could help her with the children; maybe not, maybe she did want me to go. Well I don't know, I was very young then.

The mothers see their children's need to get an education reflected in their own lack of education. They see themselves as key to their children's ability to continue their education. While all of the mothers married and had several children at a young age, they decided not to have as many children as their mothers had. They viewed limiting family size as allowing them more time and energy to devote to helping their children.

> *Ya me puse a pensar....* I thought to myself that the fewer children I have, the more chances I would have to help them become something. If I have a familia grande (large family), then I am not going to be able to help them as much.

The mothers' limiting of family size is consistent with the considerable decrease in family size within a generation observed by Gonzales in his study of Mexican and Mexican American farmworkers (1985, p. 125). But the mothers' decisions to limit family size often conflicted with their strong religious backgrounds (i.e., Roman Catholic or Evangelical) and were rarely welcomed by their husbands, who take pride in having many children. Making such reproductive choices, which for two mothers involved seeking tubal ligations, often pits the traditional value of large families against the more modern value of limiting family size to permit mothers both to contribute to family resources and to better use existing resources to support children. They observed that their own mothers were exhausted by meeting the survival needs of a large family (e.g., cooking and washing diapers) and had little time to contribute to family income or to encourage their children's education. But increasingly, Latina migrant mothers are assuming more control over decisions concerning family size and are resolving conflicts in favor of fewer children and the potential to give more time and attention to their children as they grow older.

The mothers recognized that the greatest impediment to their children's chances to complete a high school education was posed by the stop-and-start nature of their schooling caused by the need to travel. They often blamed themselves for these disruptions, as Rigoberta did in the following:

> *El bien es para ellos porque más después cuando crezcan....* It is good for the children [to stop migrating] because when they grow up, they might say, "It is my mother's fault that I don't know how to read or write." I prefer to have my children in school so they will learn. Like here, they learn English.

The mothers talk often about plans to stop traveling if they see it is doing harm to their children, but they seldom carry out these plans. They know in reality that few migrant women (or men) have the freedom to make such economic decisions. Because these families are poor, there is little choice but to continue to "travel to the jobs." One of the mothers interviewed actually did refuse to pack up her children and travel north with her husband one year, but economics and a desire not to split up her family resulted in her return to migrating the following year.

The constant moving from one place to another means that families' possessions, friends, and familial support networks are left behind.

> *Siempre cuando uno tiene que mover....* When one has to move, one has to leave things behind because you can't take everything to where you are going, and these are the hard things, because when you go to another place, you have to buy them.

> *Se mueve, que se queda y así....* One moves, something stays behind. My mother right now does not know my children. She only sees them in pictures.

In many ways, Latina migrant families experience a feeling of uprootedness. During the rare times they are not working or waiting to be called to work, families find few opportunities to engage in familiar social activities. Elia complained:

> *Se fastidia de estar en los campos....* You get frustrated being at the camps, working all week. Saturday and Friday come and you want to go out and have fun or something. When you're around here in the jobs, there are no *bailes* (dances), nothing of the sort. What we (Mexicans) like most is to dance. You have to go to the movies when they pay and you have money.

But most important for the mothers interviewed, moving from place to place means their children will go to one school for a short period of time and then move on to another school where they will need to adjust to new teachers and make new friends. When asked, "Do your children like school?", migrant mothers, unlike most mainstream U.S. mothers, respond, "Do you mean *this* (current) school or school in general?"

Migrating also means that children live with their parents in farm labor camps. These camps are rarely set up to accommodate families, which means that parents and children often stay together in a single room. One mother observed:

> *Estamos en el mismo cuarto....* [The children, my husband, and I] are in the same room. It's not like my daughter can have her own room to play Barbie. But I always accommodate them good.

Little privacy is afforded to families living in camps. Facilities are shared with other camp occupants.

> *Es duro porque uno ya siente cansada ya en su edad que tiene....* It's hard [living in the camps] because one feels tired at one's age, and the bathrooms are outside, the showers are outside, *everything* is outside.

Mothers also worry that their young sons will be influenced negatively by other young male workers in the camps, some of whom are themselves teenagers who have already abandoned their education to work in the fields. Elia reported:

> *Yo regaño con el grandecito mío que no quiero....* I scold my oldest son that I don't want him to bother with them, because they think differently than a boy of 13. At times they play cards, they play dominoes, they drink, they smoke...and he can learn things from them.

And in a culture where marriage and childbearing at an early age are common, mothers also worry about the impact of camp life on their young daughters. Rosa advised:

> *Está bien tener tus hijas pero si tú te sabes llegar con ellas, darles consejos....* It's okay having your daughters [in the camp] but only if you know how to reach them, give them advice...and believe them because sometimes there will be lies and much gossip. I trust my girls. I communicate well with them, because they are lovely. And it is dangerous to live in the camps because there are many single men, many "lovebirds" as the Americans say.

Latina migrant mothers are similar to mainstream U.S. mothers. They worry about their children's health and education, and they have dreams for their children's futures. They all want children to find jobs outside of "la labor." Migrant mothers' concept of a successful person is someone who speaks good English and has a permanent job outside of "la labor." The mothers shared:

> *Yo no quiero que mis hijos sufran también, como estoy aquí trabajando en la labor....* I don't want my children to suffer like I am working in the fields. Sometimes I suffer because of the heat. I see in my life, what I am going through is tough. I don't want my children to suffer this. I prefer that they study.

> I want them to stay in school in order to find a job—an easy one, not a hard one.

> I take them to the field so that they learn how hard it is working in the

field, see the life of farmwork and how warm the ground is. They don't like this and they keep on in school.

One mother referred to careers rather than jobs and shared specific dream careers for each of her children, careers that are clearly mainstream American but reflect traditional gender roles.

A Luíz le gusta mecánicas, a Beverly le gusta bookkeeping.... Luíz likes mechanics, and Beverly likes bookkeeping. Beatriz likes modeling, and Vicki a ballerina I guess. Oh, and Johnny wants to be a movie star.

But migrant mothers temper their hopes for their children with resignation to the reality presented by their lifestyle. They are hopeful within a context of powerlessness. This powerlessness has previously been documented by Prewitt-Diaz et al., in their 1990 ethnographic study of migrant families (pp. 74-77). A mother's reflection demonstrated this state:

In order for my children to finish school, they need me to help them. But I can't think for them. I want the best for them all of the time.

Pero no se puede, no se puede.... But if it can't be, it can't be.

While discouraged by their lack of education, the mothers also dream about their own futures.

Y el rato que ellos están en la escuela, me gustaría yo estar aprendiendo.... While my children are in school, I would like to be learning something for myself. I would like to finish school if I could. I know it's late, but I'd like to finish.

I like to work with children, and I'd like to get a job cutting hair, something different. I see that I would be able to do that well, because I have tried it.

I think that after I finish raising my children, I plan to study a little more and look for a job where I would not be in "la labor."

In the future I would like to stop traveling, buy a house, and stay in Florida. I would like to get my GED and get a good job to see to it that my children don't have to stay in farmwork.

But Latina migrant mothers are also different from mainstream U.S. mothers in significant ways. They follow lives in which role definitions and values and norms of two different cultures (rural Latina and mainstream United States) often collide. The impact of a third (migrant lifestyle) places demands and limitations on what they can do to guide and encourage their children to realize their dreams of continuing their education, finding a job outside of farmwork, and settling into a permanent location. While these mothers hope that their children's lives will be different from theirs, they express acceptance of their lifestyle with a strong sense of ethnic pride. Elia concluded her interview with the following:

> *Es una vida que no a todas les gustaría....* This is not a life that everyone would like. I see almost no Americanas in this kind of work. But, I am happy because this is the life that God gave to me, a Mexicana. I am happy with the life.

Conclusion

As a result of the many contradictions their families experience, the children of these women receive mixed messages. They feel encouraged to continue their education and seek careers outside of farmwork. Yet the immediate availability of work and the opportunity to make money when the harvest is good are appealing. Putting off this opportunity in order to study, in hopes of finding a job that will help them afford to settle in a permanent location, is a difficult choice to make, and one for which their lifestyle offers little support. Although smaller families and the availability of day-care services have reduced the pressure on young migrant girls to serve as surrogate mothers for younger brothers and sisters, migrant children continue to assume worker roles at an early age. As a result of their working in adult jobs, migrant children are often permitted by parents to make the decision to continue or quit school.

Many Latina migrant mothers are strong women, as evidenced by their courage to leave family and familiar surroundings to try to improve their lives. Most would like to help lift their children out of the migrant lifestyle. They have insight into the many influences in their own lives and their children's that make this difficult, but they also recognize the changes that have occurred in their lifetimes that make this at least possible for their sons and daughters. As reflected in the interviews recorded in S. Beth Atkin's *Voices from the Fields* (1993), an essential difference between many farmworker parents and their children is their children's chance to get an education. Latina migrant mothers need the support of migrant educators to help them find ways to explore productively these new avenues for their children. There are natural alliances to be developed between educators and migrant mothers who share similar goals for their children. The concept of parental involvement should be expanded to include ways educators can empower mothers to find these avenues for their children and negotiate the many cultural and lifestyle stumbling blocks that threaten to get in their way.

While the outcome of the oral history project provides a window on the behaviors and motivations of Latina migrant mothers and their children, the process involved in the mothers' telling their stories is likely more important than the product itself. As Linda Shopes notes in "Oral History in Pennsylvania: A Historiographical Overview" (1993, pp. 450-451), an oral history project such as the one undertaken with Latina migrant mothers is not solely an effort to record their lives at an earlier time, but is also a means of cultivating cultural pride and empowerment. The mothers expressed much pride that they were asked to speak for the record about their own experiences in their honored language rather than have others speak for them. Two mothers agreed to be photographed and all four mothers readily consented to have their stories presented in public programs supported by the Pennsylvania Humanities Council, a statewide organization funded partially by the National Endowment for the Humanities.

As Shopes (1993) observes, making interview materials public becomes a way for these mothers to assert the value of their lives against the cultural forces that devalue or fail to understand them. The process also helps these mothers recognize their strengths as women who have taken the actions necessary to ensure that their families survive economically. Listening to their own stories and knowing that others are also interested in hearing them can help migrant mothers develop the self-esteem necessary to play the role of involved parent expected in the mainstream U.S. educational system.

References

Atkin, S. B. (1993). *Voices from the fields: Children of migrant farmworkers tell their stories.* Boston: Joy Street Books.

Coles, R. (1970). *Uprooted children: The early life of migrant farmworkers.* Pittsburgh: University of Pittsburgh Press.

Farmworker women speak out. (1994). Washington, DC: Farmworker Justice Fund.

Friedland, W. H., & Nelkin, D. (1971). *Migrant agricultural workers in America's Northeast.* New York: Holt, Rinehart and Winston.

Gonzales, J. L., Jr. (1985). *Mexican and Mexican American farmworkers: The California agricultural industry.* New York: Praeger.

Prewitt-Diaz, J. O., Trotter, R. T., & Rivera, V. A., Jr. (1990). *The effects of migration on children: An ethnographic study.* Harrisburg, PA: Division of Migrant Education, Pennsylvania Department of Education.

Reul, M. R. (1974). *Territorial boundaries of rural poverty: Profiles of exploitation.* East Lansing, MI: Center for Rural Manpower and Public Affairs, Michigan State University.

Shopes, L. (1993). Oral history in Pennsylvania: A historiographical overview. *Pennsylvania History: Quarterly Journal of Pennsylvania Historical Association, 60*(4), 430-454.

Appendix

Oral History Outline

The oral history interview was organized into three sections, reflecting the three areas of migrant mothers' lives on which this project focused. The interviewer asked open-ended questions about the topics listed (i.e., "Tell me about your earliest recollections as a child in a farmworker family") to elicit information about migrant mothers' lives in these three areas. The interviewer was also encouraged to explore related topics that interviewees raised.

I. Growing Up As a Child
   A. Name and age
   B. Family name and composition
   C. Where born and raised
   D. Home(s)
   E. Camp life as a child
   F. Family work
      1. How long in farmwork
      2. How long traveling, where traveled to
      3. Kinds of crops picked
      4. Other work
   G. Culture
      1. Ethnic background
      2. Importance of religion
      3. Family traditions, foods
      4. What family did for fun
   H. Relationships between males and females in family
      1. Differences between growing up as little girl rather than little boy in family, culture, camp
   I. Difficulties in dealing with people outside of culture, camp (i.e., experiences with prejudice)
   J. Education
      1. How much, what it was like
      2. Parents' expectations
      3. Mother's expectations as a child and extent met
      4. Interesting educational experiences
   K. Special people who influenced mother when a child

II. Life As an Adult Woman
   A. When/how began working as migrant woman
   B. When/why married (i.e., how met spouse)

C. How many children
    1. Their ages
    2. Whether more or fewer children than expected
    3. How decision made to have children
D. Other members of family
E. Life as an adult woman in culture
    1. Differences from man's life
F. Life as a woman in camp (i.e., responsibilities, what mother does for fun)
    1. Differences from man's life
G. Life as a migrant mother
    1. Differences from migrant father's life
H. Changes seen in lifetime for women/mothers in culture or as migrant
I. Future plans for education, training, or change in jobs
    1. Mother's highest dreams for herself
    2. What would she like life to be like for herself

III. Life for Mother's Children
A. How children's lives differ from mother's life as a child
    1. Traveling
    2. Education
    3. Opportunities
    4. Camp life
B. Mother's hopes for her children
    1. Educational expectations
    2. Traveling expectations
    3. Job expectations
    4. Marriage/family expectations
C. Difficulties children have as migrant children outside of culture, camp
    1. Adjustment to school
    2. Experiences of prejudice
    3. How mother helps children deal with difficulties
D. Mother's highest dreams for children
    1. What mother would like life to be like for them
    2. How mother will help them achieve this

CHAPTER 19

Involving Migrant Families in Their Children's Education:
Challenges and Opportunities for Schools

NANCY FEYL CHAVKIN
RICHTER INSTITUTE OF SOCIAL WORK
SOUTHWEST TEXAS STATE UNIVERSITY

Mobility is an inherent part of migrant family life. Migrant families work and then move on to a new job. The cycle of "work, move, work, move" is continuous. Mobility affects everything a migrant family does. This chapter describes the lives of migrant families and how schools might better involve these families in their children's education.

Migrants are usually defined as farmworkers who follow the crops across the country or from one country to another, returning home for the winter harvest (Bartlett & Vargas, 1991). Since 1969 the Migrant Student Record Transfer System (MSRTS) has provided a definition and a tracking system for migrant students; however, this system tells us about only those migrant children who attend schools and are reported to the MSRTS (Cahape, 1993). Lack of a consistent federal definition and the fact that various federal agencies and offices undertake data collection mean that official studies can exhibit sharp differences about *who* migrant farmworkers are and about *how many* of them there are. Shotland (1989) reported that the estimate of the number of migrant farmworkers ranges from 317,000 to 1.5 million. The Migrant Health Program (1990) estimated that there were 1,661,875 migrant farmworkers in the United States. Martin (1994) reports that there are approximately 409,000 migrant children traveling with their families, mostly from one Mexican residence to one U.S. residence.

In addition to disagreements about the definition and number of migrant families, the diverse nature of migrant families' lifestyles makes it difficult to characterize the migrant family. Bartlett and Vargas (1991) describe the typical migrant farmworker as between 25 and 44, Latino, from Mexico or from Central America or Puerto Rico, with an average of 5.5 years of schooling, and not necessarily literate in his/her native language, which is usually Spanish.

We do know that most migrant families in the United States follow familiar geographic routes. Shotland (1989) discusses three distinct streams: the East Coast Stream, the Mid-continent Stream, and the West Coast Stream.

The East Coast Stream consists of American Blacks, Mexican Americans and Mexican nationals, Anglos, Jamaican and Haitian Blacks, and Puerto Ricans. This route includes the states along the eastern seaboard and southern United States. The Mid-continent Stream primarily consists of Mexican Americans and Mexican nationals, with small numbers of American Indians; the route begins in south Texas and moves north through the midwestern and western states. The Western Stream starts in California and moves up through Oregon and Washington, and it also is composed of a majority of Mexican Americans and Mexican nationals, although recently it has also included Southeast Asians.

Family income studies (Shotland, 1989) show that the average annual income for 1986 was less than $6,500. Jobs are usually seasonal and inconsistent, and workers are not generally covered by employee benefit programs. In addition, because of residency problems, language barriers, and unfamiliarity with locally available resources, most migrant families receive few social, economic, or health services.

The living and working conditions of migrant families are a serious national health problem. Shotland (1989) reports that risks include injury from farm machinery and equipment, poor sanitation, chronic and acute exposure to toxic chemicals, constant physical demands, and exposure to bad weather. Many families lack toilets and clean drinking water. Living quarters are usually dilapidated farmhouses, field barracks, small shacks, and even improvised shelters.

Robert Coles' (1971) classic study of migrant families is still a good representation of what life is like for a migrant family. He reports that the family is always stooping and picking, always doing what has to be done.

Lives are impoverished, hungry, and uncertain; there is always the next place to go. Children learn early that each new day brings backbreaking toil for their parents and that after one field is picked, it means a trip to another one, which may be in a new county or a new state. The video documentary *New Harvest, Old Shame* (Corporation for Public Broadcasting, 1990) with its rich portrayal of the daily lives of migrant families, shows that life had not changed much for migrant families in 20 years.

Prewitt-Diaz, Trotter, and Rivera (1990) conducted an ethnographic study of migrants in 10 states. Their report was the result of more than 3,000 hours of participant observation, semi-structured interviews, and life histories. They recorded two patterns of migration—intrastate and interstate. The major reason for migration was always economic. Deciding where to move and when was based on knowledge about the length of seasons, timing of crops, changing agricultural conditions, rates of pay, and housing considerations. Migrants talked of isolation and constant adjustment to new surroundings. As one interviewee said, "It's hard to have to always leave and say goodbye all the time" (p. 48).

Stresses on migrant families are enormous. Child abuse reports reveal a dark side of migrant family life—child maltreatment. The level of maltreatment among migrant families is much higher than for the general population (Lawless, 1986). Findings indicate that there is a differential risk of maltreatment depending on migrant status, family structure, and age. Intrastate migrant families have a higher incidence of reported maltreatment than interstate migrant families. Children from single parent families and younger children have a higher probability of being maltreated. Poverty and extraordinary challenge, combined with few resources to meet the challenges, are the likely causes.

Although the findings for single parent families and younger children are consistent with research conducted with non-migrant families, researchers disagree about the reasons for the different rates of maltreatment among interstate migrants and intrastate migrants. Some researchers hypothesize that there is a lower incidence of reported maltreatment among interstate migrants than intrastate migrants, because interstate migrant families travel with their support systems and have learned to cope with stress and negative living conditions. Others suggest that the lower rates of maltreatment are attributable to the effects of constant moves on the detection and reporting process.

The Interstate Migrant Education Council's report (IMEC, 1987) details the special problems facing migrant students, who are at great risk for dropping out of school. In addition to the problems associated with migrant students' mobility, these students are also handicapped by their limited English fluency, their poverty, their lack of academic skills, and their need to work or take care of younger children to support the family.

Romo (1993) reports that Mexican immigrant students whose families migrate as seasonal agricultural workers have special needs that vary considerably across the population. Some students have never enrolled in school in Mexico; others have attended a few years of *Primaria* (approximately grades 1-6 in the United States). A few have been fortunate enough to attend *Secundaria* (approximately 7th-9th grade in the United States) and have a strong educational background. The common characteristics of these migrant students are the need to learn English and a wide variation in early educational background.

Too frequently, educators associate the lack of English proficiency with a lack of intellectual ability, when, in fact, mobility rather than lack of ability has kept students from learning. Romo (1993) reports that schools in the United States have responded to the complicated issues of language, migration, and immigration by offering intensive English for Speakers of Other Languages (ESOL) classes, bilingual programs, and newcomers' schools. Each program has its own advantages and disadvantages, and all of the programs are hampered by the students' continued mobility.

Migrant students have the lowest graduation rate of any group in the public schools and their rate of completion for postsecondary education is even lower. Five times as many migrant students are enrolled in the second grade as in the 12th grade, and migrant educators place the dropout rate for migrant students anywhere from 50 to 90 percent (IMEC, 1987).

Baca and Harris (1988) report that migrant students are more likely to be affected by multiple health problems and disabilities. They report a higher incidence of birth injuries, mental retardation, accidents, poor pre- and postnatal care, and anemia among migrant students than the general population. The Center for Educational Planning (1989) also points out that discrimination compounds the challenges of poverty, mobility, health problems, and language difference.

Family Involvement in Migrant Students' Education

Even after differences in student ability and socioeconomic status are taken into account, the evidence that family involvement in education increases student achievement is clear (Henderson & Berla, 1994; Kagan, 1984; Walberg, 1984). In a study of high-achieving and low-achieving migrant students, parents of high achievers could list the ways the school was supportive of their child's education (Center for Educational Planning, 1989), whereas parents of low achievers had difficulty naming things that the school was doing to help their child. (It is, of course, not difficult to believe that schools have trouble helping low-achieving migrant students; the challenges are great.) Interestingly, even though no migrant parents in this study helped their children with their homework, parents of high achievers reported spending "quality time" with, and providing educational experiences for, their children, whereas no parents of low achievers reported these two activities.

Researchers such as Olsen and Dowell (1989) and Lucas, Henze, and Donato (1990) describe programs that are meeting the needs of immigrant and migrant students. The programs resemble good schools anywhere. They exhibit sound educational philosophy such as high academic expectations for all students, family involvement, and strong instructional leadership. The effective programs, as might be expected, also valued students' home language and culture, made migrant students' education a priority, worked with families in their own language and in the community, and included strong staff development programs. Not only were students' circumstances understood, but education was not conceived apart from the whole of students' lives.

Herrington (1987) discusses the importance of teachers' willingness to contact and work with parents. He notes that many migrant families have strengths of resiliency, resourcefulness, and responsiveness that teachers can recognize, value, and use. Schools must find ways to bring such strengths to bear on behalf of migrant students.

Family involvement in education is a new concept for many migrant families, and educators should *not* be surprised to find that initial efforts to involve migrant parents meet with resistance. Many migrant families believe it is the school's responsibility to educate their children; for these families, parent participation in education is a new cultural concept (Simich-Dudgeon, 1986a). Parents want the best for their children, but these parents may believe that their involvement would be counter-productive or that the schools might construe involvement as interference. In the Prewitt-Diaz, Trotter, and Rivera study (1990), the students who were successful in school often reported it was someone other than their parents who had been their inspiration to complete school. Teachers should remember that, for migrant parents, a day's wage can be important to family cohesion and even survival. When this is the case, it makes sense that parents would prefer to see their children in the fields rather than in the schools.

Involving migrant families in the education of their children is both a challenge and an opportunity. Educators need to extend the word family from the traditional definition of biological parents to all those in the community who have a significant effect on students' lives. This broader definition is a definition that creates new possibilities for linking the home and school communities. Carter (1993) calls this a family-focused approach that stems from a logical sequence of beliefs. "If better child outcomes are the shared goal of the community and its institutions, then we must use all the resources necesary to achieve those outcomes to their fullest potential" (p. 7). Carter suggests that both families and communities be full partners in the educational process. Accepting the premise is easy, but as Carter suggests, "getting from here to there is the hard part" (p. 7).

Strategies for School Districts

Many studies show what schools can do to promote family involvement. The studies hold true for migrant families, and they can serve as benchmarks for whether schools are doing what they say they want to be doing.

Williams and Chavkin (1990) used a key informant approach (interviewing educators with expertise in family involvement programming) to identify and describe the essential features of promising family and community involvement programs in school districts in five southwestern states. Two key features of effective programs stood out: written policies and administrative support for family involvement. Everything else concerned ways school districts facilitated actual work with families, including training for staff and families; a partnership approach in every aspect of programming; two-way communication; networking within and outside the district; and evaluation. In each case, the school board set the official district policy on family and community involvement and then provided administrative support to implement the established policies. Individual schools within the district developed their own strategies for undertaking actual work with families, with support from the central office as necessary.

The earlier work of Davies (1987) is in agreement with the need for a school district policy about family involvement. Because school districts have unique features that make them resist change, policies about family and community involvement are absolutely necessary. Davies' research found that the organizational goals of schools are diffuse and that responsibility for achieving goals is fragmented among administrators, counselors, teachers, families, and students. In addition, the informal norms of schools are powerful, and the formal structure is complicated, sometimes so complicated that it frustrates goal achievement. These organizational realities make family involvement difficult to introduce and maintain without a formal, written policy. A mandate for family involvement is essential, according to Davies.

Because the National Coalition for Parent Involvement in Education (NCPIE) is dedicated to the development of family/school partnerships (NCPIE, 1992), its work is particularly relevant to migrant students and families. The NCPIE organizations used their broad and diverse experiences in working with teachers, administrators, families, and community leaders to develop general policy suggestions for school districts:

- opportunities for all families to become informed about how the family involvement program will be designed and carried out;
- participation of families who lack literacy skills or who do not speak English;
- regular information for families about their child's participation and progress in specific educational programs and the objectives of those programs;
- opportunities for families to assist in the instructional process at school and at home;
- professional development for teachers and staff to enhance their effectiveness with families;
- linkages with social service agencies and community groups to address key family and community issues;
- involvement of families of children at all ages and grade levels;
- recognition of diverse family structures, circumstances and responsibilities, including differences that might impede family participation. The person(s) responsible for a child may not be the child's biological parent(s), and policies and programs should include participation by all persons interested in the child's educational progress.

As many migrant educators know firsthand, policies alone are not enough. Chavkin (1995) states that policies provide only the framework; policies need to be supported by mechanisms for monitoring, enforcing, and providing technical assistance. District support for migrant family and community involvement must occur during three critical stages: (1) development, (2) implementation, and (3) maintenance. District support helps a policy come into formal existence (development), helps translate it into practical actions (implementation), and helps maintain the policy (maintenance). Support is likely, moreover, to emerge from informal sources; policy development helps secure the commitment of the formal organization.

Based on information from actual programs, NCPIE (1992) and the National School Boards Association (Amundson, 1988) both recommend several kinds of support for policies to involve families in school activities during the development phase. These begin with assessing family needs and interests about ways of working with schools and setting clear and measurable goals, with family and community input. The understanding of what a true partnership means is critical during this first stage. School districts need to see migrant families and community members as equal partners and seek their input in developing a vision of their district's ideal family involvement program. Districts need to exert leadership and seek the involvement of migrant families within a broad community effort.

Once a policy is adopted, school districts need to successfully implement it with the help of a strong support system. Some suggestions that have worked for districts with migrant students and families include the following:

- Hire and train a parent liaison to contact migrant families directly and to coordinate parent activities. The liaison should be bilingual, if interacting with another language group, and sensitive to the needs of migrant families and the community, especially those of the non-English-speaking community.
- Develop public relations to inform families, businesses, and the community about parent involvement policies and programs through newsletters, slide shows, videotapes, announcements and stories in local newspapers, and such.
- Recognize the importance of a community's historic, ethnic, linguistic, or cultural resources in generating interest in parent participation. Even when there are problems, such as farmworker health or working condition issues, a family involvement program can serve as a forum for discussion and a conduit for change.
- Use creative forms of communication between educators and families. This may include parent/teacher conferences at community centers, homes, or neutral meeting places which yield individual parent/child and teacher/child plans.
- Mobilize families as volunteers in the school to help teachers with listening to oral reading, assisting in the lunchroom, and helping with office functions. Families might act as invited speakers when they are not working in the fields because of weather conditions or equipment repairs.
- Train educators to use techniques for surmounting barriers between migrant families and schools.

The maintenance stage follows the coming together of the partnership and the establishment of an official group; the maintenance stage focuses on working together with all partners. The work is not done after policies are developed and implemented. In fact, most partnerships report that very difficult tasks define the maintenance stage. The maintenance stage is when budgets, personalities, and time become abiding issues.

After implementing policies about migrant family and community involvement, the maintenance stage must enhance initial successes. NCPIE makes the following three recommendations:

1. Integrate information and assistance with other aspects of the total learning environment. Migrant families should have access to information about such services as health care and nutrition programs provided by schools or community agencies.
2. Schedule programs and activities flexibly to reach diverse family groups.
3. Monitor and evaluate the effectiveness of migrant family involvement programs and activities on a regular basis.

Strategies for Teachers

Partnership can lead to empowerment of parents, students, educators, and community members. Helpful strategies for teachers include (1) open, continuous, two-way communication; and (2) training for teachers, parents, and community.

Communication

Partnerships must foster open, continuous, two-way communication between the schools and their partners. Lack of communication is one of the main obstacles to parent and community involvement. The Metropolitan Life Survey of the American Teacher (Harris, Kagay, & Ross, 1987), which surveyed thousands of teachers and parents of public-school children, found that parents in inner-city districts were less satisfied than suburban parents with the frequency of their contacts with teachers. In addition, parents with less than a high school education were twice as likely to feel awkward about approaching school personnel as parents with a college education. Sometimes parents were intimidated by their communication with faculty and staff, and often they were dismayed by the institutional structure of the schools, particularly if they had previously had negative contacts with the school.

In a survey by Chavkin and Williams (1993), the number one suggestion that parents had for improving involvement was "to give parents more information about children's success in school" (p. 79). This was followed by the suggestions of "helping students understand that having their parents involved was important"; "making parents feel more welcome in the school"; "having more activities that include children, parents, and teachers"; and "asking parents in what way they would like to be involved" (p. 79). All of these suggestions concern communication.

Nicolau and Ramos (1990) report on recent research by the Hispanic Policy Development Project. Hispanic parents had very high regard and respect for school authority and often did not see how they could possibly provide input to teachers. Parents tended not to respond to printed material sent home with their children. Parents were most often involved in schools when face-to-face contact established personal relationships with neighbors or community workers.

Most schools have established methods of communicating with parents; however, much of this communication is one-way (school to parents). The need for more two-way communication is great in most schools. School can be a formidable place for parents; educators must take the time to listen to parents. Educators have a lot to learn about what it feels like to be a parent or community member walking into a school—especially an *unfamiliar* school.

Bermúdez (1994) reports that teachers often overlook what they can learn from migrant families. These families are rich sources of information useful in both the classroom and the community. These parents have worked with their children in the fields; they know their learning styles, their strengths, and their weaknesses.

Partnerships require that all participants share responsibility for educational outcomes. Active, integrated roles reflect this shared responsibility. Delgado-Gaitán (1991) insists that effective programs validate the cultural and social experiences of families. Schools should not be telling parents what schools need; instead, schools should be asking parents for ideas to help their children and to make schools more effective. Because parents and community members are such important participants in the education of children and youth, the relationship among parents, community members, and schools must become a true partnership in which all groups participate equally.

There is a big difference between the rhetoric of partnership and the action of partnership. Educators must truly believe and act on the belief that parents are their children's first teacher and the teacher by far most likely to accompany children into adulthood. As Sosa (1993) advocates, educators must discard the deficit model of working with families and, instead, operate on an enrichment model where parents are truly understood and believed to want the best for their children. Not only must educators tell *parents* that their influence is as least as important as that of the school, educators must tell *students* how important their homes and communities are. A partnership allows educators to tap a too-often neglected source of strength and meaning that is the natural ally of instruction.

For parents and community members to become successfully involved in a home-school partnership, they and school representatives must agree to a clearly defined set of goals and objectives accompanied by explicit roles and responsibilities related to those goals and objectives. Each school must meet with parent, community, and teacher representatives to define local goals for parent and community involvement and begin a long-term plan. Each school's current involvement practices need to be assessed so that parents, community members, and educators understand where they are and how to reach their goals. Programs require specific development and leadership. Even schools that seem similar can easily differ in their parent involvement efforts. It is critical to tailor the goals and objectives of parent and community involvement programs to the experiences and practices of each school within a community.

If parents and community members can begin to communicate effectively with schools, fears will gradually subside and previously isolated groups will learn to trust each other. Schools must communicate frequently and effectively with parents and community members, and communication should use every form available, with particular emphasis on cultivating face-to-face personal relationships.

Training

Teachers and administrators lack training about the best ways to involve low-income and minority parents and community members effectively. Colleges of education are just now beginning to change their curriculums to emphasize the role of the family in children's education. Chavkin and Williams (1988) found that less than 5 percent of the teachers in their survey reported having a formal course in working with parents and communities. Lack of training is compounded by a scarcity of information about comprehensive "how-to-do" parent and community involvement. Even teachers who do want to learn about parent involvement have to search for materials.

The Trinity/Arlington Project (Simich-Dudgeon, 1986b) was developed for limited-English-proficient students and consisted of teacher training, parent training, and the pilot testing of a vocational-oriented bilingual curriculum. Students reported that they acquired a better understanding of the American school system and that they learned about career planning. Parents' contacts with the schools increased, and parents were observed to have increased concern for their children's education and for their children's acquisition of basic skills necessary for functioning in this country. In addition, strong relationships were found between project activities and gains in students' English proficiency and academic self-concept.

The University of Houston-Clear Lake Model (Bermúdez, 1994) is a parent-education model for preservice and practicing teachers. Students learn about barriers to parent involvement and practice minimizing those barriers. The analysis of students' field notes revealed that 80 percent had a positive change of attitude toward minority parents after participating in the program. Another 10 percent stated that they already had positive attitudes before the program, and the remaining 10 percent showed no change of attitude. Similarly, the results from parents indicated they possessed increased awareness of the school's instructional program, participated more often in their child's school activities, and had a more favorable attitude toward the school.

Educator training can help establish parent and community involvement as a responsibility and a legitimate function of the school. McLaughlin and Shields (1987) aptly point out that it takes a combination of pressure and support to generate parent involvement. Mandates alone have not been able to generate sufficient parent involvement; norm-based pressures such as information about the success of parent-involvement efforts, incentives, and professional expectations are required.

Parents and community members also need support and training to assume partnership roles with schools. Traditionally parents and community members have served primarily in the roles of audience and supporter, with a few parents assuming the role of home tutor. Parents and community members have expressed interest in moving beyond these traditional roles. They want to be involved in partnership approaches to education, but training is fundamental in order for partnerships to succeed.

Bermúdez (1994) suggests that many Hispanic parents want to learn how to help their children. She suggests that some families can monitor children's progress through simple daily or weekly checklists. Other families may benefit from training in questioning techniques, sharing oral histories, listening to children, checking out books and materials from the school or the library, toymaking, support services, or field trips. School-based training programs are not the only kind of parent programs; programs can be center-based or home-based. Delgado-Gaitán (1991) describes an empowerment program in Carpineria, California, where a group of low-income parents first learned how schools operate and then formed a group to help advocate for parents who were more fearful or less assertive.

Partnerships will be widely effective only if parent and community partners get training for their roles. Parents and community members need specific information and training in order to assume partnership roles. They want to know what their roles are and how to perform them effectively. Training for parents should complement that provided school staff, and teachers should become familiar with the activities and programs developed by others (Bermúdez, 1994; Henderson, Marburger, & Ooms, 1986; Moles & D'Angelo, 1993; Nicolau & Ramos, 1990; Montecel, Gallagher, Montemayor, Villarreal, Adam-Reyna, & Supik, 1993).

Ongoing evaluation should also be part of the training for partnerships with migrant families. Partnerships need to be assessed at frequent checkpoints to see not only if their goals and objectives are being met but also if the goals and objectives are still appropriate (Melaville & Blank, 1993). Partnerships must recognize the complexity that life brings to migrant students and their families. Programs need to be flexible and must adjust to ensuing changes for the student, the family, the school, and the community. Often partnerships start with one specific goal and then need to revise their plans as they find out more about the problem. For example, academic concerns may lead to goals that concern health, financial problems, or child care.

Conclusion

Clearly, migrant students are vulnerable to missing and eventually dropping out of school. With our nation's current economic picture, migrant family lives are not going to change substantially; migrant families will continue to move in search of subsistence and economic self-improvement. What schools and teachers can do to meet this challenge, however, could have a profound effect on migrant students' education and subsequent life chances. Opportunities for action include adopting and supporting family involvement policies; developing and nurturing partnerships; communicating two ways and not just one way with families and communities; and participating in ongoing training about family involvement. Understanding the culture and values of migrant families and reconceptualizing how we all define and work with families will help educators facilitate migrant students' learning.

References

Amundson, K. J. (1988). *First teachers: Parent involvement in the public schools.* Alexandria, VA: National School Boards Association. (ERIC Document Reproduction Service No. ED 302 883)

Baca, L., & Harris, K. C. (1988). Teaching migrant exceptional children. *Teaching Exceptional Children, 20,* 32-35.

Bartlett, K. J., & Vargas, F. O. (1991). *Literacy education for adult migrant farmworkers* (ERIC Digest). Washington, DC: Adjunct ERIC Clearinghouse for ESL Literacy Education. (ERIC Document Reproduction Service No. ED 334 873)

Bermúdez, A. (1994). *Doing our homework.* Charleston, WV: ERIC Clearinghouse on Rural Education and Small Schools. (ERIC Document Reproduction Service No. ED 372 905)

Cahape, P. (1993). *The Migrant Student Record Transfer System (MSRTS): An Update* (ERIC Digest). Charleston, WV: ERIC Clearinghouse on Rural Education and Small Schools. (ERIC Document Reproduction Service No. ED 357 909)

Carter, J. L. (1993). Moving from principles to practice: Implementing a family-focused approach in schools and community services. *Family Resource Coalition Report, 12*(3&4), 7-10.

Center for Educational Planning. (1989). *Migrant education dropout prevention project* (Final Report). Santa Clara, CA: Santa Clara County Office of Education. (ERIC Document Reproduction Service No. ED 321 951)

Chavkin, N. F. (1995). Development and implementation of comprehensive districtwide reforms in parent and community involvement. In B. Rutherford (Ed.), *Creating family/school partnerships.* Canton, OH: National Middle Schools Association.

Chavkin, N. F., & Williams, D. L., Jr. (1988). Critical issues in teacher training for parent involvement. *Educational Horizons, 16,* 87-89.

Chavkin, N. F., & Williams, D. L., Jr. (1993). Minority parents and the elementary school: Attitudes and practices. In N. F. Chavkin (Ed.), *Families and schools in a pluralistic society.* Albany, NY: State University of New York.

Coles, R. (1971). *Migrants, sharecroppers, mountaineers. Children of Crisis,* Vol. II. Boston, MA: Little, Brown.

Corporation for Public Broadcasting. (1990). *New harvest, old shame* [video cassette]. Alexandria, VA: PBS Video.

Davies, D. (1987). Parent involvement in the public schools: Opportunities for administrators. *Education and Urban Society, 19,* 147-163.

Delgado-Gaitán, C. (1991). Involving parents in school: A process of empowerment. *American Journal of Education, 100*(1), 20-24.

Harris, L., Kagay, M., & Ross, J. (1987). *The American teacher: Strengthening links between home and school.* New York, NY: Louis Harris and Associates, Inc. (ERIC Document Reproduction Service No. ED 289 841)

Henderson, A. T., & Berla, N. (1994). *A new generation of evidence: The family is critical to student achievement.* Washington, DC: National Committee for Citizens in Education. (ERIC Document Reproduction Service No. ED 375 968)

Henderson, A. T., Marburger, C. L., & Ooms, T. (1986). *Beyond the bake sale: An educator's guide to working with parents.* Columbia, MD: National Committee for Citizens in Education. (ERIC Document Reproduction Service No. ED 270 508)

Herrington, S. (1987). How educators can help children of the road. *Instructor, 97,* 36-39.

Interstate Migrant Education Council. (1987). *Migrant education: A consolidated view.* Denver, CO: Education Commission of the States. (ERIC Document Reproduction Service No. ED 285 701)

Kagan, S. L. (1984). *Parent involvement research: A field in search of itself.* Boston, MA: Institute for Responsive Education. (ERIC Document Reproduction Service No. ED 257 569)

Lawless, K. (1986). *Harvesting the harvesters: Book 4. The family support system: Education in its broadest context.* Potsdam, NY: School of Professional Studies, Potsdam College. (ERIC Document Reproduction Service No. ED 279 469)

Lucas, T., Henze, R., & Donato, R. (1990). Promoting the success of Latino language-minority students: An exploratory study of six high schools. *Harvard Educational Review, 60*(3), 315-339.

Martin, P. (1994). *Migrant farmworkers and their children* (ERIC Digest). Charleston, WV: ERIC Clearinghouse on Rural Education and Small Schools. (Document Reproduction Service No. ED 376 997)

McLaughlin, M. W., & Shields, P. M. (1987). Involving low-income parents in the schools: A role for policy. *Phi Delta Kappan, 69,* 156-160.

Melaville, A. I., & Blank, M. J. (1993). *Together we can: A guide for crafting a profamily system of education and human services.* Washington, DC: Institute for Educational Leadership. (ERIC Document Reproduction Service No. ED 357 856)

Migrant Health Program. (1990). *An atlas of state profiles which estimate the number of migrant and seasonal farmworkers and members of their families.* Rockville, MD: U.S. Department of Health and Human Services.

Moles, O., & D'Angelo, D. (Eds.). (1993). *Building school-family partnerships for learning: Workshops for urban educators.* Washington, DC: U.S. Dept. of Education. (ERIC Document Reproduction Service No. ED 364 651)

Montecel, M. R., Gallagher, A., Montemayor, A. M., Villarreal, A., Adame-Reyna, N., & Supik, J. (1993). *Hispanic families as valued partners: An educator's guide.* San Antonio, TX: Intercultural Development Research Association. (ERIC Document Reproduction Service No. ED 356 922)

National Coalition for Parent Involvement in Education. (1992). *Guide to parent involvement resources.* Washington, DC: Author. (ERIC Document Reproduction Service No. ED 365 423)

Nicolau, S., & Ramos, C. L. (1990). *Together is better: Building strong relationships between schools and Hispanic parents.* New York: Hispanic Policy Development Project, Inc. (ERIC Document Reproduction Service No. ED 325 543)

Olsen, L., & Dowell, C. (1989). *Bridges: Promising programs for the education of immigrant children.* San Francisco, CA: California Tomorrow. (ERIC Document Reproduction Service No. ED 314 544)

Prewitt-Diaz, J. O., Trotter, R. T. II, & Rivera, V. A., Jr. (1990). *The effects of migration on children: An ethnographic study.* Harrisburg: Pennsylvania Department of Education, Division of Migrant Education. (ERIC Document Reproduction Service No. ED 327 346)

Romo, H. (1993). *Mexican immigrants in high schools: Meeting their needs* (ERIC Digest). Charleston, WV: ERIC Clearinghouse on Rural Education and Small Schools. (ERIC Document Reproduction Service No. ED 357 905)

Shotland, J. (1989). *Full fields, empty cupboard: The nutritional status of migrant farmworkers in America.* Washington, DC: Public Voice for Food and Health Policy. (ERIC Document Reproduction Service No. ED 323 076)

Simich-Dudgeon, C. (1986b). *A parent involvement model for use with limited English proficient high school students (Vols. 1-5).* Arlington, VA: Arlington Public Schools. (ERIC Document Reproduction Service Nos. ED 274 219-223)

Simich-Dudgeon, C. (1986a). *Parent involvement and the education of limited-English-proficient students* (ERIC Digest). Washington, DC: ERIC Clearinghouse on Languages and Linguistics. (ERIC Document Reproduction Service No. ED 279 205)

Sosa, A. (1993). *Thorough and fair: Creating routes to success for Mexican American students.* Charleston, WV: ERIC Clearinghouse on Rural Education and Small Schools. (ERIC Document Reproduction Service No. ED 360 116)

Walberg, H. J. (1984). Improving the productivity of America's schools. *Educational Leadership, 41*, 19-27.

Williams, D. L., & Chavkin, N. F. (1990). Essential elements of strong parent involvement programs. *Educational Leadership, 47*, 18-20.

CHAPTER 20

Involving Hispanic Parents in Improving Educational Opportunities For Their Children

ALICIA SALINAS SOSA, PH.D.
THE UNIVERSITY OF TEXAS AT SAN ANTONIO

Traditionally, school personnel have expressed concern about the relatively poor record in involving Hispanic parents in schools. The root of the problem is that Hispanic parents cherish beliefs and expectations different from those cherished by the schools and by the parents whom the schools most frequently engage. This chapter explores some of the basic misunderstandings, provides alternate ways of looking at the challenge of involving migrant and immigrant parents of Hispanic descent, and informs school personnel about strategies that have been used to cultivate much more successful experiences with these parents.

The Notion of Parental Involvement

Involving parents in their children's education and in educational decision making is a relatively new phenomenon in public schools in the United States. During early efforts to involve parents in education (in the early twentieth century), schools saw parents as agents of service for the school rather than as equal partners in the educational endeavor (Bermúdez, 1994). Schools identified the areas for assistance and how parents would be asked to assist.

With the advent of the War on Poverty and other initiatives at the federal level came renewed emphasis on parental involvement. Ascher (1987) defines parental involvement as a range of activities from promoting the value of education in the home to the actual role of team decision maker in policy, curriculum, and instructional issues. According to Ascher, parents can participate at various levels, including taking advocacy roles, sitting on councils and committees, and participating in the decision-making process and operation of schools. Parents can serve as classroom aides, accompanying a class on a field trip or assisting teachers in a variety of other ways. Parent involvement may also take the form of teachers' notes to parents, or of parental support for fund-raising projects of the school. More recently, parent involvement includes learning activities at home through which parents try to improve their children's performance in school: for example, reading to them, helping them with homework, playing educational games, or discussing current events. Clearly, parent involvement is now seen as going beyond the bake sale and booster clubs.

Forces Which Hinder Involvement of Migrant/Immigrant Parents

In addition to the barriers imposed by beliefs and expectations just described, forces exist in the day-to-day exigencies of living that influence parental participation in both negative and positive ways.

Henderson, Marburger, and Ooms (1986) categorized barriers to successful parental involvement in two major categories: logistical and attitudinal. Villarreal and Barnwell (1990) added a third category of barriers: expectations.

Logistical Barriers

Logistical barriers include concerns about time, money, safety, and child care. *Time* for participating in school activities is a barrier since parents often work. When a family includes two parents, moreover, it is now common for both parents to hold jobs. In the case of migrant families, parents, siblings, and other relatives may be working quite a distance away from the school.

Money is the second logistical barrier. Recent migrant and immigrant families may experience intense financial pressures despite working long hours doing physically exhausting labor. Parents who work very hard to provide the bare essentials for their families find that their children's schooling reduces daily income, actually compounding the problem of the family's extreme poverty level (Chavkin, 1991). This understandable and reasonable concern adds another stressor associated with schooling.

Safety is a third logistical barrier. Migrant families have much to fear, and they are not always very welcome in the communities on whose behalf they labor. And some locations are ordinarily dangerous at night, when parent activities are usually staged.

Child care poses additional barriers. Making child care arrangements becomes more difficult for migrant families and recent immigrants when they no longer have an extended family to support them through free baby-sitting services. Being recent arrivals to a community, they usually lack close, trusting friendships; these can develop over time, however.

Finally, the *segmentation of programs* creates logistical barriers. The segmented nature of public education, where different programs target varying populations, makes it difficult to facilitate familywide learning programs (Orum & Navarrete, 1990). Families must, for instance, travel to one campus to enroll a child in pre-kindergarten, while the mother's English-as-a-second-language class is scheduled in another building, though health services are located in yet another part of town. Segmentation, combined with other barriers, can force migrant families into making bad decisions or just giving up.

Attitudinal Barriers

Attitudinal barriers cause migrant parents uncertainty about roles, anxiety about how they are being perceived, disagreements regarding educational policies, dissatisfaction with their own home involvement, and communication problems. Parents experience *uncertainty* about their role in U.S. public schools. Parents who have been educated in other countries view educators with high regard and defer to their professional expertise and experience where questions concern their own children's best interests (Nicolau & Ramos, 1990). Azmitia and colleagues (1994) found that, although parents held high aspirations for their children, parents had varying amounts of information about how to help their children realize such aspirations. While some parents were aware that school grades were important, *none* of the parents who hoped their children would become doctors, lawyers, and teachers were aware that these professions require a graduate education.

Disagreements over school policy will sometimes result in demonstrations or walkouts. When Hispanic parents perceive social injustices against Hispanic children or when Hispanic parents, as a whole, are being disrespected, they will probably organize social demonstrations against the school's leadership. If not handled well, disagreements can affect a school district's goals for sharing knowledge and decision making with parents in future issues.

Dissatisfaction over their own capability to carry out home involvement activities (such as helping their children with homework, reading to them in English, and establishing routines) may prevent parents from undertaking such home teaching activities. Parents of secondary students want to help their children, but their inability to speak English usually prevents them even from trying (Simich-Dudgeon, 1986). Applying disciplinary actions related to cooperation with home learning activities also poses a problem. Azmitia and colleagues (1994) reported that 25 percent of parents indicated that they could not help directly with their older children's homework because of their limited schooling or English. Parents did help by checking to see that older children had completed the assigned homework or by enlisting the help of another older sibling. However, conflicts sometimes arose when adolescents, busy with their own homework, balked because of added work from helping younger siblings (Azmitia et al., 1994). The research of Casas, Furlong, Carranza, and Solberg (1986) showed that although both Mexican American and Anglo high school students sought help with their homework, help sources differed. Anglo students sought help from their mothers or fathers, whereas Mexican American youth, successful or not, sought help from their brothers and sisters, who were also struggling with their homework (Casas and colleagues [1994], cited in Minicucci & Olsen, 1993).

Communication problems result when parents sense that the school personnel are establishing a distance between them by using educational jargon in their communications. According to Nicolau and Ramos (1990), many low-income Hispanic parents view the school system as "a bureaucracy governed by educated non-Hispanics whom they have no right to question" (p. 13).

Expectations Barriers

Expectations barriers exist either (1) when parents feel themselves judged by their occupation or their economic status or that their language is not valued at public events or (2) when the schools actually do judge parents according to group membership, either by ethnicity or social class. Oftentimes schools expect a level of minimum participation of all parents, without regard for recency of arrival. Yet, recent arrivals to this country encounter many pressing demands on their attention, such as clearing up questions about immigration status (Commins, 1992); finding adequate, affordable housing in a safe neighborhood; seeking help for treating traumas (war, political violence undergone back home); or the shock of adapting to new lives in the United States (Carrasquillo & London, 1993; Violand-Sánchez, Sutton, & Ware, 1991).

While these barriers may seem daunting, not all of them are simultaneously present in any one site. Rather, school administrators must remember several points: (1) substantial barriers inhibit parental involvement, (2) schools must discover these barriers, and (3) school staff need to take concerted action to overcome them. In undertaking this action, moreover, schools must publicly acknowledge their responsibility *and* legitimate their concern for the life circumstances of migrant families.

Forces that Facilitate and Support the Involvement of Hispanic Migrant and Immigrant Parents

Flexible scheduling and checking for the best meeting times enhance parent participation. Some programs report conducting sessions during two time periods—for example, afternoon and mid-evening, 6:30-8:30 p.m. (Guzmán, 1990). The migrant program in Laredo, Texas, held a parent session in combination with a student attendance awards function on a Friday evening, and over 100 migrant parents attended. In attendance, too, were some of the children's grandparents and siblings. Although the time block selected by parents was inconvenient to the school, it was an excellent one for parents, who saw the event as an occasion for a social outing to celebrate the award (a bronze medal with ribbon) *after* the school functions. That is, the scheduling helped parents make sense of involvement in terms of their own circumstances. Success with Friday evening sessions were, similarly, reported by Delgado-Gaitán (1991). Casas and colleagues (cited in Minicucci & Olsen, 1993) visited immigrant parents at 10 o'clock at night because parents got off work around that time; they received him with coffee and *pan dulce* (dessert pastries).

Providing *transportation and child care* increases attendance at school functions (Bermúdez, 1994; Guzmán, 1990, Inger, 1993; Sosa, 1990). *Avance*, a nonprofit parenting agency working with Mexican Americans in the *barrio*, conducts home visits in public housing to recruit participants for their center (Cohen, 1994). They have a fleet of vans to pick up the mothers either for training in their own neighborhoods or for more advanced instruction (for the GED or college preparation) held in the downtown offices. Other outreach and logistic issues have been addressed through *home visits;* these not only personalize the invitation to attend school functions, but also assist school staff to understand parents' concerns. Successful outreach is *organized by people who have volunteered*, not by people assigned to do the job (Inger, 1992).

Ideally, the first meeting should be held outside the school, preferably at sites frequented by parents. Successful first meetings are primarily social events; business goals are reserved for subsequent meetings (Nicolau & Ramos, 1990; Procidano & Fisher, 1992). Barquet (1990) has suggested that parental involvement becomes more relevant to language-minority populations when it is intergenerational and includes extended families and the communities to which the children belong.

Attitudinal barriers can be lowered by recognizing that migrant and immigrant parents—like all parents—value education. These parents, however, are unlikely to know what the educational system in the United States expects from them (Nicolau & Ramos, 1990; Sosa, 1993; Montecel, Gallagher, Montemayor, Villarreal, & Reyna, 1993). Part of a responsive program would include *sessions on expectations and roles of parents* as part of workshops for parents. Procidano and Fisher (1992) stress the need for demonstrating an understanding of both the importance of *respeto* and the individual's dignity. To convey these, the authors recommend employing formal titles for parents and a presentation of oneself with formal titles, as well as focusing on the individual and the family rather than bureaucratic procedures.

Attitudinal issues related to language use can be diminished when the following points are observed. Important school information should be sent in *both English and Spanish*. When holding parent-teacher nights or advisory meetings, parents should be able to listen through headsets to a translator speaking in Spanish. School personnel who can speak Spanish can also provide assistance. School personnel should participate in activities that provide greater visibility in the community—at festivals, celebrations, fund raisers, or shopping expeditions in the Hispanic community (Cooper & Gonzalez, 1993).

Successful parent involvement programs recognize that parents are not just passive recipients of services. They view parents as *contributors and collaborators*. Guzmán (1990) described some of the strategies used by the San Felipe Del Rio Independent School District's parent involvement program in a border community. Funding had been secured from the U.S. Department of Education's Office of Bilingual Education and Minority Languages Affairs (OBEMLA) in Washington, DC. She describes how only the first in-service topic (information about the fully-funded pre-kindergarten program and the need for parental involvement) was decided. At that first meeting, school officials asked parents to describe their needs and provide input. According to Guzmán, this action on the part of the school personnel signaled to parents that the meeting's intent was skills-building and served to help achieve ownership for the project goals, objectives, and activities.

Project OPTIMUM in Oakland, California, is another example of a successful parental training and involvement program. Personal and group interviews, observations from school visits, and direct inquiry from leaders of various ethnic communities provided the means to assess parental needs. On the basis of identified needs, one-day workshops were organized. A cadre of parents became trainers of other parents. A large number of parents, thus, became facilitators within the school system, creating vocally positive community groups working as agents of change (Gonzales, 1986). This strategy is commended by Inger (1993), who notes that before joining any formal organization, Hispanic parents want to acquire the skills and confidence to contribute as equals.

In the Carpintería School District in California, two teachers, a special program director, and the migrant director developed the Committee for Latin Parents (COPLA). This parent committee began when a small parent group met and shared their need for training in ways to communicate with the school as well as strategies to help their children with homework. At their group meetings, parents learned how the school system works and about their rights and responsibilities as parents. Most important, this program's goal has been to link parents with one another for mutual support and for the mutual support of their children's encounters with the school (Delgado-Gaitán, 1991).

Similarly, Orum and Navarette (1990) indicated how children in the *Academia* program can be nominated to be in the program by either parents or teachers. In addition to paying a minimal (token) fee, parents are asked to contribute their own time. Parents sign a contract to attend at least 50 percent of the monthly parent activities; to read with the child at home for a specified amount of time (or for parents with limited English language skills, to have the child read to the parent); to establish and enforce rules for homework and school attendance; to review and sign the child's homework; and to ensure that the child has a library card. Extended families and other community members can make numerous contributions to the schools and should be used to enrich curriculum and school programs.

To retain the involvement of low-income Hispanic parents, school meetings must *respond to or address some need or concern* of the parents. In Houston, the FailSafe program of innovative approaches connects schools with families through two principal strategies: (1) organizing parent-teacher conferences in the secondary grades so that families can meet with several teachers on the same visit and (2) sponsoring programs that allow families to borrow school computers for the home use of both children *and* adults (Epstein, 1991). Rather than burdening parents with "shoulds" or with allegations of inability to help, this program *equips parents with the tools* they need to provide support and resources to their own children.

Literacy programs in the home language can provide meaningful, useful experiences to immigrant parents. When properly implemented, literacy programs can *tap parents' resources* and can ease the tension caused by role reversal when even young children translate for their parents. Ideally, the books selected should be meaningful and relevant to the lives of children and their families. They must also validate and respect learners' identity, country of origin, and the experiences they bring to school (Lee & Patel, 1994). Parents-as-authors programs are able to accomplish this very well. Literature-based parent involvement programs include (1) programs that focus on teaching parents to use children's literature, (2) programs that interview and assist parents to write remembrances of their childhood to share with school children, and (3) programs where parents serve as teachers. Through children's literature, parents in Richmond, California, shared what they knew about farm animals, a choice that facilitated the participation of parents who did not read (Contreras-Polk & Díaz, 1995). The aim of the *Colorín Colorado*, a children's literature program, as described by Contreras-Polk and Díaz, is to help parents integrate what they already know with their current reality. For each story read, parents talked about parenting implications. After reading one story, they discussed the dangers of children's interactions with strangers.

Thus, successful programs addressed logistic concerns by providing transportation, child care, and flexible and workable meeting times. They assessed needs, ideally through home visits, and made their first contacts with the home a social event. These programs worked on building relationships and *being of service* to parents. Attitudinal barriers were overcome through hands-on training activities that resulted in parents acquiring new skills that they could see being put to use in subsequent interactions with the schools. Overall, these programs were successful because they stopped viewing parents as deficient and began to include them as equal partners. The change enhanced the joint power brought to bear for the benefit of children and youth by parents and schools.

A Paradigm Shift for Involving Hispanic Migrant and Immigrant Families

In the past, school programs have instituted support programs on the basis of the middle class norm or what "the literature" identifies as working in schools. Too often, however, programs have disregarded the varying circumstances of the families and children they actually serve. In the case of the Hispanic community, pressing factors such as poverty, mobility, cultural differences, and language constraints make the effort of recruiting and involving parents in their children's schools a very challenging task. Generalized solutions and one-best-systems are dramatically inappropriate.

Enterprising and interested school personnel have explored ways of minimizing constraints and maximizing strengths. The examples cited previously demonstrate that Hispanic parents will participate when school personnel seek their contribution, when every meeting responds to some needs of the parents, and when programs consult with parents about agendas and meeting formats. Successful programs that reach out to parents' needs will eventually address issues that the school considers vital, whereas unsuccessful programs hold formal events at school and address parents in condescending ways (largely as a result of thoughtless habits).

Most important, successful programs recognize that treating all parents the same (in bureaucratically neutral ways) undercuts both success and equity. When school districts recognize that the Hispanic community is a diverse group with varying strengths and constraints, they can begin to plan diversified strategies for conducting outreach, recruiting volunteers, and ultimately determining how it is, specifically, that they will help parents support their children's education.

Adult education is a largely neglected strategy. Schools have persisted in training parents in reading, writing, and arithmetic to help their children with homework. But there is a connection between children's learning and adult education. That is, English-as-a-Second-Language classes, classes for the General Equivalency Diploma (GED), or Family Math Programs may have long-term benefits for the whole family. Of course, family literacy efforts should not preclude initiation of more short-term strategies that parents not yet literate in English can use at home—for example, having the children read to them, learning ways to handle discipline disputes regarding homework completion, and securing assistance from other sources.

Finally, school personnel must discard the all-too-prevalent assumptions that parents not traditionally involved in the schools have to be "remediated" and that the schools are the most authoritative source of knowledge. Successful programs have used other parents as resources, as sources of knowledge, and as trainers of other trainers.

Summary, Principles to Guide Practice

School personnel should regard migrant and immigrant families with *understanding and compassion*. They can begin the process of understanding the family and the relations of its members through carefully observing how roles are fulfilled cooperatively. This nonjudgmental stance toward the family is especially important because of the tremendous odds (including economic distress, prejudice, culture shock, language barriers, and institutional racism) confronting migrant and immigrant families.

The family should be shown and treated with *high regard* because all families, irrespective of their income, station in life, language, or cultural heritage, are *equally important* to the common good and to the arduous and challenging task of educating our youth. In particular, parents from previously unserved populations (especially poor, minority, limited-English-proficient, and migrant students) must be heard and heeded in the difficult effort to resolve dilemmas that are not yet widely understood.

The concept of family should be extended to *include other family members*, including grandparents, aunts, and siblings. Parental involvement activities should be intergenerational.

Programs should *make room for parents*. Not only should parents feel welcome, they should be visibly and responsively provided for. Parent rooms or space specifically allocated for parents need to be identified and made available for their use. Parents should be able to share and discuss ideas, get information and resources (including borrowing print materials and video- and audiotapes), and learn from each other about family problems and solutions.

Parent involvement should be *developmental and preventive*, an integral part of a school improvement or restructuring strategy, rather than a remedial intervention. Ideally, the form of parent involvement will positively affect not just the child, but will help the parent grow and develop as well.

School personnel need to keep in mind that parental involvement is not an end in itself; that is, it is not carried out in isolation. Rather, parental involvement must be *viewed as a support component*, supporting student academic achievement, in the same vein as curriculum, assessment, administration, and staff development.

School districts must allocate *the additional resources and staff* needed to accomplish the goals of parental involvement. Ideally, programs represent a collaborative effort where tasks are organized in a location convenient to families and where resources are shared.

References

Ascher, C. (1987). *Improving the school-home connection for poor and minority urban students*. New York: ERIC Clearinghouse for Urban and Minority Education. (ERIC Document Reproduction Service No. ED 300 484)

Azmitia, M., Cooper, C. R., Garcia, E. E., Ittel, A., Johanson, B., Lopez, E., Martinez-Chavez, R., & Rivera, L. (1994). *Links between home and school among low-income Mexican American and European-American families*. Santa Cruz: National Center for Research on Cultural Diversity and Second Language Learning. (ERIC Document Reproduction Service No. ED 370 757)

Barquet, N. (1990). Parent involvement in American education: A national origin perspective. *Equity Coalition for Race, Gender, and National Origin, 1*(2), 4-6.

Bermúdez , A. (1994). *Doing our homework. How schools can engage Hispanic communities.* Charleston, WV: ERIC Clearinghouse on Rural and Small Schools. (ERIC Document Reproduction Service No. ED 372 905)

Carrasquillo, A. L., & London, C. B. G. (1993). The Hispanic-American experience in family context. In *Parents and Schools: A Source Book (pp 35-49).* New York: Garland Publishing, Inc.

Casas, M., Furlong, M., Carranza, O., & Solberg, S. (1986). *Santa Barbara success study: Profiling successful and at-risk junior high school students* (Final Report submitted to the Santa Barbara School District Board of Education). Santa Barbara: University of California at Santa Barbara, Department of Education.

Chavkin, N. F. (1991). *Family lives and parental involvement in migrant students' education* (ERIC Digest). Charleston, WV: ERIC Clearinghouse on Rural and Small Schools. (ERIC Document Reproduction Service No. ED 335 174)

Cohen, D. L. (1994, October). Teach their families well. *Education Week, 14*, 30-32.

Commins, N. L. (1992). Parents and public schools: The experience of four Mexican immigrant families. *Equity and Choice, 8*(2), 40-45.

Contreras-Polk, C., & Díaz, R. (1995). How to increase parent involvement through parents as authors programs. *NABE News, 18*(4), 37-38, 40.

Cooper, K., & Gonzalez, M. L. (1993). Communicating with parents when you don't speak the language. *Principal, 73*, 45-46.

Delgado-Gaitán, C. (1991). Involving parents in school: A process of empowerment. *American Journal of Education, 100*(1), 20-24.

Epstein, J. L. (1991). Paths to partnership: What we can learn from federal, state, district and school initiatives. *Phi Delta Kappan, 72*(5), 345-349.

Gonzales, B. (1986). Schools and the language minority parents: The optimum solution. *Catalyst for Change, 16*(1), 14-17.

Guzmán, F. M. (1990, June). Parenting skills workshops: Let's examine a success story. *IDRA Newsletter, 17*, 6,8.

Henderson, A., Marburger, C., & Ooms, T. (1986). *Beyond the bake sale.* Columbia, MD: National Committee for Citizens in Education. (ERIC Document Reproduction Service No. ED 270 508)

Inger, M. (1992). *Increasing the school involvement of Hispanic parents* (ERIC Digest). New York: ERIC Clearinghouse on Urban Education, Teachers College, Columbia University. (ERIC Document Reproduction Service No. ED 350 380)

Inger, M. (1993). Getting Hispanic parents involved. *Education Digest, 58*(8), 33-34.

Lee, V., & Patel, N. (1994). Making literacy programs work for immigrant families. *New Voices, 4*(1), 1-2.

Minicucci, C., & Olsen, L. (1993). *Educating students from immigrant families: Meeting the challenge in secondary schools* (conference proceedings). Santa Cruz, CA: National Center for Research on Cultural Diversity and Second Language Learning. (ERIC Document Reproduction Service No. ED 360 826)

Montecel, M. R., Gallagher, A., Montemayor, A., Villarreal, A. & Reyna, A. (1993). *Hispanic families as valued partners: An educator's guide.* San Antonio: Intercultural Development Research Association. (ERIC Document Reproduction Service No. ED 356 922)

Nicolau, S., & Ramos, C. L. (1990). *Together is better: Building strong relationships between schools and Hispanic parents.* Washington, DC: Hispanic Policy Development Project. (ERIC Document Reproduction Service No. ED 325 543)

Orum, L., & Navarette, L. (1990). Project EXCEL: A national organization seeks to improve the American educational system for Hispanic children. *Electric Perspectives, 14*(1), 4-14. (ERIC Document Reproduction Service No. ED 337 558)

Procidano, M. E., & Fisher, C. B. (1992). *Contemporary families, A handbook for school professionals.* New York: Teachers College Press.

Simich-Dudgeon, C. (1986). *Parent involvement and the education of limited-English-proficient students* (ERIC Digest). Washington, DC: ERIC Clearinghouse on Language and Linguistics. (ERIC Document Reproduction Service No. ED 279 205)

Sosa, A. (1990). *Making education work for Mexican Americans: Promising community practices* (ERIC Digest). Charleston, WV: ERIC Clearinghouse on Rural Education and Small Schools. (ERIC Document Reproduction Service No. ED 319 580)

Sosa, A. (1993). *Thorough and fair: Creating routes to success for Mexican American students*. Charleston, WV: ERIC Clearinghouse on Rural Education and Small Schools. (ERIC Document Reproduction Service No. ED 360 116)

Villarreal, A., & Barnwell, J. (1990, September). How do you effectively teach Chapter 1 students? Strong, successful parent involvement programs help. *IDRA Newsletter, 17*(8), 1-6.

Violand-Sánchez, E., Sutton, C. P., & Ware, H. W. (1991). *Fostering home-school cooperation: Involving language minority families as partners in education.* Washington, DC: National Clearinghouse on Bilingual Education. (ERIC Document Reproduction Service No. ED 337 018)